MznLnx

Missing Links Exam Preps

Exam Prep for

Financial Management: Theory & Practice

brigham & Ehrhardt, 12th Edition

The MznLnx Exam Prep is your link from the texbook and lecture to your exams.
The MznLnx Exam Preps are unauthorized and comprehensive reviews of your textbooks.

All material provided by MznLnx and Rico Publications (c) 2010
Textbook publishers and textbook authors do not particpate in or contribute to these reviews.

MznLnx

Rico
Publications

Exam Prep for Financial Management: Theory & Practice
12th Edition
brigham & Ehrhardt

Publisher: Raymond Houge
Assistant Editor: Michael Rouger
Text and Cover Designer: Lisa Buckner
Marketing Manager: Sara Swagger
Project Manager, Editorial Production: Jerry Emerson
Art Director: Vernon Lowerui

Product Manager: Dave Mason
Editorial Asitant: Rachel Guzmanji
Pedagogy: Debra Long
Cover Image: Jim Reed/Getty Images
Text and Cover Printer: City Printing, Inc.
Compositor: Media Mix, Inc.

(c) 2010 Rico Publications
ALL RIGHTS RESERVED. No part of this work covered by the copyright may be reproduced or used in any form or by an means--graphic, electronic, or mechanical, including photocopying, recording, taping, Web distribution, information storage, and retrieval systems, or in any other manner--without the written permission of the publisher.

Printed in the United States
ISBN:

For more information about our products, contact us at:
Dave.Mason@RicoPublications.com

For permission to use material from this text or product, submit a request online to:
Dave.Mason@RicoPublications.com

Contents

CHAPTER 1
An Overview of Financial Management and the Financial Environment   1

CHAPTER 2
Time Value of Money   23

CHAPTER 3
Financial Statements, Cash Flow, and Taxes   33

CHAPTER 4
Analysis of Financial Statements   52

CHAPTER 5
Bonds, Bond Valuation, and Interest Rates   66

CHAPTER 6
Risk, Return, and the Capital Asset Pricing Model   83

CHAPTER 7
Portfolio Theory and Other Asset Pricing Models   93

CHAPTER 8
Stocks, Stock Valuation, and Stock Market Equilibrium   100

CHAPTER 9
Financial Options and Applications in Corporate Finance   112

CHAPTER 10
The Cost of Capital   120

CHAPTER 11
The Basics of Capital Budgeting: Evaluating Cash Flows   134

CHAPTER 12
Cash Flow Estimation and Risk Analysis   142

CHAPTER 13
Real Options   155

CHAPTER 14
Financial Planning and Forecasting Financial Statements   160

CHAPTER 15
Corporate Valuation, Value-Based Management, and Corporate Governance   172

CHAPTER 16
Capital Structure Decisions: The Basics   181

CHAPTER 17
Capital Structure Decisions: Extensions   195

CHAPTER 18
Distributions to Shareholders: Dividends and Repurchases   203

CHAPTER 19
Initial Public Offerings, Investment Banking, and Financial Restructuring   212

CHAPTER 20
Lease Financing   226

Contents (Cont.)

CHAPTER 21
Hybrid Financing: Preferred Stock, Warrants, and Convertibles — 239

CHAPTER 22
Working Capital Management — 248

CHAPTER 23
Derivatives and Risk Management — 259

CHAPTER 24
Bankruptcy, Reorganization, and Liquidation — 272

CHAPTER 25
Mergers, LBOs, Divestitures, and Holding Companies — 279

CHAPTER 26
Multinational Financial Management — 295

ANSWER KEY — 312

TO THE STUDENT

COMPREHENSIVE

The *MznLnx* Exam Prep series is designed to help you pass your exams. Editors at MznLnx review your textbooks and then prepare these practice exams to help you master the textbook material. Unlike study guides, workbooks, and practice tests provided by the texbook publisher and textbook authors, *MznLnx* gives you **all** of the material in each chapter in exam form, not just samples, so you can be sure to nail your exam.

MECHANICAL

The MznLnx Exam Prep series creates exams that will help you learn the subject matter as well as test you on your understanding. Each question is designed to help you master the concept. Just working through the exams, you gain an understanding of the subject--its a simple mechanical process that produces success.

INTEGRATED STUDY GUIDE AND REVIEW

MznLnx is not just a set of exams designed to test you, its also a comprehensive review of the subject content. Each exam question is also a review of the concept, making sure that you will get the answer correct without having to go to other sources of material. You learn as you go! Its the easiest way to pass an exam.

HUMOR

Studying can be tedious and dry. MznLnx's instructional design includes moderate humor within the exam questions on occassion, to break the tedium and revitalize the brain

Chapter 1. An Overview of Financial Management and the Financial Environment 1

1. Procter is a surname, and may also refer to:

   - Bryan Waller Procter (pseud. Barry Cornwall), English poet
   - Goodwin Procter, American law firm
   - _____, consumer products multinational

   a. Bucket shop
   b. Clearing house
   c. Valuation
   d. Procter ' Gamble

2. _____ is the set of processes, customs, policies, laws and institutions affecting the way a corporation is directed, administered or controlled. _____ also includes the relationships among the many stakeholders involved and the goals for which the corporation is governed. The principal stakeholders are the shareholders, management and the board of directors.

   a. Patent
   b. Foreign Corrupt Practices Act
   c. Due diligence
   d. Corporate governance

3. A sole _____, or simply _____ is a type of business entity which legally has no separate existence from its owner. Hence, the limitations of liability enjoyed by a corporation and limited liability partnerships do not apply to sole proprietors. All debts of the business are debts of the owner.

   a. Just-in-time
   b. Free cash flow
   c. Product life cycle
   d. Proprietorship

4. An _____ is a corporation that makes a valid election to be taxed under Subchapter S of Chapter 1 of the Internal Revenue Code.

   In general, _____s do not pay any income taxes. Instead, the corporation's income or losses are divided among and passed through to its shareholders.

   a. 4-4-5 Calendar
   b. 529 plan
   c. 7-Eleven
   d. S corporation

5. The institution most often referenced by the word '_____' is a public or publicly traded _____, the shares of which are traded on a public stock exchange (e.g., the New York Stock Exchange or Nasdaq in the United States) where shares of stock of _____s are bought and sold by and to the general public. Most of the largest businesses in the world are publicly traded _____s. However, the majority of _____s are said to be closely held, privately held or close _____s, meaning that no ready market exists for the trading of shares.

   a. Depository Trust Company
   b. Federal Home Loan Mortgage Corporation
   c. Protect
   d. Corporation

6. In finance, _____ is the process of estimating the potential market value of a financial asset or liability. they can be done on assets (for example, investments in marketable securities such as stocks, options, business enterprises, or intangible assets such as patents and trademarks) or on liabilities (e.g., Bonds issued by a company.) _____s are required in many contexts including investment analysis, capital budgeting, merger and acquisition transactions, financial reporting, taxable events to determine the proper tax liability, and in litigation.

Chapter 1. An Overview of Financial Management and the Financial Environment

a. Share
c. Margin
b. Procter ' Gamble
d. Valuation

7. In the commercial and legal parlance of most countries, a _____ or simply a partnership, refers to an association of persons or an unincorporated company with the following major features:

- Created by agreement, proof of existence and estoppel.
- Formed by two or more persons
- The owners are all personally liable for any legal actions and debts the company may face

It is a partnership in which partners share equally in both responsibility and liability.

Partnerships have certain default characteristics relating to both the relationship between the individual partners and (b) the relationship between the partnership and the outside world. The former can generally be overridden by agreement between the partners, whereas the latter generally cannot be.

The assets of the business are owned on behalf of the other partners, and they are each personally liable, jointly and severally, for business debts, taxes or tortious liability.

a. The Depository Trust ' Clearing Corporation
c. Federal Home Loan Mortgage Corporation
b. General partnership
d. First Prudential Markets

8. _____ is a concept whereby a person's financial liability is limited to a fixed sum, most commonly the value of a person's investment in a company or partnership with _____. A shareholder in a limited company is not personally liable for any of the debts of the company, other than for the value of his investment in that company. The same is true for the members of a _____ partnership and the limited partners in a limited partnership.

a. Sarbanes-Oxley Act
c. Personal property
b. Beneficial owner
d. Limited liability

9. A _____ has elements of partnerships and corporations. In an _____ one partner is not responsible or liable for another partner's misconduct or negligence. This is an important difference from that of a limited partnership.

a. Governmental Accounting Standards Board
c. Citrix Systems
b. KPMG
d. Limited liability partnership

10. A _____ is a form of partnership similar to a general partnership, except that in addition to one or more general partners (GPs), there are one or more limited partners (_____s). It is a partnership in which only one partner is required to be a general partner.

The GPs are, in all major respects, in the same legal position as partners in a conventional firm, i.e. they have management control, share the right to use partnership property, share the profits of the firm in predefined proportions, and have joint and several liability for the debts of the partnership.

a. Limited liability company
c. Leverage
b. Fund of funds
d. Limited partnership

Chapter 1. An Overview of Financial Management and the Financial Environment 3

11. A _____ is a type of business entity in which partners (owners) share with each other the profits or losses of the business undertaking in which all have invested. _____s are often favored over corporations for taxation purposes, as the _____ structure does not generally incur a tax on profits before it is distributed to the partners (i.e. there is no dividend tax levied.) However, depending on the _____ structure and the jurisdiction in which it operates, owners of a _____ may be exposed to greater personal liability than they would as shareholders of a corporation.

   a. Partnership
   b. Fiduciary
   c. Clayton Antitrust Act
   d. National Securities Markets Improvement Act of 1996

12. In the most general sense, a _____ is anything that is a hindrance, or puts individuals at a disadvantage.

Before we discuss the financial terms, we should note that a _____ can also have a much more important slang meaning.

This is best described in an example.

   a. Covenant
   b. McFadden Act
   c. Liability
   d. Limited liability

13. _____ is part of the Federal income tax system of the United States. There is an _____ for those who owe personal income tax, and another for corporations owing corporate income tax. Only the _____ for those owing personal income tax is described here.

The _____ operates in effect as a parallel tax system, with its own definition of taxable income, exemptions, and tax rates. Taxpayers compute tax owed under the 'regular' and _____ systems and are liable for whichever is higher.

   a. A Random Walk Down Wall Street
   b. ABN Amro
   c. Alternative minimum tax
   d. AAB

14. _____ is a term used in accounting, economics and finance to spread the cost of an asset over the span of several years.

In simple words we can say that _____ is the reduction in the value of an asset due to usage, passage of time, wear and tear, technological outdating or obsolescence, depletion or other such factors.

In accounting, _____ is a term used to describe any method of attributing the historical or purchase cost of an asset across its useful life, roughly corresponding to normal wear and tear.

   a. Matching principle
   b. Depreciation
   c. Bottom line
   d. Deferred financing costs

15. A _____ is a payment made by a corporation to its shareholder members. When a corporation earns a profit or surplus, that money can be put to two uses: it can either be re-invested in the business (called retained earnings), or it can be paid to the shareholders as a _____. Many corporations retain a portion of their earnings and pay the remainder as a _____.

4   ***Chapter 1. An Overview of Financial Management and the Financial Environment***

    a. Dividend puzzle   b. Dividend yield
    c. Special dividend   d. Dividend

16. _____ is the imposition of two or more taxes on the same income (in the case of income taxes), asset (in the case of capital taxes), or financial transaction (in the case of sales taxes.) It refers to two distinct situations:

- taxation of dividend income without relief or credit for taxes paid by the company paying the dividend on the income from which the dividend is paid. This arises in the so-called 'classical' system of corporate taxation, used in the United States.
- taxation by two or more countries of the same income, asset or transaction, for example income paid by an entity of one country to a resident of a different country. The double liability is often mitigated by tax treaties between countries.

It is not unusual for a business or individual who is resident in one country to make a taxable gain (earnings, profits) in another. This person may find that he is obliged by domestic laws to pay tax on that gain locally and pay again in the country in which the gain was made. Since this is inequitable, many nations make bilateral _____ agreements with each other.

    a. 7-Eleven   b. 529 plan
    c. Double taxation   d. 4-4-5 Calendar

17. The phrase _____ refers to the aspect of corporate strategy, corporate finance and management dealing with the buying, selling and combining of different companies that can aid, finance, or help a growing company in a given industry grow rapidly without having to create another business entity.

An acquisition, also known as a takeover, is the buying of one company (the 'target') by another. An acquisition may be friendly or hostile.

    a. 4-4-5 Calendar   b. 529 plan
    c. 7-Eleven   d. Mergers and acquisitions

18. In economics and finance, _____ is the practice of taking advantage of a price differential between two or more markets: striking a combination of matching deals that capitalize upon the imbalance, the profit being the difference between the market prices. When used by academics, an _____ is a transaction that involves no negative cash flow at any probabilistic or temporal state and a positive cash flow in at least one state; in simple terms, a risk-free profit.
    a. Arbitrage   b. Issuer
    c. Efficient-market hypothesis   d. Initial margin

19. _____ or financing is to provide capital (funds), which means money for a project, a person, a business or any other private or public institutions.

Those funds can be allocated for either short term or long term purposes. The health fund is a new way of _____ private healthcare centers.

    a. Product life cycle   b. Proxy fight
    c. Synthetic CDO   d. Funding

Chapter 1. An Overview of Financial Management and the Financial Environment

20. _____, is when a company issues common stock or shares to the public for the first time. They are often issued by smaller, younger companies seeking capital to expand, but can also be done by large privately-owned companies looking to become publicly traded.

In an _____ the issuer may obtain the assistance of an underwriting firm, which helps it determine what type of security to issue (common or preferred), best offering price and time to bring it to market.

- a. Initial public offering
- b. Interest
- c. Insolvency
- d. Asian Financial Crisis

21. In finance, _____ refers to the value of a security which is intrinsic to or contained in the security itself. It is also frequently called fundamental value. It is ordinarily calculated by summing the future income generated by the asset, and discounting it to the present value.

- a. Alpha
- b. Accretion
- c. Amortization
- d. Intrinsic value

22. _____ is an economic concept with commonplace familiarity. It is the price that a good or service is offered at, or will fetch, in the marketplace. It is of interest mainly in the study of microeconomics.

- a. Delta hedging
- b. Central Securities Depository
- c. Convertible arbitrage
- d. Market price

23. A _____ is the price of a single share of a no. of saleable stocks of the company. Once the stock is purchased, the owner becomes a shareholder of the company that issued the share.

- a. Stock split
- b. Whisper numbers
- c. Trading curb
- d. Share price

24. In finance, _____ refers to the way a corporation finances its assets through some combination of equity, debt, or hybrid securities. A firm's _____ is then the composition or 'structure' of its liabilities. For example, a firm that sells $20 billion in equity and $80 billion in debt is said to be 20% equity-financed and 80% debt-financed.

- a. Book building
- b. Capital structure
- c. Rights issue
- d. Market for corporate control

25. _____ is a structured finance process that involves pooling and repackaging of cash-flow-producing financial assets into securities, which are then sold to investors. The term '_____' is derived from the fact that the form of financial instruments used to obtain funds from the investors are securities. As a portfolio risk backed by amortizing cash flows - and unlike general corporate debt - the credit quality of securitized debt is non-stationary due to changes in volatility that are time- and structure-dependent.

- a. Special journals
- b. Reputational risk
- c. The Glass-Steagall Act of 1933
- d. Securitization

26. _____ LLP, based in Chicago, was once one of the 'Big Five' accounting firms among PricewaterhouseCoopers, Deloitte Touche Tohmatsu, Ernst ' Young and KPMG, providing auditing, tax, and consulting services to large corporations. In 2002, the firm voluntarily surrendered its licenses to practice as Certified Public Accountants in the United States after being found guilty of criminal charges relating to the firm's handling of the auditing of Enron, the energy corporation, resulting in the loss of 85,000 jobs. Although the verdict was subsequently overturned by the Supreme Court of the United States, it has not returned as a viable business.

Chapter 1. An Overview of Financial Management and the Financial Environment

a. Institute of Financial Accountants
b. Information Systems Audit and Control Association
c. Accion USA
d. Arthur Andersen

27. The _____ of 2002 (Pub.L. 107-204, 116 Stat. 745, enacted July 30, 2002), also known as the Public Company Accounting Reform and Investor Protection Act of 2002 and commonly called Sarbanes-Oxley, Sarbox or SOX, is a United States federal law enacted on July 30, 2002 in response to a number of major corporate and accounting scandals including those affecting Enron, Tyco International, Adelphia, Peregrine Systems and WorldCom.

a. Foreign Corrupt Practices Act
b. Blue sky law
c. Duty of loyalty
d. Sarbanes-Oxley Act

28. _____ is a political organization established in 2002 and dedicated to the protection of children from abuse, exploitation and neglect. It is a nonprofit, 501(c)(4) membership association with members in every U.S. state and 10 nations. _____ achieved great success in its first three years, winning legislative victories in eight state legislatures.

a. Ford Foundation
b. The Depository Trust ' Clearing Corporation
c. First Prudential Markets
d. Protect

29. A _____ is a fungible, negotiable instrument representing financial value. They are broadly categorized into debt securities (such as banknotes, bonds and debentures), and equity securities; e.g., common stocks. The company or other entity issuing the _____ is called the issuer.

a. Tracking stock
b. Security
c. Securities lending
d. Book entry

30. In corporate finance, _____ is a cash flow available for distribution among all the security holders of a company. They include equity holders, debt holders, preferred stock holders, convertible security holders, and so on.

Note that the first three lines above are calculated for you on the standard Statement of Cash Flows.

a. Funding
b. Forfaiting
c. Safety stock
d. Free cash flow

31. The _____ is a capital budgeting metric used by firms to decide whether they should make investments. It is an indicator of the efficiency or quality of an investment, as opposed to net present value (NPV), which indicates value or magnitude.

The IRR is the annualized effective compounded return rate which can be earned on the invested capital, i.e., the yield on the investment.

a. A Random Walk Down Wall Street
b. AAB
c. ABN Amro
d. Internal rate of return

Chapter 1. An Overview of Financial Management and the Financial Environment 7

32. _____ is the balance of the amounts of cash being received and paid by a business during a defined period of time, sometimes tied to a specific project. Measurement of _____ can be used

- to evaluate the state or performance of a business or project.
- to determine problems with liquidity. Being profitable does not necessarily mean being liquid. A company can fail because of a shortage of cash, even while profitable.
- to generate project rate of returns. The time of _____s into and out of projects are used as inputs to financial models such as internal rate of return, and net present value.
- to examine income or growth of a business when it is believed that accrual accounting concepts do not represent economic realities. Alternately, _____ can be used to 'validate' the net income generated by accrual accounting.

_____ as a generic term may be used differently depending on context, and certain _____ definitions may be adapted by analysts and users for their own uses. Common terms include operating _____ and free _____.

_____s can be classified into:

1. Operational _____s: Cash received or expended as a result of the company's core business activities.
2. Investment _____s: Cash received or expended through capital expenditure, investments or acquisitions.
3. Financing _____s: Cash received or expended as a result of financial activities, such as interests and dividends.

All three together - the net _____ - are necessary to reconcile the beginning cash balance to the ending cash balance. Loan draw downs or equity injections, that is just shifting of capital but no expenditure as such, are not considered in the net _____.

    a. Shareholder value   b. Cash flow
    c. Corporate finance   d. Real option

33. In economics, business, and accounting, a _____ is the value of money that has been used up to produce something, and hence is not available for use anymore. In business, the _____ may be one of acquisition, in which case the amount of money expended to acquire it is counted as _____. In this case, money is the input that is gone in order to acquire the thing.

    a. Marginal cost   b. Cost
    c. Sliding scale fees   d. Fixed costs

34. The _____ is an expected return that the provider of capital plans to earn on their investment.

Capital (money) used for funding a business should earn returns for the capital providers who risk their capital. For an investment to be worthwhile, the expected return on capital must be greater than the _____.

    a. Capital intensity   b. Cost of capital
    c. 4-4-5 Calendar   d. Weighted average cost of capital

Chapter 1. An Overview of Financial Management and the Financial Environment

35. The _____ is the rate that a company is expected to pay to finance its assets. WACC is the minimum return that a company must earn on existing asset base to satisfy its creditors, owners, and other providers of capital.

Companies raise money from a number of sources: common equity, preferred equity, straight debt, convertible debt, exchangeable debt, warrants, options, pension liabilities, executive stock options, governmental subsidies, and so on.

   a. Capital intensity
   b. 4-4-5 Calendar
   c. Cost of capital
   d. Weighted average cost of capital

36. The _____ is a private, not-for-profit organization whose primary purpose is to develop generally accepted accounting principles (GAAP) within the United States in the public's interest. The Securities and Exchange Commission (SEC) designated the _____ as the organization responsible for setting accounting standards for public companies in the U.S. It was created in 1973, replacing the Accounting Principles Board and the Committee on Accounting Procedure of the American Institute of Certified Public Accountants. The _____'s mission is 'to establish and improve standards of financial accounting and reporting for the guidance and education of the public, including issuers, auditors, and users of financial information.'

The _____ is not a governmental body.

   a. Credit karma
   b. PlaNet Finance
   c. MRU Holdings
   d. FASB

37. In finance, the _____ is the global financial market for short-term borrowing and lending. It provides short-term liquidity funding for the global financial system. The _____ is where short-term obligations such as Treasury bills, commercial paper and bankers' acceptances are bought and sold.
   a. Consumer debt
   b. Debt-for-equity swap
   c. Cramdown
   d. Money market

38. _____ mature in one year or less. Like zero-coupon bonds, they do not pay interest prior to maturity; instead they are sold at a discount of the par value to create a positive yield to maturity. Many regard _____ as the least risky investment available to U.S. investors.
   a. Treasury Inflation Protected Securities
   b. Treasury securities
   c. 4-4-5 Calendar
   d. Treasury bills

39. An _____ is a contract written by a seller that conveys to the buyer the right -- but not the obligation -- to buy (in the case of a call _____) or to sell (in the case of a put _____) a particular asset, such as a piece of property such as, among others, a futures contract. In return for granting the _____, the seller collects a payment (the premium) from the buyer.

For example, buying a call _____ provides the right to buy a specified quantity of a security at a set strike price at some time on or before expiration, while buying a put _____ provides the right to sell.

   a. Amortization
   b. AT'T Mobility LLC
   c. Option
   d. Annuity

Chapter 1. An Overview of Financial Management and the Financial Environment   9

40. A _____, also known by its legal title as an 'over-allotment option' (the only way it can be referred to in a prospectus), gives underwriters the right to sell additional shares in a registered securities offering if demand for the securities is in excess of the original amount offered. The _____ can vary in size up to 15% of the original number of shares offered.

The _____ option is popular because it is the only SEC-permitted means for an underwriter to stabilize the price of a new issue post-pricing.

   a. Green Shoe
   c. Supply and demand
   b. Foreign Language and Area Studies
   d. Business valuation standards

41. The _____ is the market for securities, where companies and governments can raise longterm funds. The _____ includes the stock market and the bond market. Financial regulators, such as the U.S. Securities and Exchange Commission, oversee the _____s in their designated countries to ensure that investors are protected against fraud.
   a. Delta neutral
   c. Capital market
   b. Forward market
   d. Spot rate

42. A _____ is a financial contract whose value is derived from the value of something else (known as the underlying.) The underlying on which a _____ is based can be an asset, weather conditions bonds or other forms of credit.
   a. 4-4-5 Calendar
   c. 7-Eleven
   b. 529 plan
   d. Derivative

43. _____ is a fee paid on borrowed assets. It is the price paid for the use of borrowed money , or, money earned by deposited funds . Assets that are sometimes lent with _____ include money, shares, consumer goods through hire purchase, major assets such as aircraft, and even entire factories in finance lease arrangements.
   a. Insolvency
   c. AAB
   b. A Random Walk Down Wall Street
   d. Interest

44. An _____ is the price a borrower pays for the use of money they do not own, and the return a lender receives for deferring the use of funds, by lending it to the borrower. _____s are normally expressed as a percentage rate over the period of one year.

_____s targets are also a vital tool of monetary policy and are used to control variables like investment, inflation, and unemployment.

   a. ABN Amro
   c. AAB
   b. Interest rate
   d. A Random Walk Down Wall Street

45. _____ is a life of security. It may also refer to the final payment date of a loan or other financial instrument, at which point all remaining interest and principal is due to be paid.

1, 3, 6 months _____ band can be calculated by using 30-day per month periods.

a. False billing
b. Primary market
c. Replacement cost
d. Maturity

46. _____ occurs when an entity that has issued callable bonds calls those debt securities from the debt holders with the express purpose of reissuing new debt at a lower coupon rate. In essence, the issue of new, lower-interest debt allows the company to prematurely refund the older, higher-interest debt.

On the contrary, NonRefundable Bonds may be callable but they cannot be re-issued with a lower coupon rate.

a. No-arbitrage bounds
b. Refunding
c. Systematic risk
d. Market neutral

47. In financial accounting, the term _____ is most commonly used to describe any part of shareholders' equity, except for basic share capital. Sometimes, the term is used instead of the term provision; such a use, however, is inconsistent with the terminology suggested by International Accounting Standards Board. For more information about provisions, see provision (accounting.)

a. Treasury stock
b. Reserve
c. Closing entries
d. FIFO and LIFO accounting

48. In economics, the concept of the _____ refers to the decision-making time frame of a firm in which at least one factor of production is fixed. Costs which are fixed in the _____ have no impact on a firms decisions. For example a firm can raise output by increasing the amount of labour through overtime.

a. Long-run
b. 529 plan
c. Short-run
d. 4-4-5 Calendar

49. _____ is that which is owed; usually referencing assets owed, but the term can cover other obligations. In the case of assets, _____ is a means of using future purchasing power in the present before a summation has been earned. Some companies and corporations use _____ as a part of their overall corporate finance strategy.

a. Debt
b. Credit cycle
c. Cross-collateralization
d. Partial Payment

50. In finance, a _____ is a derivative in which two counterparties agree to exchange one stream of cash flows against another stream. These streams are called the legs of the _____.

The cash flows are calculated over a notional principal amount, which is usually not exchanged between counterparties.

a. Volatility swap
b. Volatility arbitrage
c. Local volatility
d. Swap

51. In business and accounting, _____s are everything of value that is owned by a person or company. The balance sheet of a firm records the monetary value of the _____s owned by the firm. The two major _____ classes are tangible _____s and intangible _____s.

a. EBITDA
b. Income
c. Accounts payable
d. Asset

Chapter 1. An Overview of Financial Management and the Financial Environment 11

52. The term _____ has three unrelated technical definitions, and is also used in a variety of non-technical ways.

- In financial economics, it refers to any asset used to make money, as opposed to assets used for personal enjoyment or consumption. This is an important distinction because two people can disagree sharply about the value of personal assets, one person might think a sports car is more valuable than a pickup truck, another person might have the opposite taste. But if an asset is held for the purpose of making money, taste has nothing to do with it, only differences of opinion about how much money the asset will produce. With the further assumption that people agree on the probability distribution of future cash flows, it is possible to have an objective _____ pricing model. Even without the assumption of agreement, it is possible to set rational limits on _____ value.
- In governmental accounting, it is defined as any asset used in operations with an initial useful life extending beyond one reporting period. Generally, government managers have a 'stewardship' duty to maintain _____s under their control. See International Public Sector Accounting Standards for details.
- In US tax accounting, it is defined as any property other than a list of exceptions. The main exceptions are anything held for sale, and any real estate or depreciable property used in business. Almost everything you own and use for personal purposes, pleasure or investment is a _____. If something is a _____ for tax purposes, gains or losses on sale or disposition are capital gains or capital losses. For individuals, however, capital losses on property held for personal use are generally not deductible. See the IRS publication Tax Facts about Capital Gains and Losses for details.

A well-known financial accounting textbook advises that the term be avoided except in tax accounting because it is used in so many different senses, not all of them well-defined. For example it is often used as a synonym for fixed assets or for investments in securities.

A common non-technical usage occurs when people ask that employees or the environment or something else be treated as a _____.

- a. Capital Asset
- b. Political risk
- c. Solvency
- d. Settlement date

53. In finance, the _____ is used to determine a theoretically appropriate required rate of return of an asset, if that asset is to be added to an already well-diversified portfolio, given that asset's non-diversifiable risk. The model takes into account the asset's sensitivity to non-diversifiable risk (also known as systemic risk or market risk), often represented by the quantity beta (β) in the financial industry, as well as the expected return of the market and the expected return of a theoretical risk-free asset.

The model was introduced by Jack Treynor (1961, 1962), William Sharpe (1964), John Lintner (1965a,b) and Jan Mossin (1966) independently, building on the earlier work of Harry Markowitz on diversification and modern portfolio theory.

- a. Cox-Ingersoll-Ross model
- b. Hull-White model
- c. Random walk hypothesis
- d. Capital Asset Pricing Model

54. In economics, _____ (or 'discounting') pertains to how large a premium a consumer will place on enjoyment nearer in time over more remote enjoyment.

12 *Chapter 1. An Overview of Financial Management and the Financial Environment*

There is no absolute distinction that separates 'high' and 'low' _____, only comparisons with others either individually or in aggregate. Someone with a high _____ is focused substantially on their well-being in the present and the immediate future compared to the average, while someone with low _____ places more emphasis than average on their well-being in the further future.

    a. Time preference   b. 529 plan
    c. 4-4-5 Calendar   d. 7-Eleven

55. _____ means regulating, adapting or settling in a variety of contexts:

In commercial law, _____ means the settlement of a loss incurred on insured goods. The calculation of the amounts of compensation to be paid by or to the several interests is a complicated matter. It involves much detail and arithmetic, and requires a full and accurate knowledge of the principles of the subject.

    a. Asset recovery   b. Intelligent investor
    c. Equity method   d. Adjustment

56. _____ is the planning process used to determine whether a firm's long term investments such as new machinery, replacement machinery, new plants, new products, and research development projects are worth pursuing. It is budget for major capital, or investment, expenditures.

Many formal methods are used in _____, including the techniques such as

- Net present value
- Profitability index
- Internal rate of return
- Modified Internal Rate of Return
- Equivalent annuity

These methods use the incremental cash flows from each potential investment, or project. Techniques based on accounting earnings and accounting rules are sometimes used - though economists consider this to be improper - such as the accounting rate of return, and 'return on investment.' Simplified and hybrid methods are used as well, such as payback period and discounted payback period.

    a. Preferred stock   b. Financial distress
    c. Shareholder value   d. Capital budgeting

57. In the global money market, _____ is an unsecured promissory note with a fixed maturity of one to 270 days. _____ is a money-market security issued (sold) by large banks and corporations to get money to meet short term debt obligations (for example, payroll), and is only backed by an issuing bank or corporation's promise to pay the face amount on the maturity date specified on the note. Since it is not backed by collateral, only firms with excellent credit ratings from a recognized rating agency will be able to sell their _____ at a reasonable price.

a. Commercial paper
c. Book building
b. Trade-off theory
d. Financial distress

58. _____s are deposits denominated in United States dollars at banks outside the United States, and thus are not under the jurisdiction of the Federal Reserve. Consequently, such deposits are subject to much less regulation than similar deposits within the United States, allowing for higher margins. There is nothing 'European' about _____ deposits; a US dollar-denominated deposit in Tokyo or Caracas would likewise be deemed _____ deposits.
   a. AAB
   c. ABN Amro
   b. Eurodollar
   d. A Random Walk Down Wall Street

59. A _____ s a time deposit, a financial product commonly offered to consumers by banks, thrift institutions, and credit unions.

They are similar to savings accounts in that they are insured and thus virtually risk-free; they are 'money in the bank'. They are different from savings accounts in that they have a specific, fixed term (often three months, six months, or one to five years), and, usually, a fixed interest rate.

   a. Time deposit
   c. Variable rate mortgage
   b. Certificate of deposit
   d. Reserve requirement

60. _____ is the provision of resources (such as granting a loan) by one party to another party where that second party does not reimburse the first party immediately, thereby generating a debt, and instead arranges either to repay or return those resources (or material(s) of equal value) at a later date. The first party is called a creditor, also known as a lender, while the second party is called a debtor, also known as a borrower.

Movements of financial capital are normally dependent on either _____ or equity transfers.

   a. Comparable
   c. Credit
   b. Warrant
   d. Clearing house

61. A _____ is a futures contract on a short term interest rate (STIR.) Contracts vary, but are often defined on an interest rate index such as 3-month sterling or US dollar LIBOR.

They are traded across a wide range of currencies, including the G12 country currencies and many others.

   a. Notional amount
   c. Real estate derivatives
   b. Financial future
   d. Dual currency deposit

62. In finance, a _____ is a standardized contract, to buy or sell a specified commodity of standardized quality at a certain date in the future, at a market determined price (the futures price.)

The price is determined by the instantaneous equilibrium between the forces of supply and demand among competing buy and sell orders on the exchange at the time of the purchase or sale of the contract.

In many cases, the items may be such non-traditional 'commodities' as foreign currencies, commercial or government paper [e.g., bonds], or 'baskets' of corporate equity ['stock indices'] or other financial instruments.

14   *Chapter 1. An Overview of Financial Management and the Financial Environment*

    a. Repurchase agreement   b. Futures contract
    c. Financial future   d. Heston model

63.   A _____ is a money deposit at a banking institution that cannot be withdrawn for a certain 'term' or period of time. When the term is over it can be withdrawn or it can be held for another term. Generally speaking, the longer the term the better the yield on the money.
    a. Time deposit   b. Basel Accord
    c. Private money   d. Certificate of deposit

64.   _____ is a form of corporation equity ownership represented in the securities. It is dangerous in comparison to preferred shares and some other investment options, in that in the event of bankruptcy, _____ investors receive their funds after preferred stockholders, bondholders, creditors, etc. On the other hand, common shares on average perform better than preferred shares or bonds over time.
    a. Stop-limit order   b. Stock market bubble
    c. Stock split   d. Common stock

65.   A _____ is a bond issued by a corporation. The term is usually applied to longer-term debt instruments, generally with a maturity date falling at least a year after their issue date. (The term 'commercial paper' is sometimes used for instruments with a shorter maturity.)
    a. Serial bond   b. Government bond
    c. Brady bonds   d. Corporate bond

66.   In the United States, a _____ is a bond issued by a city or other local government, or their agencies. Potential issuers of these bonds include cities, counties, redevelopment agencies, school districts, publicly owned airports and seaports, and any other governmental entity (or group of governments) below the state level. They may be general obligations of the issuer or secured by specified revenues.
    a. Puttable bond   b. Municipal bond
    c. Senior debt   d. Premium bond

67.   _____ is typically a higher ranking stock than voting shares, and its terms are negotiated between the corporation and the investor.

_____ usually carry no voting rights, but may carry superior priority over common stock in the payment of dividends and upon liquidation. _____ may carry a dividend that is paid out prior to any dividends to common stock holders.

    a. Trade-off theory   b. Preferred stock
    c. Follow-on offering   d. Second lien loan

68.   _____ are government bonds issued by the United States Department of the Treasury through the Bureau of the Public Debt. They are the debt financing instruments of the U.S. Federal government, and they are often referred to simply as Treasuries or Treasurys. There are four types of marketable _____: Treasury bills, Treasury notes, Treasury bonds, and Treasury Inflation Protected Securities (TIPS.)
    a. Treasury securities   b. 4-4-5 Calendar
    c. Treasury Inflation Protected Securities   d. Treasury Inflation-Protected Securities

Chapter 1. An Overview of Financial Management and the Financial Environment

69. In finance, a _____ is a debt security, in which the authorized issuer owes the holders a debt and, depending on the terms of the _____, is obliged to pay interest (the coupon) and/or to repay the principal at a later date, termed maturity.

Thus a _____ is a loan: the issuer is the borrower, the _____ holder is the lender, and the coupon is the interest. _____s provide the borrower with external funds to finance long-term investments, or, in the case of government _____s, to finance current expenditure.

   a. Convertible bond
   c. Catastrophe bonds
   b. Puttable bond
   d. Bond

70. In business and finance, a _____ (also referred to as equity _____) of stock means a _____ of ownership in a corporation (company.) In the plural, stocks is often used as a synonym for _____s especially in the United States, but it is less commonly used that way outside of North America.

In the United Kingdom, South Africa, and Australia, stock can also refer to completely different financial instruments such as government bonds or, less commonly, to all kinds of marketable securities.

   a. Procter ' Gamble
   c. Margin
   b. Share
   d. Bucket shop

71. _____ is the concept of adding accumulated interest back to the principal, so that interest is earned on interest from that moment on. The act of declaring interest to be principal is called compounding (i.e., interest is compounded.) A loan, for example, may have its interest compounded every month: in this case, a loan with $100 principal and 1% interest per month would have a balance of $101 at the end of the first month.
   a. Penny stock
   c. 4-4-5 Calendar
   b. Risk management
   d. Compound interest

72. _____ refers to the likelihood that changes in the business environment adversely affect operating profits or the value of assets in a specific country. For example, financial factors such as currency controls, devaluation or regulatory changes, or stability factors such as mass riots, civil war and other potential events contribute to companies' operational risks. This term is also sometimes referred to as political risk, however _____ is a more general term, which generally only refers to risks affecting all companies operating within a particular country.
   a. Single-index model
   c. Capital asset
   b. Solvency
   d. Country risk

73. In economics, _____ is a rise in the general level of prices of goods and services in an economy over a period of time. The term '_____' once referred to increases in the money supply (monetary _____); however, economic debates about the relationship between money supply and price levels have led to its primary use today in describing price _____. _____ can also be described as a decline in the real value of money--a loss of purchasing power in the medium of exchange which is also the monetary unit of account.
   a. AAB
   c. ABN Amro
   b. A Random Walk Down Wall Street
   d. Inflation

16 *Chapter 1. An Overview of Financial Management and the Financial Environment*

74. _____ is the process of decreasing an amount over a period of time. The word comes from Middle English amortisen to kill, alienate in mortmain, from Anglo-French amorteser, alteration of amortir, from Vulgar Latin admortire to kill, from Latin ad- + mort-, mors death. Particular instances of the term include:

- _____ (business), the allocation of a lump sum amount to different time periods, particularly for loans and other forms of finance, including related interest or other finance charges.
    - _____ schedule, a table detailing each periodic payment on a loan (typically a mortgage), as generated by an _____ calculator.
    - Negative _____, an _____ schedule where the loan amount actually increases through not paying the full interest
- Amortized analysis, analyzing the execution cost of algorithms over a sequence of operations.
- _____ of capital expenditures of certain assets under accounting rules, particularly intangible assets, in a manner analogous to depreciation.
- _____ (tax law)

_____ is also used in the context of zoning regulations and describes the time in which a property owner has to relocate when the property's use constitutes a preexisting nonconforming use under zoning regulations.

- Depreciation

a. Option
b. Amortization
c. AT'T Inc.
d. Intrinsic value

75. _____ , in finance, is a general theory of asset pricing, that has become influential in the pricing of stocks.

_____ holds that the expected return of a financial asset can be modeled as a linear function of various macro-economic factors or theoretical market indices, where sensitivity to changes in each factor is represented by a factor-specific beta coefficient. The model-derived rate of return will then be used to price the asset correctly - the asset price should equal the expected end of period price discounted at the rate implied by model.

a. ABN Amro
b. AAB
c. A Random Walk Down Wall Street
d. Arbitrage pricing theory

76. A _____ is a variable associated with an increased risk of disease or infection. They are correlational and not necessarily causal, because correlation does not imply causation. For example, being young cannot be said to cause measles, but young people are more at risk as they are less likely to have developed immunity during a previous epidemic.

a. Risk factor
b. 4-4-5 Calendar
c. 7-Eleven
d. 529 plan

77.

A _____ is a type of financial intermediary and a type of bank. Commercial banking is also known as business banking. It is a bank that provides checking accounts, savings accounts, and money market accounts and that accepts time deposits.

a. 7-Eleven
c. 4-4-5 Calendar
b. 529 plan
d. Commercial bank

78. In finance, the _____ between two currencies specifies how much one currency is worth in terms of the other. For example an _____ of 102 Japanese yen to the United States dollar means that JPY 102 is worth the same as USD 1. The foreign exchange market is one of the largest markets in the world.
   a. AAB
   c. ABN Amro
   b. A Random Walk Down Wall Street
   d. Exchange rate

79. _____ is a form of risk that arises from the change in price of one currency against another. Whenever investors or companies have assets or business operations across national borders, they face _____ if their positions are not hedged.

- Transaction risk is the risk that exchange rates will change unfavourably over time. It can be hedged against using forward currency contracts;
- Translation risk is an accounting risk, proportional to the amount of assets held in foreign currencies. Changes in the exchange rate over time will render a report inaccurate, and so assets are usually balanced by borrowings in that currency.

The exchange risk associated with a foreign denominated instrument is a key element in foreign investment. This risk flows from differential monetary policy and growth in real productivity, which results in differential inflation rates.

   a. Credit risk
   c. Tracking error
   b. Market risk
   d. Currency risk

80. A _____, sometimes called a pegged exchange rate, is a type of exchange rate regime wherein a currency's value is matched to the value of another single currency or to a basket of other currencies, or to another measure of value such as gold.

A _____ is usually used to stabilize the value of a currency, vis-a-vis the currency it is pegged to. This facilitates trade and investments between the two countries, and is especially useful for small economies where external trade forms a large part of their GDP.

   a. Deflation
   c. Fixed exchange rate
   b. Human capital
   d. Market structure

81. A _____ is a currency system in which governments try to keep the value of their currencies constant against one another.
   a. Horizontal merger
   c. 4-4-5 Calendar
   b. Passive income
   d. Fixed exchange rate system

Chapter 1. An Overview of Financial Management and the Financial Environment

82. A _____ is a cooperative financial institution that is owned and controlled by its members, and operated for the purpose of promoting thrift, providing credit at reasonable rates, and providing other financial services to its members. Many _____s exist to further community development or sustainable international development on a local level. Worldwide, _____ systems vary significantly in terms of total system assets and average institution asset size since _____s exist in a wide range of sizes, ranging from volunteer operations with a handful of members to institutions with several billion dollars in assets and hundreds of thousands of members.

    a. Credit Union Service Organization
    b. Credit union
    c. Corporate credit union
    d. Fi-linx

83. _____ refer to services provided by the finance industry.

The finance industry encompasses a broad range of organizations that deal with the management of money. Among these organizations are banks, credit card companies, insurance companies, consumer finance companies, stock brokerages, investment funds and some government sponsored enterprises.

    a. Delta hedging
    b. Cost of carry
    c. Financial instruments
    d. Financial services

84. A _____ is a professionally managed type of collective investment scheme that pools money from many investors and invests it in stocks, bonds, short-term money market instruments, and/or other securities. The _____ will have a fund manager that trades the pooled money on a regular basis. Currently, the worldwide value of all _____s totals more than $26 trillion.

Since 1940, there have been three basic types of investment companies in the United States: open-end funds, also known in the US as _____s; unit investment trusts (UITs); and closed-end funds.

    a. Net asset value
    b. Trust company
    c. Financial intermediary
    d. Mutual fund

85. A _____ is a financial institution that specializes in accepting savings deposits and making mortgage and other loans. The S'L or thrift term is mainly used in the United States; similar institutions in the United Kingdom, Ireland and some Commonwealth countries include building societies and trustee savings banks.

They are often mutually held, meaning that the depositors and borrowers are members with voting rights, and have the ability to direct the financial and managerial goals of the organization, not unlike the poliyholders of a mutual insurance company.

    a. Savings and loan association
    b. Mutual fund
    c. Person-to-person lending
    d. Net asset value

86. _____ is a legally declared inability or impairment of ability of an individual or organization to pay their creditors. Creditors may file a _____ petition against a debtor ('involuntary _____') in an effort to recoup a portion of what they are owed or initiate a restructuring. In the majority of cases, however, _____ is initiated by the debtor (a 'voluntary _____' that is filed by the bankrupt individual or organization.)

Chapter 1. An Overview of Financial Management and the Financial Environment

a. Bankruptcy
b. 529 plan
c. 4-4-5 Calendar
d. Debt settlement

87. In law, _____ refers to the process by which a company (or part of a company) is brought to an end, and the assets and property of the company redistributed. _____ can also be referred to as winding-up or dissolution, although dissolution technically refers to the last stage of _____. The process of _____ also arises when customs, an authority or agency in a country responsible for collecting and safeguarding customs duties, determines the final computation or ascertainment of the duties or drawback accruing on an entry.
   a. 529 plan
   b. 4-4-5 Calendar
   c. Liquidation
   d. Debt settlement

88. In finance, a _____ is a position established in one market in an attempt to offset exposure to the price risk of an equal but opposite obligation or position in another market -- usually, but not always, in the context of one's commercial activity. Hedging is a strategy designed to minimize exposure to such business risks as a sharp contraction in demand for one's inventory, while still allowing the business to profit from producing and maintaining that inventory. A typical hedger might be a farmer with 2000 acres of unharvested wheat in the ground, who would rather tend his crop without the distraction of uncertain prices.
   a. 4-4-5 Calendar
   b. 7-Eleven
   c. Hedge
   d. 529 plan

89. A _____ is a private investment fund open to a limited range of investors that is permitted by regulators to undertake a wider range of activities than other investment funds and also pays a performance fee to its investment manager. Each fund will have its own strategy which determines the type of investments and the methods of investment it undertakes. _____s as a class invest in a broad range of investments extending over shares, debt, commodities and beyond.
   a. Hedge fund
   b. 529 plan
   c. 7-Eleven
   d. 4-4-5 Calendar

90. _____ is the process of determining the fair price of a bond. As with any security or capital investment, the fair value of a bond is the present value of the stream of cash flows it is expected to generate. Hence, the price or value of a bond is determined by discounting the bond's expected cash flows to the present using the appropriate discount rate.
   a. Collateralized debt obligations
   b. Bond fund
   c. Catastrophe bonds
   d. Bond valuation

91. In finance, _____, also known as return on investment is the ratio of money gained or lost on an investment relative to the amount of money invested. The amount of money gained or lost may be referred to as interest, profit/loss, gain/loss, or net income/loss. The money invested may be referred to as the asset, capital, principal, or the cost basis of the investment.
   a. Composiition of Creditors
   b. Doctrine of the Proper Law
   c. Stock or scrip dividends
   d. Rate of return

92. The _____ is one of several stock market indices, created by nineteenth-century Wall Street Journal editor and Dow Jones ' Company co-founder Charles Dow. Dow compiled the index to gauge the performance of the industrial sector of the American stock market. It is the second-oldest U.S. market index, after the Dow Jones Transportation Average, which Dow also created.

a. Dow Jones Industrial Average
b. 7-Eleven
c. 4-4-5 Calendar
d. 529 plan

93. The _____ is a stock exchange based in New York City, New York. It is the largest stock exchange in the world by dollar value of its listed companies securities. As of October 2008, the combined capitalization of all domestic _____ listed companies was $10.1 trillion.
   a. 529 plan
   b. 7-Eleven
   c. 4-4-5 Calendar
   d. New York Stock Exchange

94. The _____ is that part of the capital markets that deals with the issuance of new securities. Companies, governments or public sector institutions can obtain funding through the sale of a new stock or bond issue. This is typically done through a syndicate of securities dealers.
   a. Sector rotation
   b. Volatility clustering
   c. Peer group analysis
   d. Primary market

95. The _____ is the financial market where previously issued securities and financial instruments such as stock, bonds, options, and futures are bought and sold. The term '_____' is also used refer to the market for any used goods or assets, or an alternative use for an existing product or asset where the customer base is the second market

With primary issuances of securities or financial instruments, or the primary market, investors purchase these securities directly from issuers such as corporations issuing shares in an IPO or private placement, or directly from the federal government in the case of treasuries.

   a. Performance attribution
   b. Financial market
   c. Delta neutral
   d. Secondary market

96. The _____ or cash market is a commodities or securities market in which goods are sold for cash and delivered immediately. Contracts bought and sold on these markets are immediately effective. _____s can operate wherever the infrastructure exists to conduct the transaction.
   a. Foreign exchange controls
   b. Currency swap
   c. Non-deliverable forward
   d. Spot market

97. A _____, securities exchange or (in Europe) bourse is a corporation or mutual organization which provides 'trading' facilities for stock brokers and traders, to trade stocks and other securities. _____s also provide facilities for the issue and redemption of securities as well as other financial instruments and capital events including the payment of income and dividends. The securities traded on a _____ include: shares issued by companies, unit trusts and other pooled investment products and bonds.
   a. 7-Eleven
   b. 4-4-5 Calendar
   c. Stock Exchange
   d. 529 plan

98. A _____ is a private or public market for the trading of company stock and derivatives of company stock at an agreed price; these are securities listed on a stock exchange as well as those only traded privately.

The size of the world _____ is estimated at about $36.6 trillion US at the beginning of October 2008 . The world derivatives market has been estimated at about $480 trillion face or nominal value, 12 times the size of the entire world economy.

a. Anton Gelonkin b. Adolph Coors
c. Stock market d. Andrew Tobias

99. A _____ is the direction in which a financial market is moving. _____s can be classified as primary trends, secondary trends (short-term), and secular trends (long-term.) This principle incorporates the idea that market cycles occur with regularity and persistence.
   a. 7-Eleven b. Market trend
   c. 4-4-5 Calendar d. 529 plan

100. _____ is a specific term used in companies' financial reporting from the company-whole point of view. Because that use excludes the effects of changing ownership interest, an economic measure of _____ is necessary for financial analysis from the shareholders' point of view

_____ is defined by the Financial Accounting Standards Board, or FASB, as 'e;the change in equity [net assets] of a business enterprise during a period from transactions and other events and circumstances from nonowner sources. It includes all changes in equity during a period except those resulting from investments by owners and distributions to owners.'e;

_____ is the sum of net income and other items that must bypass the income statement because they have not been realized, including items like an unrealized holding gain or loss from available for sale securities and foreign currency translation gains or losses.

   a. 529 plan b. 4-4-5 Calendar
   c. 7-Eleven d. Comprehensive income

101. _____, refers to consumption opportunity gained by an entity within a specified time frame, which is generally expressed in monetary terms. However, for households and individuals, '_____ is the sum of all the wages, salaries, profits, interests payments, rents and other forms of earnings received... in a given period of time.' For firms, _____ generally refers to net-profit: what remains of revenue after expenses have been subtracted.
   a. OIBDA b. Accrual
   c. Annual report d. Income

102. _____ is a process by which a firm can obtain the use of a certain fixed assets for which it must pay a series of contractual, periodic, tax deductable payments. The lessee is the receiver of the services or the assets under the lease contract and the lessor is the owner of the assets. The relationship between the tenant and the landlord is called a tenancy, and can be for a fixed or an indefinite period of time (called the term of the lease).
   a. Foreign Corrupt Practices Act b. Leasing
   c. Quiet period d. Royalties

103. An _____ is the term used in financial circles for a type of computer system that facilitates trading of financial products outside of stock exchanges. The primary products that are traded on an _____ are stocks and currencies. They came into existence in 1998 when the SEC authorized their creation.
   a. Insider trading b. Intellidex
   c. Open outcry d. Electronic communication network

104. A _____ or Capital increase is a new equity issue by a company after its IPO. It differs from a secondary equity offering, in which owners (not the company) sell their shares. In the latter case, the company gets no money and no ownership dilution happens, for the company does not issue new shares.
   a. Seasoned equity offering
   b. Sinking fund
   c. FATF Blacklist
   d. Debt-for-equity swap

105. _____ are those dividends paid out in form of additional stock shares of the issuing corporation or other corporation They are usually issued in proportion to shares owned (for example for every 100 shares of stock owned, 5% stock dividend will yield 5 extra shares). If this payment involves the issue of new shares, this is very similar to a stock split in that it increases the total number of shares while lowering the price of each share and does not change the market capitalization or the total value of the shares held
   a. The Hong Kong Securities Institute
   b. Database auditing
   c. Time-based currency
   d. Stock or scrip dividends

106. In United States banking, _____ is a marketing term for certain services offered primarily to larger business customers. It may be used to describe all bank accounts (such as checking accounts) provided to businesses of a certain size, but it is more often used to describe specific services such as cash concentration, zero balance accounting, and automated clearing house facilities. Sometimes, private banking customers are given _____ services.
   a. Profitability index
   b. Capitalization rate
   c. Global tactical asset allocation
   d. Cash management

107. The _____ is an American stock exchange. It is the largest electronic screen-based equity securities trading market in the United States. With approximately 3,200 companies, it has more trading volume per day than any other stock exchange in the world.
   a. 529 plan
   b. 4-4-5 Calendar
   c. 7-Eleven
   d. Nasdaq

108. The _____ is an electronic quotation system in the United States that displays real-time quotes, last-sale prices, and volume information for many over-the-counter (OTC) equity securities that are not listed on the NASDAQ stock exchange or a national securities exchange. Broker-dealers who subscribe to the system can use the _____ to look up prices or enter quotes for OTC securities.
   a. AT'T Inc.
   b. OTC Bulletin Board
   c. Insolvency
   d. Internal control

109. _____ is a list for goods and materials held available in stock by a business. It is also used for a list of the contents of a household and for a list for testamentary purposes of the possessions of someone who has died. In accounting _____ is considered an asset.
   a. Inventory
   b. A Random Walk Down Wall Street
   c. AAB
   d. ABN Amro

Chapter 2. Time Value of Money

1. The institution most often referenced by the word '_____' is a public or publicly traded _____, the shares of which are traded on a public stock exchange (e.g., the New York Stock Exchange or Nasdaq in the United States) where shares of stock of _____s are bought and sold by and to the general public. Most of the largest businesses in the world are publicly traded _____s. However, the majority of _____s are said to be closely held, privately held or close _____s, meaning that no ready market exists for the trading of shares.

   a. Protect
   b. Depository Trust Company
   c. Federal Home Loan Mortgage Corporation
   d. Corporation

2. In economics, a _____ is a type of retirement plan in which the amount of the employer's annual contribution is specified. Individual accounts are set up for participants and benefits are based on the amounts credited to these accounts (through employer contributions and, if applicable, employee contributions) plus any investment earnings on the money in the account. Only employer contributions to the account are guaranteed, not the future benefits. In _____s, future benefits fluctuate on the basis of investment earnings.

   a. Total revenue
   b. Defined contribution plan
   c. Capital costs
   d. Fixed asset turnover

3. _____ is the area of law in which manufacturers, distributors, suppliers, retailers, and others who make products available to the public are held responsible for the injuries those products cause.

   In the United States, the claims most commonly associated with _____ are negligence, strict liability, breach of warranty, and various consumer protection claims. The majority of _____ laws are determined at the state level and vary widely from state to state.

   a. Foreclosure
   b. Business valuation
   c. Product liability
   d. Family and Medical Leave Act

4. In financial accounting, a _____ or statement of financial position is a summary of a person's or organization's balances. Assets, liabilities and ownership equity are listed as of a specific date, such as the end of its financial year. A _____ is often described as a snapshot of a company's financial condition.

   a. Financial statements
   b. Balance sheet
   c. Statement on Auditing Standards No. 70: Service Organizations
   d. Statement of retained earnings

5. In economics, business, and accounting, a _____ is the value of money that has been used up to produce something, and hence is not available for use anymore. In business, the _____ may be one of acquisition, in which case the amount of money expended to acquire it is counted as _____. In this case, money is the input that is gone in order to acquire the thing.

   a. Sliding scale fees
   b. Marginal cost
   c. Cost
   d. Fixed costs

6. In the most general sense, a _____ is anything that is a hindrance, or puts individuals at a disadvantage.

   Before we discuss the financial terms, we should note that a _____ can also have a much more important slang meaning.

   This is best described in an example.

Chapter 2. Time Value of Money

    a. Covenant
    b. Limited liability
    c. McFadden Act
    d. Liability

7. In finance, the value of an option consists of two components, its intrinsic value and its _____. Time value is simply the difference between option value and intrinsic value. _____ is also known as theta, extrinsic value, or instrumental value.
    a. Conservatism
    b. Time value
    c. Global Squeeze
    d. Debt buyer

8. Simply put, _____ is the value of money figuring in a given amount of interest for a given amount of time. For example 100 dollars of todays money held for a year at 5 percent interest is worth 105 dollars, therefore 100 dollars paid now or 105 dollars paid exactly one year from now is the same amount of payment of money with that given intersest at that given amount of time. This notion dates at least to Martín de Azpilcueta of the School of Salamanca.

All of the standard calculations for _____ derive from the most basic algebraic expression for the present value of a future sum, 'discounted' to the present by an amount equal to the _____. For example, a sum of FV to be received in one year is discounted (at the rate of interest r) to give a sum of PV at present: PV = FV -- rÂ·PV = FV/(1+r).

    a. Zero-coupon bond
    b. Time value of money
    c. Current account
    d. Coefficient of variation

9. In finance, _____ is the process of estimating the potential market value of a financial asset or liability. they can be done on assets (for example, investments in marketable securities such as stocks, options, business enterprises, or intangible assets such as patents and trademarks) or on liabilities (e.g., Bonds issued by a company.) _____s are required in many contexts including investment analysis, capital budgeting, merger and acquisition transactions, financial reporting, taxable events to determine the proper tax liability, and in litigation.
    a. Margin
    b. Procter ' Gamble
    c. Share
    d. Valuation

10. In finance, a _____ is a debt security, in which the authorized issuer owes the holders a debt and, depending on the terms of the _____, is obliged to pay interest (the coupon) and/or to repay the principal at a later date, termed maturity.

Thus a _____ is a loan: the issuer is the borrower, the _____ holder is the lender, and the coupon is the interest. _____s provide the borrower with external funds to finance long-term investments, or, in the case of government _____s, to finance current expenditure.

    a. Catastrophe bonds
    b. Bond
    c. Puttable bond
    d. Convertible bond

11. _____ is the concept of adding accumulated interest back to the principal, so that interest is earned on interest from that moment on. The act of declaring interest to be principal is called compounding (i.e., interest is compounded.) A loan, for example, may have its interest compounded every month: in this case, a loan with $100 principal and 1% interest per month would have a balance of $101 at the end of the first month.

a. Risk management
b. Penny stock
c. 4-4-5 Calendar
d. Compound interest

12. A _____ is a financial contract whose value is derived from the value of something else (known as the underlying.) The underlying on which a _____ is based can be an asset, weather conditions bonds or other forms of credit.
    a. Derivative
    b. 529 plan
    c. 7-Eleven
    d. 4-4-5 Calendar

13. _____ measures the nominal future sum of money that a given sum of money is 'worth' at a specified time in the future assuming a certain interest rate rate of return; it is the present value multiplied by the accumulation function.

The value does not include corrections for inflation or other factors that affect the true value of money in the future. This is used in time value of money calculations.

    a. Present value of costs
    b. Future value
    c. Discounted cash flow
    d. Future-oriented

14. _____ or net present worth (NPW) is defined as the total present value (PV) of a time series of cash flows. It is a standard method for using the time value of money to appraise long-term projects. Used for capital budgeting, and widely throughout economics, it measures the excess or shortfall of cash flows, in present value terms, once financing charges are met.
    a. Negative gearing
    b. Tax shield
    c. Present value of costs
    d. Net present value

15. _____ is the value on a given date of a future payment or series of future payments, discounted to reflect the time value of money and other factors such as investment risk. _____ calculations are widely used in business and economics to provide a means to compare cash flows at different times on a meaningful 'like to like' basis.

The most commonly applied model of the time value of money is compound interest.

    a. Present value
    b. Negative gearing
    c. Present value of benefits
    d. Net present value

16. _____ occurs when an entity that has issued callable bonds calls those debt securities from the debt holders with the express purpose of reissuing new debt at a lower coupon rate. In essence, the issue of new, lower-interest debt allows the company to prematurely refund the older, higher-interest debt.

On the contrary, NonRefundable Bonds may be callable but they cannot be re-issued with a lower coupon rate.

    a. Systematic risk
    b. Refunding
    c. Market neutral
    d. No-arbitrage bounds

Chapter 2. Time Value of Money

17. _____ is the process of decreasing an amount over a period of time. The word comes from Middle English amortisen to kill, alienate in mortmain, from Anglo-French amorteser, alteration of amortir, from Vulgar Latin admortire to kill, from Latin ad- + mort-, mors death. Particular instances of the term include:

- _____ (business), the allocation of a lump sum amount to different time periods, particularly for loans and other forms of finance, including related interest or other finance charges.
    - _____ schedule, a table detailing each periodic payment on a loan (typically a mortgage), as generated by an _____ calculator.
    - Negative _____, an _____ schedule where the loan amount actually increases through not paying the full interest
- Amortized analysis, analyzing the execution cost of algorithms over a sequence of operations.
- _____ of capital expenditures of certain assets under accounting rules, particularly intangible assets, in a manner analogous to depreciation.
- _____ (tax law)

_____ is also used in the context of zoning regulations and describes the time in which a property owner has to relocate when the property's use constitutes a preexisting nonconforming use under zoning regulations.

- Depreciation

    a. Intrinsic value   b. Amortization
    c. AT'T Inc.   d. Option

18. _____ is the process of determining the fair price of a bond. As with any security or capital investment, the fair value of a bond is the present value of the stream of cash flows it is expected to generate. Hence, the price or value of a bond is determined by discounting the bond's expected cash flows to the present using the appropriate discount rate.
    a. Collateralized debt obligations   b. Catastrophe bonds
    c. Bond fund   d. Bond valuation

19. _____ is a business valuation method. _____ is the net present value of a project if financed solely by ownership equity plus the present value of all the benefits of financing. Usually, the main benefit is a tax shield resulted from tax deductibility of interest payments. Another one can be a subsidized borrowing.
    a. A Random Walk Down Wall Street   b. ABN Amro
    c. Adjusted present value   d. AAB

20. A _____ is a payment made by a corporation to its shareholder members. When a corporation earns a profit or surplus, that money can be put to two uses: it can either be re-invested in the business (called retained earnings), or it can be paid to the shareholders as a _____. Many corporations retain a portion of their earnings and pay the remainder as a _____.
    a. Dividend yield   b. Dividend
    c. Dividend puzzle   d. Special dividend

21. The phrase _____ refers to the aspect of corporate strategy, corporate finance and management dealing with the buying, selling and combining of different companies that can aid, finance, or help a growing company in a given industry grow rapidly without having to create another business entity.

Chapter 2. Time Value of Money

An acquisition, also known as a takeover, is the buying of one company (the 'target') by another. An acquisition may be friendly or hostile.

  a. 7-Eleven
  b. 4-4-5 Calendar
  c. 529 plan
  d. Mergers and acquisitions

22. _____ is an estimate of the fair value of corporations and their stocks, by using fundamental economic criteria. This theoretical valuation has to be perfected with market criteria, as the final purpose is to determine potential market prices.
  a. Growth stocks
  b. Security Analysis
  c. 4-4-5 Calendar
  d. Stock valuation

23. An _____ can be defined as a contract which provides an income stream in return for an initial payment.

An immediate _____ is an _____ for which the time between the contract date and the date of the first payment is not longer than the time interval between payments. A common use for an immediate _____ is to provide a pension to a retired person or persons.

  a. Intrinsic value
  b. Amortization
  c. AT'T Inc.
  d. Annuity

24. _____ are the inflation-indexed bonds issued by the U.S. Treasury. The principal is adjusted to the Consumer Price Index, the commonly used measure of inflation. The coupon rate is constant, but generates a different amount of interest when multiplied by the inflation-adjusted principal, thus protecting the holder against inflation. _____ are currently offered in 5-year, 10-year and 20-year maturities.
  a. Treasury Inflation Protected Securities
  b. Treasury Inflation-Protected Securities
  c. 4-4-5 Calendar
  d. Treasury securities

25. A _____ s a time deposit, a financial product commonly offered to consumers by banks, thrift institutions, and credit unions.

They are similar to savings accounts in that they are insured and thus virtually risk-free; they are 'money in the bank'. They are different from savings accounts in that they have a specific, fixed term (often three months, six months, or one to five years), and, usually, a fixed interest rate.

  a. Time deposit
  b. Reserve requirement
  c. Variable rate mortgage
  d. Certificate of deposit

26. _____ or economic opportunity loss is the value of the next best alternative foregone as the result of making a decision. _____ analysis is an important part of a company's decision-making processes but is not treated as an actual cost in any financial statement. The next best thing that a person can engage in is referred to as the _____ of doing the best thing and ignoring the next best thing to be done.
  a. ABN Amro
  b. AAB
  c. Opportunity cost
  d. A Random Walk Down Wall Street

27. A '_____' is a 'Charge' that is paid to obtain the right to delay a payment. Essentially, the payer purchases the right to make a given payment in the future instead of in the Present. The '_____', or 'Charge' that must be paid to delay the payment, is simply the difference between what the payment amount would be if it were paid in the present and what the payment amount would be paid if it were paid in the future.
   a. Discount
   b. Value at risk
   c. Risk modeling
   d. Risk aversion

28. A _____ is a futures contract on a short term interest rate (STIR.) Contracts vary, but are often defined on an interest rate index such as 3-month sterling or US dollar LIBOR.

They are traded across a wide range of currencies, including the G12 country currencies and many others.

   a. Financial future
   b. Notional amount
   c. Real estate derivatives
   d. Dual currency deposit

29. In finance, a _____ is a standardized contract, to buy or sell a specified commodity of standardized quality at a certain date in the future, at a market determined price (the futures price.)

The price is determined by the instantaneous equilibrium between the forces of supply and demand among competing buy and sell orders on the exchange at the time of the purchase or sale of the contract.

In many cases, the items may be such non-traditional 'commodities' as foreign currencies, commercial or government paper [e.g., bonds], or 'baskets' of corporate equity ['stock indices'] or other financial instruments.

   a. Heston model
   b. Financial future
   c. Futures contract
   d. Repurchase agreement

30. In United States banking, _____ is a marketing term for certain services offered primarily to larger business customers. It may be used to describe all bank accounts (such as checking accounts) provided to businesses of a certain size, but it is more often used to describe specific services such as cash concentration, zero balance accounting, and automated clearing house facilities. Sometimes, private banking customers are given _____ services.
   a. Global tactical asset allocation
   b. Profitability index
   c. Cash management
   d. Capitalization rate

31. _____ is the balance of the amounts of cash being received and paid by a business during a defined period of time, sometimes tied to a specific project. Measurement of _____ can be used

- to evaluate the state or performance of a business or project.
- to determine problems with liquidity. Being profitable does not necessarily mean being liquid. A company can fail because of a shortage of cash, even while profitable.
- to generate project rate of returns. The time of _____s into and out of projects are used as inputs to financial models such as internal rate of return, and net present value.
- to examine income or growth of a business when it is believed that accrual accounting concepts do not represent economic realities. Alternately, _____ can be used to 'validate' the net income generated by accrual accounting.

_____ as a generic term may be used differently depending on context, and certain _____ definitions may be adapted by analysts and users for their own uses. Common terms include operating _____ and free _____.

_____s can be classified into:

1. Operational _____s: Cash received or expended as a result of the company's core business activities.
2. Investment _____s: Cash received or expended through capital expenditure, investments or acquisitions.
3. Financing _____s: Cash received or expended as a result of financial activities, such as interests and dividends.

All three together - the net _____ - are necessary to reconcile the beginning cash balance to the ending cash balance. Loan draw downs or equity injections, that is just shifting of capital but no expenditure as such, are not considered in the net _____.

a. Corporate finance
b. Shareholder value
c. Real option
d. Cash flow

32. _____ are a form of British government bond (gilt), dating originally from the 18th century. _____ are one of the rare examples of an actual perpetuity: although they may be redeemed by the British government, they are unlikely to do so in the foreseeable future.

In 1752, the Chancellor of the Exchequer and Prime Minister Sir Henry Pelham converted all outstanding issues of redeemable government stock into one bond, Consolidated 3.5% Annuities, in order to reduce the coupon rate paid on the government debt.

a. Brady bonds
b. Consols
c. Serial bond
d. Revenue bonds

33. A _____ is an annuity in which the periodic payments begin on a fixed date and continue indefinitely. It is sometimes referred to as a perpetual annuity. Fixed coupon payments on permanently invested (irredeemable) sums of money are prime examples of these. Scholarships paid perpetually from an endowment fit the definition of _____.

a. Perpetuity
b. Stochastic volatility
c. Current yield
d. LIBOR market model

34. _____ is a fee paid on borrowed assets. It is the price paid for the use of borrowed money, or, money earned by deposited funds. Assets that are sometimes lent with _____ include money, shares, consumer goods through hire purchase, major assets such as aircraft, and even entire factories in finance lease arrangements.

a. A Random Walk Down Wall Street
b. Interest
c. AAB
d. Insolvency

Chapter 2. Time Value of Money

35. An _____ is the price a borrower pays for the use of money they do not own, and the return a lender receives for deferring the use of funds, by lending it to the borrower. _____s are normally expressed as a percentage rate over the period of one year.

_____s targets are also a vital tool of monetary policy and are used to control variables like investment, inflation, and unemployment.

   a. AAB
   c. Interest rate
   b. ABN Amro
   d. A Random Walk Down Wall Street

36. In finance, the _____ (continuing value or horizon value) of a security is the present value at a future point in time of all future cash flows when we expect stable growth rate forever. It is most often used in multi-stage discounted cash flow analysis, and allows for the limitation of cash flow projections to a several-year period. Forecasting results beyond such a period is impractical and exposes such projections to a variety of risks limiting their validity, primarily the great uncertainty involved in predicting industry and macroeconomic conditions beyond a few years.
   a. Negative gearing
   c. Refinancing risk
   b. Discounted cash flow
   d. Terminal value

37. The _____ is a capital budgeting metric used by firms to decide whether they should make investments. It is an indicator of the efficiency or quality of an investment, as opposed to net present value (NPV), which indicates value or magnitude.

The IRR is the annualized effective compounded return rate which can be earned on the invested capital, i.e., the yield on the investment.

   a. ABN Amro
   c. A Random Walk Down Wall Street
   b. AAB
   d. Internal rate of return

38. In finance, _____, also known as return on investment is the ratio of money gained or lost on an investment relative to the amount of money invested. The amount of money gained or lost may be referred to as interest, profit/loss, gain/loss, or net income/loss. The money invested may be referred to as the asset, capital, principal, or the cost basis of the investment.
   a. Rate of return
   c. Composiition of Creditors
   b. Stock or scrip dividends
   d. Doctrine of the Proper Law

39. In finance and economics _____ refers to the rate of interest before adjustment for inflation (in contrast with the real interest rate); or, for interest balls stated' without adjustment for the full effect of compounding (also referred to as the nominal annual rate.) An interest rate is called nominal if the frequency of compounding (e.g. a month) is not identical to the basic time unit (normally a year.)

The real interest rate includes compensation for the lender's lost value due to inflation, whereas the _____ excludes inflation.

   a. Cash accumulation equation
   c. SIBOR
   b. Shanghai Interbank Offered Rate
   d. Nominal interest rate

Chapter 2. Time Value of Money

40. The terms _____ , nominal _____ , and effective _____ describe the interest rate for a whole year (annualized), rather than just a monthly fee/rate, as applied on a loan, mortgage, credit card, etc. Those terms have formal, legal definitions in some countries or legal jurisdictions, but in general:

- The nominal _____ is the simple-interest rate (for a year.)
- The effective _____ is the fee+compound interest rate (calculated across a year.)

The nominal _____ is calculated as: the rate, for a payment period, multiplied by the number of payment periods in a year. However, the exact legal definition of 'effective _____' can vary greatly in each jurisdiction, depending on the type of fees included, such as participation fees, loan origination fees, monthly service charges, or late fees. The effective _____ has been called the 'mathematically-true' interest rate for each year. The computation for the effective _____, as the fee+compound interest rate, can also vary depending on whether the up-front fees, such as origination or participation fees, are added to the entire amount, or treated as a short-term loan due in the first payment.

a. A Random Walk Down Wall Street
b. AAB
c. ABN Amro
d. Annual Percentage Rate

41. _____ is the provision of resources (such as granting a loan) by one party to another party where that second party does not reimburse the first party immediately, thereby generating a debt, and instead arranges either to repay or return those resources (or material(s) of equal value) at a later date. The first party is called a creditor, also known as a lender, while the second party is called a debtor, also known as a borrower.

Movements of financial capital are normally dependent on either _____ or equity transfers.

a. Clearing house
b. Credit
c. Comparable
d. Warrant

42. The _____, effective annual interest rate, Annual Equivalent Rate (AER) or simply effective rate is the interest rate on a loan or financial product restated from the nominal interest rate as an interest rate with annual compound interest. It is used to compare the annual interest between loans with different compounding terms (daily, monthly, annually, or other.)

The _____ differs in two important respects from the annual percentage rate (APR):

1. the _____ generally does not incorporate one-time charges such as front-end fees;
2. the _____ is (generally) not defined by legal or regulatory authorities (as APR is in many jurisdictions.)

By contrast, the 'effective APR' is used as a legal term, where front-fees and other costs can be included, as defined by local law.

Annual Percentage Yield or effective annual yield is the analogous concept used for savings or investment products, such as a certificate of deposit.

a. AAB
b. ABN Amro
c. Effective interest rate
d. A Random Walk Down Wall Street

43. _____ is the task of determining how a business will afford to achieve its strategic goals and objectives. Usually, a company creates a Financial Plan immediately after the vision and objectives have been set. The Financial Plan describes each of the activities, resources, equipment and materials that are needed to achieve these objectives, as well as the timeframes involved.
   a. Corporate Transparency
   b. Performance measurement
   c. Management by exception
   d. Financial planning

44. In financial accounting, _____s are precautions for which the amount or probability of occurrence are not known. Typical examples are _____s for warranty costs and _____ for taxes the term reserve is used instead of term _____; such a use, however, is inconsistent with the terminology suggested by International Accounting Standards Board.
   a. Provision
   b. Money measurement concept
   c. Petty cash
   d. Momentum Accounting and Triple-Entry Bookkeeping

45. _____ or financing is to provide capital (funds), which means money for a project, a person, a business or any other private or public institutions.

Those funds can be allocated for either short term or long term purposes. The health fund is a new way of _____ private healthcare centers.

   a. Product life cycle
   b. Funding
   c. Synthetic CDO
   d. Proxy fight

46. _____, refers to consumption opportunity gained by an entity within a specified time frame, which is generally expressed in monetary terms. However, for households and individuals, '_____ is the sum of all the wages, salaries, profits, interests payments, rents and other forms of earnings received... in a given period of time.' For firms, _____ generally refers to net-profit: what remains of revenue after expenses have been subtracted.
   a. Annual report
   b. OIBDA
   c. Income
   d. Accrual

47. _____ is the income of individuals or nations after adjusting for inflation. It is calculated by subtracting inflation from the nominal income. Real variables, such as _____, real GDP, and real interest rate are variables that are measured in physical units, while nominal variables such as nominal income, nominal GDP, and nominal interest rate are measured in monetary units.
   a. Real income
   b. 4-4-5 Calendar
   c. 7-Eleven
   d. 529 plan

Chapter 3. Financial Statements, Cash Flow, and Taxes

1. _____ is the provision of resources (such as granting a loan) by one party to another party where that second party does not reimburse the first party immediately, thereby generating a debt, and instead arranges either to repay or return those resources (or material(s) of equal value) at a later date. The first party is called a creditor, also known as a lender, while the second party is called a debtor, also known as a borrower.

Movements of financial capital are normally dependent on either _____ or equity transfers.

a. Clearing house
b. Warrant
c. Comparable
d. Credit

2. An _____ is a document a company presents at an annual general meeting for approval by its shareholders, or a charitable organization presents its trustees. The report is made up of reports, which may include the following:

- Chairman's report
- CEO's report
- Auditor's report on corporate governance
- Mission statement
- Corporate governance statement of compliance
- Statement of directors' responsibilities
- Invitation to the company's AGM

as well as financial statements including:

- Auditor's report on the financial statements
- Balance sheet
- Statement of retained earnings
- Income statement
- Cash flow statement
- Notes to the financial statements
- Accounting policies

Other information deemed relevant to stakeholders may be included, such as a report on operations for manufacturing firms. In the case of larger companies, it is usually a sleek, colorful, high gloss publication.

The details provided in the report are of use to investors to understand the company's financial position and future direction.

a. Outstanding balance
b. Amortization schedule
c. Accrued liabilities
d. Annual report

3. _____ are formal records of a business' financial activities.

_____ provide an overview of a business' financial condition in both short and long term. There are four basic _____:

1. **Balance sheet**: also referred to as statement of financial position or condition, reports on a company's assets, liabilities, and net equity as of a given point in time.
2. **Income statement**: also referred to as Profit and Loss statement (or a 'P'L'), reports on a company's income, expenses, and profits over a period of time.
3. **Statement of retained earnings**: explains the changes in a company's retained earnings over the reporting period.
4. **Statement of cash flows**: reports on a company's cash flow activities, particularly its operating, investing and financing activities.

a. Statement on Auditing Standards No. 70: Service Organizations
b. Statement of retained earnings
c. Notes to the Financial Statements
d. Financial statements

4. In financial accounting, a _____ or statement of financial position is a summary of a person's or organization's balances. Assets, liabilities and ownership equity are listed as of a specific date, such as the end of its financial year. A _____ is often described as a snapshot of a company's financial condition.

a. Statement on Auditing Standards No. 70: Service Organizations
b. Statement of retained earnings
c. Financial statements
d. Balance sheet

5. A _____ is a payment made by a corporation to its shareholder members. When a corporation earns a profit or surplus, that money can be put to two uses: it can either be re-invested in the business (called retained earnings), or it can be paid to the shareholders as a _____. Many corporations retain a portion of their earnings and pay the remainder as a _____.

a. Dividend yield
b. Special dividend
c. Dividend puzzle
d. Dividend

6. _____ is a measure of the ability of a debtor to pay their debts as and when they fall due. It is usually expressed as a ratio or a percentage of current liabilities.

For a corporation with a published balance sheet there are various ratios used to calculate a measure of liquidity.

a. Invested capital
b. Operating profit margin
c. Operating leverage
d. Accounting liquidity

7. The phrase _____ refers to the aspect of corporate strategy, corporate finance and management dealing with the buying, selling and combining of different companies that can aid, finance, or help a growing company in a given industry grow rapidly without having to create another business entity.

An acquisition, also known as a takeover, is the buying of one company (the 'target') by another. An acquisition may be friendly or hostile.

Chapter 3. Financial Statements, Cash Flow, and Taxes   35

    a. 529 plan
    b. 4-4-5 Calendar
    c. Mergers and acquisitions
    d. 7-Eleven

8. _____ is an estimate of the fair value of corporations and their stocks, by using fundamental economic criteria. This theoretical valuation has to be perfected with market criteria, as the final purpose is to determine potential market prices.
    a. Stock valuation
    b. 4-4-5 Calendar
    c. Security Analysis
    d. Growth stocks

9. In finance, the value of an option consists of two components, its intrinsic value and its _____. Time value is simply the difference between option value and intrinsic value. _____ is also known as theta, extrinsic value, or instrumental value.
    a. Conservatism
    b. Global Squeeze
    c. Debt buyer
    d. Time value

10. Simply put, _____ is the value of money figuring in a given amount of interest for a given amount of time. For example 100 dollars of todays money held for a year at 5 percent interest is worth 105 dollars, therefore 100 dollars paid now or 105 dollars paid exactly one year from now is the same amount of payment of money with that given intersest at that given amount of time. This notion dates at least to Martín de Azpilcueta of the School of Salamanca.

All of the standard calculations for _____ derive from the most basic algebraic expression for the present value of a future sum, 'discounted' to the present by an amount equal to the _____. For example, a sum of FV to be received in one year is discounted (at the rate of interest r) to give a sum of PV at present: PV = FV -- r·PV = FV/(1+r).

    a. Coefficient of variation
    b. Current account
    c. Zero-coupon bond
    d. Time value of money

11. In finance, a _____ is a debt security, in which the authorized issuer owes the holders a debt and, depending on the terms of the _____, is obliged to pay interest (the coupon) and/or to repay the principal at a later date, termed maturity.

Thus a _____ is a loan: the issuer is the borrower, the _____ holder is the lender, and the coupon is the interest. _____s provide the borrower with external funds to finance long-term investments, or, in the case of government _____s, to finance current expenditure.

    a. Convertible bond
    b. Puttable bond
    c. Catastrophe bonds
    d. Bond

12. _____ is the process of determining the fair price of a bond. As with any security or capital investment, the fair value of a bond is the present value of the stream of cash flows it is expected to generate. Hence, the price or value of a bond is determined by discounting the bond's expected cash flows to the present using the appropriate discount rate.
    a. Bond valuation
    b. Collateralized debt obligations
    c. Bond fund
    d. Catastrophe bonds

Chapter 3. Financial Statements, Cash Flow, and Taxes

13. In finance, _____ is the process of estimating the potential market value of a financial asset or liability. they can be done on assets (for example, investments in marketable securities such as stocks, options, business enterprises, or intangible assets such as patents and trademarks) or on liabilities (e.g., Bonds issued by a company.) _____s are required in many contexts including investment analysis, capital budgeting, merger and acquisition transactions, financial reporting, taxable events to determine the proper tax liability, and in litigation.
    a. Valuation
    b. Share
    c. Margin
    d. Procter ' Gamble

14. In business and accounting, _____s are everything of value that is owned by a person or company. The balance sheet of a firm records the monetary value of the _____s owned by the firm. The two major _____ classes are tangible _____s and intangible _____s.
    a. Income
    b. Accounts payable
    c. EBITDA
    d. Asset

15. In accounting, _____ or *Carrying value* is the value of an asset according to its balance sheet account balance. For assets, the value is based on the original cost of the asset less any depreciation, amortization or impairment costs made against the asset. A company's _____ is its total assets minus intangible assets and liabilities.
    a. Current liabilities
    b. Retained earnings
    c. Pro forma
    d. Book value

16. _____ or First In, First Out, is an abstraction in ways of organizing and manipulation of data relative to time and prioritization. This expression describes the principle of a queue processing technique or servicing conflicting demands by ordering process by first-come, first-served (FCFS) behaviour: what comes in first is handled first, what comes in next waits until the first is finished, etc.

Thus it is analogous to the behaviour of persons queueing (or 'standing in line', in common American parlance), where the persons leave the queue in the order they arrive, or waiting one's turn at a traffic control signal.

    a. 4-4-5 Calendar
    b. FIFO
    c. Penny stock
    d. Risk management

17. _____ is an acronym which stands for last in, first out. In computer science and queueing theory this refers to the way items stored in some types of data structures are processed. By definition, in a _____ structured linear list, elements can be added or taken off from only one end, called the 'top'.
    a. LIFO
    b. 4-4-5 Calendar
    c. 7-Eleven
    d. 529 plan

18. _____ is the price at which an asset would trade in a competitive Walrasian auction setting. _____ is often used interchangeably with open _____, fair value or fair _____, although these terms have distinct definitions in different standards, and may differ in some circumstances.

International Valuation Standards defines _____ as 'the estimated amount for which a property should exchange on the date of valuation between a willing buyer and a willing seller in an arm'e;s-length transaction after proper marketing wherein the parties had each acted knowledgeably, prudently, and without compulsion.'

_____ is a concept distinct from market price, which is 'e;the price at which one can transact'e;, while _____ is 'e;the true underlying value'e; according to theoretical standards.

a. Wrap account
b. T-Model
c. Debt restructuring
d. Market value

19. The _____ percentage shows how profitable a company's assets are in generating revenue.

_____ can be computed as:

$$ROA = \frac{\text{Net Income}}{\text{Total Assets}}$$

This number tells you 'what the company can do with what it's got', i.e. how many dollars of earnings they derive from each dollar of assets they control. It's a useful number for comparing competing companies in the same industry.

a. Return on sales
b. P/E ratio
c. Receivables turnover ratio
d. Return on assets

20. In banking and finance, _____ denotes all activities from the time a commitment is made for a transaction until it is settled. _____ is necessary because the speed of trades is much faster than the cycle time for completing the underlying transaction.

In its widest sense _____ involves the management of post-trading, pre-settlement credit exposures, to ensure that trades are settled in accordance with market rules, even if a buyer or seller should become insolvent prior to settlement.

a. Clearing house
b. Share
c. Procter ' Gamble
d. Clearing

21. In finance, a _____ is a type of bond that can be converted into shares of stock in the issuing company, usually at some pre-announced ratio. It is a hybrid security with debt- and equity-like features. Although it typically has a low coupon rate, the holder is compensated with the ability to convert the bond to common stock, usually at a substantial discount to the stock's market value.

a. Bond fund
b. Gilts
c. Corporate bond
d. Convertible bond

22. The institution most often referenced by the word '_____' is a public or publicly traded _____, the shares of which are traded on a public stock exchange (e.g., the New York Stock Exchange or Nasdaq in the United States) where shares of stock of _____s are bought and sold by and to the general public. Most of the largest businesses in the world are publicly traded _____s. However, the majority of _____s are said to be closely held, privately held or close _____s, meaning that no ready market exists for the trading of shares.

a. Federal Home Loan Mortgage Corporation
b. Protect
c. Corporation
d. Depository Trust Company

23. In economics, business, and accounting, a _____ is the value of money that has been used up to produce something, and hence is not available for use anymore. In business, the _____ may be one of acquisition, in which case the amount of money expended to acquire it is counted as _____. In this case, money is the input that is gone in order to acquire the thing.

a. Marginal cost
b. Fixed costs
c. Sliding scale fees
d. Cost

24. In finance, the _____ is the minimum rate of return a firm must offer shareholders to compensate for waiting for their returns, and for bearing some risk.

The _____ capital for a particular company is the rate of return on investment that is required by the company's ordinary shareholders. The return consists both of dividend and capital gains, e.g. increases in the share price.

a. Round-tripping
b. Residual value
c. Net pay
d. Cost of equity

25. _____, based primarily at 55 Water Street in New York City, is the worlde;s largest post-trade financial services company. It was set up to provide an efficient and safe way for buyers and sellers of securities to make their exchange, and thus 'clear and settle' transactions. It also provides custody of securities.

a. FASB
b. Federal Deposit Insurance Corporation
c. The Depository Trust ' Clearing Corporation
d. Governmental Accounting Standards Board

26. _____ is a term used in accounting, economics and finance to spread the cost of an asset over the span of several years.

In simple words we can say that _____ is the reduction in the value of an asset due to usage, passage of time, wear and tear, technological outdating or obsolescence, depletion or other such factors.

In accounting, _____ is a term used to describe any method of attributing the historical or purchase cost of an asset across its useful life, roughly corresponding to normal wear and tear.

a. Deferred financing costs
b. Bottom line
c. Depreciation
d. Matching principle

27. _____ is typically a higher ranking stock than voting shares, and its terms are negotiated between the corporation and the investor.

_____ usually carry no voting rights, but may carry superior priority over common stock in the payment of dividends and upon liquidation. _____ may carry a dividend that is paid out prior to any dividends to common stock holders.

a. Follow-on offering
b. Trade-off theory
c. Second lien loan
d. Preferred stock

28. _____ is the area of law in which manufacturers, distributors, suppliers, retailers, and others who make products available to the public are held responsible for the injuries those products cause.

In the United States, the claims most commonly associated with _____ are negligence, strict liability, breach of warranty, and various consumer protection claims. The majority of _____ laws are determined at the state level and vary widely from state to state.

a. Business valuation
b. Product liability
c. Family and Medical Leave Act
d. Foreclosure

29. A _____ is the price of a single share of a no. of saleable stocks of the company. Once the stock is purchased, the owner becomes a shareholder of the company that issued the share.
a. Share price
b. Whisper numbers
c. Trading curb
d. Stock split

30. In finance, _____ are stocks that appreciate in value and yield a high return on equity (ROE.) Analysts compute ROE by taking the company's net income and dividing it by the company's equity. To be classified as a growth stock, analysts expect to see at least 15 percent return on equity.
a. Stock valuation
b. 4-4-5 Calendar
c. Growth stocks
d. Security Analysis

31. In the most general sense, a _____ is anything that is a hindrance, or puts individuals at a disadvantage.

Before we discuss the financial terms, we should note that a _____ can also have a much more important slang meaning.

This is best described in an example.

a. Covenant
b. Liability
c. Limited liability
d. McFadden Act

32. A _____ is a fungible, negotiable instrument representing financial value. They are broadly categorized into debt securities (such as banknotes, bonds and debentures), and equity securities; e.g., common stocks. The company or other entity issuing the _____ is called the issuer.
a. Book entry
b. Securities lending
c. Tracking stock
d. Security

33. In business and finance, a _____ (also referred to as equity _____) of stock means a _____ of ownership in a corporation (company.) In the plural, stocks is often used as a synonym for _____s especially in the United States, but it is less commonly used that way outside of North America.

In the United Kingdom, South Africa, and Australia, stock can also refer to completely different financial instruments such as government bonds or, less commonly, to all kinds of marketable securities.

Chapter 3. Financial Statements, Cash Flow, and Taxes

a. Margin
c. Procter ' Gamble
b. Bucket shop
d. Share

34. Earnings before interest, taxes, depreciation and amortization (_____) is a non-GAAP metric that can be used to evaluate a company's profitability.

_____ = Operating Revenue - Operating Expenses + Other Revenue

Its name comes from the fact that Operating Expenses do not include interest, taxes, or amortization. _____ is not a defined measure according to Generally Accepted Accounting Principles (GAAP), and thus can be calculated however a company wishes.

a. Invoice processing
c. Accounts payable
b. Accrual
d. EBITDA

35. _____, refers to consumption opportunity gained by an entity within a specified time frame, which is generally expressed in monetary terms. However, for households and individuals, '_____ is the sum of all the wages, salaries, profits, interests payments, rents and other forms of earnings received... in a given period of time.' For firms, _____ generally refers to net-profit: what remains of revenue after expenses have been subtracted.

a. OIBDA
c. Accrual
b. Annual report
d. Income

36. An _____ is a financial statement for companies that indicates how Revenue is transformed into net income The purpose of the _____ is to show managers and investors whether the company made or lost money during the period being reported.

The important thing to remember about an _____ is that it represents a period of time.

a. Income statement
c. A Random Walk Down Wall Street
b. ABN Amro
d. AAB

37. _____ is equal to the income that a firm has after subtracting costs and expenses from the total revenue. _____ can be distributed among holders of common stock as a dividend or held by the firm as retained earnings. _____ is an accounting term; in some countries (such as the UK) profit is the usual term.

a. Historical cost
c. Furniture, Fixtures and Equipment
b. Write-off
d. Net income

38. In business, _____ is the total assets minus total outside liabilities of an individual or a company. For a company, this is called shareholders' equity and may be referred to as book value. _____ is stated as at a particular point in time.

a. Restructuring
c. Net worth
b. Moneylender
d. Certified International Investment Analyst

39. _____ is the difference between price and the costs of bringing to market whatever it is that is accounted as an enterprise (whether by harvest, extraction, manufacture, or purchase) in terms of the component costs of delivered goods and/or services and any operating or other expenses.

Chapter 3. Financial Statements, Cash Flow, and Taxes

A key difficulty in measuring profit is in defining costs. Pure economic monetary profits can be zero or negative even in competitive equilibrium when accounted monetized costs exceed monetized price.

a. Economic profit
b. A Random Walk Down Wall Street
c. AAB
d. Accounting profit

40. _____ is the process of decreasing an amount over a period of time. The word comes from Middle English amortisen to kill, alienate in mortmain, from Anglo-French amorteser, alteration of amortir, from Vulgar Latin admortire to kill, from Latin ad- + mort-, mors death. Particular instances of the term include:

- _____ (business), the allocation of a lump sum amount to different time periods, particularly for loans and other forms of finance, including related interest or other finance charges.
    - _____ schedule, a table detailing each periodic payment on a loan (typically a mortgage), as generated by an _____ calculator.
    - Negative _____, an _____ schedule where the loan amount actually increases through not paying the full interest
- Amortized analysis, analyzing the execution cost of algorithms over a sequence of operations.
- _____ of capital expenditures of certain assets under accounting rules, particularly intangible assets, in a manner analogous to depreciation.
- _____ (tax law)

_____ is also used in the context of zoning regulations and describes the time in which a property owner has to relocate when the property's use constitutes a preexisting nonconforming use under zoning regulations.

- Depreciation

a. AT'T Inc.
b. Option
c. Intrinsic value
d. Amortization

41. _____ is a fee paid on borrowed assets. It is the price paid for the use of borrowed money , or, money earned by deposited funds . Assets that are sometimes lent with _____ include money, shares, consumer goods through hire purchase, major assets such as aircraft, and even entire factories in finance lease arrangements.

a. Insolvency
b. Interest
c. AAB
d. A Random Walk Down Wall Street

42. In United States banking, _____ is a marketing term for certain services offered primarily to larger business customers. It may be used to describe all bank accounts (such as checking accounts) provided to businesses of a certain size, but it is more often used to describe specific services such as cash concentration, zero balance accounting, and automated clearing house facilities. Sometimes, private banking customers are given _____ services.

a. Global tactical asset allocation
b. Cash management
c. Capitalization rate
d. Profitability index

43. In accounting, _____ refers to the portion of net income which is retained by the corporation rather than distributed to its owners as dividends. Similarly, if the corporation makes a loss, then that loss is retained and called variously retained losses, accumulated losses or accumulated deficit. _____ and losses are cumulative from year to year with losses offsetting earnings.
   a. Matching principle
   b. Historical cost
   c. Generally Accepted Accounting Principles
   d. Retained earnings

44. _____, in bookkeeping, refers to assets, liabilities, income, and expenses recorded on individual pages of the so called book of final entry or ledger. Changes in _____ value are made by chronologically posting debit (DR) and credit (CR) entries to its page. Examples of _____s are cash, _____s receivable, mortgages, loans, land and buildings, common stock, sales, services provided, wages, and payroll overhead.
   a. Account
   b. Alpha
   c. Accretion
   d. Option

45. The _____ is the current method of accelerated asset depreciation required by the United States income tax code. Under _____, all assets are divided into classes which dictate the number of years over which an asset's cost will be recovered.

Prior to the Accelerated Cost Recovery System (ACRS), most capital purchases were depreciated using a straight line technique, that allowed for the depreciation of the asset over its useful life.

   a. 4-4-5 Calendar
   b. Modified Accelerated Cost Recovery System
   c. 7-Eleven
   d. 529 plan

46. _____ is the balance of the amounts of cash being received and paid by a business during a defined period of time, sometimes tied to a specific project. Measurement of _____ can be used

   • to evaluate the state or performance of a business or project.
   • to determine problems with liquidity. Being profitable does not necessarily mean being liquid. A company can fail because of a shortage of cash, even while profitable.
   • to generate project rate of returns. The time of _____s into and out of projects are used as inputs to financial models such as internal rate of return, and net present value.
   • to examine income or growth of a business when it is believed that accrual accounting concepts do not represent economic realities. Alternately, _____ can be used to 'validate' the net income generated by accrual accounting.

_____ as a generic term may be used differently depending on context, and certain _____ definitions may be adapted by analysts and users for their own uses. Common terms include operating _____ and free _____.

_____s can be classified into:

1. Operational _____s: Cash received or expended as a result of the company's core business activities.
2. Investment _____s: Cash received or expended through capital expenditure, investments or acquisitions.
3. Financing _____s: Cash received or expended as a result of financial activities, such as interests and dividends.

All three together - the net _____ - are necessary to reconcile the beginning cash balance to the ending cash balance. Loan draw downs or equity injections, that is just shifting of capital but no expenditure as such, are not considered in the net _____.

a. Corporate finance
b. Shareholder value
c. Real option
d. Cash flow

47. _____ refers to an assessment of the viability, stability and profitability of a business, sub-business or project.

It is performed by professionals who prepare reports using ratios that make use of information taken from financial statements and other reports. These reports are usually presented to top management as one of their bases in making business decisions.

a. Value investing
b. 529 plan
c. Financial analysis
d. 4-4-5 Calendar

48. _____ is that which is owed; usually referencing assets owed, but the term can cover other obligations. In the case of assets, _____ is a means of using future purchasing power in the present before a summation has been earned. Some companies and corporations use _____ as a part of their overall corporate finance strategy.

a. Credit cycle
b. Debt
c. Cross-collateralization
d. Partial Payment

49. A _____ is a financial contract whose value is derived from the value of something else (known as the underlying.) The underlying on which a _____ is based can be an asset, weather conditions bonds or other forms of credit.

a. 4-4-5 Calendar
b. 529 plan
c. 7-Eleven
d. Derivative

50. _____ are the earnings returned on the initial investment amount.

In the US, the Financial Accounting Standards Board (FASB) requires companies' income statements to report _____ for each of the major categories of the income statement: continuing operations, discontinued operations, extraordinary items, and net income.

The _____ formula does not include preferred dividends for categories outside of continued operations and net income.

a. Inventory turnover
b. Average accounting return
c. Earnings per share
d. Assets turnover

51. _____ occurs when an entity that has issued callable bonds calls those debt securities from the debt holders with the express purpose of reissuing new debt at a lower coupon rate. In essence, the issue of new, lower-interest debt allows the company to prematurely refund the older, higher-interest debt.

On the contrary, NonRefundable Bonds may be callable but they cannot be re-issued with a lower coupon rate.

a. Systematic risk
b. Refunding
c. No-arbitrage bounds
d. Market neutral

52. In financial accounting, a _____ or statement of cash flows is a financial statement that shows a company's flow of cash. The money coming into the business is called cash inflow, and money going out from the business is called cash outflow. The statement shows how changes in balance sheet and income accounts affect cash and cash equivalents, and breaks the analysis down to operating, investing, and financing activities.

a. 7-Eleven
b. Cash flow statement
c. 4-4-5 Calendar
d. 529 plan

53. _____ or financing is to provide capital (funds), which means money for a project, a person, a business or any other private or public institutions.

Those funds can be allocated for either short term or long term purposes. The health fund is a new way of _____ private healthcare centers.

a. Synthetic CDO
b. Proxy fight
c. Product life cycle
d. Funding

54. In corporate finance, _____ is a company's after-tax operating profit for all investors, including shareholders and debt holders. It is defined as follows:

_____ = Operating profit x (1 - Tax Rate)

An alternative formula is as follows

_____ = Net Profit After Tax + after tax Interest Expense - after tax Interest Income

For companies with no debt and thus no interest expense, _____ is equal to net profit. In other words, _____ represents the company's operating profit that would accrue to shareholders (after taxes) if the company had no debt.

a. Revaluation
b. Channel stuffing
c. Sector rotation
d. Net operating profit after tax

55. In financial and business accounting, _____ is a measure of a firm's profitability that excludes interest and income tax expenses.

Chapter 3. Financial Statements, Cash Flow, and Taxes

EBIT = Operating Revenue - Operating Expenses (OPEX) + Non-operating Income

Operating Income = Operating Revenue - Operating Expenses

Operating income is the difference between operating revenues and operating expenses, but it is also sometimes used as a synonym for EBIT and operating profit. This is true if the firm has no non-operating income.

   a. ABN Amro   b. Earnings before interest and taxes
   c. AAB   d. A Random Walk Down Wall Street

56. In economic models, the _____ time frame assumes no fixed factors of production. Firms can enter or leave the marketplace, and the cost (and availability) of land, labor, raw materials, and capital goods can be assumed to vary. In contrast, in the short-run time frame, certain factors are assumed to be fixed, because there is not sufficient time for them to change.
   a. Short-run   b. Long-run
   c. 529 plan   d. 4-4-5 Calendar

57. In accounting, a _____ is an asset on the balance sheet which is expected to be sold or otherwise used up in the near future, usually within one year, or one business cycle - whichever is longer. Typical _____s include cash, cash equivalents, accounts receivable, inventory, the portion of prepaid accounts which will be used within a year, and short-term investments.

On the balance sheet, assets will typically be classified into _____s and long-term assets.

   a. Long-term liabilities   b. Current asset
   c. Historical cost   d. Write-off

58. In accounting, _____ are considered liabilities of the business that are to be settled in cash within the fiscal year or the operating cycle, whichever period is longer.

For example accounts payable for goods, services or supplies that were purchased for use in the operation of the business and payable within a normal period of time would be _____.

Bonds, mortgages and loans that are payable over a term exceeding one year would be fixed liabilities.

   a. Net income   b. Closing entries
   c. Current liabilities   d. Gross sales

59. _____ is a financial metric which represents operating liquidity available to a business. Along with fixed assets such as plant and equipment, _____ is considered a part of operating capital. It is calculated as current assets minus current liabilities.
   a. 4-4-5 Calendar   b. 529 plan
   c. Working capital management   d. Working capital

Chapter 3. Financial Statements, Cash Flow, and Taxes

60. _____ is a measure of a company's earning power from ongoing operations, equal to earnings before the deduction of interest payments and income taxes.

To accountants, economic profit, or EP, is a single-period metric to determine the value created by a company in one period - usually a year. It is the net profit after tax less the equity charge, a risk-weighted cost of capital.

    a. A Random Walk Down Wall Street   b. Operating profit
    c. Economic profit   d. AAB

61. _____ LLP, based in Chicago, was once one of the 'Big Five' accounting firms among PricewaterhouseCoopers, Deloitte Touche Tohmatsu, Ernst ' Young and KPMG, providing auditing, tax, and consulting services to large corporations. In 2002, the firm voluntarily surrendered its licenses to practice as Certified Public Accountants in the United States after being found guilty of criminal charges relating to the firm's handling of the auditing of Enron, the energy corporation, resulting in the loss of 85,000 jobs. Although the verdict was subsequently overturned by the Supreme Court of the United States, it has not returned as a viable business.

    a. Arthur Andersen   b. Accion USA
    c. Information Systems Audit and Control Association   d. Institute of Financial Accountants

62. In corporate finance, _____ is a cash flow available for distribution among all the security holders of a company. They include equity holders, debt holders, preferred stock holders, convertible security holders, and so on.

Note that the first three lines above are calculated for you on the standard Statement of Cash Flows.

    a. Forfaiting   b. Free cash flow
    c. Safety stock   d. Funding

63. _____ is a business valuation method. _____ is the net present value of a project if financed solely by ownership equity plus the present value of all the benefits of financing. Usually, the main benefit is a tax shield resulted from tax deductibility of interest payments. Another one can be a subsidized borrowing.

    a. A Random Walk Down Wall Street   b. ABN Amro
    c. Adjusted present value   d. AAB

64. The _____ is the rate that a company is expected to pay to finance its assets. WACC is the minimum return that a company must earn on existing asset base to satisfy its creditors, owners, and other providers of capital.

Companies raise money from a number of sources: common equity, preferred equity, straight debt, convertible debt, exchangeable debt, warrants, options, pension liabilities, executive stock options, governmental subsidies, and so on.

    a. Weighted average cost of capital   b. Capital intensity
    c. 4-4-5 Calendar   d. Cost of capital

65. _____ represents the total cash investment that shareholders and debtholders have made in a company. There are two different but completely equivalent methods for calculating _____. The operating approach is calculated as:

_____ = Operating Net Working Capital + Net PP'E + Capitalized Operating Leases + Other Operating Assets + Operating Intangibles - Other Operating Liabilities - Cumulative Adjustment for Amortization of R'D

Equivalently, the financing approach is calculated as:

In symbols:

$$K = D + E - M$$

_____ is used in several important measurements of financial performance, including return on _____, economic value added, and free cash flow.

a. Inventory turnover
b. Information ratio
c. Operating leverage
d. Invested capital

66. _____ is a financial measure that quantifies how well a company generates cash flow relative to the capital it has invested in its business. It is defined as Net operating profit less adjusted taxes divided by Invested Capital and is usually expressed as a percentage. In this calculation, capital invested includes all monetary capital invested: long-term debt, common and preferred shares.
a. Cash conversion cycle
b. Debt service coverage ratio
c. Sharpe ratio
d. Return on invested capital

67. _____ is the difference between the current market value of a firm and the capital contributed by investors. If _____ is positive, the firm has added value. If it is negative, the firm has destroyed value.
a. Wrap account
b. Monetary system
c. Market value added
d. Decision process tool

68. _____ refers to the additional value of a commodity over the cost of commodities used to produce it from the previous stage of production. An example is the price of gasoline at the pump over the price of the oil in it. In national accounts used in macroeconomics, it refers to the contribution of the factors of production, i.e., land, labor, and capital goods, to raising the value of a product and corresponds to the incomes received by the owners of these factors.
a. Deregulation
b. Supply shock
c. Demand shock
d. Value added

69. In corporate finance, _____ is an estimate of true economic profit after making corrective adjustments to GAAP accounting, including deducting the opportunity cost of equity capital. GAAP is estimated to ignore US$300 billion in shareholder opportunity costs. _____ can be measured as Net Operating Profit After Taxes(or NOPAT) less the money cost of capital.
a. A Random Walk Down Wall Street
b. AAB
c. ABN Amro
d. Economic value added

70. _____ is the standard framework of guidelines for financial accounting used in the United States of America. It includes the standards, conventions, and rules accountants follow in recording and summarizing transactions, and in the preparation of financial statements. _____ are now issued by the Financial Accounting Standards Board (FASB).

a. Revenue
b. Net income
c. Generally Accepted Accounting Principles
d. Depreciation

71. The _____ of 2002 (Pub.L. 107-204, 116 Stat. 745, enacted July 30, 2002), also known as the Public Company Accounting Reform and Investor Protection Act of 2002 and commonly called Sarbanes-Oxley, Sarbox or SOX, is a United States federal law enacted on July 30, 2002 in response to a number of major corporate and accounting scandals including those affecting Enron, Tyco International, Adelphia, Peregrine Systems and WorldCom.
   a. Blue sky law
   b. Foreign Corrupt Practices Act
   c. Duty of loyalty
   d. Sarbanes-Oxley Act

72. _____ relates to the cost of borrowing money. It is the price that a lender charges a borrower for the use of the lender's money. _____ is different from OPEX and CAPEX, for it relates to the capital structure of a company.
   a. ABN Amro
   b. A Random Walk Down Wall Street
   c. AAB
   d. Interest expense

73. A _____ is a profit that results from investments into a capital asset, such as stocks, bonds or real estate, which exceeds the purchase price. It is the difference between a higher selling price and a lower purchase price, resulting in a financial gain for the seller. Conversely, a capital loss arises if the proceeds from the sale of a capital asset are less than the purchase price.
   a. Capital gain
   b. Payroll tax
   c. Tax brackets
   d. Capital gains tax

74. An _____ is a tax levied on the financial income of people, corporations, or other legal entities. Various _____ systems exist, with varying degrees of tax incidence. Income taxation can be progressive, proportional, or regressive.
   a. ABN Amro
   b. A Random Walk Down Wall Street
   c. Income tax
   d. AAB

75. The _____, in terms of finance and investing, describes how the expected return of a stock or portfolio is correlated to the return of the financial market as a whole.

An asset with a beta of 0 means that its price is not at all correlated with the market; that asset is independent. A positive beta means that the asset generally follows the market.

   a. Perpetuity
   b. Current yield
   c. LIBOR market model
   d. Beta coefficient

76. _____ refers to a tax levied by various jurisdictions on the profits made by companies or associations. It is a tax on the value of the corporation's profits.

The measure of taxable profits varies from country to country.

   a. Trade finance
   b. Corporate tax
   c. First-mover advantage
   d. Proxy fight

77. In financial accounting, _____s are precautions for which the amount or probability of occurrence are not known. Typical examples are _____s for warranty costs and _____ for taxes the term reserve is used instead of term _____; such a use, however, is inconsistent with the terminology suggested by International Accounting Standards Board.
   a. Money measurement concept
   b. Momentum Accounting and Triple-Entry Bookkeeping
   c. Petty cash
   d. Provision

78. A _____ is a corporation in the United States that, for Federal income tax purposes, is taxed under 26 U.S.C. Â§ 11 and Subchapter C (26 U.S.C. Â§ 11 and Subchapter C (26 U.S.C. Â§ 301 et seq.) of Chapter 1 of the Internal Revenue Code. Most major companies (and many smaller companies) are treated as _____ for Federal income tax purposes.

The income of a _____ is taxed, whereas the income of an S corporation (with a few exceptions) is not taxed under the Federal income tax laws. The income, or loss, is applied, Pro Rata, to each Shareholder and appears on their tax return as Schedule E income/(loss).

   a. 7-Eleven
   b. 529 plan
   c. C corporation
   d. 4-4-5 Calendar

79. The term _____ has three unrelated technical definitions, and is also used in a variety of non-technical ways.

- In financial economics, it refers to any asset used to make money, as opposed to assets used for personal enjoyment or consumption. This is an important distinction because two people can disagree sharply about the value of personal assets, one person might think a sports car is more valuable than a pickup truck, another person might have the opposite taste. But if an asset is held for the purpose of making money, taste has nothing to do with it, only differences of opinion about how much money the asset will produce. With the further assumption that people agree on the probability distribution of future cash flows, it is possible to have an objective _____ pricing model. Even without the assumption of agreement, it is possible to set rational limits on _____ value.
- In governmental accounting, it is defined as any asset used in operations with an initial useful life extending beyond one reporting period. Generally, government managers have a 'stewardship' duty to maintain _____s under their control. See International Public Sector Accounting Standards for details.
- In US tax accounting, it is defined as any property other than a list of exceptions. The main exceptions are anything held for sale, and any real estate or depreciable property used in business. Almost everything you own and use for personal purposes, pleasure or investment is a _____. If something is a _____ for tax purposes, gains or losses on sale or disposition are capital gains or capital losses. For individuals, however, capital losses on property held for personal use are generally not deductible. See the IRS publication Tax Facts about Capital Gains and Losses for details.

A well-known financial accounting textbook advises that the term be avoided except in tax accounting because it is used in so many different senses, not all of them well-defined. For example it is often used as a synonym for fixed assets or for investments in securities.

A common non-technical usage occurs when people ask that employees or the environment or something else be treated as a _____.

a. Solvency
b. Capital asset
c. Settlement date
d. Political risk

80. _____ is the difference between a lower selling price and a higher purchase price, resulting in a financial loss for the seller. Pursuant to IRS TAX TIP 2009-35 'If your _____ exceeds your capital gain, the excess can be deducted on your tax return, up to an annual limit of $3,000 ($1,500 if you are married filing separately.)'.
  a. Capital loss
  b. 4-4-5 Calendar
  c. 7-Eleven
  d. 529 plan

81. In the United States, a _____ is a bond issued by a city or other local government, or their agencies. Potential issuers of these bonds include cities, counties, redevelopment agencies, school districts, publicly owned airports and seaports, and any other governmental entity (or group of governments) below the state level. They may be general obligations of the issuer or secured by specified revenues.
  a. Puttable bond
  b. Municipal bond
  c. Senior debt
  d. Premium bond

82. Under the United States Internal Revenue Code, the type of income is defined by its character. _____ is usually characterized as income other than capital gain. _____ can consist of income from wages, salaries, tips, commissions, bonuses, and other types of compensation from employment, interest, dividends, or net income from a sole proprietorship, partnership or LLC.
  a. ABN Amro
  b. AAB
  c. A Random Walk Down Wall Street
  d. Ordinary income

83. An _____ is a corporation that makes a valid election to be taxed under Subchapter S of Chapter 1 of the Internal Revenue Code.

In general, _____s do not pay any income taxes. Instead, the corporation's income or losses are divided among and passed through to its shareholders.

  a. 529 plan
  b. 4-4-5 Calendar
  c. 7-Eleven
  d. S corporation

84. _____ is the portion of income that is the subject of taxation according to the laws that determine what is income and the taxation rate for that income. Generally, _____ refers to an individual's (or corporation's) gross income, adjusted for various deductions allowable by statute. The main questions put by most individuals in any jurisdiction are 'what makes up my _____' and what tax rates should be applied such that I can work out my tax liability to the state.
  a. 529 plan
  b. 4-4-5 Calendar
  c. 7-Eleven
  d. Taxable income

85. An _____ is a contract written by a seller that conveys to the buyer the right -- but not the obligation -- to buy (in the case of a call _____) or to sell (in the case of a put _____) a particular asset, such as a piece of property such as, among others, a futures contract. In return for granting the _____, the seller collects a payment (the premium) from the buyer.

For example, buying a call _____ provides the right to buy a specified quantity of a security at a set strike price at some time on or before expiration, while buying a put _____ provides the right to sell.

a. Amortization
b. AT'T Mobility LLC
c. Annuity
d. Option

86. A _____ is a type of business entity in which partners (owners) share with each other the profits or losses of the business undertaking in which all have invested. _____s are often favored over corporations for taxation purposes, as the _____ structure does not generally incur a tax on profits before it is distributed to the partners (i.e. there is no dividend tax levied.) However, depending on the _____ structure and the jurisdiction in which it operates, owners of a _____ may be exposed to greater personal liability than they would as shareholders of a corporation.
   a. National Securities Markets Improvement Act of 1996
   b. Partnership
   c. Clayton Antitrust Act
   d. Fiduciary

87. A sole _____, or simply _____ is a type of business entity which legally has no separate existence from its owner. Hence, the limitations of liability enjoyed by a corporation and limited liability partnerships do not apply to sole proprietors. All debts of the business are debts of the owner.
   a. Just-in-time
   b. Product life cycle
   c. Free cash flow
   d. Proprietorship

Chapter 4. Analysis of Financial Statements

1. The United States _____ of 1995, Pub. L. 104-67, 109 Stat. 737 (codified as amended in scattered sections of 15 U.S.C.) ('_____') implemented several substantive changes affecting certain cases brought under the federal securities laws, including changes related to pleading, discovery, liability, class representation, and awards fees and expenses.

It was designed to reduce the number of 'frivolous' securities lawsuits filed in federal courts. In essence, it says that investors cannot proceed with a case unless they already have facts in-hand that strongly suggest a deliberate fraud.

- a. Fraud deterrence
- b. National Securities Markets Improvement Act of 1996
- c. Royalties
- d. Private Securities Litigation Reform Act

2. The U.S. Securities and Exchange Commission's (SEC's) _____, was an SEC ruling implemented in October 2000. It mandated that all publicly traded companies must disclose material information to all investors at the same time.

The regulation sought to stamp out selective disclosure, in which some investors (often large institutional investors) received market moving information before others (often smaller, individual investors).

- a. Trading strategy
- b. Regulation FD
- c. Tail risk
- d. Regulation Fair Disclosure

3. The U.S. _____ is an independent agency of the United States government which holds primary responsibility for enforcing the federal securities laws and regulating the securities industry, the nation's stock and options exchanges, and other electronic securities markets. The SEC was created by section 4 of the SEC of 1934 (now codified as 15 U.S.C. § 78d and commonly referred to as the 1934 Act.)

- a. 529 plan
- b. 7-Eleven
- c. Securities and Exchange Commission
- d. 4-4-5 Calendar

4. A _____ is a fungible, negotiable instrument representing financial value. They are broadly categorized into debt securities (such as banknotes, bonds and debentures), and equity securities; e.g., common stocks. The company or other entity issuing the _____ is called the issuer.

- a. Book entry
- b. Securities lending
- c. Security
- d. Tracking stock

5. The term _____ is a term applied to practices that are perfunctory, or seek to satisfy the minimum requirements or to conform to a convention or doctrine. It has different meanings in different fields.

In accounting, _____ earnings are those earnings of companies in addition to actual earnings calculated under the Generally Accepted Accounting Principles (GAAP) in their quarterly and yearly financial reports.

- a. Long-term liabilities
- b. Deferred financing costs
- c. Pro forma
- d. Deferred income

6. In business and accounting, _____s are everything of value that is owned by a person or company. The balance sheet of a firm records the monetary value of the _____s owned by the firm. The two major _____ classes are tangible _____s and intangible _____s.

Chapter 4. Analysis of Financial Statements

a. Accounts payable
b. Income
c. EBITDA
d. Asset

7. A _____ is a payment made by a corporation to its shareholder members. When a corporation earns a profit or surplus, that money can be put to two uses: it can either be re-invested in the business (called retained earnings), or it can be paid to the shareholders as a _____. Many corporations retain a portion of their earnings and pay the remainder as a _____.

a. Dividend
b. Dividend puzzle
c. Dividend yield
d. Special dividend

8. _____ are formal records of a business' financial activities.

_____ provide an overview of a business' financial condition in both short and long term. There are four basic _____:

1. **Balance sheet**: also referred to as statement of financial position or condition, reports on a company's assets, liabilities, and net equity as of a given point in time.
2. **Income statement**: also referred to as Profit and Loss statement (or a 'P'L'), reports on a company's income, expenses, and profits over a period of time.
3. **Statement of retained earnings**: explains the changes in a company's retained earnings over the reporting period.
4. **Statement of cash flows**: reports on a company's cash flow activities, particularly its operating, investing and financing activities.

a. Notes to the Financial Statements
b. Financial statements
c. Statement of retained earnings
d. Statement on Auditing Standards No. 70: Service Organizations

9. _____ is a measure of the ability of a debtor to pay their debts as and when they fall due. It is usually expressed as a ratio or a percentage of current liabilities.

For a corporation with a published balance sheet there are various ratios used to calculate a measure of liquidity.

a. Invested capital
b. Operating leverage
c. Operating profit margin
d. Accounting liquidity

10. The phrase _____ refers to the aspect of corporate strategy, corporate finance and management dealing with the buying, selling and combining of different companies that can aid, finance, or help a growing company in a given industry grow rapidly without having to create another business entity.

An acquisition, also known as a takeover, is the buying of one company (the 'target') by another. An acquisition may be friendly or hostile.

a. 7-Eleven
b. Mergers and acquisitions
c. 4-4-5 Calendar
d. 529 plan

11. _____ is an estimate of the fair value of corporations and their stocks, by using fundamental economic criteria. This theoretical valuation has to be perfected with market criteria, as the final purpose is to determine potential market prices.
   a. 4-4-5 Calendar
   b. Security Analysis
   c. Growth stocks
   d. Stock valuation

12. In financial accounting, a _____ or statement of financial position is a summary of a person's or organization's balances. Assets, liabilities and ownership equity are listed as of a specific date, such as the end of its financial year. A _____ is often described as a snapshot of a company's financial condition.
   a. Statement on Auditing Standards No. 70: Service Organizations
   b. Financial statements
   c. Statement of retained earnings
   d. Balance sheet

13. In finance, a _____ is a debt security, in which the authorized issuer owes the holders a debt and, depending on the terms of the _____, is obliged to pay interest (the coupon) and/or to repay the principal at a later date, termed maturity.

   Thus a _____ is a loan: the issuer is the borrower, the _____ holder is the lender, and the coupon is the interest. _____s provide the borrower with external funds to finance long-term investments, or, in the case of government _____s, to finance current expenditure.

   a. Bond
   b. Convertible bond
   c. Puttable bond
   d. Catastrophe bonds

14. _____ is the process of determining the fair price of a bond. As with any security or capital investment, the fair value of a bond is the present value of the stream of cash flows it is expected to generate. Hence, the price or value of a bond is determined by discounting the bond's expected cash flows to the present using the appropriate discount rate.
   a. Collateralized debt obligations
   b. Catastrophe bonds
   c. Bond valuation
   d. Bond fund

15. In finance, _____ is the process of estimating the potential market value of a financial asset or liability. they can be done on assets (for example, investments in marketable securities such as stocks, options, business enterprises, or intangible assets such as patents and trademarks) or on liabilities (e.g., Bonds issued by a company.) _____s are required in many contexts including investment analysis, capital budgeting, merger and acquisition transactions, financial reporting, taxable events to determine the proper tax liability, and in litigation.
   a. Margin
   b. Procter ' Gamble
   c. Share
   d. Valuation

16. _____, refers to consumption opportunity gained by an entity within a specified time frame, which is generally expressed in monetary terms. However, for households and individuals, '_____ is the sum of all the wages, salaries, profits, interests payments, rents and other forms of earnings received... in a given period of time.' For firms, _____ generally refers to net-profit: what remains of revenue after expenses have been subtracted.

Chapter 4. Analysis of Financial Statements

a. Income
b. OIBDA
c. Accrual
d. Annual report

17. An _____ is a financial statement for companies that indicates how Revenue is transformed into net income The purpose of the _____ is to show managers and investors whether the company made or lost money during the period being reported.

The important thing to remember about an _____ is that it represents a period of time.

a. AAB
b. ABN Amro
c. A Random Walk Down Wall Street
d. Income statement

18. A _____ is a monetary authority which is required to maintain a fixed exchange rate with a foreign currency. This policy objective requires the conventional objectives of a central bank to be subordinated to the exchange rate target.

a. Devaluation
b. Functional currency
c. Hard currency
d. Currency board

19. In accounting, a _____ is an asset on the balance sheet which is expected to be sold or otherwise used up in the near future, usually within one year, or one business cycle - whichever is longer. Typical _____s include cash, cash equivalents, accounts receivable, inventory, the portion of prepaid accounts which will be used within a year, and short-term investments.

On the balance sheet, assets will typically be classified into _____s and long-term assets.

a. Current asset
b. Historical cost
c. Long-term liabilities
d. Write-off

20. In accounting, _____ are considered liabilities of the business that are to be settled in cash within the fiscal year or the operating cycle, whichever period is longer.

For example accounts payable for goods, services or supplies that were purchased for use in the operation of the business and payable within a normal period of time would be _____.

Bonds, mortgages and loans that are payable over a term exceeding one year would be fixed liabilities.

a. Gross sales
b. Closing entries
c. Net income
d. Current liabilities

21. The _____ is a financial ratio that measures whether or not a firm has enough resources to pay its debts over the next 12 months. It compares a firm's current assets to its current liabilities. It is expressed as follows:

$$\text{Current ratio} = \frac{\text{Current Assets}}{\text{Current Liabilities}}$$

For example, if WXY Company's current assets are $50,000,000 and its current liabilities are $40,000,000, then its _____ would be $50,000,000 divided by $40,000,000, which equals 1.25.

a. Debt service coverage ratio
b. PEG ratio
c. Sustainable growth rate
d. Current ratio

22. The term _____ is often used to refer to the investment management of collective investments, (not necessarily) whilst the more generic fund management may refer to all forms of institutional investment as well as investment management for private investors. Investment managers who specialize in advisory or discretionary management on behalf of (normally wealthy) private investors may often refer to their services as wealth management or portfolio management often within the context of so-called 'private banking'.

The provision of 'investment management services' includes elements of financial analysis, asset selection, stock selection, plan implementation and ongoing monitoring of investments.

a. AAB
b. ABN Amro
c. A Random Walk Down Wall Street
d. Asset management

23. In finance, the Acid-test or _____ or liquid ratio measures the ability of a company to use its near cash or quick assets to immediately extinguish or retire its current liabilities. Quick assets include those current assets that presumably can be quickly converted to cash at close to their book values.

>

Generally, the acid test ratio should be 1:1 or better, however this varies widely by industry.

a. Net assets
b. Financial ratio
c. P/E ratio
d. Quick ratio

24. _____ is a list for goods and materials held available in stock by a business. It is also used for a list of the contents of a household and for a list for testamentary purposes of the possessions of someone who has died. In accounting _____ is considered an asset.

a. AAB
b. Inventory
c. ABN Amro
d. A Random Walk Down Wall Street

25. The _____ is an equation that equals the cost of goods sold divided by the average inventory. Average inventory equals beginning inventory plus ending inventory divided by 2.

The formula for _____:

$$\text{Inventory Turnover} = \frac{\text{Cost of Goods Sold}}{\text{Average Inventory}}$$

The formula for average inventory:

$$\text{Average Inventory} = \frac{\text{Beginning inventory} + \text{Ending inventory}}{2}$$

Chapter 4. Analysis of Financial Statements

A low turnover rate may point to overstocking, obsolescence, or deficiencies in the product line or marketing effort.

   a. Earnings yield
   b. Inventory turnover
   c. Operating leverage
   d. Information ratio

26. _____ is one of the Accounting Liquidity ratios, a financial ratio. This ratio measures the number of times, on average, the inventory is sold during the period. Its purpose is to measure the liquidity of the inventory.
   a. A Random Walk Down Wall Street
   b. AAB
   c. ABN Amro
   d. Inventory turnover ratio

27. _____, in bookkeeping, refers to assets, liabilities, income, and expenses recorded on individual pages of the so called book of final entry or ledger. Changes in _____ value are made by chronologically posting debit (DR) and credit (CR) entries to its page. Examples of _____s are cash, _____s receivable, mortgages, loans, land and buildings, common stock, sales, services provided, wages, and payroll overhead.
   a. Alpha
   b. Option
   c. Accretion
   d. Account

28. _____ is one of a series of accounting transactions dealing with the billing of customers who owe money to a person, company or organization for goods and services that have been provided to the customer. In most business entities this is typically done by generating an invoice and mailing or electronically delivering it to the customer, who in turn must pay it within an established timeframe called credit or payment terms.

An example of a common payment term is Net 30, meaning payment is due in the amount of the invoice 30 days from the date of invoice.

   a. Income
   b. Accounts receivable
   c. Accounting methods
   d. Impaired asset

29. In accountancy, _____ is a company's average collection period. A low number of days indicates that the company collects its outstanding receivables quickly. Typically, _____ is calculated monthly. The _____ figure is an index of the relationship between outstanding receivables and sales achieved over a given period. The _____ analysis provides general information about the number of days on average that customers take to pay invoices.
   a. Round-tripping
   b. Net pay
   c. Residual value
   d. Days sales outstanding

30. _____ plant, and equipment, is a term used in accountancy for assets and property which cannot easily be converted into cash. This can be compared with current assets such as cash or bank accounts, which are described as liquid assets. In most cases, only tangible assets are referred to as fixed.
   a. Remittance advice
   b. Petty cash
   c. Fixed asset
   d. Percentage of Completion

31. _____ is a business term and may be used as a broad measure of asset efficiency and is calculated by dividing sales revenue by the total assets.

It's also used in the Du Pont Identity:

$$\frac{Net\ Earnings}{Shareholders\ Eq.} = \frac{Net\ Earnings}{Sales(Income)} * \frac{Sales(Income)}{Total Assets} * \frac{Total\ Assets}{Shareholders\ Eq.}$$

In which,

$$Net\ Margin = \frac{Net\ Earnings}{Sales(Income)}$$
$$Total\ Asset\ Turnover = \frac{Sales(Income)}{Total Assets}$$
$$Financial\ Leverage = \frac{Average\ Total\ Assets}{Average\ Total\ Equity}$$

The net margin is a summary indicator of an income statement, Asset turnover is an indicator of the left side of the balance sheet (total assets' side) and Leverage is an indicator of the right side of the Balance Sheet (liabilities and shareholders' equity' side.)

The Du Pont Identity helps many companies or individuals, visualize and comprehend the analysis of a financial statement or annual report of a company, in return on assets and return on investments.

- a. Invested capital
- b. Operating profit margin
- c. Earnings yield
- d. Assets turnover

32. _____ is that which is owed; usually referencing assets owed, but the term can cover other obligations. In the case of assets, _____ is a means of using future purchasing power in the present before a summation has been earned. Some companies and corporations use _____ as a part of their overall corporate finance strategy.
- a. Cross-collateralization
- b. Partial Payment
- c. Credit cycle
- d. Debt

33. _____ is a financial ratio that indicates the percentage of a company's assets are provided via debt. It is the ratio of total debt (the sum of current liabilities and long-term liabilities) and total assets (the sum of current assets, fixed assets, and other assets such as 'goodwill'.)

or alternatively:

For example, a company with $2 million in total assets and $500,000 in total liabilities would have a _____ of 25%

Like all financial ratios, a company's _____ should be compared with their industry average or other competing firms.

a. Cash management
b. Cash concentration
c. Capitalization rate
d. Debt ratio

34. Earnings before interest, taxes, depreciation and amortization (_____) is a non-GAAP metric that can be used to evaluate a company's profitability.

_____ = Operating Revenue - Operating Expenses + Other Revenue

Its name comes from the fact that Operating Expenses do not include interest, taxes, or amortization. _____ is not a defined measure according to Generally Accepted Accounting Principles (GAAP), and thus can be calculated however a company wishes.

a. Accounts payable
b. Accrual
c. Invoice processing
d. EBITDA

35. In economics and finance, _____ is the practice of taking advantage of a price differential between two or more markets: striking a combination of matching deals that capitalize upon the imbalance, the profit being the difference between the market prices. When used by academics, an _____ is a transaction that involves no negative cash flow at any probabilistic or temporal state and a positive cash flow in at least one state; in simple terms, a risk-free profit.

a. Issuer
b. Initial margin
c. Arbitrage
d. Efficient-market hypothesis

36. The role of the _____ is to issue accounting standards in the United Kingdom. It is recognised for that purpose under the Companies Act 1985. It took over the task of setting accounting standards from the Accounting Standards Committee (ASC) in 1990.

a. A Random Walk Down Wall Street
b. ABN Amro
c. AAB
d. Accounting Standards Board

37. _____ is the field of accountancy concerned with the preparation of financial statements for decision makers, such as stockholders, suppliers, banks, employees, government agencies, owners, and other stakeholders. The fundamental need for _____ is to reduce principal-agent problem by measuring and monitoring agents' performance and reporting the results to interested users.

_____ is used to prepare accounting information for people outside the organization or not involved in the day to day running of the company.

a. Financial Accounting
b. 4-4-5 Calendar
c. 7-Eleven
d. 529 plan

Chapter 4. Analysis of Financial Statements

38. The _____ is a private, not-for-profit organization whose primary purpose is to develop generally accepted accounting principles (GAAP) within the United States in the public's interest. The Securities and Exchange Commission (SEC) designated the _____ as the organization responsible for setting accounting standards for public companies in the U.S. It was created in 1973, replacing the Accounting Principles Board and the Committee on Accounting Procedure of the American Institute of Certified Public Accountants. The _____'s mission is 'to establish and improve standards of financial accounting and reporting for the guidance and education of the public, including issuers, auditors, and users of financial information.'

The _____ is not a governmental body.

   a. KPMG
   b. Federal Deposit Insurance Corporation
   c. Financial Accounting Standards Board
   d. World Congress of Accountants

39. The _____ is a capital budgeting metric used by firms to decide whether they should make investments. It is an indicator of the efficiency or quality of an investment, as opposed to net present value (NPV), which indicates value or magnitude.

The IRR is the annualized effective compounded return rate which can be earned on the invested capital, i.e., the yield on the investment.

   a. Internal rate of return
   b. AAB
   c. A Random Walk Down Wall Street
   d. ABN Amro

40. The _____ founded on April 1, 2001 is the successor of the International Accounting Standards Committee (IASC) founded in June 1973 in London. It is responsible for developing the International Financial Reporting Standards (new name for the International Accounting Standards issued after 2001), and promoting the use and application of these standards.

The _____ is an independent, privately-funded accounting standard-setter based in London, UK.

   a. International Accounting Standards Board
   b. Association of Certified Public Accountants
   c. American Accounting Association
   d. International Federation of Accountants

41. In finance, _____, also known as return on investment is the ratio of money gained or lost on an investment relative to the amount of money invested. The amount of money gained or lost may be referred to as interest, profit/loss, gain/loss, or net income/loss. The money invested may be referred to as the asset, capital, principal, or the cost basis of the investment.
   a. Rate of return
   b. Composiition of Creditors
   c. Stock or scrip dividends
   d. Doctrine of the Proper Law

42. _____ is the difference between price and the costs of bringing to market whatever it is that is accounted as an enterprise (whether by harvest, extraction, manufacture, or purchase) in terms of the component costs of delivered goods and/or services and any operating or other expenses.

A key difficulty in measuring profit is in defining costs. Pure economic monetary profits can be zero or negative even in competitive equilibrium when accounted monetized costs exceed monetized price.

Chapter 4. Analysis of Financial Statements

    a. A Random Walk Down Wall Street
    b. Economic profit
    c. AAB
    d. Accounting profit

43. _____, Net Margin, Net _____ or Net Profit Ratio all refer to a measure of profitability. It is calculated using a formula and written as a percentage or a number.

$$\text{Net profit margin} = \frac{\text{Net profit after taxes}}{\text{Net Sales}}$$

The _____ is mostly used for internal comparison.

    a. 4-4-5 Calendar
    b. Net profit margin
    c. Profit maximization
    d. Profit margin

44. In finance, a _____ is collateral that the holder of a position in securities, options, or futures contracts has to deposit to cover the credit risk of his counterparty (most often his broker.) This risk can arise if the holder has done any of the following:

- borrowed cash from the counterparty to buy securities or options,
- sold securities or options short, or
- entered into a futures contract.

The collateral can be in the form of cash or securities, and it is deposited in a _____ account. On U.S. futures exchanges, '_____' was formally called performance bond.

_____ buying is buying securities with cash borrowed from a broker, using other securities as collateral.

    a. Margin
    b. Credit
    c. Procter ' Gamble
    d. Share

45. The _____ percentage shows how profitable a company's assets are in generating revenue.

_____ can be computed as:

$$\text{ROA} = \frac{\text{Net Income}}{\text{Total Assets}}$$

This number tells you 'what the company can do with what it's got', i.e. how many dollars of earnings they derive from each dollar of assets they control. It's a useful number for comparing competing companies in the same industry.

    a. Return on sales
    b. Receivables turnover ratio
    c. P/E ratio
    d. Return on assets

Chapter 4. Analysis of Financial Statements

46. The _____ of a stock is a measure of the price paid for a share relative to the annual income or profit earned by the firm per share. It is a financial ratio used for valuation: a higher _____ means that investors are paying more for each unit of income, so the stock is more expensive compared to one with lower _____.

The _____ has units of years, which can be interpreted as 'number of years of earnings to pay back purchase price'.

- a. Sustainable growth rate
- b. Quick ratio
- c. Return of capital
- d. P/E ratio

47. The _____, is a ratio used to compare a company's market value to its cash flow. It is calculated by dividing the company's market cap by the company's operating cash flow in the most recent fiscal year; or, equivalently, divide the per-share stock price by the per-share operating cash flow. In theory, the lower a stock's _____ is, the better value that stock is.

- a. Diluted Earnings Per Share
- b. Current ratio
- c. P/E ratio
- d. Price/cash flow ratio

48. _____, is when a company issues common stock or shares to the public for the first time. They are often issued by smaller, younger companies seeking capital to expand, but can also be done by large privately-owned companies looking to become publicly traded.

In an _____ the issuer may obtain the assistance of an underwriting firm, which helps it determine what type of security to issue (common or preferred), best offering price and time to bring it to market.

- a. Initial public offering
- b. Insolvency
- c. Interest
- d. Asian Financial Crisis

49. _____ is the discipline of identifying, monitoring and limiting risks. In some cases the acceptable risk may be near zero. Risks can come from accidents, natural causes and disasters as well as deliberate attacks from an adversary.

- a. FIFO
- b. 4-4-5 Calendar
- c. Penny stock
- d. Risk Management

50. In economics, business, and accounting, a _____ is the value of money that has been used up to produce something, and hence is not available for use anymore. In business, the _____ may be one of acquisition, in which case the amount of money expended to acquire it is counted as _____. In this case, money is the input that is gone in order to acquire the thing.

- a. Marginal cost
- b. Cost
- c. Fixed costs
- d. Sliding scale fees

51. In finance, the _____ is the minimum rate of return a firm must offer shareholders to compensate for waiting for their returns, and for bearing some risk.

The _____ capital for a particular company is the rate of return on investment that is required by the company's ordinary shareholders. The return consists both of dividend and capital gains, e.g. increases in the share price.

Chapter 4. Analysis of Financial Statements

a. Round-tripping
c. Net pay
b. Cost of equity
d. Residual value

52. _____ is typically a higher ranking stock than voting shares, and its terms are negotiated between the corporation and the investor.

_____ usually carry no voting rights, but may carry superior priority over common stock in the payment of dividends and upon liquidation. _____ may carry a dividend that is paid out prior to any dividends to common stock holders.

a. Preferred stock
c. Second lien loan
b. Trade-off theory
d. Follow-on offering

53. _____ measures the rate of return on the ownership interest (shareholders' equity) of the common stock owners. _____ is viewed as one of the most important financial ratios. It measures a firm's efficiency at generating profits from every dollar of shareholders' equity (also known as net assets or assets minus liabilities.)
a. Diluted Earnings Per Share
c. Return of capital
b. Return on equity
d. Return on sales

54. In business and finance, a _____ (also referred to as equity _____) of stock means a _____ of ownership in a corporation (company.) In the plural, stocks is often used as a synonym for _____s especially in the United States, but it is less commonly used that way outside of North America.

In the United Kingdom, South Africa, and Australia, stock can also refer to completely different financial instruments such as government bonds or, less commonly, to all kinds of marketable securities.

a. Procter ' Gamble
c. Bucket shop
b. Margin
d. Share

55. _____ is the process of comparing the cost, time or quality of what one organization does against what another organization does. The result is often a business case for making changes in order to make improvements.

Also referred to as 'best practice _____' or 'process _____', it is a process used in management and particularly strategic management, in which organizations evaluate various aspects of their processes in relation to best practice, usually within their own sector.

a. 529 plan
c. 7-Eleven
b. 4-4-5 Calendar
d. Benchmarking

56. The _____ is a private, not-for-profit organization whose primary purpose is to develop generally accepted accounting principles (GAAP) within the United States in the public's interest. The Securities and Exchange Commission (SEC) designated the _____ as the organization responsible for setting accounting standards for public companies in the U.S. It was created in 1973, replacing the Accounting Principles Board and the Committee on Accounting Procedure of the American Institute of Certified Public Accountants. The _____'s mission is 'to establish and improve standards of financial accounting and reporting for the guidance and education of the public, including issuers, auditors, and users of financial information.'

Chapter 4. Analysis of Financial Statements

The _____ is not a governmental body.

a. Credit karma
b. MRU Holdings
c. PlaNet Finance
d. FASB

57. _____ is a specific term used in companies' financial reporting from the company-whole point of view. Because that use excludes the effects of changing ownership interest, an economic measure of _____ is necessary for financial analysis from the shareholders' point of view

_____ is defined by the Financial Accounting Standards Board, or FASB, as 'e;the change in equity [net assets] of a business enterprise during a period from transactions and other events and circumstances from nonowner sources. It includes all changes in equity during a period except those resulting from investments by owners and distributions to owners.'e;

_____ is the sum of net income and other items that must bypass the income statement because they have not been realized, including items like an unrealized holding gain or loss from available for sale securities and foreign currency translation gains or losses.

a. 4-4-5 Calendar
b. 7-Eleven
c. Comprehensive income
d. 529 plan

58. _____ refers to an assessment of the viability, stability and profitability of a business, sub-business or project.

It is performed by professionals who prepare reports using ratios that make use of information taken from financial statements and other reports. These reports are usually presented to top management as one of their bases in making business decisions.

a. 529 plan
b. Value investing
c. 4-4-5 Calendar
d. Financial analysis

59. The institution most often referenced by the word '_____' is a public or publicly traded _____, the shares of which are traded on a public stock exchange (e.g., the New York Stock Exchange or Nasdaq in the United States) where shares of stock of _____s are bought and sold by and to the general public. Most of the largest businesses in the world are publicly traded _____s. However, the majority of _____s are said to be closely held, privately held or close _____s, meaning that no ready market exists for the trading of shares.

a. Protect
b. Depository Trust Company
c. Federal Home Loan Mortgage Corporation
d. Corporation

60. _____ or financing is to provide capital (funds), which means money for a project, a person, a business or any other private or public institutions.

Those funds can be allocated for either short term or long term purposes. The health fund is a new way of _____ private healthcare centers.

a. Synthetic CDO
c. Funding

b. Product life cycle
d. Proxy fight

61. _____ is the set of processes, customs, policies, laws and institutions affecting the way a corporation is directed, administered or controlled. _____ also includes the relationships among the many stakeholders involved and the goals for which the corporation is governed. The principal stakeholders are the shareholders, management and the board of directors.

a. Patent
c. Due diligence

b. Corporate governance
d. Foreign Corrupt Practices Act

Chapter 5. Bonds, Bond Valuation, and Interest Rates

1. In finance, a _____ is a debt security, in which the authorized issuer owes the holders a debt and, depending on the terms of the _____, is obliged to pay interest (the coupon) and/or to repay the principal at a later date, termed maturity.

   Thus a _____ is a loan: the issuer is the borrower, the _____ holder is the lender, and the coupon is the interest. _____s provide the borrower with external funds to finance long-term investments, or, in the case of government _____s, to finance current expenditure.

   a. Puttable bond
   b. Catastrophe bonds
   c. Convertible bond
   d. Bond

2. A _____ is an international bond that is denominated in a currency not native to the country where it is issued. It can be categorised according to the currency in which it is issued. London is one of the centers of the _____ market, but _____s may be traded throughout the world - for example in Singapore or Tokyo.

   a. Interest rate option
   b. Eurobond
   c. Economic entity
   d. Education production function

3. In financial accounting, the term _____ is most commonly used to describe any part of shareholders' equity, except for basic share capital. Sometimes, the term is used instead of the term provision; such a use, however, is inconsistent with the terminology suggested by International Accounting Standards Board. For more information about provisions, see provision (accounting.)

   a. FIFO and LIFO accounting
   b. Treasury stock
   c. Closing entries
   d. Reserve

4. _____ are government bonds issued by the United States Department of the Treasury through the Bureau of the Public Debt. They are the debt financing instruments of the U.S. Federal government, and they are often referred to simply as Treasuries or Treasurys. There are four types of marketable _____: Treasury bills, Treasury notes, Treasury bonds, and Treasury Inflation Protected Securities (TIPS.)

   a. Treasury Inflation Protected Securities
   b. Treasury Inflation-Protected Securities
   c. Treasury securities
   d. 4-4-5 Calendar

5. _____ is a fee paid on borrowed assets. It is the price paid for the use of borrowed money, or, money earned by deposited funds. Assets that are sometimes lent with _____ include money, shares, consumer goods through hire purchase, major assets such as aircraft, and even entire factories in finance lease arrangements.

   a. AAB
   b. A Random Walk Down Wall Street
   c. Insolvency
   d. Interest

6. An _____ is the price a borrower pays for the use of money they do not own, and the return a lender receives for deferring the use of funds, by lending it to the borrower. _____s are normally expressed as a percentage rate over the period of one year.

   _____s targets are also a vital tool of monetary policy and are used to control variables like investment, inflation, and unemployment.

   a. ABN Amro
   b. Interest rate
   c. A Random Walk Down Wall Street
   d. AAB

Chapter 5. Bonds, Bond Valuation, and Interest Rates 67

7. In finance, a _____ is a security that entitles the holder to buy stock of the company that issued it at a specified price, which is usually higher than the stock price at time of issue.

_____s are frequently attached to bonds or preferred stock as a sweetener, allowing the issuer to pay lower interest rates or dividends. They can be used to enhance the yield of the bond, and make them more attractive to potential buyers.

a. Credit
b. Clearing
c. Warrant
d. Clearing house

8. In business and accounting, _____s are everything of value that is owned by a person or company. The balance sheet of a firm records the monetary value of the _____s owned by the firm. The two major _____ classes are tangible _____s and intangible _____s.

a. EBITDA
b. Asset
c. Accounts payable
d. Income

9. In finance, _____ is the process of estimating the potential market value of a financial asset or liability. they can be done on assets (for example, investments in marketable securities such as stocks, options, business enterprises, or intangible assets such as patents and trademarks) or on liabilities (e.g., Bonds issued by a company.) _____s are required in many contexts including investment analysis, capital budgeting, merger and acquisition transactions, financial reporting, taxable events to determine the proper tax liability, and in litigation.

a. Valuation
b. Margin
c. Share
d. Procter ' Gamble

10. The term _____ has three unrelated technical definitions, and is also used in a variety of non-technical ways.

- In financial economics, it refers to any asset used to make money, as opposed to assets used for personal enjoyment or consumption. This is an important distinction because two people can disagree sharply about the value of personal assets, one person might think a sports car is more valuable than a pickup truck, another person might have the opposite taste. But if an asset is held for the purpose of making money, taste has nothing to do with it, only differences of opinion about how much money the asset will produce. With the further assumption that people agree on the probability distribution of future cash flows, it is possible to have an objective _____ pricing model. Even without the assumption of agreement, it is possible to set rational limits on _____ value.
- In governmental accounting, it is defined as any asset used in operations with an initial useful life extending beyond one reporting period. Generally, government managers have a 'stewardship' duty to maintain _____s under their control. See International Public Sector Accounting Standards for details.
- In US tax accounting, it is defined as any property other than a list of exceptions. The main exceptions are anything held for sale, and any real estate or depreciable property used in business. Almost everything you own and use for personal purposes, pleasure or investment is a _____. If something is a _____ for tax purposes, gains or losses on sale or disposition are capital gains or capital losses. For individuals, however, capital losses on property held for personal use are generally not deductible. See the IRS publication Tax Facts about Capital Gains and Losses for details.

A well-known financial accounting textbook advises that the term be avoided except in tax accounting because it is used in so many different senses, not all of them well-defined. For example it is often used as a synonym for fixed assets or for investments in securities.

A common non-technical usage occurs when people ask that employees or the environment or something else be treated as a _____.

   a. Solvency
   c. Settlement date
   b. Political risk
   d. Capital Asset

11. In finance, the _____ is used to determine a theoretically appropriate required rate of return of an asset, if that asset is to be added to an already well-diversified portfolio, given that asset's non-diversifiable risk. The model takes into account the asset's sensitivity to non-diversifiable risk (also known as systemic risk or market risk), often represented by the quantity beta (β) in the financial industry, as well as the expected return of the market and the expected return of a theoretical risk-free asset.

The model was introduced by Jack Treynor (1961, 1962), William Sharpe (1964), John Lintner (1965a,b) and Jan Mossin (1966) independently, building on the earlier work of Harry Markowitz on diversification and modern portfolio theory.

   a. Random walk hypothesis
   c. Cox-Ingersoll-Ross model
   b. Capital Asset Pricing Model
   d. Hull-White model

12. A _____ is a bond issued by a corporation. The term is usually applied to longer-term debt instruments, generally with a maturity date falling at least a year after their issue date. (The term 'commercial paper' is sometimes used for instruments with a shorter maturity.)
   a. Serial bond
   c. Brady bonds
   b. Government bond
   d. Corporate bond

13. In finance, _____ occurs when a debtor has not met its legal obligations according to the debt contract, e.g. it has not made a scheduled payment, or has violated a loan covenant (condition) of the debt contract. _____ may occur if the debtor is either unwilling or unable to pay their debt. This can occur with all debt obligations including bonds, mortgages, loans, and promissory notes.
   a. Default
   c. Vendor finance
   b. Debt validation
   d. Credit crunch

14. _____ is the risk of loss due to a debtor's non-payment of a loan or other line of credit (either the principal or interest (coupon) or both)

Most lenders employ their own models (credit scorecards) to rank potential and existing customers according to risk, and then apply appropriate strategies. With products such as unsecured personal loans or mortgages, lenders charge a higher price for higher risk customers and vice versa. With revolving products such as credit cards and overdrafts, risk is controlled through careful setting of credit limits.

   a. Market risk
   c. Transaction risk
   b. Liquidity risk
   d. Credit risk

15. _____ is the concept of adding accumulated interest back to the principal, so that interest is earned on interest from that moment on. The act of declaring interest to be principal is called compounding (i.e., interest is compounded.) A loan, for example, may have its interest compounded every month: in this case, a loan with $100 principal and 1% interest per month would have a balance of $101 at the end of the first month.
   a. Penny stock
   b. Risk management
   c. Compound interest
   d. 4-4-5 Calendar

16. The coupon or _____ of a bond is the amount of interest paid per year expressed as a percentage of the face value of the bond.

For example if you hold $10,000 nominal of a bond described as a 4.5% loan stock, you will receive $450 in interest each year (probably in two installments of $225 each.)

Not all bonds have coupons.

   a. Revenue bonds
   b. Zero-coupon bond
   c. Puttable bond
   d. Coupon rate

17. A _____ is a financial contract whose value is derived from the value of something else (known as the underlying.) The underlying on which a _____ is based can be an asset, weather conditions bonds or other forms of credit.
   a. 529 plan
   b. 7-Eleven
   c. Derivative
   d. 4-4-5 Calendar

18. A _____ is a payment made by a corporation to its shareholder members. When a corporation earns a profit or surplus, that money can be put to two uses: it can either be re-invested in the business (called retained earnings), or it can be paid to the shareholders as a _____. Many corporations retain a portion of their earnings and pay the remainder as a _____.
   a. Special dividend
   b. Dividend
   c. Dividend yield
   d. Dividend puzzle

19. The phrase _____ refers to the aspect of corporate strategy, corporate finance and management dealing with the buying, selling and combining of different companies that can aid, finance, or help a growing company in a given industry grow rapidly without having to create another business entity.

An acquisition, also known as a takeover, is the buying of one company (the 'target') by another. An acquisition may be friendly or hostile.

   a. 7-Eleven
   b. 4-4-5 Calendar
   c. Mergers and acquisitions
   d. 529 plan

20. In the United States, a _____ is a bond issued by a city or other local government, or their agencies. Potential issuers of these bonds include cities, counties, redevelopment agencies, school districts, publicly owned airports and seaports, and any other governmental entity (or group of governments) below the state level. They may be general obligations of the issuer or secured by specified revenues.

a. Puttable bond
c. Senior debt
b. Premium bond
d. Municipal bond

21. _____, in finance and accounting, means stated value or face value. From this comes the expressions at par (at the _____), over par (over _____) and under par (under _____.)

The term '_____' has several meanings depending on context and geography.

a. Par value
c. Sinking fund
b. FIDC
d. Global Squeeze

22. _____ occurs when an entity that has issued callable bonds calls those debt securities from the debt holders with the express purpose of reissuing new debt at a lower coupon rate. In essence, the issue of new, lower-interest debt allows the company to prematurely refund the older, higher-interest debt.

On the contrary, NonRefundable Bonds may be callable but they cannot be re-issued with a lower coupon rate.

a. Systematic risk
c. No-arbitrage bounds
b. Market neutral
d. Refunding

23. _____ is an estimate of the fair value of corporations and their stocks, by using fundamental economic criteria. This theoretical valuation has to be perfected with market criteria, as the final purpose is to determine potential market prices.

a. 4-4-5 Calendar
c. Security Analysis
b. Growth stocks
d. Stock valuation

24. _____ is the process of decreasing an amount over a period of time. The word comes from Middle English amortisen to kill, alienate in mortmain, from Anglo-French amorteser, alteration of amortir, from Vulgar Latin admortire to kill, from Latin ad- + mort-, mors death. Particular instances of the term include:

- _____ (business), the allocation of a lump sum amount to different time periods, particularly for loans and other forms of finance, including related interest or other finance charges.
  - _____ schedule, a table detailing each periodic payment on a loan (typically a mortgage), as generated by an _____ calculator.
  - Negative _____, an _____ schedule where the loan amount actually increases through not paying the full interest
- Amortized analysis, analyzing the execution cost of algorithms over a sequence of operations.
- _____ of capital expenditures of certain assets under accounting rules, particularly intangible assets, in a manner analogous to depreciation.
- _____ (tax law)

Chapter 5. Bonds, Bond Valuation, and Interest Rates

_____ is also used in the context of zoning regulations and describes the time in which a property owner has to relocate when the property's use constitutes a preexisting nonconforming use under zoning regulations.

- Depreciation

a. AT'T Inc.
b. Amortization
c. Intrinsic value
d. Option

25. _____ is the process of determining the fair price of a bond. As with any security or capital investment, the fair value of a bond is the present value of the stream of cash flows it is expected to generate. Hence, the price or value of a bond is determined by discounting the bond's expected cash flows to the present using the appropriate discount rate.
a. Collateralized debt obligations
b. Catastrophe bonds
c. Bond fund
d. Bond valuation

26. A _____ is a bond bought at a price lower than its face value, with the face value repaid at the time of maturity. It does not make periodic interest payments, or so-called 'coupons,' hence the term zero-coupon bond. Investors earn return from the compounded interest all paid at maturity plus the difference between the discounted price of the bond and its par value.
a. Zero coupon bond
b. Callable bond
c. Bowie bonds
d. Municipal bond

27. A _____ is something for which there is demand, but which is supplied without qualitative differentiation across a market. It is a product that is the same no matter who produces it, such as petroleum, notebook paper, or milk. In other words, copper is copper.
a. 4-4-5 Calendar
b. 7-Eleven
c. Commodity
d. 529 plan

28. A '_____' is a 'Charge' that is paid to obtain the right to delay a payment. Essentially, the payer purchases the right to make a given payment in the future instead of in the Present. The '_____', or 'Charge' that must be paid to delay the payment, is simply the difference between what the payment amount would be if it were paid in the present and what the payment amount would be paid if it were paid in the future.
a. Value at risk
b. Risk modeling
c. Discount
d. Risk aversion

29. In financial accounting, _____s are precautions for which the amount or probability of occurrence are not known. Typical examples are _____s for warranty costs and _____ for taxes the term reserve is used instead of term _____; such a use, however, is inconsistent with the terminology suggested by International Accounting Standards Board.
a. Petty cash
b. Momentum Accounting and Triple-Entry Bookkeeping
c. Money measurement concept
d. Provision

30. _____, in accrual accounting, is any account where the asset or liability is not realized until a future date, e.g. annuities, charges, taxes, income, etc. The _____ item may be carried, dependent on type of deferral, as either an asset or liability. See also: accrual

_____ is also used in the university admissions process. It is the action by which a school rejects a student for early admission but still opts to review that student in the general admissions pool.

a. Current asset
c. Revenue
b. Net profit
d. Deferred

31. _____ is a life of security. It may also refer to the final payment date of a loan or other financial instrument, at which point all remaining interest and principal is due to be paid.

1, 3, 6 months _____ band can be calculated by using 30-day per month periods.

a. False billing
c. Replacement cost
b. Primary market
d. Maturity

32. An _____ is a contract written by a seller that conveys to the buyer the right -- but not the obligation -- to buy (in the case of a call _____) or to sell (in the case of a put _____) a particular asset, such as a piece of property such as, among others, a futures contract. In return for granting the _____, the seller collects a payment (the premium) from the buyer.

For example, buying a call _____ provides the right to buy a specified quantity of a security at a set strike price at some time on or before expiration, while buying a put _____ provides the right to sell.

a. Annuity
c. Option
b. AT'T Mobility LLC
d. Amortization

33. A _____ is a fungible, negotiable instrument representing financial value. They are broadly categorized into debt securities (such as banknotes, bonds and debentures), and equity securities; e.g., common stocks. The company or other entity issuing the _____ is called the issuer.

a. Book entry
c. Security
b. Tracking stock
d. Securities lending

34. The U.S. _____ is an independent agency of the United States government which holds primary responsibility for enforcing the federal securities laws and regulating the securities industry, the nation's stock and options exchanges, and other electronic securities markets. The SEC was created by section 4 of the SEC of 1934 (now codified as 15 U.S.C. § 78d and commonly referred to as the 1934 Act.)

a. 529 plan
c. 4-4-5 Calendar
b. 7-Eleven
d. Securities and Exchange Commission

35. A _____ is a fund established by a government agency or business for the purpose of reducing debt.

Chapter 5. Bonds, Bond Valuation, and Interest Rates

The _____ was first used in Great Britain in the 18th century to reduce national debt. While used by Robert Walpole in 1716 and effectively in the 1720s and early 1730s, it originated in the commercial tax syndicates of the Italian peninsula of the 14th century to retire redeemable public debt of those cities.

a. Sinking fund
b. Debtor
c. Modern portfolio theory
d. Security interest

36. _____ measures the nominal future sum of money that a given sum of money is 'worth' at a specified time in the future assuming a certain interest rate rate of return; it is the present value multiplied by the accumulation function.

The value does not include corrections for inflation or other factors that affect the true value of money in the future. This is used in time value of money calculations.

a. Future value
b. Future-oriented
c. Present value of costs
d. Discounted cash flow

37. In business, a _____ is the purchase of one company (the target) by another (the acquirer or bidder). In the UK the term refers to the acquisition of a public company whose shares are listed on a stock exchange, in contrast to the acquisition of a private company.

Before a bidder makes an offer for another company, it usually first informs that company's board of directors.

a. Stock swap
b. 529 plan
c. 4-4-5 Calendar
d. Takeover

38. In finance, a _____ is a type of bond that can be converted into shares of stock in the issuing company, usually at some pre-announced ratio. It is a hybrid security with debt- and equity-like features. Although it typically has a low coupon rate, the holder is compensated with the ability to convert the bond to common stock, usually at a substantial discount to the stock's market value.

a. Convertible bond
b. Corporate bond
c. Gilts
d. Bond fund

39. _____, refers to consumption opportunity gained by an entity within a specified time frame, which is generally expressed in monetary terms. However, for households and individuals, '_____ is the sum of all the wages, salaries, profits, interests payments, rents and other forms of earnings received... in a given period of time.' For firms, _____ generally refers to net-profit: what remains of revenue after expenses have been subtracted.

a. Accrual
b. OIBDA
c. Annual report
d. Income

40. _____ is typically a higher ranking stock than voting shares, and its terms are negotiated between the corporation and the investor.

_____ usually carry no voting rights, but may carry superior priority over common stock in the payment of dividends and upon liquidation. _____ may carry a dividend that is paid out prior to any dividends to common stock holders.

a. Follow-on offering
b. Preferred stock
c. Trade-off theory
d. Second lien loan

41. _____ refers to a business or organization attempting to acquire goods or services to accomplish the goals of the enterprise. Though there are several organizations that attempt to set standards in the _____ process, processes can vary greatly between organizations. Typically the word '_____' is not used interchangeably with the word 'procurement', since procurement typically includes Expediting, Supplier Quality, and Traffic and Logistics (T'L) in addition to _____.
   a. 4-4-5 Calendar
   b. 529 plan
   c. 7-Eleven
   d. Purchasing

42. _____ is the value of goods/services compared to the amount paid with a currency. Currency can be either a commodity money, like gold or silver, or fiat currency like US dollars which are the world reserve currency. As Adam Smith noted, having money gives one the ability to 'command' others' labor, so _____ to some extent is power over other people, to the extent that they are willing to trade their labor or goods for money or currency.
   a. 529 plan
   b. Purchasing power
   c. 4-4-5 Calendar
   d. 7-Eleven

43. A _____ is the price of a single share of a no. of saleable stocks of the company. Once the stock is purchased, the owner becomes a shareholder of the company that issued the share.
   a. Stock split
   b. Share price
   c. Whisper numbers
   d. Trading curb

44. In financial accounting, a _____ or statement of financial position is a summary of a person's or organization's balances. Assets, liabilities and ownership equity are listed as of a specific date, such as the end of its financial year. A _____ is often described as a snapshot of a company's financial condition.
   a. Financial statements
   b. Balance sheet
   c. Statement of retained earnings
   d. Statement on Auditing Standards No. 70: Service Organizations

45. In economics, business, and accounting, a _____ is the value of money that has been used up to produce something, and hence is not available for use anymore. In business, the _____ may be one of acquisition, in which case the amount of money expended to acquire it is counted as _____. In this case, money is the input that is gone in order to acquire the thing.
   a. Fixed costs
   b. Sliding scale fees
   c. Marginal cost
   d. Cost

46. In finance, _____ are stocks that appreciate in value and yield a high return on equity (ROE.) Analysts compute ROE by taking the company's net income and dividing it by the company's equity. To be classified as a growth stock, analysts expect to see at least 15 percent return on equity.
   a. Security Analysis
   b. Growth stocks
   c. 4-4-5 Calendar
   d. Stock valuation

47. In business and finance, a _____ (also referred to as equity _____) of stock means a _____ of ownership in a corporation (company.) In the plural, stocks is often used as a synonym for _____s especially in the United States, but it is less commonly used that way outside of North America.

Chapter 5. Bonds, Bond Valuation, and Interest Rates

In the United Kingdom, South Africa, and Australia, stock can also refer to completely different financial instruments such as government bonds or, less commonly, to all kinds of marketable securities.

- a. Bucket shop
- b. Procter ' Gamble
- c. Margin
- d. Share

48. The _____ is a capital budgeting metric used by firms to decide whether they should make investments. It is an indicator of the efficiency or quality of an investment, as opposed to net present value (NPV), which indicates value or magnitude.

The IRR is the annualized effective compounded return rate which can be earned on the invested capital, i.e., the yield on the investment.

- a. AAB
- b. A Random Walk Down Wall Street
- c. ABN Amro
- d. Internal rate of return

49. In finance, _____, also known as return on investment is the ratio of money gained or lost on an investment relative to the amount of money invested. The amount of money gained or lost may be referred to as interest, profit/loss, gain/loss, or net income/loss. The money invested may be referred to as the asset, capital, principal, or the cost basis of the investment.

- a. Stock or scrip dividends
- b. Rate of return
- c. Doctrine of the Proper Law
- d. Composiition of Creditors

50. An _____ can be defined as a contract which provides an income stream in return for an initial payment.

An immediate _____ is an _____ for which the time between the contract date and the date of the first payment is not longer than the time interval between payments. A common use for an immediate _____ is to provide a pension to a retired person or persons.

- a. Annuity
- b. Intrinsic value
- c. AT'T Inc.
- d. Amortization

51. A _____ is a generic term for any bond selling for more than 100% of par value, i.e., at a price greater than 100.00, which typically occurs for high coupon bonds in a falling interest rate climate.

- a. Revenue bonds
- b. Nominal yield
- c. Municipal bond
- d. Premium bond

52. In finance, the term _____ describes the amount in cash that returns to the owners of a security. Normally it does not include the price variations, at the difference of the total return. _____ applies to various stated rates of return on stocks (common and preferred, and convertible), fixed income instruments (bonds, notes, bills, strips, zero coupon), and some other investment type insurance products (e.g. annuities.)

- a. 4-4-5 Calendar
- b. Yield
- c. Macaulay duration
- d. Yield to maturity

Chapter 5. Bonds, Bond Valuation, and Interest Rates

53. The _____ or redemption yield is the yield promised to the bondholder on the assumption that the bond or other fixed-interest security such as gilts will be held to maturity, that all coupon and principal payments will be made and coupon payments are reinvested at the bond's promised yield at the same rate as invested. It is a measure of the return of the bond. This technique in theory allows investors to calculate the fair value of different financial instruments.

  a. Yield to maturity
  b. Yield
  c. 4-4-5 Calendar
  d. Macaulay duration

54. The _____, interest yield, income yield, flat yield or running yield is a financial term used in reference to bonds and other fixed-interest securities such as gilts. It is the ratio of the annual interest payment and the bond's current price.

The _____ only therefore refers to the yield of the bond at the current moment. It does not reflect the total return over the life of the bond. In particular, it takes no account of reinvestment risk (the uncertainty about the rate at which future cashflows can be reinvested) or the fact that bonds usually mature at par value, which can be an important component of a bond's return.

  a. Perpetuity
  b. Modified Internal Rate of Return
  c. Stochastic volatility
  d. Current yield

55. A _____ or Capital increase is a new equity issue by a company after its IPO. It differs from a secondary equity offering, in which owners (not the company) sell their shares. In the latter case, the company gets no money and no ownership dilution happens, for the company does not issue new shares.

  a. FATF Blacklist
  b. Debt-for-equity swap
  c. Sinking fund
  d. Seasoned equity offering

56. A _____ is a profit that results from investments into a capital asset, such as stocks, bonds or real estate, which exceeds the purchase price. It is the difference between a higher selling price and a lower purchase price, resulting in a financial gain for the seller. Conversely, a capital loss arises if the proceeds from the sale of a capital asset are less than the purchase price.

  a. Capital gains tax
  b. Capital gain
  c. Tax brackets
  d. Payroll tax

57. The term _____ usually refers to a company that is permitted to offer its registered securities for sale to the general public, typically through a stock exchange, or occasionally a company whose stock is traded over the counter via market makers who use non-exchange quotation services.

The term '_____' may also refer to a company owned by the government.

  a. Public Company
  b. General partnership
  c. First Prudential Markets
  d. Corporation

58. The _____ (sometimes called 'Peekaboo') is a private-sector, non-profit corporation created by the Sarbanes-Oxley Act, a 2002 United States federal law, to oversee the auditors of public companies. Its stated purpose is to 'protect the interests of investors and further the public interest in the preparation of informative, fair, and independent audit reports'. Although a private entity, the _____ has many government-like regulatory functions, making it in some ways similar to the private Self Regulatory Organizations (SROs) that regulate stock markets and other aspects of the financial markets in the United States.

Chapter 5. Bonds, Bond Valuation, and Interest Rates

a. World Trade Organization
b. Gamelan Council
c. Financial Crimes Enforcement Network
d. Public Company Accounting Oversight Board

59. The term _____ is a term applied to practices that are perfunctory, or seek to satisfy the minimum requirements or to conform to a convention or doctrine. It has different meanings in different fields.

In accounting, _____ earnings are those earnings of companies in addition to actual earnings calculated under the Generally Accepted Accounting Principles (GAAP) in their quarterly and yearly financial reports.

a. Deferred income
b. Pro forma
c. Deferred financing costs
d. Long-term liabilities

60. In economics, _____ is a rise in the general level of prices of goods and services in an economy over a period of time. The term '_____' once referred to increases in the money supply (monetary _____); however, economic debates about the relationship between money supply and price levels have led to its primary use today in describing price _____. _____ can also be described as a decline in the real value of money--a loss of purchasing power in the medium of exchange which is also the monetary unit of account.

a. Inflation
b. ABN Amro
c. A Random Walk Down Wall Street
d. AAB

61. _____ are the inflation-indexed bonds issued by the U.S. Treasury. The principal is adjusted to the Consumer Price Index, the commonly used measure of inflation. The coupon rate is constant, but generates a different amount of interest when multiplied by the inflation-adjusted principal, thus protecting the holder against inflation. _____ are currently offered in 5-year, 10-year and 20-year maturities.

a. Treasury Inflation Protected Securities
b. Treasury securities
c. 4-4-5 Calendar
d. Treasury Inflation-Protected Securities

62.

In finance, the _____ can be the expected rate of return above the risk-free interest rate. When measuring risk, a common sense approach is to compare the risk-free return on T-bills and the very risky return on other investments. The difference between these two returns can be interpreted as a measure of the excess return on the average risky asset. This excess return is known as the _____.

a. Risk premium
b. Risk adjusted return on capital
c. Risk aversion
d. Risk modeling

63. A _____ is defined as a certificate of agreement of loans which is given under the company's stamp and carries an undertaking that the _____ holder will get a fixed return (fixed on the basis of interest rates) and the principal amount whenever the _____ matures.

In finance, a _____ is a long-term debt instrument used by governments and large companies to obtain funds. It is defined as 'a debt secured only by the debtor's earning power, not by a lien on any specific asset.' It is similar to a bond except the securitization conditions are different.

a. Collection agency
b. Partial Payment
c. Collateral Management
d. Debenture

64. _____ is a legally declared inability or impairment of ability of an individual or organization to pay their creditors. Creditors may file a _____ petition against a debtor ('involuntary _____') in an effort to recoup a portion of what they are owed or initiate a restructuring. In the majority of cases, however, _____ is initiated by the debtor (a 'voluntary _____' that is filed by the bankrupt individual or organization.)
   a. 4-4-5 Calendar
   b. 529 plan
   c. Debt settlement
   d. Bankruptcy

65. A _____ is an exchange of promises between two or more parties to do an act which is enforceable in a court of law. It is where an unqualified offer meets a qualified acceptance and the parties reach Consensus ad Idem. The parties must have the necessary capacity to _____ and the _____ must not be either trifling, indeterminate, impossible or illegal.
   a. 4-4-5 Calendar
   b. 7-Eleven
   c. Contract
   d. 529 plan

66. _____ is the set of processes, customs, policies, laws and institutions affecting the way a corporation is directed, administered or controlled. _____ also includes the relationships among the many stakeholders involved and the goals for which the corporation is governed. The principal stakeholders are the shareholders, management and the board of directors.
   a. Due diligence
   b. Patent
   c. Foreign Corrupt Practices Act
   d. Corporate governance

67. A _____, in its most general sense, is a solemn promise to engage in or refrain from a specified action.

More specifically, a _____, in contrast to a contract, is a one-way agreement whereby the _____er is the only party bound by the promise. A _____ may have conditions and prerequisites that qualify the undertaking, including the actions of second or third parties, but there is no inherent agreement by such other parties to fulfill those requirements.

   a. Partnership
   b. Federal Trade Commission Act
   c. Clayton Antitrust Act
   d. Covenant

68. A bond is considered _____ if its credit rating is BBB- or higher by Standard and Poor's or Baa3 or higher by Moody's or BBB(low) or higher by DBRS. Generally they are bonds that are judged by the rating agency as likely enough to meet payment obligations that banks are allowed to invest in them.

Ratings play a critical role in determining how much companies and other entities that issue debt, including sovereign governments, have to pay to access credit markets, i.e., the amount of interest they pay on their issued debt.

   a. Investment grade
   b. ABN Amro
   c. A Random Walk Down Wall Street
   d. AAB

Chapter 5. Bonds, Bond Valuation, and Interest Rates

69. _____ are a class of computational algorithms that rely on repeated random sampling to compute their results. _____ are often used when simulating physical and mathematical systems. Because of their reliance on repeated computation and random or pseudo-random numbers, _____ are most suited to calculation by a computer.

_____ in finance are often used to calculate the value of companies, to evaluate investments in projects at corporate level or to evaluate financial derivatives. The method is intended for financial analysts who want to construct stochastic or probabilistic financial models as opposed to the traditional static and deterministic models.

   a. Sample size
   c. Correlation
   b. Semivariance
   d. Monte Carlo methods

70. _____ is the discipline of identifying, monitoring and limiting risks. In some cases the acceptable risk may be near zero. Risks can come from accidents, natural causes and disasters as well as deliberate attacks from an adversary.
   a. FIFO
   c. 4-4-5 Calendar
   b. Risk management
   d. Penny stock

71. In probability and statistics, the _____ of a collection of numbers is a measure of the dispersion of the numbers from their expected (mean) value. It can apply to a probability distribution, a random variable, a population or a data set. The _____ is usually denoted with the letter σ (lowercase sigma.)
   a. Sample size
   c. Mean
   b. Kurtosis
   d. Standard deviation

72. In finance, a _____ (non-investment grade bond, speculative grade bond or junk bond) is a bond that is rated below investment grade at the time of purchase. These bonds have a higher risk of default or other adverse credit events, but typically pay higher yields than better quality bonds in order to make them attractive to investors.
   a. High yield bond
   c. Sharpe ratio
   b. Private equity
   d. Volatility

73. _____ is the risk (variability in value) borne by an interest-bearing asset, such as a loan or a bond, due to variability of interest rates. In general, as rates rise, the price of a fixed rate bond will fall, and vice versa. _____ is commonly measured by the bond's duration.
   a. A Random Walk Down Wall Street
   c. International Fisher effect
   b. Official bank rate
   d. Interest rate risk

74. _____ is a measure of the ability of a debtor to pay their debts as and when they fall due. It is usually expressed as a ratio or a percentage of current liabilities.

For a corporation with a published balance sheet there are various ratios used to calculate a measure of liquidity.

   a. Operating leverage
   c. Invested capital
   b. Operating profit margin
   d. Accounting liquidity

75. _____ is a term used to explain a difference between two types of financial securities (e.g. stocks), that have all the same qualities except liquidity. For example:

_____ is a segment of a three-part theory that works to explain the behavior of yield curves for interest rates. The upwards-curving component of the interest yield can be explained by the _____.

a. 7-Eleven
b. 529 plan
c. 4-4-5 Calendar
d. Liquidity premium

76. In finance, the yield curve is the relation between the interest rate (or cost of borrowing) and the time to maturity of the debt for a given borrower in a given currency. For example, the current U.S. dollar interest rates paid on U.S. Treasury securities for various maturities are closely watched by many traders, and are commonly plotted on a graph such as the one on the right which is informally called 'the yield curve.' More formal mathematical descriptions of this relation are often called the _____.

The yield of a debt instrument is the annualized percentage increase in the value of the investment.

a. 529 plan
b. 7-Eleven
c. 4-4-5 Calendar
d. Term structure of interest rates

77. In finance, the _____ is the relation between the interest rate (or cost of borrowing) and the time to maturity of the debt for a given borrower in a given currency. For example, the current U.S. dollar interest rates paid on U.S. Treasury securities for various maturities are closely watched by many traders, and are commonly plotted on a graph such as the one on the right which is informally called 'the _____.' More formal mathematical descriptions of this relation are often called the term structure of interest rates.

The yield of a debt instrument is the annualized percentage increase in the value of the investment.

a. Yield curve
b. 4-4-5 Calendar
c. 529 plan
d. 7-Eleven

78. _____ or financing is to provide capital (funds), which means money for a project, a person, a business or any other private or public institutions.

Those funds can be allocated for either short term or long term purposes. The health fund is a new way of _____ private healthcare centers.

a. Synthetic CDO
b. Product life cycle
c. Proxy fight
d. Funding

79. _____ means the inability to pay one's debts as they fall due. Usually used in Business terms, _____ refers to the inability for a 'limited liability' company to pay off debts.

Chapter 5. Bonds, Bond Valuation, and Interest Rates 81

This is defined in two different ways:

Cash flow _____ -
　　Unable to pay debts as they fall due.
Balance sheet _____ -
　　Having negative net assets: liabilities exceed assets; or net liabilities.

　a. A Random Walk Down Wall Street
　c. Insolvency
　b. Interest
　d. AAB

80. In law, _____ refers to the process by which a company (or part of a company) is brought to an end, and the assets and property of the company redistributed. _____ can also be referred to as winding-up or dissolution, although dissolution technically refers to the last stage of _____. The process of _____ also arises when customs, an authority or agency in a country responsible for collecting and safeguarding customs duties, determines the final computation or ascertainment of the duties or drawback accruing on an entry.
　a. Liquidation
　c. Debt settlement
　b. 529 plan
　d. 4-4-5 Calendar

81. In economics, a _____ is a general slowdown in economic activity in a country over a sustained period of time, or a business cycle contraction. During _____s, many macroeconomic indicators vary in a similar way. Production as measured by Gross Domestic Product (GDP), employment, investment spending, capacity utilization, household incomes and business profits all fall during _____s.
　a. Fixed exchange rate
　c. Recession
　b. Mercantilism
　d. Behavioral finance

82. _____ is the corporate management term for the act of reorganizing the legal, ownership, operational, or other structures of a company for the purpose of making it more profitable or better organized for its present needs. Alternate reasons for restructing include a change of ownership or ownership structure, demerger repositioning debt _____ and financial _____.
　a. Cross-border leasing
　c. Day trading
　b. Concentrated stock
　d. Restructuring

83. The institution most often referenced by the word '_____' is a public or publicly traded _____, the shares of which are traded on a public stock exchange (e.g., the New York Stock Exchange or Nasdaq in the United States) where shares of stock of _____s are bought and sold by and to the general public. Most of the largest businesses in the world are publicly traded _____s. However, the majority of _____s are said to be closely held, privately held or close _____s, meaning that no ready market exists for the trading of shares.
　a. Depository Trust Company
　c. Protect
　b. Federal Home Loan Mortgage Corporation
　d. Corporation

84. _____ is that which is owed; usually referencing assets owed, but the term can cover other obligations. In the case of assets, _____ is a means of using future purchasing power in the present before a summation has been earned. Some companies and corporations use _____ as a part of their overall corporate finance strategy.

Chapter 5. Bonds, Bond Valuation, and Interest Rates

a. Partial Payment
b. Credit cycle
c. Debt
d. Cross-collateralization

85. _____ is a process that allows a private or public company - or a sovereign entity - facing cash flow problems and financial distress, to reduce and renegotiate its delinquent debts in order to improve or restore liquidity and rehabilitate so that it can continue its operations.

Out-of court restructurings, also known as workouts, are increasingly becoming a global reality. A _____ is usually less expensive and a preferable alternative to bankruptcy.

a. Commuted cash value
b. Cost of living
c. Prepayment
d. Debt Restructuring

Chapter 6. Risk, Return, and the Capital Asset Pricing Model

1. A _____, is a mathematical formalization of a trajectory that consists of taking successive random steps. The results of _____ analysis have been applied to computer science, physics, ecology, economics and a number of other fields as a fundamental model for random processes in time. For example, the path traced by a molecule as it travels in a liquid or a gas, the search path of a foraging animal, the price of a fluctuating stock and the financial status of a gambler can all be modeled as _____s.

    a. 7-Eleven
    b. 4-4-5 Calendar
    c. 529 plan
    d. Random Walk

2. The _____ is a capital budgeting metric used by firms to decide whether they should make investments. It is an indicator of the efficiency or quality of an investment, as opposed to net present value (NPV), which indicates value or magnitude.

    The IRR is the annualized effective compounded return rate which can be earned on the invested capital, i.e., the yield on the investment.

    a. A Random Walk Down Wall Street
    b. ABN Amro
    c. Internal rate of return
    d. AAB

3. In finance, a _____ is a debt security, in which the authorized issuer owes the holders a debt and, depending on the terms of the _____, is obliged to pay interest (the coupon) and/or to repay the principal at a later date, termed maturity.

    Thus a _____ is a loan: the issuer is the borrower, the _____ holder is the lender, and the coupon is the interest. _____s provide the borrower with external funds to finance long-term investments, or, in the case of government _____s, to finance current expenditure.

    a. Convertible bond
    b. Catastrophe bonds
    c. Puttable bond
    d. Bond

4. _____ is the process of determining the fair price of a bond. As with any security or capital investment, the fair value of a bond is the present value of the stream of cash flows it is expected to generate. Hence, the price or value of a bond is determined by discounting the bond's expected cash flows to the present using the appropriate discount rate.

    a. Collateralized debt obligations
    b. Catastrophe bonds
    c. Bond fund
    d. Bond valuation

5. In finance, _____, also known as return on investment is the ratio of money gained or lost on an investment relative to the amount of money invested. The amount of money gained or lost may be referred to as interest, profit/loss, gain/loss, or net income/loss. The money invested may be referred to as the asset, capital, principal, or the cost basis of the investment.

    a. Stock or scrip dividends
    b. Composiition of Creditors
    c. Rate of return
    d. Doctrine of the Proper Law

6. In finance, _____ is the process of estimating the potential market value of a financial asset or liability. they can be done on assets (for example, investments in marketable securities such as stocks, options, business enterprises, or intangible assets such as patents and trademarks) or on liabilities (e.g., Bonds issued by a company.) _____s are required in many contexts including investment analysis, capital budgeting, merger and acquisition transactions, financial reporting, taxable events to determine the proper tax liability, and in litigation.

a. Margin	b. Share
c. Procter ' Gamble	d. Valuation

7. In business and accounting, _____s are everything of value that is owned by a person or company. The balance sheet of a firm records the monetary value of the _____s owned by the firm. The two major _____ classes are tangible _____s and intangible _____s.

a. EBITDA	b. Income
c. Accounts payable	d. Asset

8. The term _____ has three unrelated technical definitions, and is also used in a variety of non-technical ways.

- In financial economics, it refers to any asset used to make money, as opposed to assets used for personal enjoyment or consumption. This is an important distinction because two people can disagree sharply about the value of personal assets, one person might think a sports car is more valuable than a pickup truck, another person might have the opposite taste. But if an asset is held for the purpose of making money, taste has nothing to do with it, only differences of opinion about how much money the asset will produce. With the further assumption that people agree on the probability distribution of future cash flows, it is possible to have an objective _____ pricing model. Even without the assumption of agreement, it is possible to set rational limits on _____ value.
- In governmental accounting, it is defined as any asset used in operations with an initial useful life extending beyond one reporting period. Generally, government managers have a 'stewardship' duty to maintain _____s under their control. See International Public Sector Accounting Standards for details.
- In US tax accounting, it is defined as any property other than a list of exceptions. The main exceptions are anything held for sale, and any real estate or depreciable property used in business. Almost everything you own and use for personal purposes, pleasure or investment is a _____. If something is a _____ for tax purposes, gains or losses on sale or disposition are capital gains or capital losses. For individuals, however, capital losses on property held for personal use are generally not deductible. See the IRS publication Tax Facts about Capital Gains and Losses for details.

A well-known financial accounting textbook advises that the term be avoided except in tax accounting because it is used in so many different senses, not all of them well-defined. For example it is often used as a synonym for fixed assets or for investments in securities.

A common non-technical usage occurs when people ask that employees or the environment or something else be treated as a _____.

a. Capital Asset	b. Political risk
c. Solvency	d. Settlement date

9. In finance, the _____ is used to determine a theoretically appropriate required rate of return of an asset, if that asset is to be added to an already well-diversified portfolio, given that asset's non-diversifiable risk. The model takes into account the asset's sensitivity to non-diversifiable risk (also known as systemic risk or market risk), often represented by the quantity beta (β) in the financial industry, as well as the expected return of the market and the expected return of a theoretical risk-free asset.

Chapter 6. Risk, Return, and the Capital Asset Pricing Model

The model was introduced by Jack Treynor (1961, 1962), William Sharpe (1964), John Lintner (1965a,b) and Jan Mossin (1966) independently, building on the earlier work of Harry Markowitz on diversification and modern portfolio theory.

a. Cox-Ingersoll-Ross model
b. Random walk hypothesis
c. Hull-White model
d. Capital Asset Pricing Model

10. In probability theory and statistics, a _____ identifies either the probability of each value of an unidentified random variable (when the variable is discrete), or the probability of the value falling within a particular interval (when the variable is continuous.) The _____ describes the range of possible values that a random variable can attain and the probability that the value of the random variable is within any (measurable) subset of that range. The Normal distribution, often called the 'bell curve'

When the random variable takes values in the set of real numbers, the _____ is completely described by the cumulative distribution function, whose value at each real x is the probability that the random variable is smaller than or equal to x.

a. P-value
b. Correlation
c. Standard deviation
d. Probability distribution

11. _____ are a class of computational algorithms that rely on repeated random sampling to compute their results. _____ are often used when simulating physical and mathematical systems. Because of their reliance on repeated computation and random or pseudo-random numbers, _____ are most suited to calculation by a computer.

_____ in finance are often used to calculate the value of companies, to evaluate investments in projects at corporate level or to evaluate financial derivatives. The method is intended for financial analysts who want to construct stochastic or probabilistic financial models as opposed to the traditional static and deterministic models.

a. Monte Carlo methods
b. Sample size
c. Correlation
d. Semivariance

12. A _____ is a fungible, negotiable instrument representing financial value. They are broadly categorized into debt securities (such as banknotes, bonds and debentures), and equity securities; e.g., common stocks. The company or other entity issuing the _____ is called the issuer.

a. Book entry
b. Securities lending
c. Tracking stock
d. Security

13. In Modern Portfolio Theory, the _____ is the graphical representation of the Capital Asset Pricing Model. It displays the expected rate of return for an overall market as a function of systematic (non-diversifiable) risk (beta.)

The Y-Intercept (beta=0) of the _____ is equal to the risk-free interest rate.

Chapter 6. Risk, Return, and the Capital Asset Pricing Model

a. Security Market Line
b. Certificate in Investment Performance Measurement
c. Rebalancing
d. Divestment

14. In probability and statistics, the _____ of a collection of numbers is a measure of the dispersion of the numbers from their expected (mean) value. It can apply to a probability distribution, a random variable, a population or a data set. The _____ is usually denoted with the letter σ (lowercase sigma.)

   a. Kurtosis
   b. Standard deviation
   c. Sample size
   d. Mean

15. An _____ is a contract written by a seller that conveys to the buyer the right -- but not the obligation -- to buy (in the case of a call _____) or to sell (in the case of a put _____) a particular asset, such as a piece of property such as, among others, a futures contract. In return for granting the _____, the seller collects a payment (the premium) from the buyer.

For example, buying a call _____ provides the right to buy a specified quantity of a security at a set strike price at some time on or before expiration, while buying a put _____ provides the right to sell.

   a. Amortization
   b. Annuity
   c. AT'T Mobility LLC
   d. Option

16. In probability theory and statistics, the _____ of a random variable, probability distribution averaging the squared distance of its possible values from the expected value (mean.) Whereas the mean is a way to describe the location of a distribution, the _____ is a way to capture its scale or degree of being spread out. The unit of _____ is the square of the unit of the original variable.

   a. Semivariance
   b. Harmonic mean
   c. Variance
   d. Monte Carlo methods

17. _____ is a form of corporation equity ownership represented in the securities. It is dangerous in comparison to preferred shares and some other investment options, in that in the event of bankruptcy, _____ investors receive their funds after preferred stockholders, bondholders, creditors, etc. On the other hand, common shares on average perform better than preferred shares or bonds over time.

   a. Stock market bubble
   b. Common stock
   c. Stop-limit order
   d. Stock split

18. The _____ is an important family of continuous probability distributions, applicable in many fields. Each member of the family may be defined by two parameters, location and scale: the mean and variance respectively. The standard _____ is the _____ with a mean of zero and a variance of one

   a. Normal distribution
   b. Correlation
   c. Random variables
   d. Probability distribution

19. In probability theory and statistics, the _____ is a normalized measure of dispersion of a probability distribution. It is defined as the ratio of the standard deviation ☒ > to the mean ☒ >:

This is only defined for non-zero mean, and is most useful for variables that are always positive. It is also known as unitized risk.

a. Random variables
b. Coefficient of variation
c. Harmonic mean
d. Sample size

20. _____ is a concept in economics, finance, and psychology related to the behaviour of consumers and investors under uncertainty. _____ is the reluctance of a person to accept a bargain with an uncertain payoff rather than another bargain with a more certain, but possibly lower, expected payoff.

The inverse of a person's _____ is sometimes called their risk tolerance

a. Discount factor
b. Risk adjusted return on capital
c. Risk premium
d. Risk aversion

21. _____ mature in one year or less. Like zero-coupon bonds, they do not pay interest prior to maturity; instead they are sold at a discount of the par value to create a positive yield to maturity. Many regard _____ as the least risky investment available to U.S. investors.

a. Treasury Inflation Protected Securities
b. 4-4-5 Calendar
c. Treasury securities
d. Treasury bills

22.

In finance, the _____ can be the expected rate of return above the risk-free interest rate. When measuring risk, a common sense approach is to compare the risk-free return on T-bills and the very risky return on other investments. The difference between these two returns can be interpreted as a measure of the excess return on the average risky asset. This excess return is known as the _____.

a. Risk aversion
b. Risk modeling
c. Risk adjusted return on capital
d. Risk premium

23. A _____ is a situation that involves losing one quality or aspect of something in return for gaining another quality or aspect. It implies a decision to be made with full comprehension of both the upside and downside of a particular choice.

In economics the term is expressed as opportunity cost, referring the most preferred alternative given up.

a. Break-even point
b. Capital outflow
c. Total revenue
d. Trade-off

24. The _____ is the market for securities, where companies and governments can raise longterm funds. The _____ includes the stock market and the bond market. Financial regulators, such as the U.S. Securities and Exchange Commission, oversee the _____s in their designated countries to ensure that investors are protected against fraud.

a. Spot rate
b. Forward market
c. Delta neutral
d. Capital Market

25. _____ proposes how rational investors will use diversification to optimize their portfolios, and how a risky asset should be priced. The basic concepts of the theory are Markowitz diversification, the efficient frontier, capital asset pricing model, the alpha and beta coefficients, the Capital Market Line and the Securities Market Line.

_____ models an asset's return as a random variable, and models a portfolio as a weighted combination of assets so that the return of a portfolio is the weighted combination of the assets' returns.

a. Market value
b. Modern portfolio theory
c. Consumer basket
d. Payback period

26. In probability theory and statistics, _____ indicates the strength and direction of a linear relationship between two random variables. That is in contrast with the usage of the term in colloquial speech, which denotes any relationship, not necessarily linear. In general statistical usage, _____ or co-relation refers to the departure of two random variables from independence.

a. Variance
b. Probability distribution
c. Correlation
d. Geometric mean

27. In business and finance, a _____ (also referred to as equity _____) of stock means a _____ of ownership in a corporation (company.) In the plural, stocks is often used as a synonym for _____s especially in the United States, but it is less commonly used that way outside of North America.

In the United Kingdom, South Africa, and Australia, stock can also refer to completely different financial instruments such as government bonds or, less commonly, to all kinds of marketable securities.

a. Bucket shop
b. Margin
c. Procter ' Gamble
d. Share

28. _____ in finance is a risk management technique, related to hedging, that mixes a wide variety of investments within a portfolio. Because the fluctuations of a single security have less impact on a diverse portfolio, _____ minimizes the risk from any one investment.

A simple example of _____ is the following: On a particular island the entire economy consists of two companies: one that sells umbrellas and another that sells sunscreen.

a. Diversification
b. 4-4-5 Calendar
c. 7-Eleven
d. 529 plan

Chapter 6. Risk, Return, and the Capital Asset Pricing Model

29. _____ is the risk that the value of an investment will decrease due to moves in market factors. The five standard _____ factors are:

- Equity risk, the risk that stock prices will change.
- Interest rate risk, the risk that interest rates will change.
- Currency risk, the risk that foreign exchange rates will change.
- Commodity risk, the risk that commodity prices (e.g. grains, metals) will change.

As with other forms of risk, _____ may be measured in a number of ways. Traditionally, this is done using a Value at Risk methodology. Value at risk is well established as a risk management technique, but it contains a number of limiting assumptions that constrain its accuracy.

   a. Currency risk   b. Tracking error
   c. Transaction risk   d. Market risk

30. The institution most often referenced by the word '_____' is a public or publicly traded _____, the shares of which are traded on a public stock exchange (e.g., the New York Stock Exchange or Nasdaq in the United States) where shares of stock of _____s are bought and sold by and to the general public. Most of the largest businesses in the world are publicly traded _____s. However, the majority of _____s are said to be closely held, privately held or close _____s, meaning that no ready market exists for the trading of shares.

   a. Federal Home Loan Mortgage Corporation   b. Corporation
   c. Depository Trust Company   d. Protect

31. _____ or financing is to provide capital (funds), which means money for a project, a person, a business or any other private or public institutions.

Those funds can be allocated for either short term or long term purposes. The health fund is a new way of _____ private healthcare centers.

   a. Product life cycle   b. Funding
   c. Synthetic CDO   d. Proxy fight

32. The _____, in terms of finance and investing, describes how the expected return of a stock or portfolio is correlated to the return of the financial market as a whole.

An asset with a beta of 0 means that its price is not at all correlated with the market; that asset is independent. A positive beta means that the asset generally follows the market.

   a. LIBOR market model   b. Perpetuity
   c. Current yield   d. Beta coefficient

33. In probability theory and statistics, _____ is a measure of how much two variables change together (variance is a special case of the _____ when the two variables are identical.)

If two variables tend to vary together (that is, when one of them is above its expected value, then the other variable tends to be above its expected value too), then the _____ between the two variables will be positive. On the other hand, when one of them is above its expected value the other variable tends to be below its expected value, then the _____ between the two variables will be negative.

 a. Covariance   b. Stratified sampling
 c. Probability distribution   d. Frequency distribution

34. The _____ is one of several stock market indices, created by nineteenth-century Wall Street Journal editor and Dow Jones ' Company co-founder Charles Dow. Dow compiled the index to gauge the performance of the industrial sector of the American stock market. It is the second-oldest U.S. market index, after the Dow Jones Transportation Average, which Dow also created.

 a. Dow Jones Industrial Average   b. 7-Eleven
 c. 529 plan   d. 4-4-5 Calendar

35. In the portfolio management field, Eugene Fama and Kenneth French developed the highly successful _____ to describe market behavior.

CAPM uses a single factor, beta, to compare the excess returns of a portfolio with the excess returns of the market as a whole. But it oversimplifies the complex market. Fama and French started with the observation that two classes of stocks have tended to do better than the market as a whole: small caps and (ii) stocks with a high book-to-market ratio (BM, customarily called value stocks, and different from growth stocks). They then added two factors to CAPM to reflect a portfolio's exposure to these two classes:

>

Here r is the portfolio's return rate, R_f is the risk-free return rate, and K_m is the return of the whole stock market. The 'three factor' >β is analogous to the classical >β but not equal to it, since there are now two additional factors to do some of the work. SMB stands for 'small minus big' and HML for 'high (book-to-price ratio) minus low'; they measure the historic excess returns of small caps over big caps and of value stocks over growth stocks.

 a. Reputational risk   b. Guaranteed investment contracts
 c. Mitigating Control   d. Fama-French three factor model

36. In economics and finance, _____ is the practice of taking advantage of a price differential between two or more markets: striking a combination of matching deals that capitalize upon the imbalance, the profit being the difference between the market prices. When used by academics, an _____ is a transaction that involves no negative cash flow at any probabilistic or temporal state and a positive cash flow in at least one state; in simple terms, a risk-free profit.
 a. Initial margin   b. Arbitrage
 c. Efficient-market hypothesis   d. Issuer

37. _____ , in finance, is a general theory of asset pricing, that has become influential in the pricing of stocks.

Chapter 6. Risk, Return, and the Capital Asset Pricing Model

_____ holds that the expected return of a financial asset can be modeled as a linear function of various macro-economic factors or theoretical market indices, where sensitivity to changes in each factor is represented by a factor-specific beta coefficient. The model-derived rate of return will then be used to price the asset correctly - the asset price should equal the expected end of period price discounted at the rate implied by model.

  a. AAB
  b. A Random Walk Down Wall Street
  c. ABN Amro
  d. Arbitrage pricing theory

38. Procter is a surname, and may also refer to:

  - Bryan Waller Procter (pseud. Barry Cornwall), English poet
  - Goodwin Procter, American law firm
  - _____, consumer products multinational

  a. Procter ' Gamble
  b. Valuation
  c. Clearing house
  d. Bucket shop

39. In statistics, _____ refers to techniques for the modeling and analysis of numerical data consisting of values of a dependent variable and of one or more independent variables The dependent variable in the regression equation is modeled as a function of the independent variables, corresponding parameters, and an error term. The error term is treated as a random variable.
  a. 529 plan
  b. 7-Eleven
  c. 4-4-5 Calendar
  d. Regression analysis

40. In economics, _____ is a rise in the general level of prices of goods and services in an economy over a period of time. The term '_____' once referred to increases in the money supply (monetary _____); however, economic debates about the relationship between money supply and price levels have led to its primary use today in describing price _____. _____ can also be described as a decline in the real value of money--a loss of purchasing power in the medium of exchange which is also the monetary unit of account.
  a. Inflation
  b. A Random Walk Down Wall Street
  c. ABN Amro
  d. AAB

41. In economics, business, and accounting, a _____ is the value of money that has been used up to produce something, and hence is not available for use anymore. In business, the _____ may be one of acquisition, in which case the amount of money expended to acquire it is counted as _____. In this case, money is the input that is gone in order to acquire the thing.
  a. Marginal cost
  b. Cost
  c. Fixed costs
  d. Sliding scale fees

42. Behavioral economics and _____ are closely related fields that have evolved to be a separate branch of economic and financial analysis which applies scientific research on human and social, cognitive and emotional factors to better understand economic decisions by, say, consumers, borrowers, investors, and how they affect market prices, returns and the allocation of resources.

The field is primarily concerned with the bounds of rationality (selfishness, self-control) of economic agents. Behavioral models typically integrate insights from psychology with neo-classical economic theory.

a. Medium of exchange
b. Behavioral finance
c. Market structure
d. Recession

Chapter 7. Portfolio Theory and Other Asset Pricing Models

1. An _____ or index tracker is a collective investment scheme (usually a mutual fund or exchange-traded fund) that aims to replicate the movements of an index of a specific financial market regardless of market conditions.

Tracking can be achieved by trying to hold all of the securities in the index, in the same proportions as the index. Other methods include statistically sampling the market and holding 'representative' securities.

   a. Investment company
   b. A Random Walk Down Wall Street
   c. AAB
   d. Index fund

2. An investment strategy or portfolio is considered _____ if it seeks to entirely avoid some form of market risk, typically by hedging. In order to evaluate market neutrality, it is first necessary to specify the risk being avoided. For example, convertible arbitrage attempts to fully hedge fluctuations in the price of the underlying common stock.
   a. Flight-to-quality
   b. Market neutral
   c. Credit event
   d. Black-Litterman model

3. A _____ is a professionally managed type of collective investment scheme that pools money from many investors and invests it in stocks, bonds, short-term money market instruments, and/or other securities. The _____ will have a fund manager that trades the pooled money on a regular basis. Currently, the worldwide value of all _____ s totals more than $26 trillion.

Since 1940, there have been three basic types of investment companies in the United States: open-end funds, also known in the US as _____ s; unit investment trusts (UITs); and closed-end funds.

   a. Financial intermediary
   b. Trust company
   c. Net asset value
   d. Mutual fund

4. In business and accounting, _____ s are everything of value that is owned by a person or company. The balance sheet of a firm records the monetary value of the _____ s owned by the firm. The two major _____ classes are tangible _____ s and intangible _____ s.
   a. Income
   b. EBITDA
   c. Accounts payable
   d. Asset

5. In finance, _____ is the process of estimating the potential market value of a financial asset or liability. they can be done on assets (for example, investments in marketable securities such as stocks, options, business enterprises, or intangible assets such as patents and trademarks) or on liabilities (e.g., Bonds issued by a company.) _____ s are required in many contexts including investment analysis, capital budgeting, merger and acquisition transactions, financial reporting, taxable events to determine the proper tax liability, and in litigation.
   a. Margin
   b. Procter ' Gamble
   c. Valuation
   d. Share

Chapter 7. Portfolio Theory and Other Asset Pricing Models

6. The term _____ has three unrelated technical definitions, and is also used in a variety of non-technical ways.

    - In financial economics, it refers to any asset used to make money, as opposed to assets used for personal enjoyment or consumption. This is an important distinction because two people can disagree sharply about the value of personal assets, one person might think a sports car is more valuable than a pickup truck, another person might have the opposite taste. But if an asset is held for the purpose of making money, taste has nothing to do with it, only differences of opinion about how much money the asset will produce. With the further assumption that people agree on the probability distribution of future cash flows, it is possible to have an objective _____ pricing model. Even without the assumption of agreement, it is possible to set rational limits on _____ value.
    - In governmental accounting, it is defined as any asset used in operations with an initial useful life extending beyond one reporting period. Generally, government managers have a 'stewardship' duty to maintain _____s under their control. See International Public Sector Accounting Standards for details.
    - In US tax accounting, it is defined as any property other than a list of exceptions. The main exceptions are anything held for sale, and any real estate or depreciable property used in business. Almost everything you own and use for personal purposes, pleasure or investment is a _____. If something is a _____ for tax purposes, gains or losses on sale or disposition are capital gains or capital losses. For individuals, however, capital losses on property held for personal use are generally not deductible. See the IRS publication Tax Facts about Capital Gains and Losses for details.

A well-known financial accounting textbook advises that the term be avoided except in tax accounting because it is used in so many different senses, not all of them well-defined. For example it is often used as a synonym for fixed assets or for investments in securities.

A common non-technical usage occurs when people ask that employees or the environment or something else be treated as a _____.

   a. Settlement date
   b. Solvency
   c. Political risk
   d. Capital Asset

7. In finance, the _____ is used to determine a theoretically appropriate required rate of return of an asset, if that asset is to be added to an already well-diversified portfolio, given that asset's non-diversifiable risk. The model takes into account the asset's sensitivity to non-diversifiable risk (also known as systemic risk or market risk), often represented by the quantity beta (β) in the financial industry, as well as the expected return of the market and the expected return of a theoretical risk-free asset.

The model was introduced by Jack Treynor (1961, 1962), William Sharpe (1964), John Lintner (1965a,b) and Jan Mossin (1966) independently, building on the earlier work of Harry Markowitz on diversification and modern portfolio theory.

   a. Cox-Ingersoll-Ross model
   b. Random walk hypothesis
   c. Hull-White model
   d. Capital Asset Pricing Model

8. The _____ is the market for securities, where companies and governments can raise longterm funds. The _____ includes the stock market and the bond market. Financial regulators, such as the U.S. Securities and Exchange Commission, oversee the _____s in their designated countries to ensure that investors are protected against fraud.

Chapter 7. Portfolio Theory and Other Asset Pricing Models

a. Capital Market
c. Forward market
b. Delta neutral
d. Spot rate

9. _____ proposes how rational investors will use diversification to optimize their portfolios, and how a risky asset should be priced. The basic concepts of the theory are Markowitz diversification, the efficient frontier, capital asset pricing model, the alpha and beta coefficients, the Capital Market Line and the Securities Market Line.

_____ models an asset's return as a random variable, and models a portfolio as a weighted combination of assets so that the return of a portfolio is the weighted combination of the assets' returns.

a. Payback period
c. Modern portfolio theory
b. Market value
d. Consumer basket

10. _____ are a class of computational algorithms that rely on repeated random sampling to compute their results. _____ are often used when simulating physical and mathematical systems. Because of their reliance on repeated computation and random or pseudo-random numbers, _____ are most suited to calculation by a computer.

_____ in finance are often used to calculate the value of companies, to evaluate investments in projects at corporate level or to evaluate financial derivatives. The method is intended for financial analysts who want to construct stochastic or probabilistic financial models as opposed to the traditional static and deterministic models.

a. Semivariance
c. Correlation
b. Monte Carlo methods
d. Sample size

11. A _____ is a fungible, negotiable instrument representing financial value. They are broadly categorized into debt securities (such as banknotes, bonds and debentures), and equity securities; e.g., common stocks. The company or other entity issuing the _____ is called the issuer.
a. Securities lending
c. Book entry
b. Security
d. Tracking stock

12. In Modern Portfolio Theory, the _____ is the graphical representation of the Capital Asset Pricing Model. It displays the expected rate of return for an overall market as a function of systematic (non-diversifiable) risk (beta.)

The Y-Intercept (beta=0) of the _____ is equal to the risk-free interest rate.

a. Certificate in Investment Performance Measurement
c. Security Market Line
b. Divestment
d. Rebalancing

13. In economics and finance, _____ is the practice of taking advantage of a price differential between two or more markets: striking a combination of matching deals that capitalize upon the imbalance, the profit being the difference between the market prices. When used by academics, an _____ is a transaction that involves no negative cash flow at any probabilistic or temporal state and a positive cash flow in at least one state; in simple terms, a risk-free profit.
a. Initial margin
c. Arbitrage
b. Issuer
d. Efficient-market hypothesis

14. _____ , in finance, is a general theory of asset pricing, that has become influential in the pricing of stocks.

96 *Chapter 7. Portfolio Theory and Other Asset Pricing Models*

_____ holds that the expected return of a financial asset can be modeled as a linear function of various macro-economic factors or theoretical market indices, where sensitivity to changes in each factor is represented by a factor-specific beta coefficient. The model-derived rate of return will then be used to price the asset correctly - the asset price should equal the expected end of period price discounted at the rate implied by model.

    a. Arbitrage pricing theory   b. A Random Walk Down Wall Street
    c. ABN Amro   d. AAB

15. Modern portfolio theory (MPT) proposes how rational investors will use diversification to optimize their portfolios, and how a risky asset should be priced. The basic concepts of the theory are Markowitz diversification, the _____, capital asset pricing model, the alpha and beta coefficients, the Capital Market Line and the Securities Market Line.

MPT models an asset's return as a random variable, and models a portfolio as a weighted combination of assets so that the return of a portfolio is the weighted combination of the assets' returns.

    a. ABN Amro   b. Efficient frontier
    c. A Random Walk Down Wall Street   d. AAB

16. In microeconomic theory, an _____ is a graph showing different bundles of goods, each measured as to quantity, between which a consumer is indifferent. That is, at each point on the curve, the consumer has no preference for one bundle over another. In other words, they are all equally preferred. One can equivalently refer to each point on the _____ as rendering the same level of utility (satisfaction) for the consumer.

    a. A Random Walk Down Wall Street   b. AAB
    c. ABN Amro   d. Indifference curve

17. In the portfolio management field, Eugene Fama and Kenneth French developed the highly successful _____ to describe market behavior.

CAPM uses a single factor, beta, to compare the excess returns of a portfolio with the excess returns of the market as a whole. But it oversimplifies the complex market. Fama and French started with the observation that two classes of stocks have tended to do better than the market as a whole: small caps and (ii) stocks with a high book-to-market ratio (BM, customarily called value stocks, and different from growth stocks). They then added two factors to CAPM to reflect a portfolio's exposure to these two classes:

Here r is the portfolio's return rate, R_f is the risk-free return rate, and K_m is the return of the whole stock market. The 'three factor' >β is analogous to the classical >β but not equal to it, since there are now two additional factors to do some of the work. SMB stands for 'small minus big' and HML for 'high (book-to-price ratio) minus low'; they measure the historic excess returns of small caps over big caps and of value stocks over growth stocks.

Chapter 7. Portfolio Theory and Other Asset Pricing Models

a. Fama-French three factor model
b. Reputational risk
c. Mitigating Control
d. Guaranteed investment contracts

18. The _____, in terms of finance and investing, describes how the expected return of a stock or portfolio is correlated to the return of the financial market as a whole.

An asset with a beta of 0 means that its price is not at all correlated with the market; that asset is independent. A positive beta means that the asset generally follows the market.

a. Current yield
b. Perpetuity
c. LIBOR market model
d. Beta coefficient

19. In statistics, _____ refers to techniques for the modeling and analysis of numerical data consisting of values of a dependent variable and of one or more independent variables The dependent variable in the regression equation is modeled as a function of the independent variables, corresponding parameters, and an error term. The error term is treated as a random variable.

a. 529 plan
b. 4-4-5 Calendar
c. 7-Eleven
d. Regression analysis

20. _____ is a risk-adjusted measure of the so-called active return on an investment. It is the return in excess of the compensation for the risk borne, and thus commonly used to assess active managers' performances. Often, the return of a benchmark is subtracted in order to consider relative performance, which yields Jensen's _____.

a. Option
b. Amortization
c. Annuity
d. Alpha

21. The _____ is one of the measures of national income and input for a given country's economy. _____ is defined as the total cost of all finished goods and services produced within the country in a stipulated period of time (usually a 365-day year.) It is sometimes regarded as the sum of profits added at every level of production (the intermediate stages) of all final goods and services produced within a country in a stipulated timeframe, and it is rarely given a monetary value.

a. Recession
b. Macroeconomics
c. Behavioral finance
d. Gross domestic product

22. In economics, _____ is a rise in the general level of prices of goods and services in an economy over a period of time. The term '_____' once referred to increases in the money supply (monetary _____); however, economic debates about the relationship between money supply and price levels have led to its primary use today in describing price _____. _____ can also be described as a decline in the real value of money--a loss of purchasing power in the medium of exchange which is also the monetary unit of account.

a. Inflation
b. A Random Walk Down Wall Street
c. ABN Amro
d. AAB

23. _____ is a concept in economics, finance, and psychology related to the behaviour of consumers and investors under uncertainty. _____ is the reluctance of a person to accept a bargain with an uncertain payoff rather than another bargain with a more certain, but possibly lower, expected payoff.

The inverse of a person's _____ is sometimes called their risk tolerance

a. Risk adjusted return on capital
c. Risk premium
b. Discount factor
d. Risk aversion

24. _____ is a statistical method used to describe variability among observed variables in terms of fewer unobserved variables called factors. The observed variables are modeled as linear combinations of the factors, plus 'error' terms. The information gained about the interdependencies can be used later to reduce the set of variables in a dataset.
   a. 4-4-5 Calendar
   c. 529 plan
   b. 7-Eleven
   d. Factor analysis

25. The _____ is a financial ratio used to compare a company's book value to its current market price. Book value is an accounting term denoting the portion of the company held by the shareholders; in other words, the company's total tangible assets less its total liabilities. The calculation can be performed in two ways, but the result should be the same each way. In the first way, the company's market capitalization can be divided by the company's total book value from its balance sheet. The second way, using per-share values, is to divide the company's current share price by the book value per share (i.e. its book value divided by the number of outstanding shares).
   a. Stop order
   c. Stock repurchase
   b. Whisper numbers
   d. Price-to-book ratio

26. Behavioral economics and _____ are closely related fields that have evolved to be a separate branch of economic and financial analysis which applies scientific research on human and social, cognitive and emotional factors to better understand economic decisions by, say, consumers, borrowers, investors, and how they affect market prices, returns and the allocation of resources.

The field is primarily concerned with the bounds of rationality (selfishness, self-control) of economic agents. Behavioral models typically integrate insights from psychology with neo-classical economic theory.

   a. Behavioral finance
   c. Medium of exchange
   b. Market structure
   d. Recession

27. In prospect theory, _____ refers to the tendency for people to strongly prefer avoiding losses than acquiring gains. Some studies suggest that losses are twice as powerful, psychologically, as gains. _____ was first convincingly demonstrated by Amos Tversky and Daniel Kahneman.
   a. Herd behavior
   c. Quantitative behavioral finance
   b. Perth Leadership Outcome Model
   d. Loss aversion

28. _____ is the inclination to see events that have occurred as more predictable than they in fact were before they took place. _____ has been demonstrated experimentally in a variety of settings, including politics, games and medicine. In psychological experiments of _____, subjects also tend to remember their predictions of future events as having been stronger than they actually were, in those cases where those predictions turn out correct.
   a. Sunk costs
   c. Hyperbolic discounting
   b. 4-4-5 Calendar
   d. Hindsight bias

29. A _____, also known by its legal title as an 'over-allotment option' (the only way it can be referred to in a prospectus), gives underwriters the right to sell additional shares in a registered securities offering if demand for the securities is in excess of the original amount offered. The _____ can vary in size up to 15% of the original number of shares offered.

The _____ option is popular because it is the only SEC-permitted means for an underwriter to stabilize the price of a new issue post-pricing.

- a. Business valuation standards
- b. Green Shoe
- c. Supply and demand
- d. Foreign Language and Area Studies

30. An _____ is a contract written by a seller that conveys to the buyer the right -- but not the obligation -- to buy (in the case of a call _____) or to sell (in the case of a put _____) a particular asset, such as a piece of property such as, among others, a futures contract. In return for granting the _____, the seller collects a payment (the premium) from the buyer.

For example, buying a call _____ provides the right to buy a specified quantity of a security at a set strike price at some time on or before expiration, while buying a put _____ provides the right to sell.

- a. Annuity
- b. Amortization
- c. AT'T Mobility LLC
- d. Option

Chapter 8. Stocks, Stock Valuation, and Stock Market Equilibrium

1. A _____ is the direction in which a financial market is moving. _____s can be classified as primary trends, secondary trends (short-term), and secular trends (long-term.) This principle incorporates the idea that market cycles occur with regularity and persistence.
   a. 4-4-5 Calendar
   b. 529 plan
   c. 7-Eleven
   d. Market trend

2. The _____ is one of several stock market indices, created by nineteenth-century Wall Street Journal editor and Dow Jones ' Company co-founder Charles Dow. Dow compiled the index to gauge the performance of the industrial sector of the American stock market. It is the second-oldest U.S. market index, after the Dow Jones Transportation Average, which Dow also created.
   a. Dow Jones Industrial Average
   b. 529 plan
   c. 7-Eleven
   d. 4-4-5 Calendar

3. A _____ is a private or public market for the trading of company stock and derivatives of company stock at an agreed price; these are securities listed on a stock exchange as well as those only traded privately.

   The size of the world _____ is estimated at about $36.6 trillion US at the beginning of October 2008 . The world derivatives market has been estimated at about $480 trillion face or nominal value, 12 times the size of the entire world economy.

   a. Andrew Tobias
   b. Anton Gelonkin
   c. Adolph Coors
   d. Stock market

4. In finance, a _____ is a type of bond that can be converted into shares of stock in the issuing company, usually at some pre-announced ratio. It is a hybrid security with debt- and equity-like features. Although it typically has a low coupon rate, the holder is compensated with the ability to convert the bond to common stock, usually at a substantial discount to the stock's market value.
   a. Gilts
   b. Bond fund
   c. Corporate bond
   d. Convertible bond

5. A _____ is a payment made by a corporation to its shareholder members. When a corporation earns a profit or surplus, that money can be put to two uses: it can either be re-invested in the business (called retained earnings), or it can be paid to the shareholders as a _____. Many corporations retain a portion of their earnings and pay the remainder as a _____.
   a. Special dividend
   b. Dividend puzzle
   c. Dividend yield
   d. Dividend

6. The phrase _____ refers to the aspect of corporate strategy, corporate finance and management dealing with the buying, selling and combining of different companies that can aid, finance, or help a growing company in a given industry grow rapidly without having to create another business entity.

   An acquisition, also known as a takeover, is the buying of one company (the 'target') by another. An acquisition may be friendly or hostile.

   a. 529 plan
   b. 4-4-5 Calendar
   c. 7-Eleven
   d. Mergers and acquisitions

7. _____ is typically a higher ranking stock than voting shares, and its terms are negotiated between the corporation and the investor.

_____ usually carry no voting rights, but may carry superior priority over common stock in the payment of dividends and upon liquidation. _____ may carry a dividend that is paid out prior to any dividends to common stock holders.

- a. Second lien loan
- b. Trade-off theory
- c. Follow-on offering
- d. Preferred stock

8. A _____ is an event that may occur when a corporation's stockholders develop opposition to some aspect of the corporate governance, often focusing on directorial and management positions. Corporate activists may attempt to persuade shareholders to use their proxy votes (i.e. votes by one individual or institution as the authorized representative of another) to install new management for any of a variety of reasons.

In a _____, incumbent directors and management have the odds stacked in their favor over those trying to force the corporate change.

- a. Forfaiting
- b. Procurement
- c. Trade finance
- d. Proxy fight

9. A _____ is the price of a single share of a no. of saleable stocks of the company. Once the stock is purchased, the owner becomes a shareholder of the company that issued the share.
- a. Whisper numbers
- b. Stock split
- c. Trading curb
- d. Share price

10. _____ is an estimate of the fair value of corporations and their stocks, by using fundamental economic criteria. This theoretical valuation has to be perfected with market criteria, as the final purpose is to determine potential market prices.
- a. Growth stocks
- b. Stock valuation
- c. 4-4-5 Calendar
- d. Security Analysis

11. In financial accounting, a _____ or statement of financial position is a summary of a person's or organization's balances. Assets, liabilities and ownership equity are listed as of a specific date, such as the end of its financial year. A _____ is often described as a snapshot of a company's financial condition.
- a. Financial statements
- b. Statement of retained earnings
- c. Statement on Auditing Standards No. 70: Service Organizations
- d. Balance sheet

12. _____ measures the nominal future sum of money that a given sum of money is 'worth' at a specified time in the future assuming a certain interest rate rate of return; it is the present value multiplied by the accumulation function.

The value does not include corrections for inflation or other factors that affect the true value of money in the future. This is used in time value of money calculations.

a. Future value
b. Present value of costs
c. Discounted cash flow
d. Future-oriented

13. In finance, _____ are stocks that appreciate in value and yield a high return on equity (ROE.) Analysts compute ROE by taking the company's net income and dividing it by the company's equity. To be classified as a growth stock, analysts expect to see at least 15 percent return on equity.

a. Growth stocks
b. 4-4-5 Calendar
c. Stock valuation
d. Security Analysis

14. A _____ is a fungible, negotiable instrument representing financial value. They are broadly categorized into debt securities (such as banknotes, bonds and debentures), and equity securities; e.g., common stocks. The company or other entity issuing the _____ is called the issuer.

a. Tracking stock
b. Book entry
c. Securities lending
d. Security

15. A mutual shareholder or _____ is an individual or company (including a corporation) that legally owns one or more shares of stock in a joint stock company. A company's shareholders collectively own that company. Thus, the typical goal of such companies is to enhance shareholder value.

a. Trading curb
b. Limit order
c. Stock market bubble
d. Stockholder

16. In business and finance, a _____ (also referred to as equity _____) of stock means a _____ of ownership in a corporation (company.) In the plural, stocks is often used as a synonym for _____s especially in the United States, but it is less commonly used that way outside of North America.

In the United Kingdom, South Africa, and Australia, stock can also refer to completely different financial instruments such as government bonds or, less commonly, to all kinds of marketable securities.

a. Bucket shop
b. Margin
c. Procter ' Gamble
d. Share

17. In business, a _____ is the purchase of one company (the target) by another (the acquirer or bidder). In the UK the term refers to the acquisition of a public company whose shares are listed on a stock exchange, in contrast to the acquisition of a private company.

Before a bidder makes an offer for another company, it usually first informs that company's board of directors.

a. 4-4-5 Calendar
b. Stock swap
c. 529 plan
d. Takeover

18. In finance, _____ is the process of estimating the potential market value of a financial asset or liability. they can be done on assets (for example, investments in marketable securities such as stocks, options, business enterprises, or intangible assets such as patents and trademarks) or on liabilities (e.g., Bonds issued by a company.) _____s are required in many contexts including investment analysis, capital budgeting, merger and acquisition transactions, financial reporting, taxable events to determine the proper tax liability, and in litigation.

a. Share
b. Margin
c. Procter ' Gamble
d. Valuation

19. _____ is a business valuation method. _____ is the net present value of a project if financed solely by ownership equity plus the present value of all the benefits of financing. Usually, the main benefit is a tax shield resulted from tax deductibility of interest payments. Another one can be a subsidized borrowing.
   a. Adjusted present value
   b. AAB
   c. A Random Walk Down Wall Street
   d. ABN Amro

20. A _____ is a right to acquire certain property in preference to any other person. It usually refers to property newly coming into existence. A right to acquire existing property in preference to any other person is usually referred to as a right of first refusal.

In practice, the most common form of _____ is the right of existing shareholders to acquire newly issued shares issued by a company in a rights issue, a usually but not always public offering.
   a. Court of Audit of Belgium
   b. Down payment
   c. Fraud deterrence
   d. Pre-emption right

21. A _____ is a security issued by a parent company to track the results of one of its subsidiaries or lines of business. The financial results of the subsidiary or line of business are attributed to the _____. Often, the reason for doing so is to separate a high-growth division from a larger parent company.
   a. Marketable
   b. Book entry
   c. Securities lending
   d. Tracking stock

22. A _____ is the highest price that a buyer (i.e., bidder) is willing to pay for a good. It is usually referred to simply as the 'bid.'

In bid and ask, the _____ stands in contrast to the ask price or 'offer', and the difference between the two is called the bid/ask spread.

An unsolicited bid or offer is when a person or company receives a bid even though they are not looking to sell.
   a. Mid price
   b. Settlement date
   c. Political risk
   d. Bid price

23. The institution most often referenced by the word '_____' is a public or publicly traded _____, the shares of which are traded on a public stock exchange (e.g., the New York Stock Exchange or Nasdaq in the United States) where shares of stock of _____s are bought and sold by and to the general public. Most of the largest businesses in the world are publicly traded _____s. However, the majority of _____s are said to be closely held, privately held or close _____s, meaning that no ready market exists for the trading of shares.
   a. Depository Trust Company
   b. Protect
   c. Federal Home Loan Mortgage Corporation
   d. Corporation

24. _____ are formal records of a business' financial activities.

_____ provide an overview of a business' financial condition in both short and long term. There are four basic _____:

1. **Balance sheet**: also referred to as statement of financial position or condition, reports on a company's assets, liabilities, and net equity as of a given point in time.
2. **Income statement**: also referred to as Profit and Loss statement (or a 'P'L'), reports on a company's income, expenses, and profits over a period of time.
3. **Statement of retained earnings**: explains the changes in a company's retained earnings over the reporting period.
4. **Statement of cash flows**: reports on a company's cash flow activities, particularly its operating, investing and financing activities.

a. Financial statements
b. Statement of retained earnings
c. Statement on Auditing Standards No. 70: Service Organizations
d. Notes to the Financial Statements

25. An _____ is a document a company presents at an annual general meeting for approval by its shareholders, or a charitable organization presents its trustees. The report is made up of reports, which may include the following:

- Chairman's report
- CEO's report
- Auditor's report on corporate governance
- Mission statement
- Corporate governance statement of compliance
- Statement of directors' responsibilities
- Invitation to the company's AGM

as well as financial statements including:

- Auditor's report on the financial statements
- Balance sheet
- Statement of retained earnings
- Income statement
- Cash flow statement
- Notes to the financial statements
- Accounting policies

Other information deemed relevant to stakeholders may be included, such as a report on operations for manufacturing firms. In the case of larger companies, it is usually a sleek, colorful, high gloss publication.

The details provided in the report are of use to investors to understand the company's financial position and future direction.

Chapter 8. Stocks, Stock Valuation, and Stock Market Equilibrium

a. Accrued liabilities
b. Amortization schedule
c. Annual report
d. Outstanding balance

26. In finance, a _____ is a debt security, in which the authorized issuer owes the holders a debt and, depending on the terms of the _____, is obliged to pay interest (the coupon) and/or to repay the principal at a later date, termed maturity.

Thus a _____ is a loan: the issuer is the borrower, the _____ holder is the lender, and the coupon is the interest. _____s provide the borrower with external funds to finance long-term investments, or, in the case of government _____s, to finance current expenditure.

a. Convertible bond
b. Puttable bond
c. Catastrophe bonds
d. Bond

27. _____ are the earnings returned on the initial investment amount.

In the US, the Financial Accounting Standards Board (FASB) requires companies' income statements to report _____ for each of the major categories of the income statement: continuing operations, discontinued operations, extraordinary items, and net income.

The _____ formula does not include preferred dividends for categories outside of continued operations and net income.

a. Assets turnover
b. Inventory turnover
c. Earnings per share
d. Average accounting return

28. In finance, _____ refers to the value of a security which is intrinsic to or contained in the security itself. It is also frequently called fundamental value. It is ordinarily calculated by summing the future income generated by the asset, and discounting it to the present value.
a. Amortization
b. Accretion
c. Alpha
d. Intrinsic value

29. A _____ is a financial contract between two parties, the buyer and the seller of this type of option. Often it is simply labeled a 'call'. The buyer of the option has the right, but not the obligation to buy an agreed quantity of a particular commodity or financial instrument (the underlying instrument) from the seller of the option at a certain time (the expiration date) for a certain price (the strike price.)
a. Bear call spread
b. Bear spread
c. Bull spread
d. Call option

30. _____ is a form of corporation equity ownership represented in the securities. It is dangerous in comparison to preferred shares and some other investment options, in that in the event of bankruptcy, _____ investors receive their funds after preferred stockholders, bondholders, creditors, etc. On the other hand, common shares on average perform better than preferred shares or bonds over time.
a. Common stock
b. Stop-limit order
c. Stock split
d. Stock market bubble

31. An _____ is a contract written by a seller that conveys to the buyer the right -- but not the obligation -- to buy (in the case of a call _____) or to sell (in the case of a put _____) a particular asset, such as a piece of property such as, among others, a futures contract. In return for granting the _____, the seller collects a payment (the premium) from the buyer.

For example, buying a call _____ provides the right to buy a specified quantity of a security at a set strike price at some time on or before expiration, while buying a put _____ provides the right to sell.

    a. Amortization   b. Option
    c. AT'T Mobility LLC   d. Annuity

32. The _____ is the market for securities, where companies and governments can raise longterm funds. The _____ includes the stock market and the bond market. Financial regulators, such as the U.S. Securities and Exchange Commission, oversee the _____s in their designated countries to ensure that investors are protected against fraud.

    a. Delta neutral   b. Capital Market
    c. Spot rate   d. Forward market

33. _____ proposes how rational investors will use diversification to optimize their portfolios, and how a risky asset should be priced. The basic concepts of the theory are Markowitz diversification, the efficient frontier, capital asset pricing model, the alpha and beta coefficients, the Capital Market Line and the Securities Market Line.

_____ models an asset's return as a random variable, and models a portfolio as a weighted combination of assets so that the return of a portfolio is the weighted combination of the assets' returns.

    a. Modern portfolio theory   b. Market value
    c. Consumer basket   d. Payback period

34. A _____ is a profit that results from investments into a capital asset, such as stocks, bonds or real estate, which exceeds the purchase price. It is the difference between a higher selling price and a lower purchase price, resulting in a financial gain for the seller. Conversely, a capital loss arises if the proceeds from the sale of a capital asset are less than the purchase price.

    a. Payroll tax   b. Capital gains tax
    c. Tax brackets   d. Capital gain

35. The _____ on a company stock is the company's annual dividend payments divided by its market cap, or the dividend per share divided by the price per share. It is often expressed as a percentage.

Dividend payments on preferred shares are stipulated by the prospectus.

    a. Dividend yield   b. Dividend imputation
    c. Dividend reinvestment plan   d. Special dividend

36. In finance, _____, also known as return on investment is the ratio of money gained or lost on an investment relative to the amount of money invested. The amount of money gained or lost may be referred to as interest, profit/loss, gain/loss, or net income/loss. The money invested may be referred to as the asset, capital, principal, or the cost basis of the investment.

Chapter 8. Stocks, Stock Valuation, and Stock Market Equilibrium 107

a. Rate of return
b. Stock or scrip dividends
c. Composiition of Creditors
d. Doctrine of the Proper Law

37. In finance, the term _____ describes the amount in cash that returns to the owners of a security. Normally it does not include the price variations, at the difference of the total return. _____ applies to various stated rates of return on stocks (common and preferred, and convertible), fixed income instruments (bonds, notes, bills, strips, zero coupon), and some other investment type insurance products (e.g. annuities.)

a. Macaulay duration
b. Yield to maturity
c. 4-4-5 Calendar
d. Yield

38. _____ is a variant of the Discounted cash flow model, a method for valuing a stock or business. Often used to provide difficult-to-resolve valuation issues for litigation, tax planning, and business transactions that are currently off market.

It assumes that the company issues a dividend that has a current value of D that grows at a constant rate g. It also assumes that the required rate of return for the stock remains constant at k which is equal to the cost of equity for that company. It involves summing the infinite series which gives the value of price current P.

a. Gordon growth model
b. Special journals
c. Stock or scrip dividends
d. Securitization

39. _____ or net present worth (NPW) is defined as the total present value (PV) of a time series of cash flows. It is a standard method for using the time value of money to appraise long-term projects. Used for capital budgeting, and widely throughout economics, it measures the excess or shortfall of cash flows, in present value terms, once financing charges are met.

a. Negative gearing
b. Net present value
c. Tax shield
d. Present value of costs

40. _____ is the value on a given date of a future payment or series of future payments, discounted to reflect the time value of money and other factors such as investment risk. _____ calculations are widely used in business and economics to provide a means to compare cash flows at different times on a meaningful 'like to like' basis.

The most commonly applied model of the time value of money is compound interest.

a. Net present value
b. Present value of benefits
c. Negative gearing
d. Present value

41. _____ are those dividends paid out in form of additional stock shares of the issuing corporation or other corporation They are usually issued in proportion to shares owned (for example for every 100 shares of stock owned, 5% stock dividend will yield 5 extra shares). If this payment involves the issue of new shares, this is very similar to a stock split in that it increases the total number of shares while lowering the price of each share and does not change the market capitalization or the total value of the shares held

a. Database auditing
b. Time-based currency
c. The Hong Kong Securities Institute
d. Stock or scrip dividends

Chapter 8. Stocks, Stock Valuation, and Stock Market Equilibrium

42. _____ is part of the Federal income tax system of the United States. There is an _____ for those who owe personal income tax, and another for corporations owing corporate income tax. Only the _____ for those owing personal income tax is described here.

The _____ operates in effect as a parallel tax system, with its own definition of taxable income, exemptions, and tax rates. Taxpayers compute tax owed under the 'regular' and _____ systems and are liable for whichever is higher.

a. Alternative minimum tax
b. A Random Walk Down Wall Street
c. ABN Amro
d. AAB

43. _____ is a term used in accounting, economics and finance to spread the cost of an asset over the span of several years.

In simple words we can say that _____ is the reduction in the value of an asset due to usage, passage of time, wear and tear, technological outdating or obsolescence, depletion or other such factors.

In accounting, _____ is a term used to describe any method of attributing the historical or purchase cost of an asset across its useful life, roughly corresponding to normal wear and tear.

a. Deferred financing costs
b. Bottom line
c. Matching principle
d. Depreciation

44. The _____ is the rate that a company is expected to pay to finance its assets. WACC is the minimum return that a company must earn on existing asset base to satisfy its creditors, owners, and other providers of capital.

Companies raise money from a number of sources: common equity, preferred equity, straight debt, convertible debt, exchangeable debt, warrants, options, pension liabilities, executive stock options, governmental subsidies, and so on.

a. 4-4-5 Calendar
b. Cost of capital
c. Capital intensity
d. Weighted average cost of capital

45. _____ is a theory that all economic activities and policies should be oriented towards achieving a state of equilibrium, a steady state.

The theory asserts that the continuous growth model is inherently unstable resulting in a 'boom/bust' cycle, and that continuous growth in the context of finite resources is unlikely to support current levels of prosperity indefinitely.

Proponents of this theory also explicitly challenge the popular equation of economic growth with progress - an equation they have labelled Growth Fetish - and posit that sustainability has inherent value.

a. 4-4-5 Calendar
c. 7-Eleven
b. Zero growth
d. 529 plan

46. In economics and finance, _____ is the practice of taking advantage of a price differential between two or more markets: striking a combination of matching deals that capitalize upon the imbalance, the profit being the difference between the market prices. When used by academics, an _____ is a transaction that involves no negative cash flow at any probabilistic or temporal state and a positive cash flow in at least one state; in simple terms, a risk-free profit.
   a. Efficient-market hypothesis
   c. Issuer
   b. Arbitrage
   d. Initial margin

47. _____ or financing is to provide capital (funds), which means money for a project, a person, a business or any other private or public institutions.

Those funds can be allocated for either short term or long term purposes. The health fund is a new way of _____ private healthcare centers.

   a. Proxy fight
   c. Funding
   b. Synthetic CDO
   d. Product life cycle

48. _____ is the balance of the amounts of cash being received and paid by a business during a defined period of time, sometimes tied to a specific project. Measurement of _____ can be used

   - to evaluate the state or performance of a business or project.
   - to determine problems with liquidity. Being profitable does not necessarily mean being liquid. A company can fail because of a shortage of cash, even while profitable.
   - to generate project rate of returns. The time of _____s into and out of projects are used as inputs to financial models such as internal rate of return, and net present value.
   - to examine income or growth of a business when it is believed that accrual accounting concepts do not represent economic realities. Alternately, _____ can be used to 'validate' the net income generated by accrual accounting.

_____ as a generic term may be used differently depending on context, and certain _____ definitions may be adapted by analysts and users for their own uses. Common terms include operating _____ and free _____.

_____s can be classified into:

1. Operational _____s: Cash received or expended as a result of the company's core business activities.
2. Investment _____s: Cash received or expended through capital expenditure, investments or acquisitions.
3. Financing _____s: Cash received or expended as a result of financial activities, such as interests and dividends.

All three together - the net _____ - are necessary to reconcile the beginning cash balance to the ending cash balance. Loan draw downs or equity injections, that is just shifting of capital but no expenditure as such, are not considered in the net _____.

a. Real option
b. Shareholder value
c. Corporate finance
d. Cash flow

49. In corporate finance, _____ is a cash flow available for distribution among all the security holders of a company. They include equity holders, debt holders, preferred stock holders, convertible security holders, and so on.

Note that the first three lines above are calculated for you on the standard Statement of Cash Flows.

a. Funding
b. Free cash flow
c. Safety stock
d. Forfaiting

50. Earnings before interest, taxes, depreciation and amortization (_____) is a non-GAAP metric that can be used to evaluate a company's profitability.

_____ = Operating Revenue - Operating Expenses + Other Revenue

Its name comes from the fact that Operating Expenses do not include interest, taxes, or amortization. _____ is not a defined measure according to Generally Accepted Accounting Principles (GAAP), and thus can be calculated however a company wishes.

a. Accrual
b. Accounts payable
c. Invoice processing
d. EBITDA

51. In business and accounting, _____s are everything of value that is owned by a person or company. The balance sheet of a firm records the monetary value of the _____s owned by the firm. The two major _____ classes are tangible _____s and intangible _____s.

a. EBITDA
b. Accounts payable
c. Income
d. Asset

52. _____, is when a company issues common stock or shares to the public for the first time. They are often issued by smaller, younger companies seeking capital to expand, but can also be done by large privately-owned companies looking to become publicly traded.

In an _____ the issuer may obtain the assistance of an underwriting firm, which helps it determine what type of security to issue (common or preferred), best offering price and time to bring it to market.

a. Asian Financial Crisis
b. Insolvency
c. Initial public offering
d. Interest

53. In finance, _____ refers to the way a corporation finances its assets through some combination of equity, debt, or hybrid securities. A firm's _____ is then the composition or 'structure' of its liabilities. For example, a firm that sells $20 billion in equity and $80 billion in debt is said to be 20% equity-financed and 80% debt-financed.

a. Rights issue
b. Market for corporate control
c. Book building
d. Capital structure

54. _____ most frequently refers to the standard deviation of the continuously compounded returns of a financial instrument with a specific time horizon. It is often used to quantify the risk of the instrument over that time period. _____ is typically expressed in annualized terms, and it may either be an absolute number ($5) or a fraction of the mean (5%).
   a. Volatility
   b. Portfolio insurance
   c. Currency swap
   d. Seasoned equity offering

55. The _____ is a stock exchange based in New York City, New York. It is the largest stock exchange in the world by dollar value of its listed companies securities. As of October 2008, the combined capitalization of all domestic _____ listed companies was $10.1 trillion.
   a. 529 plan
   b. 4-4-5 Calendar
   c. 7-Eleven
   d. New York Stock Exchange

56. A _____, securities exchange or (in Europe) bourse is a corporation or mutual organization which provides 'trading' facilities for stock brokers and traders, to trade stocks and other securities. _____s also provide facilities for the issue and redemption of securities as well as other financial instruments and capital events including the payment of income and dividends. The securities traded on a _____ include: shares issued by companies, unit trusts and other pooled investment products and bonds.
   a. 4-4-5 Calendar
   b. 529 plan
   c. 7-Eleven
   d. Stock Exchange

Chapter 9. Financial Options and Applications in Corporate Finance

1. A _____ is a financial contract between two parties, the buyer and the seller of this type of option. Often it is simply labeled a 'call'. The buyer of the option has the right, but not the obligation to buy an agreed quantity of a particular commodity or financial instrument (the underlying instrument) from the seller of the option at a certain time (the expiration date) for a certain price (the strike price.)

   a. Call option
   b. Bear call spread
   c. Bull spread
   d. Bear spread

2. A _____ is a financial contract whose value is derived from the value of something else (known as the underlying.) The underlying on which a _____ is based can be an asset, weather conditions bonds or other forms of credit.

   a. 7-Eleven
   b. 529 plan
   c. 4-4-5 Calendar
   d. Derivative

3. An _____ is a contract written by a seller that conveys to the buyer the right -- but not the obligation -- to buy (in the case of a call _____) or to sell (in the case of a put _____) a particular asset, such as a piece of property such as, among others, a futures contract. In return for granting the _____, the seller collects a payment (the premium) from the buyer.

   For example, buying a call _____ provides the right to buy a specified quantity of a security at a set strike price at some time on or before expiration, while buying a put _____ provides the right to sell.

   a. Amortization
   b. Annuity
   c. AT'T Mobility LLC
   d. Option

4. An _____ option has no intrinsic value. A call option is _____ when the strike price is above the spot price of the underlying security. A put option is _____ when the strike price is below the spot price.

   a. A Random Walk Down Wall Street
   b. AAB
   c. Out-of-the-money
   d. ABN Amro

5. A _____ is a financial contract between two parties, the seller (writer) and the buyer of the option. The put allows its buyer the right but not the obligation to sell a commodity or financial instrument (the underlying instrument) to the writer (seller) of the option at a certain time for a certain price (the strike price.) The writer (seller) has the obligation to purchase the underlying asset at that strike price, if the buyer exercises the option.

   a. Debit spread
   b. Bear spread
   c. Bear call spread
   d. Put option

6. In options, the _____ is a key variable in a derivatives contract between two parties. Where the contract requires delivery of the underlying instrument, the trade will be at the _____, regardless of the spot price (market price) of the underlying instrument at that time.

   Definition - The fixed price at which the owner of an option can purchase, in the case of a call in the case of a put, the underlying security or commodity.

   a. Strike price
   b. Swaption
   c. Naked put
   d. Moneyness

Chapter 9. Financial Options and Applications in Corporate Finance 113

7. _____, is when a company issues common stock or shares to the public for the first time. They are often issued by smaller, younger companies seeking capital to expand, but can also be done by large privately-owned companies looking to become publicly traded.

In an _____ the issuer may obtain the assistance of an underwriting firm, which helps it determine what type of security to issue (common or preferred), best offering price and time to bring it to market.

 a. Asian Financial Crisis
 b. Interest
 c. Insolvency
 d. Initial public offering

8. In finance, a _____ is a debt security, in which the authorized issuer owes the holders a debt and, depending on the terms of the _____, is obliged to pay interest (the coupon) and/or to repay the principal at a later date, termed maturity.

Thus a _____ is a loan: the issuer is the borrower, the _____ holder is the lender, and the coupon is the interest. _____s provide the borrower with external funds to finance long-term investments, or, in the case of government _____s, to finance current expenditure.

 a. Catastrophe bonds
 b. Convertible bond
 c. Puttable bond
 d. Bond

9. A _____ is a payment made by a corporation to its shareholder members. When a corporation earns a profit or surplus, that money can be put to two uses: it can either be re-invested in the business (called retained earnings), or it can be paid to the shareholders as a _____. Many corporations retain a portion of their earnings and pay the remainder as a _____.

 a. Dividend yield
 b. Dividend puzzle
 c. Special dividend
 d. Dividend

10. In finance, a _____ is a standardized contract, to buy or sell a specified commodity of standardized quality at a certain date in the future, at a market determined price (the futures price.)

The price is determined by the instantaneous equilibrium between the forces of supply and demand among competing buy and sell orders on the exchange at the time of the purchase or sale of the contract.

In many cases, the items may be such non-traditional 'commodities' as foreign currencies, commercial or government paper [e.g., bonds], or 'baskets' of corporate equity ['stock indices'] or other financial instruments.

 a. Financial future
 b. Repurchase agreement
 c. Futures contract
 d. Heston model

11. In economic models, the _____ time frame assumes no fixed factors of production. Firms can enter or leave the marketplace, and the cost (and availability) of land, labor, raw materials, and capital goods can be assumed to vary. In contrast, in the short-run time frame, certain factors are assumed to be fixed, because there is not sufficient time for them to change.

a. 4-4-5 Calendar
b. 529 plan
c. Long-run
d. Short-run

12. The phrase _____ refers to the aspect of corporate strategy, corporate finance and management dealing with the buying, selling and combining of different companies that can aid, finance, or help a growing company in a given industry grow rapidly without having to create another business entity.

An acquisition, also known as a takeover, is the buying of one company (the 'target') by another. An acquisition may be friendly or hostile.

a. 4-4-5 Calendar
b. 7-Eleven
c. Mergers and acquisitions
d. 529 plan

13. A _____ is a fungible, negotiable instrument representing financial value. They are broadly categorized into debt securities (such as banknotes, bonds and debentures), and equity securities; e.g., common stocks. The company or other entity issuing the _____ is called the issuer.
   a. Book entry
   b. Tracking stock
   c. Securities lending
   d. Security

14. _____ is an estimate of the fair value of corporations and their stocks, by using fundamental economic criteria. This theoretical valuation has to be perfected with market criteria, as the final purpose is to determine potential market prices.
   a. Growth stocks
   b. Stock valuation
   c. 4-4-5 Calendar
   d. Security Analysis

15. _____ is the process of determining the fair price of a bond. As with any security or capital investment, the fair value of a bond is the present value of the stream of cash flows it is expected to generate. Hence, the price or value of a bond is determined by discounting the bond's expected cash flows to the present using the appropriate discount rate.
   a. Catastrophe bonds
   b. Collateralized debt obligations
   c. Bond fund
   d. Bond valuation

16. A _____ is something for which there is demand, but which is supplied without qualitative differentiation across a market. It is a product that is the same no matter who produces it, such as petroleum, notebook paper, or milk. In other words, copper is copper.
   a. 7-Eleven
   b. 4-4-5 Calendar
   c. 529 plan
   d. Commodity

17. In economics, business, and accounting, a _____ is the value of money that has been used up to produce something, and hence is not available for use anymore. In business, the _____ may be one of acquisition, in which case the amount of money expended to acquire it is counted as _____. In this case, money is the input that is gone in order to acquire the thing.
   a. Fixed costs
   b. Sliding scale fees
   c. Marginal cost
   d. Cost

18. _____ is an economic concept with commonplace familiarity. It is the price that a good or service is offered at, or will fetch, in the marketplace. It is of interest mainly in the study of microeconomics.

Chapter 9. Financial Options and Applications in Corporate Finance

    a. Market price
    b. Convertible arbitrage
    c. Central Securities Depository
    d. Delta hedging

19. In finance, _____ is the process of estimating the potential market value of a financial asset or liability. they can be done on assets (for example, investments in marketable securities such as stocks, options, business enterprises, or intangible assets such as patents and trademarks) or on liabilities (e.g., Bonds issued by a company.) _____s are required in many contexts including investment analysis, capital budgeting, merger and acquisition transactions, financial reporting, taxable events to determine the proper tax liability, and in litigation.
    a. Share
    b. Valuation
    c. Margin
    d. Procter ' Gamble

20. In business and accounting, _____s are everything of value that is owned by a person or company. The balance sheet of a firm records the monetary value of the _____s owned by the firm. The two major _____ classes are tangible _____s and intangible _____s.
    a. EBITDA
    b. Income
    c. Asset
    d. Accounts payable

21. The term _____ has three unrelated technical definitions, and is also used in a variety of non-technical ways.

- In financial economics, it refers to any asset used to make money, as opposed to assets used for personal enjoyment or consumption. This is an important distinction because two people can disagree sharply about the value of personal assets, one person might think a sports car is more valuable than a pickup truck, another person might have the opposite taste. But if an asset is held for the purpose of making money, taste has nothing to do with it, only differences of opinion about how much money the asset will produce. With the further assumption that people agree on the probability distribution of future cash flows, it is possible to have an objective _____ pricing model. Even without the assumption of agreement, it is possible to set rational limits on _____ value.
- In governmental accounting, it is defined as any asset used in operations with an initial useful life extending beyond one reporting period. Generally, government managers have a 'stewardship' duty to maintain _____s under their control. See International Public Sector Accounting Standards for details.
- In US tax accounting, it is defined as any property other than a list of exceptions. The main exceptions are anything held for sale, and any real estate or depreciable property used in business. Almost everything you own and use for personal purposes, pleasure or investment is a _____. If something is a _____ for tax purposes, gains or losses on sale or disposition are capital gains or capital losses. For individuals, however, capital losses on property held for personal use are generally not deductible. See the IRS publication Tax Facts about Capital Gains and Losses for details.

A well-known financial accounting textbook advises that the term be avoided except in tax accounting because it is used in so many different senses, not all of them well-defined. For example it is often used as a synonym for fixed assets or for investments in securities.

A common non-technical usage occurs when people ask that employees or the environment or something else be treated as a _____.

    a. Political risk
    b. Solvency
    c. Settlement date
    d. Capital Asset

Chapter 9. Financial Options and Applications in Corporate Finance

22. In finance, the _____ is used to determine a theoretically appropriate required rate of return of an asset, if that asset is to be added to an already well-diversified portfolio, given that asset's non-diversifiable risk. The model takes into account the asset's sensitivity to non-diversifiable risk (also known as systemic risk or market risk), often represented by the quantity beta (β) in the financial industry, as well as the expected return of the market and the expected return of a theoretical risk-free asset.

The model was introduced by Jack Treynor (1961, 1962), William Sharpe (1964), John Lintner (1965a,b) and Jan Mossin (1966) independently, building on the earlier work of Harry Markowitz on diversification and modern portfolio theory.

- a. Hull-White model
- b. Random walk hypothesis
- c. Cox-Ingersoll-Ross model
- d. Capital Asset Pricing Model

23. _____ are formal records of a business' financial activities.

_____ provide an overview of a business' financial condition in both short and long term. There are four basic _____:

1. **Balance sheet**: also referred to as statement of financial position or condition, reports on a company's assets, liabilities, and net equity as of a given point in time.
2. **Income statement**: also referred to as Profit and Loss statement (or a 'P'L'), reports on a company's income, expenses, and profits over a period of time.
3. **Statement of retained earnings**: explains the changes in a company's retained earnings over the reporting period.
4. **Statement of cash flows**: reports on a company's cash flow activities, particularly its operating, investing and financing activities.

- a. Financial statements
- b. Statement of retained earnings
- c. Notes to the Financial Statements
- d. Statement on Auditing Standards No. 70: Service Organizations

24. In finance, _____ refers to the way a corporation finances its assets through some combination of equity, debt, or hybrid securities. A firm's _____ is then the composition or 'structure' of its liabilities. For example, a firm that sells $20 billion in equity and $80 billion in debt is said to be 20% equity-financed and 80% debt-financed.
- a. Capital structure
- b. Market for corporate control
- c. Book building
- d. Rights issue

25. An _____ is a call option on the common stock of a company, issued as a form of non-cash compensation. Restrictions on the option (such as vesting and limited transferability) attempt to align the holder's interest with those of the business' shareholders. If the company's stock rises, holders of options experience a direct financial benefit.
- a. Internal financing
- b. Employee stock option
- c. Underwriting contract
- d. Operating ratio

26. _____ is a life of security. It may also refer to the final payment date of a loan or other financial instrument, at which point all remaining interest and principal is due to be paid.

1, 3, 6 months _____ band can be calculated by using 30-day per month periods.

a. Primary market
b. Replacement cost
c. False billing
d. Maturity

27. A _____ is the price of a single share of a no. of saleable stocks of the company. Once the stock is purchased, the owner becomes a shareholder of the company that issued the share.

a. Share price
b. Trading curb
c. Whisper numbers
d. Stock split

28. In finance, a _____ is a position established in one market in an attempt to offset exposure to the price risk of an equal but opposite obligation or position in another market -- usually, but not always, in the context of one's commercial activity. Hedging is a strategy designed to minimize exposure to such business risks as a sharp contraction in demand for one's inventory, while still allowing the business to profit from producing and maintaining that inventory. A typical hedger might be a farmer with 2000 acres of unharvested wheat in the ground, who would rather tend his crop without the distraction of uncertain prices.

a. 7-Eleven
b. 4-4-5 Calendar
c. 529 plan
d. Hedge

29. _____ or net present worth (NPW) is defined as the total present value (PV) of a time series of cash flows. It is a standard method for using the time value of money to appraise long-term projects. Used for capital budgeting, and widely throughout economics, it measures the excess or shortfall of cash flows, in present value terms, once financing charges are met.

a. Tax shield
b. Negative gearing
c. Present value of costs
d. Net present value

30. _____ is the value on a given date of a future payment or series of future payments, discounted to reflect the time value of money and other factors such as investment risk. _____ calculations are widely used in business and economics to provide a means to compare cash flows at different times on a meaningful 'like to like' basis.

The most commonly applied model of the time value of money is compound interest.

a. Present value
b. Negative gearing
c. Present value of benefits
d. Net present value

31. _____ is part of the Federal income tax system of the United States. There is an _____ for those who owe personal income tax, and another for corporations owing corporate income tax. Only the _____ for those owing personal income tax is described here.

The _____ operates in effect as a parallel tax system, with its own definition of taxable income, exemptions, and tax rates. Taxpayers compute tax owed under the 'regular' and _____ systems and are liable for whichever is higher.

Chapter 9. Financial Options and Applications in Corporate Finance

a. ABN Amro
c. AAB

b. Alternative minimum tax
d. A Random Walk Down Wall Street

32. _____ or financing is to provide capital (funds), which means money for a project, a person, a business or any other private or public institutions.

Those funds can be allocated for either short term or long term purposes. The health fund is a new way of _____ private healthcare centers.

a. Product life cycle
c. Proxy fight

b. Synthetic CDO
d. Funding

33. In probability theory and statistics, the _____ of a random variable, probability distribution averaging the squared distance of its possible values from the expected value (mean.) Whereas the mean is a way to describe the location of a distribution, the _____ is a way to capture its scale or degree of being spread out. The unit of _____ is the square of the unit of the original variable.

a. Harmonic mean
c. Semivariance

b. Monte Carlo methods
d. Variance

34. In financial mathematics, _____ defines a relationship between the price of a call option and a put option--both with the identical strike price and expiry. To derive the _____ relationship, the assumption is that the options are not exercised before expiration day, which necessarily applies to European options. _____ can be derived in a manner that is largely model independent.

a. Rendleman-Bartter model
c. Hull-White model

b. Cox-Ingersoll-Ross model
d. Put-call parity

35. In finance, _____ is the risk involved in using models to value financial securities. Rebonato considers alternative definitions including:

1) After observing a set of prices for the underlying and hedging instruments, different but identically calibrated models might produce different prices for the same exotic product. 2) Losses will be incurred because of an 'incorrect' hedging strategy suggested by a model.

a. Model risk
c. Takeover

b. Price-to-book ratio
d. Duty of loyalty

36. In corporate finance, _____ analysis applies put option and call option valuation techniques to capital budgeting decisions. A _____ itself, is the right--but not the obligation--to undertake some business decision; typically the option to make, or abandon, a capital investment. For example, the opportunity to invest in the expansion of a firm's factory, or alternatively to sell the factory, is a _____.

a. Book building
c. Capital budgeting

b. Cash flow
d. Real option

Chapter 9. Financial Options and Applications in Corporate Finance

37. The institution most often referenced by the word '_____' is a public or publicly traded _____, the shares of which are traded on a public stock exchange (e.g., the New York Stock Exchange or Nasdaq in the United States) where shares of stock of _____s are bought and sold by and to the general public. Most of the largest businesses in the world are publicly traded _____s. However, the majority of _____s are said to be closely held, privately held or close _____s, meaning that no ready market exists for the trading of shares.
   a. Federal Home Loan Mortgage Corporation
   b. Protect
   c. Depository Trust Company
   d. Corporation

38. _____ is the discipline of identifying, monitoring and limiting risks. In some cases the acceptable risk may be near zero. Risks can come from accidents, natural causes and disasters as well as deliberate attacks from an adversary.
   a. Penny stock
   b. FIFO
   c. 4-4-5 Calendar
   d. Risk management

39. _____ is a multiple-winner voting system intended to promote proportional representation while also being simple to understand.

   _____ is used frequently in corporate governance, where it is mandated by many U.S. states, and it was used to elect the Illinois House of Representatives from 1870 until its repeal in 1980. It was used in England in the late 19th century to elect school boards.

   a. 529 plan
   b. 7-Eleven
   c. 4-4-5 Calendar
   d. Cumulative voting

40. In finance, the _____ between two currencies specifies how much one currency is worth in terms of the other. For example an _____ of 102 Japanese yen to the United States dollar means that JPY 102 is worth the same as USD 1. The foreign exchange market is one of the largest markets in the world.
   a. Exchange rate
   b. A Random Walk Down Wall Street
   c. ABN Amro
   d. AAB

41. _____ is a term used in accounting relating to the increase in value of an asset. In this sense it is the reverse of depreciation, which measures the fall in value of assets over their normal life-time.

   _____ is a rise of a currency in a floating exchange rate.

   a. Operating cash flow
   b. Other Comprehensive Basis of Accounting
   c. A Random Walk Down Wall Street
   d. Appreciation

Chapter 10. The Cost of Capital

1. In economics, business, and accounting, a _____ is the value of money that has been used up to produce something, and hence is not available for use anymore. In business, the _____ may be one of acquisition, in which case the amount of money expended to acquire it is counted as _____. In this case, money is the input that is gone in order to acquire the thing.
   a. Cost
   b. Sliding scale fees
   c. Marginal cost
   d. Fixed costs

2. The _____ is an expected return that the provider of capital plans to earn on their investment.

   Capital (money) used for funding a business should earn returns for the capital providers who risk their capital. For an investment to be worthwhile, the expected return on capital must be greater than the _____.

   a. Weighted average cost of capital
   b. 4-4-5 Calendar
   c. Capital intensity
   d. Cost of capital

3. _____ is the price at which an asset would trade in a competitive Walrasian auction setting. _____ is often used interchangeably with open _____, fair value or fair _____, although these terms have distinct definitions in different standards, and may differ in some circumstances.

   International Valuation Standards defines _____ as 'the estimated amount for which a property should exchange on the date of valuation between a willing buyer and a willing seller in an arm'e;s-length transaction after proper marketing wherein the parties had each acted knowledgeably, prudently, and without compulsion.'

   _____ is a concept distinct from market price, which is 'e;the price at which one can transact'e;, while _____ is 'e;the true underlying value'e; according to theoretical standards.

   a. Debt restructuring
   b. T-Model
   c. Wrap account
   d. Market value

4. _____ is the difference between the current market value of a firm and the capital contributed by investors. If _____ is positive, the firm has added value. If it is negative, the firm has destroyed value.
   a. Monetary system
   b. Decision process tool
   c. Wrap account
   d. Market value added

5. _____ refers to the additional value of a commodity over the cost of commodities used to produce it from the previous stage of production. An example is the price of gasoline at the pump over the price of the oil in it. In national accounts used in macroeconomics, it refers to the contribution of the factors of production, i.e., land, labor, and capital goods, to raising the value of a product and corresponds to the incomes received by the owners of these factors.
   a. Value added
   b. Supply shock
   c. Deregulation
   d. Demand shock

6. In economics, _____ is a measure of the relative satisfaction from or desirability of consumption of various goods and services. Given this measure, one may speak meaningfully of increasing or decreasing _____, and thereby explain economic behavior in terms of attempts to increase one's _____. For illustrative purposes, changes in _____ are sometimes expressed in units called utils.

Chapter 10. The Cost of Capital 121

    a. AAB
    b. Utility function
    c. A Random Walk Down Wall Street
    d. Utility

7. The _____ is the rate that a company is expected to pay to finance its assets. WACC is the minimum return that a company must earn on existing asset base to satisfy its creditors, owners, and other providers of capital.

Companies raise money from a number of sources: common equity, preferred equity, straight debt, convertible debt, exchangeable debt, warrants, options, pension liabilities, executive stock options, governmental subsidies, and so on.

    a. Capital intensity
    b. 4-4-5 Calendar
    c. Cost of capital
    d. Weighted average cost of capital

8. _____ is that which is owed; usually referencing assets owed, but the term can cover other obligations. In the case of assets, _____ is a means of using future purchasing power in the present before a summation has been earned. Some companies and corporations use _____ as a part of their overall corporate finance strategy.
    a. Debt
    b. Partial Payment
    c. Credit cycle
    d. Cross-collateralization

9. _____ is a financial ratio that indicates the percentage of a company's assets are provided via debt. It is the ratio of total debt (the sum of current liabilities and long-term liabilities) and total assets (the sum of current assets, fixed assets, and other assets such as 'goodwill'.)

[image] >

or alternatively:

[image] >

For example, a company with $2 million in total assets and $500,000 in total liabilities would have a _____ of 25%

Like all financial ratios, a company's _____ should be compared with their industry average or other competing firms.

    a. Cash concentration
    b. Cash management
    c. Capitalization rate
    d. Debt ratio

10. The _____ is a capital budgeting metric used by firms to decide whether they should make investments. It is an indicator of the efficiency or quality of an investment, as opposed to net present value (NPV), which indicates value or magnitude.

The IRR is the annualized effective compounded return rate which can be earned on the invested capital, i.e., the yield on the investment.

Chapter 10. The Cost of Capital

a. Internal rate of return
c. ABN Amro
b. A Random Walk Down Wall Street
d. AAB

11. _____ is a life of security. It may also refer to the final payment date of a loan or other financial instrument, at which point all remaining interest and principal is due to be paid.

1, 3, 6 months _____ band can be calculated by using 30-day per month periods.

a. False billing
c. Primary market
b. Replacement cost
d. Maturity

12. In corporate finance, _____ analysis applies put option and call option valuation techniques to capital budgeting decisions. A _____ itself, is the right--but not the obligation--to undertake some business decision; typically the option to make, or abandon, a capital investment. For example, the opportunity to invest in the expansion of a firm's factory, or alternatively to sell the factory, is a _____.

a. Capital budgeting
c. Cash flow
b. Book building
d. Real option

13. _____ occurs when an entity that has issued callable bonds calls those debt securities from the debt holders with the express purpose of reissuing new debt at a lower coupon rate. In essence, the issue of new, lower-interest debt allows the company to prematurely refund the older, higher-interest debt.

On the contrary, NonRefundable Bonds may be callable but they cannot be re-issued with a lower coupon rate.

a. Refunding
c. No-arbitrage bounds
b. Market neutral
d. Systematic risk

14. The U.S. _____ is an independent agency of the United States government which holds primary responsibility for enforcing the federal securities laws and regulating the securities industry, the nation's stock and options exchanges, and other electronic securities markets. The SEC was created by section 4 of the SEC of 1934 (now codified as 15 U.S.C. § 78d and commonly referred to as the 1934 Act.)

a. 7-Eleven
c. Securities and Exchange Commission
b. 4-4-5 Calendar
d. 529 plan

15. In finance, a _____ is a debt security, in which the authorized issuer owes the holders a debt and, depending on the terms of the _____, is obliged to pay interest (the coupon) and/or to repay the principal at a later date, termed maturity.

Thus a _____ is a loan: the issuer is the borrower, the _____ holder is the lender, and the coupon is the interest. _____s provide the borrower with external funds to finance long-term investments, or, in the case of government _____s, to finance current expenditure.

a. Puttable bond
c. Catastrophe bonds
b. Convertible bond
d. Bond

Chapter 10. The Cost of Capital

16. _____ is the process of determining the fair price of a bond. As with any security or capital investment, the fair value of a bond is the present value of the stream of cash flows it is expected to generate. Hence, the price or value of a bond is determined by discounting the bond's expected cash flows to the present using the appropriate discount rate.
   a. Collateralized debt obligations
   b. Bond fund
   c. Bond valuation
   d. Catastrophe bonds

17. In finance, _____ refers to the way a corporation finances its assets through some combination of equity, debt, or hybrid securities. A firm's _____ is then the composition or 'structure' of its liabilities. For example, a firm that sells $20 billion in equity and $80 billion in debt is said to be 20% equity-financed and 80% debt-financed.
   a. Capital structure
   b. Book building
   c. Market for corporate control
   d. Rights issue

18. An _____ is a contract written by a seller that conveys to the buyer the right -- but not the obligation -- to buy (in the case of a call _____) or to sell (in the case of a put _____) a particular asset, such as a piece of property such as, among others, a futures contract. In return for granting the _____, the seller collects a payment (the premium) from the buyer.

For example, buying a call _____ provides the right to buy a specified quantity of a security at a set strike price at some time on or before expiration, while buying a put _____ provides the right to sell.

   a. Amortization
   b. Option
   c. AT'T Mobility LLC
   d. Annuity

19. In finance, _____, also known as return on investment is the ratio of money gained or lost on an investment relative to the amount of money invested. The amount of money gained or lost may be referred to as interest, profit/loss, gain/loss, or net income/loss. The money invested may be referred to as the asset, capital, principal, or the cost basis of the investment.
   a. Composiition of Creditors
   b. Doctrine of the Proper Law
   c. Stock or scrip dividends
   d. Rate of return

20. In finance, _____ is the process of estimating the potential market value of a financial asset or liability. they can be done on assets (for example, investments in marketable securities such as stocks, options, business enterprises, or intangible assets such as patents and trademarks) or on liabilities (e.g., Bonds issued by a company.) _____s are required in many contexts including investment analysis, capital budgeting, merger and acquisition transactions, financial reporting, taxable events to determine the proper tax liability, and in litigation.
   a. Procter ' Gamble
   b. Share
   c. Valuation
   d. Margin

21. _____, is when a company issues common stock or shares to the public for the first time. They are often issued by smaller, younger companies seeking capital to expand, but can also be done by large privately-owned companies looking to become publicly traded.

In an _____ the issuer may obtain the assistance of an underwriting firm, which helps it determine what type of security to issue (common or preferred), best offering price and time to bring it to market.

a. Asian Financial Crisis
b. Insolvency
c. Interest
d. Initial public offering

22. _____ is typically a higher ranking stock than voting shares, and its terms are negotiated between the corporation and the investor.

_____ usually carry no voting rights, but may carry superior priority over common stock in the payment of dividends and upon liquidation. _____ may carry a dividend that is paid out prior to any dividends to common stock holders.

a. Trade-off theory
b. Second lien loan
c. Preferred stock
d. Follow-on offering

23. _____ is the financing of long-term infrastructure and industrial projects based upon a complex financial structure where project debt and equity are used to finance the project, rather than the balance sheets of project sponsors. Usually, a _____ structure involves a number of equity investors, known as sponsors, as well as a syndicate of banks that provide loans to the operation. The loans are most commonly non-recourse loans, which are secured by the project assets and paid entirely from project cash flow, rather than from the general assets or creditworthiness of the project sponsors, a decision in part supported by financial modeling.

a. Project finance
b. Standard of deferred payment
c. Duration gap
d. FATF Blacklist

24. _____ refers to a tax levied by various jurisdictions on the profits made by companies or associations. It is a tax on the value of the corporation's profits.

The measure of taxable profits varies from country to country.

a. First-mover advantage
b. Corporate tax
c. Proxy fight
d. Trade finance

25. _____ or financing is to provide capital (funds), which means money for a project, a person, a business or any other private or public institutions.

Those funds can be allocated for either short term or long term purposes. The health fund is a new way of _____ private healthcare centers.

a. Proxy fight
b. Synthetic CDO
c. Product life cycle
d. Funding

26. _____, refers to consumption opportunity gained by an entity within a specified time frame, which is generally expressed in monetary terms. However, for households and individuals, '_____ is the sum of all the wages, salaries, profits, interests payments, rents and other forms of earnings received... in a given period of time.' For firms, _____ generally refers to net-profit: what remains of revenue after expenses have been subtracted.

a. Annual report
b. Accrual
c. OIBDA
d. Income

Chapter 10. The Cost of Capital

27. An _____ is a tax levied on the financial income of people, corporations, or other legal entities. Various _____ systems exist, with varying degrees of tax incidence. Income taxation can be progressive, proportional, or regressive.
   a. ABN Amro
   b. A Random Walk Down Wall Street
   c. AAB
   d. Income tax

28. In business and finance, a _____ (also referred to as equity _____) of stock means a _____ of ownership in a corporation (company.) In the plural, stocks is often used as a synonym for _____s especially in the United States, but it is less commonly used that way outside of North America.

   In the United Kingdom, South Africa, and Australia, stock can also refer to completely different financial instruments such as government bonds or, less commonly, to all kinds of marketable securities.

   a. Procter ' Gamble
   b. Margin
   c. Bucket shop
   d. Share

29. _____ is a form of corporation equity ownership represented in the securities. It is dangerous in comparison to preferred shares and some other investment options, in that in the event of bankruptcy, _____ investors receive their funds after preferred stockholders, bondholders, creditors, etc. On the other hand, common shares on average perform better than preferred shares or bonds over time.
   a. Stock split
   b. Stock market bubble
   c. Stop-limit order
   d. Common stock

30. In business and accounting, _____s are everything of value that is owned by a person or company. The balance sheet of a firm records the monetary value of the _____s owned by the firm. The two major _____ classes are tangible _____s and intangible _____s.
   a. EBITDA
   b. Accounts payable
   c. Income
   d. Asset

31. In finance, the _____ is used to determine a theoretically appropriate required rate of return of an asset, if that asset is to be added to an already well-diversified portfolio, given that asset's non-diversifiable risk. The model takes into account the asset's sensitivity to non-diversifiable risk (also known as systemic risk or market risk), often represented by the quantity beta (β) in the financial industry, as well as the expected return of the market and the expected return of a theoretical risk-free asset.

   The model was introduced by Jack Treynor (1961, 1962), William Sharpe (1964), John Lintner (1965a,b) and Jan Mossin (1966) independently, building on the earlier work of Harry Markowitz on diversification and modern portfolio theory.

   a. Hull-White model
   b. Random walk hypothesis
   c. Cox-Ingersoll-Ross model
   d. Capital asset pricing model

32. The term _____ has three unrelated technical definitions, and is also used in a variety of non-technical ways.

- In financial economics, it refers to any asset used to make money, as opposed to assets used for personal enjoyment or consumption. This is an important distinction because two people can disagree sharply about the value of personal assets, one person might think a sports car is more valuable than a pickup truck, another person might have the opposite taste. But if an asset is held for the purpose of making money, taste has nothing to do with it, only differences of opinion about how much money the asset will produce. With the further assumption that people agree on the probability distribution of future cash flows, it is possible to have an objective _____ pricing model. Even without the assumption of agreement, it is possible to set rational limits on _____ value.
- In governmental accounting, it is defined as any asset used in operations with an initial useful life extending beyond one reporting period. Generally, government managers have a 'stewardship' duty to maintain _____s under their control. See International Public Sector Accounting Standards for details.
- In US tax accounting, it is defined as any property other than a list of exceptions. The main exceptions are anything held for sale, and any real estate or depreciable property used in business. Almost everything you own and use for personal purposes, pleasure or investment is a _____. If something is a _____ for tax purposes, gains or losses on sale or disposition are capital gains or capital losses. For individuals, however, capital losses on property held for personal use are generally not deductible. See the IRS publication Tax Facts about Capital Gains and Losses for details.

A well-known financial accounting textbook advises that the term be avoided except in tax accounting because it is used in so many different senses, not all of them well-defined. For example it is often used as a synonym for fixed assets or for investments in securities.

A common non-technical usage occurs when people ask that employees or the environment or something else be treated as a _____.

a. Solvency
b. Capital Asset
c. Political risk
d. Settlement date

33. In finance, the _____ approach describes a method of valuing a project, company, or asset using the concepts of the time value of money. All future cash flows are estimated and discounted to give their present values. The discount rate used is generally the appropriate cost of capital and may incorporate judgments of the uncertainty (riskiness) of the future cash flows.

a. Present value of benefits
b. Net present value
c. Future-oriented
d. Discounted cash flow

34. _____ or economic opportunity loss is the value of the next best alternative foregone as the result of making a decision. _____ analysis is an important part of a company's decision-making processes but is not treated as an actual cost in any financial statement. The next best thing that a person can engage in is referred to as the _____ of doing the best thing and ignoring the next best thing to be done.

a. A Random Walk Down Wall Street
b. ABN Amro
c. AAB
d. Opportunity cost

Chapter 10. The Cost of Capital

35. _____ is the balance of the amounts of cash being received and paid by a business during a defined period of time, sometimes tied to a specific project. Measurement of _____ can be used

- to evaluate the state or performance of a business or project.
- to determine problems with liquidity. Being profitable does not necessarily mean being liquid. A company can fail because of a shortage of cash, even while profitable.
- to generate project rate of returns. The time of _____s into and out of projects are used as inputs to financial models such as internal rate of return, and net present value.
- to examine income or growth of a business when it is believed that accrual accounting concepts do not represent economic realities. Alternately, _____ can be used to 'validate' the net income generated by accrual accounting.

_____ as a generic term may be used differently depending on context, and certain _____ definitions may be adapted by analysts and users for their own uses. Common terms include operating _____ and free _____.

_____s can be classified into:

1. Operational _____s: Cash received or expended as a result of the company's core business activities.
2. Investment _____s: Cash received or expended through capital expenditure, investments or acquisitions.
3. Financing _____s: Cash received or expended as a result of financial activities, such as interests and dividends.

All three together - the net _____ - are necessary to reconcile the beginning cash balance to the ending cash balance. Loan draw downs or equity injections, that is just shifting of capital but no expenditure as such, are not considered in the net _____.

a. Corporate finance
c. Real option
b. Shareholder value
d. Cash flow

36. In the portfolio management field, Eugene Fama and Kenneth French developed the highly successful _____ to describe market behavior.

CAPM uses a single factor, beta, to compare the excess returns of a portfolio with the excess returns of the market as a whole. But it oversimplifies the complex market. Fama and French started with the observation that two classes of stocks have tended to do better than the market as a whole: small caps and (ii) stocks with a high book-to-market ratio (BM, customarily called value stocks, and different from growth stocks). They then added two factors to CAPM to reflect a portfolio's exposure to these two classes:

Here r is the portfolio's return rate, R_f is the risk-free return rate, and K_m is the return of the whole stock market. The 'three factor' $>\beta$ is analogous to the classical $>\beta$ but not equal to it, since there are now two additional factors to do some of the work. SMB stands for 'small minus big' and HML for 'high (book-to-price ratio) minus low'; they measure the historic excess returns of small caps over big caps and of value stocks over growth stocks.

   a. Reputational risk
   b. Mitigating Control
   c. Guaranteed investment contracts
   d. Fama-French three factor model

37. _____ mature in one year or less. Like zero-coupon bonds, they do not pay interest prior to maturity; instead they are sold at a discount of the par value to create a positive yield to maturity. Many regard _____ as the least risky investment available to U.S. investors.
   a. 4-4-5 Calendar
   b. Treasury bills
   c. Treasury securities
   d. Treasury Inflation Protected Securities

38. _____ are government bonds issued by the United States Department of the Treasury through the Bureau of the Public Debt. They are the debt financing instruments of the U.S. Federal government, and they are often referred to simply as Treasuries or Treasurys. There are four types of marketable _____: Treasury bills, Treasury notes, Treasury bonds, and Treasury Inflation Protected Securities (TIPS.)
   a. Treasury Inflation-Protected Securities
   b. 4-4-5 Calendar
   c. Treasury Inflation Protected Securities
   d. Treasury securities

39. The _____ is the market for securities, where companies and governments can raise longterm funds. The _____ includes the stock market and the bond market. Financial regulators, such as the U.S. Securities and Exchange Commission, oversee the _____s in their designated countries to ensure that investors are protected against fraud.
   a. Capital Market
   b. Forward market
   c. Delta neutral
   d. Spot rate

40. _____ proposes how rational investors will use diversification to optimize their portfolios, and how a risky asset should be priced. The basic concepts of the theory are Markowitz diversification, the efficient frontier, capital asset pricing model, the alpha and beta coefficients, the Capital Market Line and the Securities Market Line.

_____ models an asset's return as a random variable, and models a portfolio as a weighted combination of assets so that the return of a portfolio is the weighted combination of the assets' returns.

   a. Consumer basket
   b. Payback period
   c. Market value
   d. Modern portfolio theory

41. In finance, the _____ is the minimum rate of return a firm must offer shareholders to compensate for waiting for their returns, and for bearing some risk.

The _____ capital for a particular company is the rate of return on investment that is required by the company's ordinary shareholders. The return consists both of dividend and capital gains, e.g. increases in the share price.

a. Net pay
b. Cost of equity
c. Round-tripping
d. Residual value

42. In financial accounting, a _____ or statement of financial position is a summary of a person's or organization's balances. Assets, liabilities and ownership equity are listed as of a specific date, such as the end of its financial year. A _____ is often described as a snapshot of a company's financial condition.

a. Statement of retained earnings
b. Statement on Auditing Standards No. 70: Service Organizations
c. Financial statements
d. Balance sheet

43. _____ is a concept in economics, finance, and psychology related to the behaviour of consumers and investors under uncertainty. _____ is the reluctance of a person to accept a bargain with an uncertain payoff rather than another bargain with a more certain, but possibly lower, expected payoff.

The inverse of a person's _____ is sometimes called their risk tolerance

a. Risk adjusted return on capital
b. Discount factor
c. Risk premium
d. Risk aversion

44.

In finance, the _____ can be the expected rate of return above the risk-free interest rate. When measuring risk, a common sense approach is to compare the risk-free return on T-bills and the very risky return on other investments. The difference between these two returns can be interpreted as a measure of the excess return on the average risky asset. This excess return is known as the _____.

a. Risk adjusted return on capital
b. Risk modeling
c. Risk aversion
d. Risk premium

45. _____ measures the rate of return on the ownership interest (shareholders' equity) of the common stock owners. _____ is viewed as one of the most important financial ratios. It measures a firm's efficiency at generating profits from every dollar of shareholders' equity (also known as net assets or assets minus liabilities.)

a. Return on sales
b. Diluted Earnings Per Share
c. Return on equity
d. Return of capital

46. A _____ is a fungible, negotiable instrument representing financial value. They are broadly categorized into debt securities (such as banknotes, bonds and debentures), and equity securities; e.g., common stocks. The company or other entity issuing the _____ is called the issuer.

a. Tracking stock
b. Book entry
c. Securities lending
d. Security

47. In Modern Portfolio Theory, the _____ is the graphical representation of the Capital Asset Pricing Model. It displays the expected rate of return for an overall market as a function of systematic (non-diversifiable) risk (beta.)

The Y-Intercept (beta=0) of the _____ is equal to the risk-free interest rate.

Chapter 10. The Cost of Capital

a. Rebalancing
b. Divestment
c. Certificate in Investment Performance Measurement
d. Security Market Line

48. In finance, _____ are stocks that appreciate in value and yield a high return on equity (ROE.) Analysts compute ROE by taking the company's net income and dividing it by the company's equity. To be classified as a growth stock, analysts expect to see at least 15 percent return on equity.

a. Stock valuation
b. Security Analysis
c. 4-4-5 Calendar
d. Growth stocks

49. The _____ is the financial market where previously issued securities and financial instruments such as stock, bonds, options, and futures are bought and sold. The term '_____' is also used refer to the market for any used goods or assets, or an alternative use for an existing product or asset where the customer base is the second market

With primary issuances of securities or financial instruments, or the primary market, investors purchase these securities directly from issuers such as corporations issuing shares in an IPO or private placement, or directly from the federal government in the case of treasuries.

a. Delta neutral
b. Secondary market
c. Financial market
d. Performance attribution

50. The institution most often referenced by the word '_____' is a public or publicly traded _____, the shares of which are traded on a public stock exchange (e.g., the New York Stock Exchange or Nasdaq in the United States) where shares of stock of _____s are bought and sold by and to the general public. Most of the largest businesses in the world are publicly traded _____s. However, the majority of _____s are said to be closely held, privately held or close _____s, meaning that no ready market exists for the trading of shares.

a. Protect
b. Federal Home Loan Mortgage Corporation
c. Depository Trust Company
d. Corporation

51. _____ is a fee paid on borrowed assets. It is the price paid for the use of borrowed money, or, money earned by deposited funds. Assets that are sometimes lent with _____ include money, shares, consumer goods through hire purchase, major assets such as aircraft, and even entire factories in finance lease arrangements.

a. Interest
b. AAB
c. Insolvency
d. A Random Walk Down Wall Street

52. An _____ is the price a borrower pays for the use of money they do not own, and the return a lender receives for deferring the use of funds, by lending it to the borrower. _____s are normally expressed as a percentage rate over the period of one year.

_____s targets are also a vital tool of monetary policy and are used to control variables like investment, inflation, and unemployment.

a. ABN Amro
b. AAB
c. A Random Walk Down Wall Street
d. Interest rate

Chapter 10. The Cost of Capital

53. _____ is the risk that the value of an investment will decrease due to moves in market factors. The five standard _____ factors are:

- Equity risk, the risk that stock prices will change.
- Interest rate risk, the risk that interest rates will change.
- Currency risk, the risk that foreign exchange rates will change.
- Commodity risk, the risk that commodity prices (e.g. grains, metals) will change.

As with other forms of risk, _____ may be measured in a number of ways. Traditionally, this is done using a Value at Risk methodology. Value at risk is well established as a risk management technique, but it contains a number of limiting assumptions that constrain its accuracy.

a. Currency risk
c. Transaction risk
b. Market risk
d. Tracking error

54. _____ is a financial measure used to determine the attractiveness of an investment. It is generally used as part of a capital budgeting process to rank various alternative choices. It is a modification of the Internal Rate of Return (IRR).

_____ ranks project efficiency consistently with the present worth ratio (variant of NPV/Discounted Negative Cash Flow), considered the gold standard in many finance textbooks.

MIRR is calculated as follows:

width=747 border=0>

where n is the number of (equal) periods in which the cash flows occur.

a. Current yield
c. Binomial options pricing model
b. Modified Internal Rate of Return
d. Black-Scholes

55. _____ means regulating, adapting or settling in a variety of contexts:

In commercial law, _____ means the settlement of a loss incurred on insured goods. The calculation of the amounts of compensation to be paid by or to the several interests is a complicated matter. It involves much detail and arithmetic, and requires a full and accurate knowledge of the principles of the subject.

a. Intelligent investor
c. Adjustment
b. Equity method
d. Asset recovery

Chapter 10. The Cost of Capital

56. A _____ is a payment made by a corporation to its shareholder members. When a corporation earns a profit or surplus, that money can be put to two uses: it can either be re-invested in the business (called retained earnings), or it can be paid to the shareholders as a _____. Many corporations retain a portion of their earnings and pay the remainder as a _____.

   a. Special dividend
   b. Dividend yield
   c. Dividend puzzle
   d. Dividend

57. An _____ is any government regulation or law that encourages or discourages foreign investment in the local economy, e.g. currency exchange limits.

As globalization integrates the economies of neighboring and of trading states, they are typically forced to trade off such rules as part of a common tax, tariff and trade regime, e.g. as defined by a free trade pact. _____ favoring local investors over global ones is typically discouraged in such pacts, and the idea of a separate _____ rapidly becomes a fiction or fantasy, as real decisions reflect the real need for nations to compete for investment, even from their own local investors.

   a. ABN Amro
   b. A Random Walk Down Wall Street
   c. AAB
   d. Investment policy

58. _____ identifies the relationship of investment to payoff of a proposed project. The ratio is calculated as follows:

   - >

_____ is also known as Profit Investment Ratio, abbreviated to P.I. and Value Investment Ratio (V.I.R.). _____ is a good tool for ranking projects because it allows you to clearly identify the amount of value created per unit of investment, thus if you are capital constrained you wish to invest in those projects which create value most efficiently first.

   a. Capitalization rate
   b. Profitability index
   c. Total return
   d. Conditional prepayment rate

59. In e-business terms, a _____ is an organization that originated and does business purely through the internet, they have no physical store (brick and mortar) where customers can shop. Examples of large _____ companies include Amazon.com and Netflix.com. There are also many smaller, niche oriented _____ mail order companies such as women's travel accessories company Christine Columbus and fashion jewelry merchant Jewels of Denial.
   a. Pure play
   b. 4-4-5 Calendar
   c. 529 plan
   d. The Dogs of the Dow

60. _____ is the discipline of identifying, monitoring and limiting risks. In some cases the acceptable risk may be near zero. Risks can come from accidents, natural causes and disasters as well as deliberate attacks from an adversary.
   a. FIFO
   b. 4-4-5 Calendar
   c. Penny stock
   d. Risk management

61. The coupon or _____ of a bond is the amount of interest paid per year expressed as a percentage of the face value of the bond.

For example if you hold $10,000 nominal of a bond described as a 4.5% loan stock, you will receive $450 in interest each year (probably in two installments of $225 each.)

Not all bonds have coupons.

a. Zero-coupon bond
c. Coupon rate
b. Revenue bonds
d. Puttable bond

62.   The _____ is an American stock exchange. It is the largest electronic screen-based equity securities trading market in the United States. With approximately 3,200 companies, it has more trading volume per day than any other stock exchange in the world.

a. 7-Eleven
c. 4-4-5 Calendar
b. Nasdaq
d. 529 plan

63.   In accounting, _____ or *Carrying value* is the value of an asset according to its balance sheet account balance. For assets, the value is based on the original cost of the asset less any depreciation, amortization or impairment costs made against the asset. A company's _____ is its total assets minus intangible assets and liabilities.

a. Retained earnings
c. Pro forma
b. Current liabilities
d. Book value

Chapter 11. The Basics of Capital Budgeting: Evaluating Cash Flows

1. _____ is the planning process used to determine whether a firm's long term investments such as new machinery, replacement machinery, new plants, new products, and research development projects are worth pursuing. It is budget for major capital, or investment, expenditures.

Many formal methods are used in _____, including the techniques such as

- Net present value
- Profitability index
- Internal rate of return
- Modified Internal Rate of Return
- Equivalent annuity

These methods use the incremental cash flows from each potential investment, or project. Techniques based on accounting earnings and accounting rules are sometimes used - though economists consider this to be improper - such as the accounting rate of return, and 'return on investment.' Simplified and hybrid methods are used as well, such as payback period and discounted payback period.

a. Shareholder value
b. Preferred stock
c. Financial distress
d. Capital budgeting

2. _____ is a business valuation method. _____ is the net present value of a project if financed solely by ownership equity plus the present value of all the benefits of financing. Usually, the main benefit is a tax shield resulted from tax deductibility of interest payments. Another one can be a subsidized borrowing.

a. A Random Walk Down Wall Street
b. Adjusted present value
c. ABN Amro
d. AAB

3. _____ is a financial measure used to determine the attractiveness of an investment. It is generally used as part of a capital budgeting process to rank various alternative choices. It is a modification of the Internal Rate of Return (IRR).

_____ ranks project efficiency consistently with the present worth ratio (variant of NPV/Discounted Negative Cash Flow), considered the gold standard in many finance textbooks.

MIRR is calculated as follows:

[image] width=747 border=0>

where n is the number of (equal) periods in which the cash flows occur.

a. Binomial options pricing model
b. Black-Scholes
c. Current yield
d. Modified Internal Rate of Return

Chapter 11. The Basics of Capital Budgeting: Evaluating Cash Flows

4. _____ or net present worth (NPW) is defined as the total present value (PV) of a time series of cash flows. It is a standard method for using the time value of money to appraise long-term projects. Used for capital budgeting, and widely throughout economics, it measures the excess or shortfall of cash flows, in present value terms, once financing charges are met.
   a. Tax shield
   b. Net present value
   c. Present value of costs
   d. Negative gearing

5. _____ is the value on a given date of a future payment or series of future payments, discounted to reflect the time value of money and other factors such as investment risk. _____ calculations are widely used in business and economics to provide a means to compare cash flows at different times on a meaningful 'like to like' basis.

   The most commonly applied model of the time value of money is compound interest.

   a. Present value
   b. Present value of benefits
   c. Negative gearing
   d. Net present value

6. The _____ is a capital budgeting metric used by firms to decide whether they should make investments. It is an indicator of the efficiency or quality of an investment, as opposed to net present value (NPV), which indicates value or magnitude.

   The IRR is the annualized effective compounded return rate which can be earned on the invested capital, i.e., the yield on the investment.

   a. A Random Walk Down Wall Street
   b. Internal rate of return
   c. AAB
   d. ABN Amro

7. _____ identifies the relationship of investment to payoff of a proposed project. The ratio is calculated as follows:

   - [×] >

   _____ is also known as Profit Investment Ratio, abbreviated to P.I. and Value Investment Ratio (V.I.R.). _____ is a good tool for ranking projects because it allows you to clearly identify the amount of value created per unit of investment, thus if you are capital constrained you wish to invest in those projects which create value most efficiently first.

   a. Profitability index
   b. Capitalization rate
   c. Conditional prepayment rate
   d. Total return

8. In finance, _____, also known as return on investment is the ratio of money gained or lost on an investment relative to the amount of money invested. The amount of money gained or lost may be referred to as interest, profit/loss, gain/loss, or net income/loss. The money invested may be referred to as the asset, capital, principal, or the cost basis of the investment.
   a. Rate of return
   b. Composiition of Creditors
   c. Stock or scrip dividends
   d. Doctrine of the Proper Law

Chapter 11. The Basics of Capital Budgeting: Evaluating Cash Flows

9. In finance, the _____ approach describes a method of valuing a project, company, or asset using the concepts of the time value of money. All future cash flows are estimated and discounted to give their present values. The discount rate used is generally the appropriate cost of capital and may incorporate judgments of the uncertainty (riskiness) of the future cash flows.
   a. Net present value
   b. Future-oriented
   c. Present value of benefits
   d. Discounted cash flow

10. In corporate finance, _____ analysis applies put option and call option valuation techniques to capital budgeting decisions. A _____ itself, is the right--but not the obligation--to undertake some business decision; typically the option to make, or abandon, a capital investment. For example, the opportunity to invest in the expansion of a firm's factory, or alternatively to sell the factory, is a _____.
   a. Book building
   b. Capital budgeting
   c. Cash flow
   d. Real option

11. _____ is the balance of the amounts of cash being received and paid by a business during a defined period of time, sometimes tied to a specific project. Measurement of _____ can be used

   - to evaluate the state or performance of a business or project.
   - to determine problems with liquidity. Being profitable does not necessarily mean being liquid. A company can fail because of a shortage of cash, even while profitable.
   - to generate project rate of returns. The time of _____s into and out of projects are used as inputs to financial models such as internal rate of return, and net present value.
   - to examine income or growth of a business when it is believed that accrual accounting concepts do not represent economic realities. Alternately, _____ can be used to 'validate' the net income generated by accrual accounting.

   _____ as a generic term may be used differently depending on context, and certain _____ definitions may be adapted by analysts and users for their own uses. Common terms include operating _____ and free _____.

   _____s can be classified into:

   1. Operational _____s: Cash received or expended as a result of the company's core business activities.
   2. Investment _____s: Cash received or expended through capital expenditure, investments or acquisitions.
   3. Financing _____s: Cash received or expended as a result of financial activities, such as interests and dividends.

   All three together - the net _____ - are necessary to reconcile the beginning cash balance to the ending cash balance. Loan draw downs or equity injections, that is just shifting of capital but no expenditure as such, are not considered in the net _____.

   a. Cash flow
   b. Real option
   c. Corporate finance
   d. Shareholder value

Chapter 11. The Basics of Capital Budgeting: Evaluating Cash Flows

12. An _____ is a contract written by a seller that conveys to the buyer the right -- but not the obligation -- to buy (in the case of a call _____) or to sell (in the case of a put _____) a particular asset, such as a piece of property such as, among others, a futures contract. In return for granting the _____, the seller collects a payment (the premium) from the buyer.

For example, buying a call _____ provides the right to buy a specified quantity of a security at a set strike price at some time on or before expiration, while buying a put _____ provides the right to sell.

   a. AT'T Mobility LLC   b. Amortization
   c. Option   d. Annuity

13. The institution most often referenced by the word '_____' is a public or publicly traded _____, the shares of which are traded on a public stock exchange (e.g., the New York Stock Exchange or Nasdaq in the United States) where shares of stock of _____s are bought and sold by and to the general public. Most of the largest businesses in the world are publicly traded _____s. However, the majority of _____s are said to be closely held, privately held or close _____s, meaning that no ready market exists for the trading of shares.

   a. Federal Home Loan Mortgage Corporation   b. Protect
   c. Depository Trust Company   d. Corporation

14. The _____ is the rate of return that must be met for a company to undertake a particular project. The _____ is usually determined by evaluating existing opportunities in operations expansion, rate of return for investments, and other factors deemed relevant by management. A risk premium can also be attached to the _____ if management feels that specific opportunities inherently contain more risk than others that could be pursued with the same resources.

   a. Gross profit   b. Capital structure
   c. Corporate finance   d. Hurdle rate

15. In economics, business, and accounting, a _____ is the value of money that has been used up to produce something, and hence is not available for use anymore. In business, the _____ may be one of acquisition, in which case the amount of money expended to acquire it is counted as _____. In this case, money is the input that is gone in order to acquire the thing.

   a. Marginal cost   b. Cost
   c. Fixed costs   d. Sliding scale fees

16. The _____ is an expected return that the provider of capital plans to earn on their investment.

Capital (money) used for funding a business should earn returns for the capital providers who risk their capital. For an investment to be worthwhile, the expected return on capital must be greater than the _____.

   a. Capital intensity   b. Cost of capital
   c. 4-4-5 Calendar   d. Weighted average cost of capital

17. _____ in business and economics refers to the period of time required for the return on an investment to 'repay' the sum of the original investment. For example, a $1000 investment which returned $500 per year would have a two year _____. It intuitively measures how long something takes to 'pay for itself.' _____ is widely used due to its ease of use despite recognized limitations.

a. Payback period
b. Consignment stock
c. Financial Gerontology
d. Seasoned equity offering

18. In finance, a _____ is collateral that the holder of a position in securities, options, or futures contracts has to deposit to cover the credit risk of his counterparty (most often his broker.) This risk can arise if the holder has done any of the following:

- borrowed cash from the counterparty to buy securities or options,
- sold securities or options short, or
- entered into a futures contract.

The collateral can be in the form of cash or securities, and it is deposited in a _____ account. On U.S. futures exchanges, '_____' was formally called performance bond.

_____ buying is buying securities with cash borrowed from a broker, using other securities as collateral.

a. Credit
b. Procter ' Gamble
c. Share
d. Margin

19. In business and accounting, _____s are everything of value that is owned by a person or company. The balance sheet of a firm records the monetary value of the _____s owned by the firm. The two major _____ classes are tangible _____s and intangible _____s.

a. Accounts payable
b. Asset
c. Income
d. EBITDA

20. In finance, _____ is the process of estimating the potential market value of a financial asset or liability. they can be done on assets (for example, investments in marketable securities such as stocks, options, business enterprises, or intangible assets such as patents and trademarks) or on liabilities (e.g., Bonds issued by a company.) _____s are required in many contexts including investment analysis, capital budgeting, merger and acquisition transactions, financial reporting, taxable events to determine the proper tax liability, and in litigation.

a. Share
b. Margin
c. Procter ' Gamble
d. Valuation

Chapter 11. The Basics of Capital Budgeting: Evaluating Cash Flows

21. The term _____ has three unrelated technical definitions, and is also used in a variety of non-technical ways.

- In financial economics, it refers to any asset used to make money, as opposed to assets used for personal enjoyment or consumption. This is an important distinction because two people can disagree sharply about the value of personal assets, one person might think a sports car is more valuable than a pickup truck, another person might have the opposite taste. But if an asset is held for the purpose of making money, taste has nothing to do with it, only differences of opinion about how much money the asset will produce. With the further assumption that people agree on the probability distribution of future cash flows, it is possible to have an objective _____ pricing model. Even without the assumption of agreement, it is possible to set rational limits on _____ value.
- In governmental accounting, it is defined as any asset used in operations with an initial useful life extending beyond one reporting period. Generally, government managers have a 'stewardship' duty to maintain _____s under their control. See International Public Sector Accounting Standards for details.
- In US tax accounting, it is defined as any property other than a list of exceptions. The main exceptions are anything held for sale, and any real estate or depreciable property used in business. Almost everything you own and use for personal purposes, pleasure or investment is a _____. If something is a _____ for tax purposes, gains or losses on sale or disposition are capital gains or capital losses. For individuals, however, capital losses on property held for personal use are generally not deductible. See the IRS publication Tax Facts about Capital Gains and Losses for details.

A well-known financial accounting textbook advises that the term be avoided except in tax accounting because it is used in so many different senses, not all of them well-defined. For example it is often used as a synonym for fixed assets or for investments in securities.

A common non-technical usage occurs when people ask that employees or the environment or something else be treated as a _____.

   a. Solvency
   c. Political risk
   b. Settlement date
   d. Capital Asset

22. In finance, the _____ is used to determine a theoretically appropriate required rate of return of an asset, if that asset is to be added to an already well-diversified portfolio, given that asset's non-diversifiable risk. The model takes into account the asset's sensitivity to non-diversifiable risk (also known as systemic risk or market risk), often represented by the quantity beta (β) in the financial industry, as well as the expected return of the market and the expected return of a theoretical risk-free asset.

The model was introduced by Jack Treynor (1961, 1962), William Sharpe (1964), John Lintner (1965a,b) and Jan Mossin (1966) independently, building on the earlier work of Harry Markowitz on diversification and modern portfolio theory.

   a. Capital Asset Pricing Model
   c. Random walk hypothesis
   b. Hull-White model
   d. Cox-Ingersoll-Ross model

23. A _____ is a set of exclusive rights granted by a state to an inventor or his assignee for a limited period of time in exchange for a disclosure of an invention.

The procedure for granting _____s, the requirements placed on the _____ee and the extent of the exclusive rights vary widely between countries according to national laws and international agreements. Typically, however, a _____ application must include one or more claims defining the invention which must be new, inventive, and useful or industrially applicable.

- a. Patent
- b. Foreclosure
- c. Vesting
- d. National Securities Markets Improvement Act of 1996

24. _____ is a measure of the ability of a debtor to pay their debts as and when they fall due. It is usually expressed as a ratio or a percentage of current liabilities.

For a corporation with a published balance sheet there are various ratios used to calculate a measure of liquidity.

- a. Accounting liquidity
- b. Operating profit margin
- c. Operating leverage
- d. Invested capital

25. _____ is the study of how the variation (uncertainty) in the output of a mathematical model can be apportioned, qualitatively or quantitatively, to different sources of variation in the input of a model.

In more general terms uncertainty and sensitivity analyses investigate the robustness of a study when the study includes some form of mathematical modelling. While uncertainty analysis studies the overall uncertainty in the conclusions of the study, _____ tries to identify what source of uncertainty weights more on the study's conclusions.

- a. Golden parachute
- b. Synthetic CDO
- c. Sensitivity analysis
- d. Proxy fight

26. In economics and finance, _____ is the change in total cost that arises when the quantity produced changes by one unit. It is the cost of producing one more unit of a good. Mathematically, the _____ function is expressed as the first derivative of the total cost (TC) function with respect to quantity (Q). Note that the _____ may change with volume, and so at each level of production, the _____ is the cost of the next unit produced.

A typical _____ Curve

- a. Marginal cost
- b. Sliding scale fees
- c. Cost accounting
- d. Fixed costs

27. In mathematics, _____ is a technique for optimization of a linear objective function, subject to linear equality and linear inequality constraints. Informally, _____ determines the way to achieve the best outcome (such as maximum profit or lowest cost) in a given mathematical model and given some list of requirements represented as linear equations.

Chapter 11. The Basics of Capital Budgeting: Evaluating Cash Flows 141

More formally, given a polytope (for example, a polygon or a polyhedron), and a real-valued affine function

defined on this polytope, a _____ method will find a point in the polytope where this function has the smallest (or largest) value.

a. 529 plan
c. 7-Eleven
b. Linear programming
d. 4-4-5 Calendar

Chapter 12. Cash Flow Estimation and Risk Analysis

1. _____ is the balance of the amounts of cash being received and paid by a business during a defined period of time, sometimes tied to a specific project. Measurement of _____ can be used

- to evaluate the state or performance of a business or project.
- to determine problems with liquidity. Being profitable does not necessarily mean being liquid. A company can fail because of a shortage of cash, even while profitable.
- to generate project rate of returns. The time of _____s into and out of projects are used as inputs to financial models such as internal rate of return, and net present value.
- to examine income or growth of a business when it is believed that accrual accounting concepts do not represent economic realities. Alternately, _____ can be used to 'validate' the net income generated by accrual accounting.

_____ as a generic term may be used differently depending on context, and certain _____ definitions may be adapted by analysts and users for their own uses. Common terms include operating _____ and free _____.

_____s can be classified into:

1. Operational _____s: Cash received or expended as a result of the company's core business activities.
2. Investment _____s: Cash received or expended through capital expenditure, investments or acquisitions.
3. Financing _____s: Cash received or expended as a result of financial activities, such as interests and dividends.

All three together - the net _____ - are necessary to reconcile the beginning cash balance to the ending cash balance. Loan draw downs or equity injections, that is just shifting of capital but no expenditure as such, are not considered in the net _____.

    a. Real option
    b. Cash flow
    c. Shareholder value
    d. Corporate finance

2. A _____ is a payment made by a corporation to its shareholder members. When a corporation earns a profit or surplus, that money can be put to two uses: it can either be re-invested in the business (called retained earnings), or it can be paid to the shareholders as a _____. Many corporations retain a portion of their earnings and pay the remainder as a _____.

    a. Dividend puzzle
    b. Special dividend
    c. Dividend yield
    d. Dividend

3. _____ is a business valuation method. _____ is the net present value of a project if financed solely by ownership equity plus the present value of all the benefits of financing. Usually, the main benefit is a tax shield resulted from tax deductibility of interest payments. Another one can be a subsidized borrowing.

    a. AAB
    b. ABN Amro
    c. A Random Walk Down Wall Street
    d. Adjusted present value

4. In economics and finance, _____ is the practice of taking advantage of a price differential between two or more markets: striking a combination of matching deals that capitalize upon the imbalance, the profit being the difference between the market prices. When used by academics, an _____ is a transaction that involves no negative cash flow at any probabilistic or temporal state and a positive cash flow in at least one state; in simple terms, a risk-free profit.

a. Initial margin
b. Arbitrage
c. Efficient-market hypothesis
d. Issuer

5. _____ is a financial measure used to determine the attractiveness of an investment. It is generally used as part of a capital budgeting process to rank various alternative choices. It is a modification of the Internal Rate of Return (IRR).

_____ ranks project efficiency consistently with the present worth ratio (variant of NPV/Discounted Negative Cash Flow), considered the gold standard in many finance textbooks.

MIRR is calculated as follows:

[ ] width=747 border=0>

where n is the number of (equal) periods in which the cash flows occur.

a. Black-Scholes
b. Modified Internal Rate of Return
c. Current yield
d. Binomial options pricing model

6. Straight-line depreciation is the simplest and most-often-used technique, in which the company estimates the _____ of the asset at the end of the period during which it will be used to generate revenues (useful life) and will expense a portion of original cost in equal increments over that period. The _____ is an estimate of the value of the asset at the time it will be sold or disposed of; it may be zero or even negative. _____ is scrap value, by another name.

a. Net profit
b. Depreciation
c. Fixed investment
d. Salvage value

7. The _____ is the current method of accelerated asset depreciation required by the United States income tax code. Under _____, all assets are divided into classes which dictate the number of years over which an asset's cost will be recovered.

Prior to the Accelerated Cost Recovery System (ACRS), most capital purchases were depreciated using a straight line technique, that allowed for the depreciation of the asset over its useful life.

a. 529 plan
b. 4-4-5 Calendar
c. 7-Eleven
d. Modified Accelerated Cost Recovery System

8. In economics, business, and accounting, a _____ is the value of money that has been used up to produce something, and hence is not available for use anymore. In business, the _____ may be one of acquisition, in which case the amount of money expended to acquire it is counted as _____. In this case, money is the input that is gone in order to acquire the thing.

a. Marginal cost
b. Fixed costs
c. Cost
d. Sliding scale fees

9. _____ is a fee paid on borrowed assets. It is the price paid for the use of borrowed money, or, money earned by deposited funds. Assets that are sometimes lent with _____ include money, shares, consumer goods through hire purchase, major assets such as aircraft, and even entire factories in finance lease arrangements.
   a. AAB
   b. A Random Walk Down Wall Street
   c. Interest
   d. Insolvency

10. _____ relates to the cost of borrowing money. It is the price that a lender charges a borrower for the use of the lender's money. _____ is different from OPEX and CAPEX, for it relates to the capital structure of a company.
   a. AAB
   b. A Random Walk Down Wall Street
   c. ABN Amro
   d. Interest expense

11. _____ are a class of computational algorithms that rely on repeated random sampling to compute their results. _____ are often used when simulating physical and mathematical systems. Because of their reliance on repeated computation and random or pseudo-random numbers, _____ are most suited to calculation by a computer.

_____ in finance are often used to calculate the value of companies, to evaluate investments in projects at corporate level or to evaluate financial derivatives. The method is intended for financial analysts who want to construct stochastic or probabilistic financial models as opposed to the traditional static and deterministic models.

   a. Correlation
   b. Semivariance
   c. Sample size
   d. Monte Carlo methods

12. In finance and economics _____ refers to the rate of interest before adjustment for inflation (in contrast with the real interest rate); or, for interest balls stated' without adjustment for the full effect of compounding (also referred to as the nominal annual rate.) An interest rate is called nominal if the frequency of compounding (e.g. a month) is not identical to the basic time unit (normally a year.)

The real interest rate includes compensation for the lender's lost value due to inflation, whereas the _____ excludes inflation.

   a. Cash accumulation equation
   b. Nominal interest rate
   c. Shanghai Interbank Offered Rate
   d. SIBOR

13. In corporate finance, _____ analysis applies put option and call option valuation techniques to capital budgeting decisions. A _____ itself, is the right--but not the obligation--to undertake some business decision; typically the option to make, or abandon, a capital investment. For example, the opportunity to invest in the expansion of a firm's factory, or alternatively to sell the factory, is a _____.
   a. Capital budgeting
   b. Cash flow
   c. Book building
   d. Real option

14. In business and accounting, _____s are everything of value that is owned by a person or company. The balance sheet of a firm records the monetary value of the _____s owned by the firm. The two major _____ classes are tangible _____s and intangible _____s.
   a. Income
   b. Asset
   c. Accounts payable
   d. EBITDA

Chapter 12. Cash Flow Estimation and Risk Analysis

15. _____ plant, and equipment, is a term used in accountancy for assets and property which cannot easily be converted into cash. This can be compared with current assets such as cash or bank accounts, which are described as liquid assets. In most cases, only tangible assets are referred to as fixed.
    a. Remittance advice
    b. Petty cash
    c. Percentage of Completion
    d. Fixed asset

16. An _____ is the price a borrower pays for the use of money they do not own, and the return a lender receives for deferring the use of funds, by lending it to the borrower. _____s are normally expressed as a percentage rate over the period of one year.

    _____s targets are also a vital tool of monetary policy and are used to control variables like investment, inflation, and unemployment.

    a. Interest rate
    b. AAB
    c. ABN Amro
    d. A Random Walk Down Wall Street

17. An _____ is a contract written by a seller that conveys to the buyer the right -- but not the obligation -- to buy (in the case of a call _____) or to sell (in the case of a put _____) a particular asset, such as a piece of property such as, among others, a futures contract. In return for granting the _____, the seller collects a payment (the premium) from the buyer.

    For example, buying a call _____ provides the right to buy a specified quantity of a security at a set strike price at some time on or before expiration, while buying a put _____ provides the right to sell.

    a. AT'T Mobility LLC
    b. Option
    c. Amortization
    d. Annuity

18. _____ refers to a business or organization attempting to acquire goods or services to accomplish the goals of the enterprise. Though there are several organizations that attempt to set standards in the _____ process, processes can vary greatly between organizations. Typically the word '_____' is not used interchangeably with the word 'procurement', since procurement typically includes Expediting, Supplier Quality, and Traffic and Logistics (T'L) in addition to _____.
    a. 7-Eleven
    b. Purchasing
    c. 4-4-5 Calendar
    d. 529 plan

19. _____ is a financial metric which represents operating liquidity available to a business. Along with fixed assets such as plant and equipment, _____ is considered a part of operating capital. It is calculated as current assets minus current liabilities.
    a. Working capital management
    b. Working capital
    c. 4-4-5 Calendar
    d. 529 plan

20. In marketing and strategy, _____ refers to a reduction in the sales volume, sales revenue, or market share of one product as a result of the introduction of a new product by the same producer.

    For example, if Coca Cola were to introduce a similar product (say, Diet Coke or Cherry Coke), this new product could take some of the sales away from the original Coke. _____ is a key consideration in product portfolio analysis.

a. 4-4-5 Calendar
c. 7-Eleven

b. Cannibalization
d. 529 plan

21. In economics and business decision-making, _____ are costs that cannot be recovered once they have been incurred. _____ are sometimes contrasted with variable costs, which are the costs that will change due to the proposed course of action, and prospective costs which are costs that will be incurred if an action is taken. In microeconomic theory, only variable costs are relevant to a decision.

a. 4-4-5 Calendar
c. Hindsight bias

b. Hyperbolic discounting
d. Sunk costs

22. In economics, an _____ or spillover of an economic transaction is an impact on a party that is not directly involved in the transaction. In such a case, prices do not reflect the full costs or benefits in production or consumption of a product or service. A positive impact is called an external benefit, while a negative impact is called an external cost.

a. Externality
c. ABN Amro

b. AAB
d. A Random Walk Down Wall Street

23. _____ or economic opportunity loss is the value of the next best alternative foregone as the result of making a decision. _____ analysis is an important part of a company's decision-making processes but is not treated as an actual cost in any financial statement. The next best thing that a person can engage in is referred to as the _____ of doing the best thing and ignoring the next best thing to be done.

a. ABN Amro
c. Opportunity cost

b. A Random Walk Down Wall Street
d. AAB

24. _____ is the study of how the variation (uncertainty) in the output of a mathematical model can be apportioned, qualitatively or quantitatively, to different sources of variation in the input of a model .

In more general terms uncertainty and sensitivity analyses investigate the robustness of a study when the study includes some form of mathematical modelling. While uncertainty analysis studies the overall uncertainty in the conclusions of the study, _____ tries to identify what source of uncertainty weights more on the study's conclusions.

a. Proxy fight
c. Synthetic CDO

b. Golden parachute
d. Sensitivity analysis

25. The _____ is a capital budgeting metric used by firms to decide whether they should make investments. It is an indicator of the efficiency or quality of an investment, as opposed to net present value (NPV), which indicates value or magnitude.

The IRR is the annualized effective compounded return rate which can be earned on the invested capital, i.e., the yield on the investment.

a. ABN Amro
c. AAB

b. A Random Walk Down Wall Street
d. Internal rate of return

26. _____ or net present worth (NPW) is defined as the total present value (PV) of a time series of cash flows. It is a standard method for using the time value of money to appraise long-term projects. Used for capital budgeting, and widely throughout economics, it measures the excess or shortfall of cash flows, in present value terms, once financing charges are met.

   a. Negative gearing
   b. Net present value
   c. Tax shield
   d. Present value of costs

27. Depreciation methods that provide for a higher depreciation charge in the first year of an asset's life and gradually decreasing charges in subsequent years are called accelerated depreciation methods. This may be a more realistic reflection of an asset's actual expected benefit from the use of the asset: many assets are most useful when they are new. One popular accelerated method is the declining-balance method. Under this method the Book Value is multiplied by a fixed rate.

The most common rate used is double the straight-line rate. For this reason, this technique is referred to as the _____. To illustrate, suppose a business has an asset with $1,000 Original Cost, $100 Salvage Value, and 5 years useful life. First, calculate straight-line depreciation rate. Since the asset has 5 years useful life, the straight-line depreciation rate equals (100% / 5) 20% per year. With _____, as the name suggests, double that rate, or 40% depreciation rate is used.

   a. Doctrine of the Proper Law
   b. The Goodyear Tire ' Rubber Company
   c. Database auditing
   d. Double-declining-balance method

28. _____ is the planning process used to determine whether a firm's long term investments such as new machinery, replacement machinery, new plants, new products, and research development projects are worth pursuing. It is budget for major capital, or investment, expenditures.

Many formal methods are used in _____, including the techniques such as

- Net present value
- Profitability index
- Internal rate of return
- Modified Internal Rate of Return
- Equivalent annuity

These methods use the incremental cash flows from each potential investment, or project. Techniques based on accounting earnings and accounting rules are sometimes used - though economists consider this to be improper - such as the accounting rate of return, and 'return on investment.' Simplified and hybrid methods are used as well, such as payback period and discounted payback period.

   a. Preferred stock
   b. Shareholder value
   c. Capital budgeting
   d. Financial distress

29. _____ is a term used in accounting, economics and finance to spread the cost of an asset over the span of several years.

In simple words we can say that _____ is the reduction in the value of an asset due to usage, passage of time, wear and tear, technological outdating or obsolescence, depletion or other such factors.

In accounting, _____ is a term used to describe any method of attributing the historical or purchase cost of an asset across its useful life, roughly corresponding to normal wear and tear.

a. Bottom line
b. Deferred financing costs
c. Matching principle
d. Depreciation

30. _____ is the value on a given date of a future payment or series of future payments, discounted to reflect the time value of money and other factors such as investment risk. _____ calculations are widely used in business and economics to provide a means to compare cash flows at different times on a meaningful 'like to like' basis.

The most commonly applied model of the time value of money is compound interest.

a. Present value of benefits
b. Negative gearing
c. Present value
d. Net present value

31. _____ is a type of property. In the common law systems _____ may also be called chattels or personalty. It is distinguished from real property, or real estate.
a. Loan agreement
b. Beneficial owner
c. McFadden Act
d. Personal property

32. In tax accounting the _____ is the default applicable convention used for federal income tax purposes. Like other conventions, the _____ affects the depreciation deduction computation in the year in which the property is placed into service. Using the _____, a taxpayer claims a half of a year's depreciation for the first taxable year, regardless of when the property was actually put into service.
a. 4-4-5 Calendar
b. 7-Eleven
c. Half-year convention
d. 529 plan

33. In economics, _____ is a rise in the general level of prices of goods and services in an economy over a period of time. The term '_____' once referred to increases in the money supply (monetary _____); however, economic debates about the relationship between money supply and price levels have led to its primary use today in describing price _____. _____ can also be described as a decline in the real value of money--a loss of purchasing power in the medium of exchange which is also the monetary unit of account.
a. A Random Walk Down Wall Street
b. ABN Amro
c. AAB
d. Inflation

34. _____ means regulating, adapting or settling in a variety of contexts:

In commercial law, _____ means the settlement of a loss incurred on insured goods. The calculation of the amounts of compensation to be paid by or to the several interests is a complicated matter. It involves much detail and arithmetic, and requires a full and accurate knowledge of the principles of the subject.

a. Asset recovery
b. Intelligent investor
c. Equity method
d. Adjustment

35. _____ , in finance, is a general theory of asset pricing, that has become influential in the pricing of stocks.

_____ holds that the expected return of a financial asset can be modeled as a linear function of various macro-economic factors or theoretical market indices, where sensitivity to changes in each factor is represented by a factor-specific beta coefficient. The model-derived rate of return will then be used to price the asset correctly - the asset price should equal the expected end of period price discounted at the rate implied by model.

a. AAB
b. A Random Walk Down Wall Street
c. ABN Amro
d. Arbitrage pricing theory

36. _____ is the process of adjusting economic indicators and the prices of goods and services from different time periods to the same price level. To adjust for inflation, an indicator is divided by the inflation index.

It is easy to show that 7% inflation, lasting 10 years, would nearly double the cost of living (1.07^{10}=1.96.)

a. ABN Amro
b. AAB
c. A Random Walk Down Wall Street
d. Inflation adjustment

37. _____ is a process of analyzing possible future events by considering alternative possible outcomes (scenarios.) The analysis is designed to allow improved decision-making by allowing consideration of outcomes and their implications.

For example, in economics and finance, a financial institution might attempt to forecast several possible scenarios for the economy (e.g. rapid growth, moderate growth, slow growth) and it might also attempt to forecast financial market returns (for bonds, stocks and cash) in each of those scenarios.

a. 529 plan
b. 4-4-5 Calendar
c. Detection Risk
d. Scenario analysis

38. In economics and business, specifically cost accounting, the _____ is the point at which cost or expenses and revenue are equal: there is no net loss or gain, and one has 'broken even'. A profit or a loss has not been made, although opportunity costs have been paid, and capital has received the risk-adjusted, expected return.

For example, if the business sells less than 200 tables each month, it will make a loss, if it sells more, it will be a profit.

a. Market microstructure
b. Defined contribution plan
c. Fixed asset turnover
d. Break-even point

39. In probability theory and statistics, a _____ identifies either the probability of each value of an unidentified random variable (when the variable is discrete), or the probability of the value falling within a particular interval (when the variable is continuous.) The _____ describes the range of possible values that a random variable can attain and the probability that the value of the random variable is within any (measurable) subset of that range. The Normal distribution, often called the 'bell curve'

When the random variable takes values in the set of real numbers, the _____ is completely described by the cumulative distribution function, whose value at each real x is the probability that the random variable is smaller than or equal to x.

a. Standard deviation
c. P-value

b. Correlation
d. Probability distribution

40. In finance, _____ is the process of estimating the potential market value of a financial asset or liability. they can be done on assets (for example, investments in marketable securities such as stocks, options, business enterprises, or intangible assets such as patents and trademarks) or on liabilities (e.g., Bonds issued by a company.) _____s are required in many contexts including investment analysis, capital budgeting, merger and acquisition transactions, financial reporting, taxable events to determine the proper tax liability, and in litigation.

a. Share
c. Margin

b. Procter ' Gamble
d. Valuation

41. The term _____ has three unrelated technical definitions, and is also used in a variety of non-technical ways.

- In financial economics, it refers to any asset used to make money, as opposed to assets used for personal enjoyment or consumption. This is an important distinction because two people can disagree sharply about the value of personal assets, one person might think a sports car is more valuable than a pickup truck, another person might have the opposite taste. But if an asset is held for the purpose of making money, taste has nothing to do with it, only differences of opinion about how much money the asset will produce. With the further assumption that people agree on the probability distribution of future cash flows, it is possible to have an objective _____ pricing model. Even without the assumption of agreement, it is possible to set rational limits on _____ value.
- In governmental accounting, it is defined as any asset used in operations with an initial useful life extending beyond one reporting period. Generally, government managers have a 'stewardship' duty to maintain _____s under their control. See International Public Sector Accounting Standards for details.
- In US tax accounting, it is defined as any property other than a list of exceptions. The main exceptions are anything held for sale, and any real estate or depreciable property used in business. Almost everything you own and use for personal purposes, pleasure or investment is a _____. If something is a _____ for tax purposes, gains or losses on sale or disposition are capital gains or capital losses. For individuals, however, capital losses on property held for personal use are generally not deductible. See the IRS publication Tax Facts about Capital Gains and Losses for details.

A well-known financial accounting textbook advises that the term be avoided except in tax accounting because it is used in so many different senses, not all of them well-defined. For example it is often used as a synonym for fixed assets or for investments in securities.

A common non-technical usage occurs when people ask that employees or the environment or something else be treated as a _____.

a. Solvency
c. Political risk

b. Capital Asset
d. Settlement date

Chapter 12. Cash Flow Estimation and Risk Analysis

42. In finance, the _____ is used to determine a theoretically appropriate required rate of return of an asset, if that asset is to be added to an already well-diversified portfolio, given that asset's non-diversifiable risk. The model takes into account the asset's sensitivity to non-diversifiable risk (also known as systemic risk or market risk), often represented by the quantity beta (β) in the financial industry, as well as the expected return of the market and the expected return of a theoretical risk-free asset.

The model was introduced by Jack Treynor (1961, 1962), William Sharpe (1964), John Lintner (1965a,b) and Jan Mossin (1966) independently, building on the earlier work of Harry Markowitz on diversification and modern portfolio theory.

- a. Hull-White model
- b. Capital Asset Pricing Model
- c. Cox-Ingersoll-Ross model
- d. Random walk hypothesis

43. The _____ is the rate that a company is expected to pay to finance its assets. WACC is the minimum return that a company must earn on existing asset base to satisfy its creditors, owners, and other providers of capital.

Companies raise money from a number of sources: common equity, preferred equity, straight debt, convertible debt, exchangeable debt, warrants, options, pension liabilities, executive stock options, governmental subsidies, and so on.

- a. Capital intensity
- b. Weighted average cost of capital
- c. Cost of capital
- d. 4-4-5 Calendar

44. The _____ is an expected return that the provider of capital plans to earn on their investment.

Capital (money) used for funding a business should earn returns for the capital providers who risk their capital. For an investment to be worthwhile, the expected return on capital must be greater than the _____.

- a. Cost of capital
- b. Capital intensity
- c. 4-4-5 Calendar
- d. Weighted average cost of capital

45. In finance, _____, also known as return on investment is the ratio of money gained or lost on an investment relative to the amount of money invested. The amount of money gained or lost may be referred to as interest, profit/loss, gain/loss, or net income/loss. The money invested may be referred to as the asset, capital, principal, or the cost basis of the investment.

- a. Doctrine of the Proper Law
- b. Stock or scrip dividends
- c. Composiition of Creditors
- d. Rate of return

46. The institution most often referenced by the word '_____' is a public or publicly traded _____, the shares of which are traded on a public stock exchange (e.g., the New York Stock Exchange or Nasdaq in the United States) where shares of stock of _____s are bought and sold by and to the general public. Most of the largest businesses in the world are publicly traded _____s. However, the majority of _____s are said to be closely held, privately held or close _____s, meaning that no ready market exists for the trading of shares.

- a. Corporation
- b. Federal Home Loan Mortgage Corporation
- c. Depository Trust Company
- d. Protect

Chapter 12. Cash Flow Estimation and Risk Analysis

47. The _____ is the guaranteed payoff at which a person is 'indifferent' between accepting the guaranteed payoff and a higher but uncertain payoff. (It is the amount of the higher payout minus the risk premium).
   a. 4-4-5 Calendar
   b. 529 plan
   c. Certainty equivalent
   d. 7-Eleven

48. A _____ is a decision support tool that uses a tree-like graph or model of decisions and their possible consequences, including chance event outcomes, resource costs, and utility. _____s are commonly used in operations research, specifically in decision analysis, to help identify a strategy most likely to reach a goal. Another use of _____s is as a descriptive means for calculating conditional probabilities.
   a. 7-Eleven
   b. Decision tree
   c. 4-4-5 Calendar
   d. 529 plan

49. A '_____' is a 'Charge' that is paid to obtain the right to delay a payment. Essentially, the payer purchases the right to make a given payment in the future instead of in the Present. The '_____', or 'Charge' that must be paid to delay the payment, is simply the difference between what the payment amount would be if it were paid in the present and what the payment amount would be paid if it were paid in the future.
   a. Discount
   b. Value at risk
   c. Risk modeling
   d. Risk aversion

50. The _____ is an interest rate a central bank charges depository institutions that borrow reserves from it.

The term _____ has two meanings:

- the same as interest rate; the term 'discount' does not refer to the meaning of the word, but to the purpose of using the quantity, such as computations of present value, e.g. net present value / discounted cash flow

- the annual effective _____, which is the annual interest divided by the capital including that interest; this rate is lower than the interest rate; it corresponds to using the value after a year as the nominal value, and seeing the initial value as the nominal value minus a discount; it is used for Treasury Bills and similar financial instruments

The annual effective _____ is the annual interest divided by the capital including that interest, which is the interest rate divided by 100% plus the interest rate. It is the annual discount factor to be applied to the future cash flow, to find the discount, subtracted from a future value to find the value one year earlier.

For example, suppose there is a government bond that sells for $95 and pays $100 in a year's time.

   a. Fisher equation
   b. Discount rate
   c. Black-Scholes
   d. Stochastic volatility

51. _____ is a legally declared inability or impairment of ability of an individual or organization to pay their creditors. Creditors may file a _____ petition against a debtor ('involuntary _____') in an effort to recoup a portion of what they are owed or initiate a restructuring. In the majority of cases, however, _____ is initiated by the debtor (a 'voluntary _____' that is filed by the bankrupt individual or organization.)

Chapter 12. Cash Flow Estimation and Risk Analysis

    a. 529 plan   b. 4-4-5 Calendar
    c. Bankruptcy   d. Debt settlement

52.   In United States banking, _____ is a marketing term for certain services offered primarily to larger business customers. It may be used to describe all bank accounts (such as checking accounts) provided to businesses of a certain size, but it is more often used to describe specific services such as cash concentration, zero balance accounting, and automated clearing house facilities. Sometimes, private banking customers are given _____ services.
    a. Profitability index   b. Cash management
    c. Capitalization rate   d. Global tactical asset allocation

53.   _____ is the set of processes, customs, policies, laws and institutions affecting the way a corporation is directed, administered or controlled. _____ also includes the relationships among the many stakeholders involved and the goals for which the corporation is governed. The principal stakeholders are the shareholders, management and the board of directors.
    a. Foreign Corrupt Practices Act   b. Due diligence
    c. Corporate governance   d. Patent

54.   _____ is a process by which a firm can obtain the use of a certain fixed assets for which it must pay a series of contractual, periodic, tax deductable payments. The lessee is the receiver of the services or the assets under the lease contract and the lessor is the owner of the assets. The relationship between the tenant and the landlord is called a tenancy, and can be for a fixed or an indefinite period of time (called the term of the lease).
    a. Leasing   b. Royalties
    c. Quiet period   d. Foreign Corrupt Practices Act

55.   The phrase _____ refers to the aspect of corporate strategy, corporate finance and management dealing with the buying, selling and combining of different companies that can aid, finance, or help a growing company in a given industry grow rapidly without having to create another business entity.

An acquisition, also known as a takeover, is the buying of one company (the 'target') by another. An acquisition may be friendly or hostile.

    a. 7-Eleven   b. 529 plan
    c. 4-4-5 Calendar   d. Mergers and acquisitions

56.   _____ is an estimate of the fair value of corporations and their stocks, by using fundamental economic criteria. This theoretical valuation has to be perfected with market criteria, as the final purpose is to determine potential market prices.
    a. 4-4-5 Calendar   b. Growth stocks
    c. Security Analysis   d. Stock valuation

57.   In finance, a _____ is a debt security, in which the authorized issuer owes the holders a debt and, depending on the terms of the _____, is obliged to pay interest (the coupon) and/or to repay the principal at a later date, termed maturity.

Thus a _____ is a loan: the issuer is the borrower, the _____ holder is the lender, and the coupon is the interest. _____s provide the borrower with external funds to finance long-term investments, or, in the case of government _____s, to finance current expenditure.

a. Puttable bond
b. Bond
c. Convertible bond
d. Catastrophe bonds

58. _____ is the process of determining the fair price of a bond. As with any security or capital investment, the fair value of a bond is the present value of the stream of cash flows it is expected to generate. Hence, the price or value of a bond is determined by discounting the bond's expected cash flows to the present using the appropriate discount rate.

a. Bond valuation
b. Catastrophe bonds
c. Collateralized debt obligations
d. Bond fund

Chapter 13. Real Options

1. An _____ is a contract written by a seller that conveys to the buyer the right -- but not the obligation -- to buy (in the case of a call _____) or to sell (in the case of a put _____) a particular asset, such as a piece of property such as, among others, a futures contract. In return for granting the _____, the seller collects a payment (the premium) from the buyer.

For example, buying a call _____ provides the right to buy a specified quantity of a security at a set strike price at some time on or before expiration, while buying a put _____ provides the right to sell.

   a. Annuity
   b. Amortization
   c. AT'T Mobility LLC
   d. Option

2. In corporate finance, _____ analysis applies put option and call option valuation techniques to capital budgeting decisions. A _____ itself, is the right--but not the obligation--to undertake some business decision; typically the option to make, or abandon, a capital investment. For example, the opportunity to invest in the expansion of a firm's factory, or alternatively to sell the factory, is a _____.
   a. Book building
   b. Real option
   c. Capital budgeting
   d. Cash flow

3. A _____ is a financial contract between two parties, the buyer and the seller of this type of option. Often it is simply labeled a 'call'. The buyer of the option has the right, but not the obligation to buy an agreed quantity of a particular commodity or financial instrument (the underlying instrument) from the seller of the option at a certain time (the expiration date) for a certain price (the strike price.)
   a. Bear call spread
   b. Bull spread
   c. Bear spread
   d. Call option

4. A _____ is a financial contract whose value is derived from the value of something else (known as the underlying.) The underlying on which a _____ is based can be an asset, weather conditions bonds or other forms of credit.
   a. 529 plan
   b. 4-4-5 Calendar
   c. 7-Eleven
   d. Derivative

5. In finance, the _____ approach describes a method of valuing a project, company, or asset using the concepts of the time value of money. All future cash flows are estimated and discounted to give their present values. The discount rate used is generally the appropriate cost of capital and may incorporate judgments of the uncertainty (riskiness) of the future cash flows.
   a. Net present value
   b. Future-oriented
   c. Present value of benefits
   d. Discounted cash flow

6. A _____ is a payment made by a corporation to its shareholder members. When a corporation earns a profit or surplus, that money can be put to two uses: it can either be re-invested in the business (called retained earnings), or it can be paid to the shareholders as a _____. Many corporations retain a portion of their earnings and pay the remainder as a _____.
   a. Dividend yield
   b. Dividend puzzle
   c. Special dividend
   d. Dividend

7. The phrase _____ refers to the aspect of corporate strategy, corporate finance and management dealing with the buying, selling and combining of different companies that can aid, finance, or help a growing company in a given industry grow rapidly without having to create another business entity.

An acquisition, also known as a takeover, is the buying of one company (the 'target') by another. An acquisition may be friendly or hostile.

   a. 529 plan
   b. 7-Eleven
   c. Mergers and acquisitions
   d. 4-4-5 Calendar

8. A _____ is a financial contract between two parties, the seller (writer) and the buyer of the option. The put allows its buyer the right but not the obligation to sell a commodity or financial instrument (the underlying instrument) to the writer (seller) of the option at a certain time for a certain price (the strike price.) The writer (seller) has the obligation to purchase the underlying asset at that strike price, if the buyer exercises the option.
   a. Bear spread
   b. Bear call spread
   c. Debit spread
   d. Put option

9. _____ is an estimate of the fair value of corporations and their stocks, by using fundamental economic criteria. This theoretical valuation has to be perfected with market criteria, as the final purpose is to determine potential market prices.
   a. Stock valuation
   b. Security Analysis
   c. Growth stocks
   d. 4-4-5 Calendar

10. In finance, a _____ is a debt security, in which the authorized issuer owes the holders a debt and, depending on the terms of the _____, is obliged to pay interest (the coupon) and/or to repay the principal at a later date, termed maturity.

Thus a _____ is a loan: the issuer is the borrower, the _____ holder is the lender, and the coupon is the interest. _____s provide the borrower with external funds to finance long-term investments, or, in the case of government _____s, to finance current expenditure.

   a. Puttable bond
   b. Convertible bond
   c. Bond
   d. Catastrophe bonds

11. _____ is the process of determining the fair price of a bond. As with any security or capital investment, the fair value of a bond is the present value of the stream of cash flows it is expected to generate. Hence, the price or value of a bond is determined by discounting the bond's expected cash flows to the present using the appropriate discount rate.
   a. Bond fund
   b. Bond valuation
   c. Collateralized debt obligations
   d. Catastrophe bonds

Chapter 13. Real Options

12. _____ is the balance of the amounts of cash being received and paid by a business during a defined period of time, sometimes tied to a specific project. Measurement of _____ can be used

   - to evaluate the state or performance of a business or project.
   - to determine problems with liquidity. Being profitable does not necessarily mean being liquid. A company can fail because of a shortage of cash, even while profitable.
   - to generate project rate of returns. The time of _____s into and out of projects are used as inputs to financial models such as internal rate of return, and net present value.
   - to examine income or growth of a business when it is believed that accrual accounting concepts do not represent economic realities. Alternately, _____ can be used to 'validate' the net income generated by accrual accounting.

_____ as a generic term may be used differently depending on context, and certain _____ definitions may be adapted by analysts and users for their own uses. Common terms include operating _____ and free _____.

_____s can be classified into:

1. Operational _____s: Cash received or expended as a result of the company's core business activities.
2. Investment _____s: Cash received or expended through capital expenditure, investments or acquisitions.
3. Financing _____s: Cash received or expended as a result of financial activities, such as interests and dividends.

All three together - the net _____ - are necessary to reconcile the beginning cash balance to the ending cash balance. Loan draw downs or equity injections, that is just shifting of capital but no expenditure as such, are not considered in the net _____.

   a. Real option
   b. Corporate finance
   c. Shareholder value
   d. Cash flow

13. In finance, _____ is the process of estimating the potential market value of a financial asset or liability. they can be done on assets (for example, investments in marketable securities such as stocks, options, business enterprises, or intangible assets such as patents and trademarks) or on liabilities (e.g., Bonds issued by a company.) _____s are required in many contexts including investment analysis, capital budgeting, merger and acquisition transactions, financial reporting, taxable events to determine the proper tax liability, and in litigation.
   a. Share
   b. Margin
   c. Procter ' Gamble
   d. Valuation

14. A _____ is a decision support tool that uses a tree-like graph or model of decisions and their possible consequences, including chance event outcomes, resource costs, and utility. _____s are commonly used in operations research, specifically in decision analysis, to help identify a strategy most likely to reach a goal. Another use of _____s is as a descriptive means for calculating conditional probabilities.
   a. 529 plan
   b. 7-Eleven
   c. Decision tree
   d. 4-4-5 Calendar

Chapter 13. Real Options

15. _____ is a process of analyzing possible future events by considering alternative possible outcomes (scenarios.) The analysis is designed to allow improved decision-making by allowing consideration of outcomes and their implications.

For example, in economics and finance, a financial institution might attempt to forecast several possible scenarios for the economy (e.g. rapid growth, moderate growth, slow growth) and it might also attempt to forecast financial market returns (for bonds, stocks and cash) in each of those scenarios.

  a. Scenario analysis
  b. 529 plan
  c. Detection Risk
  d. 4-4-5 Calendar

16. _____ is the advantage gained by the initial occupant of a market segment. This advantage may stem from the fact that the first entrant can gain control of resources that followers may not be able to match. Sometimes the first mover is not able to capitalise on its advantage, leaving the opportunity for another firm to gain second-mover advantage.
  a. First-mover advantage
  b. Planning horizon
  c. Market capitalization
  d. Golden parachute

17. _____ is the study of how the variation (uncertainty) in the output of a mathematical model can be apportioned, qualitatively or quantitatively, to different sources of variation in the input of a model.

In more general terms uncertainty and sensitivity analyses investigate the robustness of a study when the study includes some form of mathematical modelling. While uncertainty analysis studies the overall uncertainty in the conclusions of the study, _____ tries to identify what source of uncertainty weights more on the study's conclusions.

  a. Golden parachute
  b. Proxy fight
  c. Sensitivity analysis
  d. Synthetic CDO

18. In probability theory and statistics, the _____ of a random variable, probability distribution averaging the squared distance of its possible values from the expected value (mean.) Whereas the mean is a way to describe the location of a distribution, the _____ is a way to capture its scale or degree of being spread out. The unit of _____ is the square of the unit of the original variable.
  a. Monte Carlo methods
  b. Semivariance
  c. Harmonic mean
  d. Variance

19. _____ is a business valuation method. _____ is the net present value of a project if financed solely by ownership equity plus the present value of all the benefits of financing. Usually, the main benefit is a tax shield resulted from tax deductibility of interest payments. Another one can be a subsidized borrowing.
  a. Adjusted present value
  b. AAB
  c. A Random Walk Down Wall Street
  d. ABN Amro

20. The _____, in terms of finance and investing, describes how the expected return of a stock or portfolio is correlated to the return of the financial market as a whole.

An asset with a beta of 0 means that its price is not at all correlated with the market; that asset is independent. A positive beta means that the asset generally follows the market.

a. Current yield
c. LIBOR market model
b. Beta coefficient
d. Perpetuity

Chapter 14. Financial Planning and Forecasting Financial Statements

1. _____ is the planning process used to determine whether a firm's long term investments such as new machinery, replacement machinery, new plants, new products, and research development projects are worth pursuing. It is budget for major capital, or investment, expenditures.

Many formal methods are used in _____, including the techniques such as

- Net present value
- Profitability index
- Internal rate of return
- Modified Internal Rate of Return
- Equivalent annuity

These methods use the incremental cash flows from each potential investment, or project. Techniques based on accounting earnings and accounting rules are sometimes used - though economists consider this to be improper - such as the accounting rate of return, and 'return on investment.' Simplified and hybrid methods are used as well, such as payback period and discounted payback period.

a. Financial distress
b. Preferred stock
c. Shareholder value
d. Capital budgeting

2. In economics, a _____ is a mechanism that allows people to easily buy and sell (trade) financial securities (such as stocks and bonds), commodities (such as precious metals or agricultural goods), and other fungible items of value at low transaction costs and at prices that reflect the efficient-market hypothesis.

_____s have evolved significantly over several hundred years and are undergoing constant innovation to improve liquidity.

Both general markets (where many commodities are traded) and specialized markets (where only one commodity is traded) exist.

a. Financial market
b. Secondary market
c. Delta hedging
d. Cost of carry

3. _____ is the set of processes, customs, policies, laws and institutions affecting the way a corporation is directed, administered or controlled. _____ also includes the relationships among the many stakeholders involved and the goals for which the corporation is governed. The principal stakeholders are the shareholders, management and the board of directors.

a. Foreign Corrupt Practices Act
b. Corporate governance
c. Due diligence
d. Patent

4. _____ are formal records of a business' financial activities.

Chapter 14. Financial Planning and Forecasting Financial Statements 161

_____ provide an overview of a business' financial condition in both short and long term. There are four basic _____:

1. **Balance sheet**: also referred to as statement of financial position or condition, reports on a company's assets, liabilities, and net equity as of a given point in time.
2. **Income statement**: also referred to as Profit and Loss statement (or a 'P'L'), reports on a company's income, expenses, and profits over a period of time.
3. **Statement of retained earnings**: explains the changes in a company's retained earnings over the reporting period.
4. **Statement of cash flows**: reports on a company's cash flow activities, particularly its operating, investing and financing activities.

a. Notes to the Financial Statements

b. Statement on Auditing Standards No. 70: Service Organizations

c. Statement of retained earnings

d. Financial statements

5. A _____ is a brief written statement of the purpose of a company or organization. Ideally, a _____ guides the actions of the organization, spells out its overall goal, provides a sense of direction, and guides decision making for all levels of management.

_____s often contain the following:

- Purpose and aim of the organization
- The organization's primary stakeholders: clients, stockholders, etc.
- Responsibilities of the organization toward these stakeholders
- Products and services offered

In developing a _____:

- Encourage as much input as feasible from employees, volunteers, and other stakeholders
- Publicize it broadly

The _____ can be used to resolve differences between business stakeholders. Stakeholders include: employees including managers and executives, stockholders, board of directors, customers, suppliers, distributors, creditors, governments (local, state, federal, etc.), unions, competitors, NGO's, and the general public.

a. 529 plan

b. 4-4-5 Calendar

c. 7-Eleven

d. Mission statement

6. The term _____ is a term applied to practices that are perfunctory, or seek to satisfy the minimum requirements or to conform to a convention or doctrine. It has different meanings in different fields.

Chapter 14. Financial Planning and Forecasting Financial Statements

In accounting, _____ earnings are those earnings of companies in addition to actual earnings calculated under the Generally Accepted Accounting Principles (GAAP) in their quarterly and yearly financial reports.

a. Deferred income
c. Deferred financing costs

b. Long-term liabilities
d. Pro forma

7. An _____ is a corporation that makes a valid election to be taxed under Subchapter S of Chapter 1 of the Internal Revenue Code.

In general, _____s do not pay any income taxes. Instead, the corporation's income or losses are divided among and passed through to its shareholders.

a. 529 plan
c. 4-4-5 Calendar

b. S corporation
d. 7-Eleven

8. An _____ is a document a company presents at an annual general meeting for approval by its shareholders, or a charitable organization presents its trustees. The report is made up of reports, which may include the following:

- Chairman's report
- CEO's report
- Auditor's report on corporate governance
- Mission statement
- Corporate governance statement of compliance
- Statement of directors' responsibilities
- Invitation to the company's AGM

as well as financial statements including:

- Auditor's report on the financial statements
- Balance sheet
- Statement of retained earnings
- Income statement
- Cash flow statement
- Notes to the financial statements
- Accounting policies

Other information deemed relevant to stakeholders may be included, such as a report on operations for manufacturing firms. In the case of larger companies, it is usually a sleek, colorful, high gloss publication.

The details provided in the report are of use to investors to understand the company's financial position and future direction.

a. Amortization schedule	b. Outstanding balance
c. Accrued liabilities	d. Annual report

9. _____ is the balance of the amounts of cash being received and paid by a business during a defined period of time, sometimes tied to a specific project. Measurement of _____ can be used

- to evaluate the state or performance of a business or project.
- to determine problems with liquidity. Being profitable does not necessarily mean being liquid. A company can fail because of a shortage of cash, even while profitable.
- to generate project rate of returns. The time of _____s into and out of projects are used as inputs to financial models such as internal rate of return, and net present value.
- to examine income or growth of a business when it is believed that accrual accounting concepts do not represent economic realities. Alternately, _____ can be used to 'validate' the net income generated by accrual accounting.

_____ as a generic term may be used differently depending on context, and certain _____ definitions may be adapted by analysts and users for their own uses. Common terms include operating _____ and free _____.

_____s can be classified into:

1. Operational _____s: Cash received or expended as a result of the company's core business activities.
2. Investment _____s: Cash received or expended through capital expenditure, investments or acquisitions.
3. Financing _____s: Cash received or expended as a result of financial activities, such as interests and dividends.

All three together - the net _____ - are necessary to reconcile the beginning cash balance to the ending cash balance. Loan draw downs or equity injections, that is just shifting of capital but no expenditure as such, are not considered in the net _____.

a. Real option	b. Corporate finance
c. Cash flow	d. Shareholder value

10. The institution most often referenced by the word '_____' is a public or publicly traded _____, the shares of which are traded on a public stock exchange (e.g., the New York Stock Exchange or Nasdaq in the United States) where shares of stock of _____s are bought and sold by and to the general public. Most of the largest businesses in the world are publicly traded _____s. However, the majority of _____s are said to be closely held, privately held or close _____s, meaning that no ready market exists for the trading of shares.

a. Protect	b. Federal Home Loan Mortgage Corporation
c. Depository Trust Company	d. Corporation

11. In finance, _____ is the process of estimating the potential market value of a financial asset or liability. they can be done on assets (for example, investments in marketable securities such as stocks, options, business enterprises, or intangible assets such as patents and trademarks) or on liabilities (e.g., Bonds issued by a company.) _____s are required in many contexts including investment analysis, capital budgeting, merger and acquisition transactions, financial reporting, taxable events to determine the proper tax liability, and in litigation.

Chapter 14. Financial Planning and Forecasting Financial Statements

a. Procter ' Gamble
c. Margin
b. Share
d. Valuation

12. A _____ is a payment made by a corporation to its shareholder members. When a corporation earns a profit or surplus, that money can be put to two uses: it can either be re-invested in the business (called retained earnings), or it can be paid to the shareholders as a _____. Many corporations retain a portion of their earnings and pay the remainder as a _____.

a. Dividend
c. Dividend puzzle
b. Special dividend
d. Dividend yield

13. The phrase _____ refers to the aspect of corporate strategy, corporate finance and management dealing with the buying, selling and combining of different companies that can aid, finance, or help a growing company in a given industry grow rapidly without having to create another business entity.

An acquisition, also known as a takeover, is the buying of one company (the 'target') by another. An acquisition may be friendly or hostile.

a. Mergers and acquisitions
c. 4-4-5 Calendar
b. 7-Eleven
d. 529 plan

14. _____ is an estimate of the fair value of corporations and their stocks, by using fundamental economic criteria. This theoretical valuation has to be perfected with market criteria, as the final purpose is to determine potential market prices.

a. 4-4-5 Calendar
c. Growth stocks
b. Stock valuation
d. Security Analysis

15. The _____, in terms of finance and investing, describes how the expected return of a stock or portfolio is correlated to the return of the financial market as a whole.

An asset with a beta of 0 means that its price is not at all correlated with the market; that asset is independent. A positive beta means that the asset generally follows the market.

a. LIBOR market model
c. Perpetuity
b. Current yield
d. Beta coefficient

16. In finance, a _____ is a debt security, in which the authorized issuer owes the holders a debt and, depending on the terms of the _____, is obliged to pay interest (the coupon) and/or to repay the principal at a later date, termed maturity.

Thus a _____ is a loan: the issuer is the borrower, the _____ holder is the lender, and the coupon is the interest. _____s provide the borrower with external funds to finance long-term investments, or, in the case of government _____s, to finance current expenditure.

a. Bond
c. Puttable bond
b. Convertible bond
d. Catastrophe bonds

Chapter 14. Financial Planning and Forecasting Financial Statements

17. _____ is the process of determining the fair price of a bond. As with any security or capital investment, the fair value of a bond is the present value of the stream of cash flows it is expected to generate. Hence, the price or value of a bond is determined by discounting the bond's expected cash flows to the present using the appropriate discount rate.

   a. Bond fund
   b. Collateralized debt obligations
   c. Catastrophe bonds
   d. Bond valuation

18. _____ is the task of determining how a business will afford to achieve its strategic goals and objectives. Usually, a company creates a Financial Plan immediately after the vision and objectives have been set. The Financial Plan describes each of the activities, resources, equipment and materials that are needed to achieve these objectives, as well as the timeframes involved.

   a. Performance measurement
   b. Financial planning
   c. Management by exception
   d. Corporate Transparency

19. A _____ is a pool of assets forming an independent legal entity that are bought with the contributions to a pension plan for the exclusive purpose of financing pension plan benefits.

   _____s are important shareholders of listed and private companies. They are especially important to the stock market where large institutional investors like the Ontario Teachers' Pension Plan dominate.

   a. Pension fund
   b. Leverage
   c. Leveraged buyout
   d. Limited liability company

20. _____ is the term in economics for the amount of fixed or real capital present in relation to other factors of production, especially labor. At the level of either a production process or the aggregate economy, it may be estimated by the capital/labor ratio, such as from the points along a capital/labor isoquant.

   Since the use of tools and machinery makes labor more effective, rising _____ pushes up the productivity of labor, so a society that is more capital intensive tends to have a higher standard of living over the long run than one with low _____.

   a. Cost of capital
   b. 4-4-5 Calendar
   c. Weighted average cost of capital
   d. Capital intensity

21. _____ is the difference between price and the costs of bringing to market whatever it is that is accounted as an enterprise (whether by harvest, extraction, manufacture, or purchase) in terms of the component costs of delivered goods and/or services and any operating or other expenses.

   A key difficulty in measuring profit is in defining costs. Pure economic monetary profits can be zero or negative even in competitive equilibrium when accounted monetized costs exceed monetized price.

   a. AAB
   b. A Random Walk Down Wall Street
   c. Accounting profit
   d. Economic profit

22. _____, Net Margin, Net _____ or Net Profit Ratio all refer to a measure of profitability. It is calculated using a formula and written as a percentage or a number.

$$\text{Net profit margin} = \frac{\text{Net profit after taxes}}{\text{Net Sales}}$$

The _____ is mostly used for internal comparison.

a. 4-4-5 Calendar
c. Net profit margin
b. Profit maximization
d. Profit margin

23. _____ indicates the percentage of a company's earnings that are not paid out in dividends but credited to retained earnings. It is the opposite of the dividend payout ratio, so that also called the retention rate.

_____ = 1 - Dividend Payout Ratio

a. Bankassurer
c. Fair market value
b. Dow Jones Indexes
d. Retention ratio

24. In finance, a _____ is collateral that the holder of a position in securities, options, or futures contracts has to deposit to cover the credit risk of his counterparty (most often his broker.) This risk can arise if the holder has done any of the following:

- borrowed cash from the counterparty to buy securities or options,
- sold securities or options short, or
- entered into a futures contract.

The collateral can be in the form of cash or securities, and it is deposited in a _____ account. On U.S. futures exchanges, '_____' was formally called performance bond.

_____ buying is buying securities with cash borrowed from a broker, using other securities as collateral.

a. Margin
c. Credit
b. Procter ' Gamble
d. Share

25. _____ or financing is to provide capital (funds), which means money for a project, a person, a business or any other private or public institutions.

Those funds can be allocated for either short term or long term purposes. The health fund is a new way of _____ private healthcare centers.

a. Proxy fight
c. Funding
b. Synthetic CDO
d. Product life cycle

Chapter 14. Financial Planning and Forecasting Financial Statements

26. _____, refers to consumption opportunity gained by an entity within a specified time frame, which is generally expressed in monetary terms. However, for households and individuals, '_____ is the sum of all the wages, salaries, profits, interests payments, rents and other forms of earnings received... in a given period of time.' For firms, _____ generally refers to net-profit: what remains of revenue after expenses have been subtracted.
   a. OIBDA
   b. Accrual
   c. Income
   d. Annual report

27. An _____ is a financial statement for companies that indicates how Revenue is transformed into net income The purpose of the _____ is to show managers and investors whether the company made or lost money during the period being reported.

The important thing to remember about an _____ is that it represents a period of time.

   a. Income statement
   b. A Random Walk Down Wall Street
   c. ABN Amro
   d. AAB

28. The _____ is the current method of accelerated asset depreciation required by the United States income tax code. Under _____, all assets are divided into classes which dictate the number of years over which an asset's cost will be recovered.

Prior to the Accelerated Cost Recovery System (ACRS), most capital purchases were depreciated using a straight line technique, that allowed for the depreciation of the asset over its useful life.

   a. 7-Eleven
   b. Modified Accelerated Cost Recovery System
   c. 4-4-5 Calendar
   d. 529 plan

29. In economics, business, and accounting, a _____ is the value of money that has been used up to produce something, and hence is not available for use anymore. In business, the _____ may be one of acquisition, in which case the amount of money expended to acquire it is counted as _____. In this case, money is the input that is gone in order to acquire the thing.
   a. Fixed costs
   b. Sliding scale fees
   c. Marginal cost
   d. Cost

30. In economics and finance, _____ is the practice of taking advantage of a price differential between two or more markets: striking a combination of matching deals that capitalize upon the imbalance, the profit being the difference between the market prices. When used by academics, an _____ is a transaction that involves no negative cash flow at any probabilistic or temporal state and a positive cash flow in at least one state; in simple terms, a risk-free profit.
   a. Efficient-market hypothesis
   b. Arbitrage
   c. Issuer
   d. Initial margin

31. _____ is a fee paid on borrowed assets. It is the price paid for the use of borrowed money , or, money earned by deposited funds . Assets that are sometimes lent with _____ include money, shares, consumer goods through hire purchase, major assets such as aircraft, and even entire factories in finance lease arrangements.
   a. Interest
   b. Insolvency
   c. A Random Walk Down Wall Street
   d. AAB

32. _____ relates to the cost of borrowing money. It is the price that a lender charges a borrower for the use of the lender's money. _____ is different from OPEX and CAPEX, for it relates to the capital structure of a company.
   a. ABN Amro
   b. Interest expense
   c. A Random Walk Down Wall Street
   d. AAB

33. In financial accounting, a _____ or statement of financial position is a summary of a person's or organization's balances. Assets, liabilities and ownership equity are listed as of a specific date, such as the end of its financial year. A _____ is often described as a snapshot of a company's financial condition.
   a. Statement of retained earnings
   b. Financial statements
   c. Statement on Auditing Standards No. 70: Service Organizations
   d. Balance sheet

34. In business and accounting, _____s are everything of value that is owned by a person or company. The balance sheet of a firm records the monetary value of the _____s owned by the firm. The two major _____ classes are tangible _____s and intangible _____s.
   a. Accounts payable
   b. EBITDA
   c. Income
   d. Asset

35. _____, in bookkeeping, refers to assets, liabilities, income, and expenses recorded on individual pages of the so called book of final entry or ledger. Changes in _____ value are made by chronologically posting debit (DR) and credit (CR) entries to its page. Examples of _____s are cash, _____s receivable, mortgages, loans, land and buildings, common stock, sales, services provided, wages, and payroll overhead.
   a. Account
   b. Alpha
   c. Option
   d. Accretion

36. _____ is one of a series of accounting transactions dealing with the billing of customers who owe money to a person, company or organization for goods and services that have been provided to the customer. In most business entities this is typically done by generating an invoice and mailing or electronically delivering it to the customer, who in turn must pay it within an established timeframe called credit or payment terms.

An example of a common payment term is Net 30, meaning payment is due in the amount of the invoice 30 days from the date of invoice.

   a. Impaired asset
   b. Accounting methods
   c. Income
   d. Accounts receivable

37. _____ means regulating, adapting or settling in a variety of contexts:

In commercial law, _____ means the settlement of a loss incurred on insured goods. The calculation of the amounts of compensation to be paid by or to the several interests is a complicated matter. It involves much detail and arithmetic, and requires a full and accurate knowledge of the principles of the subject.

   a. Equity method
   b. Asset recovery
   c. Adjustment
   d. Intelligent investor

Chapter 14. Financial Planning and Forecasting Financial Statements

38. In accountancy, _____ is a company's average collection period. A low number of days indicates that the company collects its outstanding receivables quickly. Typically, _____ is calculated monthly. The _____ figure is an index of the relationship between outstanding receivables and sales achieved over a given period. The _____ analysis provides general information about the number of days on average that customers take to pay invoices.
   a. Days sales outstanding
   b. Net pay
   c. Round-tripping
   d. Residual value

39. In accounting, _____ are considered liabilities of the business that are to be settled in cash within the fiscal year or the operating cycle, whichever period is longer.

For example accounts payable for goods, services or supplies that were purchased for use in the operation of the business and payable within a normal period of time would be _____.

Bonds, mortgages and loans that are payable over a term exceeding one year would be fixed liabilities.

   a. Current liabilities
   b. Net income
   c. Gross sales
   d. Closing entries

40. The _____ is a financial ratio that measures whether or not a firm has enough resources to pay its debts over the next 12 months. It compares a firm's current assets to its current liabilities. It is expressed as follows:

$$\text{Current ratio} = \frac{\text{Current Assets}}{\text{Current Liabilities}}$$

For example, if WXY Company's current assets are $50,000,000 and its current liabilities are $40,000,000, then its _____ would be $50,000,000 divided by $40,000,000, which equals 1.25.

   a. Debt service coverage ratio
   b. Sustainable growth rate
   c. PEG ratio
   d. Current ratio

41. In finance, a _____ is a type of bond that can be converted into shares of stock in the issuing company, usually at some pre-announced ratio. It is a hybrid security with debt- and equity-like features. Although it typically has a low coupon rate, the holder is compensated with the ability to convert the bond to common stock, usually at a substantial discount to the stock's market value.
   a. Gilts
   b. Corporate bond
   c. Convertible bond
   d. Bond fund

42. A _____ is an international bond that is denominated in a currency not native to the country where it is issued. It can be categorised according to the currency in which it is issued. London is one of the centers of the _____ market, but _____s may be traded throughout the world - for example in Singapore or Tokyo.
   a. Interest rate option
   b. Education production function
   c. Economic entity
   d. Eurobond

Chapter 14. Financial Planning and Forecasting Financial Statements

43. In economic models, the _____ time frame assumes no fixed factors of production. Firms can enter or leave the marketplace, and the cost (and availability) of land, labor, raw materials, and capital goods can be assumed to vary. In contrast, in the short-run time frame, certain factors are assumed to be fixed, because there is not sufficient time for them to change.
   a. Long-run
   b. Short-run
   c. 4-4-5 Calendar
   d. 529 plan

44. _____ is typically a higher ranking stock than voting shares, and its terms are negotiated between the corporation and the investor.

   _____ usually carry no voting rights, but may carry superior priority over common stock in the payment of dividends and upon liquidation. _____ may carry a dividend that is paid out prior to any dividends to common stock holders.

   a. Follow-on offering
   b. Preferred stock
   c. Second lien loan
   d. Trade-off theory

45. A _____ is the price of a single share of a no. of saleable stocks of the company. Once the stock is purchased, the owner becomes a shareholder of the company that issued the share.
   a. Stock split
   b. Trading curb
   c. Whisper numbers
   d. Share price

46. In finance, _____ are stocks that appreciate in value and yield a high return on equity (ROE.) Analysts compute ROE by taking the company's net income and dividing it by the company's equity. To be classified as a growth stock, analysts expect to see at least 15 percent return on equity.
   a. Growth stocks
   b. Stock valuation
   c. 4-4-5 Calendar
   d. Security Analysis

47. A _____ is a fungible, negotiable instrument representing financial value. They are broadly categorized into debt securities (such as banknotes, bonds and debentures), and equity securities; e.g., common stocks. The company or other entity issuing the _____ is called the issuer.
   a. Security
   b. Securities lending
   c. Tracking stock
   d. Book entry

48. In business and finance, a _____ (also referred to as equity _____) of stock means a _____ of ownership in a corporation (company.) In the plural, stocks is often used as a synonym for _____s especially in the United States, but it is less commonly used that way outside of North America.

   In the United Kingdom, South Africa, and Australia, stock can also refer to completely different financial instruments such as government bonds or, less commonly, to all kinds of marketable securities.

   a. Margin
   b. Procter ' Gamble
   c. Bucket shop
   d. Share

Chapter 14. Financial Planning and Forecasting Financial Statements

49. In corporate finance, _____ is an estimate of true economic profit after making corrective adjustments to GAAP accounting, including deducting the opportunity cost of equity capital. GAAP is estimated to ignore US$300 billion in shareholder opportunity costs. _____ can be measured as Net Operating Profit After Taxes(or NOPAT) less the money cost of capital.
   a. ABN Amro
   c. AAB
   b. A Random Walk Down Wall Street
   d. Economic value added

50. _____, in microeconomics, are the cost advantages that a business obtains due to expansion. _____ may be utilized by any size firm expanding its scale of operation.
   a. Employee Retirement Income Security Act
   c. Articles of incorporation
   b. Uniform Commercial Code
   d. Economies of scale

51. _____ refers to the additional value of a commodity over the cost of commodities used to produce it from the previous stage of production. An example is the price of gasoline at the pump over the price of the oil in it. In national accounts used in macroeconomics, it refers to the contribution of the factors of production, i.e., land, labor, and capital goods, to raising the value of a product and corresponds to the incomes received by the owners of these factors.
   a. Deregulation
   c. Supply shock
   b. Demand shock
   d. Value added

Chapter 15. Corporate Valuation, Value-Based Management, and Corporate Governance

1. In finance, _____ refers to the value of a security which is intrinsic to or contained in the security itself. It is also frequently called fundamental value. It is ordinarily calculated by summing the future income generated by the asset, and discounting it to the present value.

   a. Amortization
   b. Intrinsic value
   c. Alpha
   d. Accretion

2. _____ refers to the overarching strategy of the diversified firm. Such a _____ answers the questions of 'in which businesses should we be in?' and 'how does being in these business create synergy and/or add to the competitive advantage of the corporation as a whole?'

   Business strategy refers to the aggregated strategies of single business firm or a strategic business unit (SBU) in a diversified corporation. According to Michael Porter, a firm must formulate a business strategy that incorporates either cost leadership, differentiation or focus in order to achieve a sustainable competitive advantage and long-term success in its chosen arenas or industries.

   a. 7-Eleven
   b. 4-4-5 Calendar
   c. Corporate strategy
   d. 529 plan

3. _____ is the set of processes, customs, policies, laws and institutions affecting the way a corporation is directed, administered or controlled. _____ also includes the relationships among the many stakeholders involved and the goals for which the corporation is governed. The principal stakeholders are the shareholders, management and the board of directors.

   a. Patent
   b. Due diligence
   c. Foreign Corrupt Practices Act
   d. Corporate governance

4. _____, is when a company issues common stock or shares to the public for the first time. They are often issued by smaller, younger companies seeking capital to expand, but can also be done by large privately-owned companies looking to become publicly traded.

   In an _____ the issuer may obtain the assistance of an underwriting firm, which helps it determine what type of security to issue (common or preferred), best offering price and time to bring it to market.

   a. Asian Financial Crisis
   b. Interest
   c. Insolvency
   d. Initial public offering

5. In finance, _____ refers to the way a corporation finances its assets through some combination of equity, debt, or hybrid securities. A firm's _____ is then the composition or 'structure' of its liabilities. For example, a firm that sells $20 billion in equity and $80 billion in debt is said to be 20% equity-financed and 80% debt-financed.

   a. Capital structure
   b. Book building
   c. Market for corporate control
   d. Rights issue

6. A _____ is a payment made by a corporation to its shareholder members. When a corporation earns a profit or surplus, that money can be put to two uses: it can either be re-invested in the business (called retained earnings), or it can be paid to the shareholders as a _____. Many corporations retain a portion of their earnings and pay the remainder as a _____.

Chapter 15. Corporate Valuation, Value-Based Management, and Corporate Governance

    a. Dividend puzzle
    b. Special dividend
    c. Dividend yield
    d. Dividend

7. In finance, _____ is the process of estimating the potential market value of a financial asset or liability. they can be done on assets (for example, investments in marketable securities such as stocks, options, business enterprises, or intangible assets such as patents and trademarks) or on liabilities (e.g., Bonds issued by a company.) _____s are required in many contexts including investment analysis, capital budgeting, merger and acquisition transactions, financial reporting, taxable events to determine the proper tax liability, and in litigation.
    a. Procter ' Gamble
    b. Share
    c. Valuation
    d. Margin

8. In business and accounting, _____s are everything of value that is owned by a person or company. The balance sheet of a firm records the monetary value of the _____s owned by the firm. The two major _____ classes are tangible _____s and intangible _____s.
    a. EBITDA
    b. Income
    c. Accounts payable
    d. Asset

9. An _____ is a contract written by a seller that conveys to the buyer the right -- but not the obligation -- to buy (in the case of a call _____) or to sell (in the case of a put _____) a particular asset, such as a piece of property such as, among others, a futures contract. In return for granting the _____, the seller collects a payment (the premium) from the buyer.

For example, buying a call _____ provides the right to buy a specified quantity of a security at a set strike price at some time on or before expiration, while buying a put _____ provides the right to sell.

    a. Option
    b. Amortization
    c. AT'T Mobility LLC
    d. Annuity

10. _____ is a business valuation method. _____ is the net present value of a project if financed solely by ownership equity plus the present value of all the benefits of financing. Usually, the main benefit is a tax shield resulted from tax deductibility of interest payments. Another one can be a subsidized borrowing.
    a. AAB
    b. A Random Walk Down Wall Street
    c. ABN Amro
    d. Adjusted present value

11. In finance, the _____ (continuing value or horizon value) of a security is the present value at a future point in time of all future cash flows when we expect stable growth rate forever. It is most often used in multi-stage discounted cash flow analysis, and allows for the limitation of cash flow projections to a several-year period. Forecasting results beyond such a period is impractical and exposes such projections to a variety of risks limiting their validity, primarily the great uncertainty involved in predicting industry and macroeconomic conditions beyond a few years.
    a. Terminal value
    b. Refinancing risk
    c. Discounted cash flow
    d. Negative gearing

12. In business and finance, a _____ (also referred to as equity _____) of stock means a _____ of ownership in a corporation (company.) In the plural, stocks is often used as a synonym for _____s especially in the United States, but it is less commonly used that way outside of North America.

174   Chapter 15. Corporate Valuation, Value-Based Management, and Corporate Governance

In the United Kingdom, South Africa, and Australia, stock can also refer to completely different financial instruments such as government bonds or, less commonly, to all kinds of marketable securities.

a. Bucket shop
b. Procter ' Gamble
c. Margin
d. Share

13.   In economics, business, and accounting, a _____ is the value of money that has been used up to produce something, and hence is not available for use anymore. In business, the _____ may be one of acquisition, in which case the amount of money expended to acquire it is counted as _____. In this case, money is the input that is gone in order to acquire the thing.

a. Cost
b. Sliding scale fees
c. Marginal cost
d. Fixed costs

14.   The _____ is an expected return that the provider of capital plans to earn on their investment.

Capital (money) used for funding a business should earn returns for the capital providers who risk their capital. For an investment to be worthwhile, the expected return on capital must be greater than the _____.

a. Weighted average cost of capital
b. 4-4-5 Calendar
c. Cost of capital
d. Capital intensity

15.   The _____ is the weighted-average most likely outcome in gambling, probability theory, economics or finance.

In gambling and probability theory, there is usually a discrete set of possible outcomes. In this case, _____ is a measure of the relative balance of win or loss weighted by their chances of occurring.

a. ABN Amro
b. AAB
c. A Random Walk Down Wall Street
d. Expected return

16.   _____ represents the total cash investment that shareholders and debtholders have made in a company. There are two different but completely equivalent methods for calculating _____. The operating approach is calculated as:

_____ = Operating Net Working Capital + Net PP'E + Capitalized Operating Leases + Other Operating Assets + Operating Intangibles - Other Operating Liabilities - Cumulative Adjustment for Amortization of R'D

Equivalently, the financing approach is calculated as:

In symbols:

$$K = D + E - M$$

_____ is used in several important measurements of financial performance, including return on _____, economic value added, and free cash flow.

Chapter 15. Corporate Valuation, Value-Based Management, and Corporate Governance

a. Inventory turnover
b. Operating leverage
c. Information ratio
d. Invested capital

17. _____ is a financial measure that quantifies how well a company generates cash flow relative to the capital it has invested in its business. It is defined as Net operating profit less adjusted taxes divided by Invested Capital and is usually expressed as a percentage. In this calculation, capital invested includes all monetary capital invested: long-term debt, common and preferred shares.

a. Debt service coverage ratio
b. Sharpe ratio
c. Return on invested capital
d. Cash conversion cycle

18. _____ is a global management consulting firm that focuses on solving issues of concern to senior management. McKinsey serves as an advisor to the worlde;s leading businesses, governments, and institutions. It is widely recognized as a leader and one of the most prestigious firms in the management consulting industry.

a. 4-4-5 Calendar
b. McKinsey ' Company
c. 7-Eleven
d. 529 plan

19. _____ is a legally declared inability or impairment of ability of an individual or organization to pay their creditors. Creditors may file a _____ petition against a debtor ('involuntary _____') in an effort to recoup a portion of what they are owed or initiate a restructuring. In the majority of cases, however, _____ is initiated by the debtor (a 'voluntary _____' that is filed by the bankrupt individual or organization.)

a. 529 plan
b. Debt settlement
c. Bankruptcy
d. 4-4-5 Calendar

20. The term _____ has three unrelated technical definitions, and is also used in a variety of non-technical ways.

- In financial economics, it refers to any asset used to make money, as opposed to assets used for personal enjoyment or consumption. This is an important distinction because two people can disagree sharply about the value of personal assets, one person might think a sports car is more valuable than a pickup truck, another person might have the opposite taste. But if an asset is held for the purpose of making money, taste has nothing to do with it, only differences of opinion about how much money the asset will produce. With the further assumption that people agree on the probability distribution of future cash flows, it is possible to have an objective _____ pricing model. Even without the assumption of agreement, it is possible to set rational limits on _____ value.
- In governmental accounting, it is defined as any asset used in operations with an initial useful life extending beyond one reporting period. Generally, government managers have a 'stewardship' duty to maintain _____s under their control. See International Public Sector Accounting Standards for details.
- In US tax accounting, it is defined as any property other than a list of exceptions. The main exceptions are anything held for sale, and any real estate or depreciable property used in business. Almost everything you own and use for personal purposes, pleasure or investment is a _____. If something is a _____ for tax purposes, gains or losses on sale or disposition are capital gains or capital losses. For individuals, however, capital losses on property held for personal use are generally not deductible. See the IRS publication Tax Facts about Capital Gains and Losses for details.

A well-known financial accounting textbook advises that the term be avoided except in tax accounting because it is used in so many different senses, not all of them well-defined. For example it is often used as a synonym for fixed assets or for investments in securities.

Chapter 15. Corporate Valuation, Value-Based Management, and Corporate Governance

A common non-technical usage occurs when people ask that employees or the environment or something else be treated as a _____.

   a. Settlement date
   b. Solvency
   c. Political risk
   d. Capital Asset

21. In finance, the _____ is used to determine a theoretically appropriate required rate of return of an asset, if that asset is to be added to an already well-diversified portfolio, given that asset's non-diversifiable risk. The model takes into account the asset's sensitivity to non-diversifiable risk (also known as systemic risk or market risk), often represented by the quantity beta (β) in the financial industry, as well as the expected return of the market and the expected return of a theoretical risk-free asset.

The model was introduced by Jack Treynor (1961, 1962), William Sharpe (1964), John Lintner (1965a,b) and Jan Mossin (1966) independently, building on the earlier work of Harry Markowitz on diversification and modern portfolio theory.

   a. Hull-White model
   b. Capital Asset Pricing Model
   c. Cox-Ingersoll-Ross model
   d. Random walk hypothesis

22. In United States banking, _____ is a marketing term for certain services offered primarily to larger business customers. It may be used to describe all bank accounts (such as checking accounts) provided to businesses of a certain size, but it is more often used to describe specific services such as cash concentration, zero balance accounting, and automated clearing house facilities. Sometimes, private banking customers are given _____ services.

   a. Profitability index
   b. Global tactical asset allocation
   c. Capitalization rate
   d. Cash management

23. _____ is a fee paid on borrowed assets. It is the price paid for the use of borrowed money, or, money earned by deposited funds. Assets that are sometimes lent with _____ include money, shares, consumer goods through hire purchase, major assets such as aircraft, and even entire factories in finance lease arrangements.

   a. AAB
   b. Interest
   c. Insolvency
   d. A Random Walk Down Wall Street

24. In business, a _____ is the purchase of one company (the target) by another (the acquirer or bidder). In the UK the term refers to the acquisition of a public company whose shares are listed on a stock exchange, in contrast to the acquisition of a private company.

Before a bidder makes an offer for another company, it usually first informs that company's board of directors.

   a. Stock swap
   b. Takeover
   c. 529 plan
   d. 4-4-5 Calendar

25. _____ is money paid by a company (or allied company or individual) to acquire its own shares of stock from a shareholder who is threatening to take control of, or unwanted influence of, the company.

Chapter 15. Corporate Valuation, Value-Based Management, and Corporate Governance

The term is a neologism combining the terms greenback and blackmail, invented by journalists and commentators who saw the practices of corporate raiders as a form of blackmail. The target company is financially held hostage, and is legally forced to pay the _____er to go away.

a. Stock swap
c. 529 plan
b. 4-4-5 Calendar
d. Greenmail

26. In some countries, including the United States and the United Kingdom, corporations can buy back their own stock in a share repurchase, also known as a _____ or share buyback. There has been a meteoric rise in the use of share repurchases in the U.S. in the past twenty years, from $5b in 1980 to $349b in 2005. A share repurchase distributes cash to existing shareholders in exchange for a fraction of the firm's outstanding equity.

a. Common stock
c. Trading curb
b. Stockholder
d. Stock repurchase

27. _____ are formal records of a business' financial activities.

_____ provide an overview of a business' financial condition in both short and long term. There are four basic _____:

1. **Balance sheet**: also referred to as statement of financial position or condition, reports on a company's assets, liabilities, and net equity as of a given point in time.
2. **Income statement**: also referred to as Profit and Loss statement (or a 'P'L'), reports on a company's income, expenses, and profits over a period of time.
3. **Statement of retained earnings**: explains the changes in a company's retained earnings over the reporting period.
4. **Statement of cash flows**: reports on a company's cash flow activities, particularly its operating, investing and financing activities.

a. Financial statements
c. Statement of retained earnings
b. Notes to the Financial Statements
d. Statement on Auditing Standards No. 70: Service Organizations

28. A _____ is a fungible, negotiable instrument representing financial value. They are broadly categorized into debt securities (such as banknotes, bonds and debentures), and equity securities; e.g., common stocks. The company or other entity issuing the _____ is called the issuer.

a. Tracking stock
c. Securities lending
b. Book entry
d. Security

29. The U.S. _____ is an independent agency of the United States government which holds primary responsibility for enforcing the federal securities laws and regulating the securities industry, the nation's stock and options exchanges, and other electronic securities markets. The SEC was created by section 4 of the SEC of 1934 (now codified as 15 U.S.C. Â§ 78d and commonly referred to as the 1934 Act.)

a. 4-4-5 Calendar
c. 7-Eleven
b. 529 plan
d. Securities and Exchange Commission

Chapter 15. Corporate Valuation, Value-Based Management, and Corporate Governance

30. In law, _____ is to give an immediately secured right of present or future enjoyment. One has a vested right to an asset that cannot be taken away by any third party, even though one may not yet possess the asset. When the right, interest or title to the present or future possession of a legal estate can be transferred to any other party, it is termed a vested interest.
    a. Corporate governance
    b. Limited liability
    c. Competition law
    d. Vesting

31. In economics and finance, _____ is the practice of taking advantage of a price differential between two or more markets: striking a combination of matching deals that capitalize upon the imbalance, the profit being the difference between the market prices. When used by academics, an _____ is a transaction that involves no negative cash flow at any probabilistic or temporal state and a positive cash flow in at least one state; in simple terms, a risk-free profit.
    a. Issuer
    b. Initial margin
    c. Efficient-market hypothesis
    d. Arbitrage

32. The phrase _____ refers to the aspect of corporate strategy, corporate finance and management dealing with the buying, selling and combining of different companies that can aid, finance, or help a growing company in a given industry grow rapidly without having to create another business entity.

    An acquisition, also known as a takeover, is the buying of one company (the 'target') by another. An acquisition may be friendly or hostile.

    a. 7-Eleven
    b. Mergers and acquisitions
    c. 4-4-5 Calendar
    d. 529 plan

33. The _____ of 2002 (Pub.L. 107-204, 116 Stat. 745, enacted July 30, 2002), also known as the Public Company Accounting Reform and Investor Protection Act of 2002 and commonly called Sarbanes-Oxley, Sarbox or SOX, is a United States federal law enacted on July 30, 2002 in response to a number of major corporate and accounting scandals including those affecting Enron, Tyco International, Adelphia, Peregrine Systems and WorldCom.
    a. Sarbanes-Oxley Act
    b. Duty of loyalty
    c. Foreign Corrupt Practices Act
    d. Blue sky law

34. In accounting and organizational theory, _____ is defined as a process effected by an organization's structure, work and authority flows, people and management information systems, designed to help the organization accomplish specific goals or objectives. It is a means by which an organization's resources are directed, monitored, and measured. It plays an important role in preventing and detecting fraud and protecting the organization's resources, both physical (e.g., machinery and property) and intangible (e.g., reputation or intellectual property such as trademarks.)
    a. OTC Bulletin Board
    b. Interest
    c. Internal control
    d. Asian Financial Crisis

35. The term _____ usually refers to a company that is permitted to offer its registered securities for sale to the general public, typically through a stock exchange, or occasionally a company whose stock is traded over the counter via market makers who use non-exchange quotation services.

The term '_____' may also refer to a company owned by the government.

a. First Prudential Markets
c. General partnership
b. Corporation
d. Public Company

36. The _____ (sometimes called 'Peekaboo') is a private-sector, non-profit corporation created by the Sarbanes-Oxley Act, a 2002 United States federal law, to oversee the auditors of public companies. Its stated purpose is to 'protect the interests of investors and further the public interest in the preparation of informative, fair, and independent audit reports'. Although a private entity, the _____ has many government-like regulatory functions, making it in some ways similar to the private Self Regulatory Organizations (SROs) that regulate stock markets and other aspects of the financial markets in the United States.
   a. Gamelan Council
   c. Financial Crimes Enforcement Network
   b. World Trade Organization
   d. Public Company Accounting Oversight Board

37. In finance, a _____ is a type of bond that can be converted into shares of stock in the issuing company, usually at some pre-announced ratio. It is a hybrid security with debt- and equity-like features. Although it typically has a low coupon rate, the holder is compensated with the ability to convert the bond to common stock, usually at a substantial discount to the stock's market value.
   a. Convertible bond
   c. Gilts
   b. Corporate bond
   d. Bond fund

38. _____ is typically a higher ranking stock than voting shares, and its terms are negotiated between the corporation and the investor.

   _____ usually carry no voting rights, but may carry superior priority over common stock in the payment of dividends and upon liquidation. _____ may carry a dividend that is paid out prior to any dividends to common stock holders.
   a. Second lien loan
   c. Trade-off theory
   b. Follow-on offering
   d. Preferred stock

39. A _____ is the price of a single share of a no. of saleable stocks of the company. Once the stock is purchased, the owner becomes a shareholder of the company that issued the share.
   a. Trading curb
   c. Stock split
   b. Whisper numbers
   d. Share price

40. _____ is an estimate of the fair value of corporations and their stocks, by using fundamental economic criteria. This theoretical valuation has to be perfected with market criteria, as the final purpose is to determine potential market prices.
   a. Growth stocks
   c. Security Analysis
   b. Stock valuation
   d. 4-4-5 Calendar

41. In financial accounting, a _____ or statement of financial position is a summary of a person's or organization's balances. Assets, liabilities and ownership equity are listed as of a specific date, such as the end of its financial year. A _____ is often described as a snapshot of a company's financial condition.

180   Chapter 15. Corporate Valuation, Value-Based Management, and Corporate Governance

a. Statement on Auditing Standards No. 70: Service Organizations
b. Statement of retained earnings
c. Financial statements
d. Balance sheet

42. In finance, _____ are stocks that appreciate in value and yield a high return on equity (ROE.) Analysts compute ROE by taking the company's net income and dividing it by the company's equity. To be classified as a growth stock, analysts expect to see at least 15 percent return on equity.

a. Growth stocks
b. Stock valuation
c. 4-4-5 Calendar
d. Security Analysis

43. A _____ is a set of companies with interlocking business relationships and shareholdings. It is a type of business group.

The prototypical _____ are those which appeared in Japan during the 'economic miracle' following World War II.

a. Relative strength Index
b. Keiretsu
c. Stock split
d. Zero-coupon bond

44. The institution most often referenced by the word '_____' is a public or publicly traded _____, the shares of which are traded on a public stock exchange (e.g., the New York Stock Exchange or Nasdaq in the United States) where shares of stock of _____s are bought and sold by and to the general public. Most of the largest businesses in the world are publicly traded _____s. However, the majority of _____s are said to be closely held, privately held or close _____s, meaning that no ready market exists for the trading of shares.

a. Depository Trust Company
b. Federal Home Loan Mortgage Corporation
c. Corporation
d. Protect

45. _____ or financing is to provide capital (funds), which means money for a project, a person, a business or any other private or public institutions.

Those funds can be allocated for either short term or long term purposes. The health fund is a new way of _____ private healthcare centers.

a. Synthetic CDO
b. Proxy fight
c. Product life cycle
d. Funding

46. _____ measures the nominal future sum of money that a given sum of money is 'worth' at a specified time in the future assuming a certain interest rate rate of return; it is the present value multiplied by the accumulation function.

The value does not include corrections for inflation or other factors that affect the true value of money in the future. This is used in time value of money calculations.

a. Future value
b. Present value of costs
c. Discounted cash flow
d. Future-oriented

Chapter 16. Capital Structure Decisions: The Basics

1. In economics, _____ is a measure of the relative satisfaction from or desirability of consumption of various goods and services. Given this measure, one may speak meaningfully of increasing or decreasing _____, and thereby explain economic behavior in terms of attempts to increase one's _____. For illustrative purposes, changes in _____ are sometimes expressed in units called utils.
   a. AAB
   b. Utility function
   c. A Random Walk Down Wall Street
   d. Utility

2. _____ is that which is owed; usually referencing assets owed, but the term can cover other obligations. In the case of assets, _____ is a means of using future purchasing power in the present before a summation has been earned. Some companies and corporations use _____ as a part of their overall corporate finance strategy.
   a. Cross-collateralization
   b. Debt
   c. Partial Payment
   d. Credit cycle

3. _____ is a financial ratio that indicates the percentage of a company's assets are provided via debt. It is the ratio of total debt (the sum of current liabilities and long-term liabilities) and total assets (the sum of current assets, fixed assets, and other assets such as 'goodwill'.)

   ☒ >

   or alternatively:

   ☒ >

   For example, a company with $2 million in total assets and $500,000 in total liabilities would have a _____ of 25%

   Like all financial ratios, a company's _____ should be compared with their industry average or other competing firms.

   a. Capitalization rate
   b. Cash concentration
   c. Cash management
   d. Debt ratio

4. _____ is a business valuation method. _____ is the net present value of a project if financed solely by ownership equity plus the present value of all the benefits of financing. Usually, the main benefit is a tax shield resulted from tax deductibility of interest payments. Another one can be a subsidized borrowing.
   a. ABN Amro
   b. A Random Walk Down Wall Street
   c. Adjusted present value
   d. AAB

5. In economics and finance, _____ is the practice of taking advantage of a price differential between two or more markets: striking a combination of matching deals that capitalize upon the imbalance, the profit being the difference between the market prices. When used by academics, an _____ is a transaction that involves no negative cash flow at any probabilistic or temporal state and a positive cash flow in at least one state; in simple terms, a risk-free profit.
   a. Efficient-market hypothesis
   b. Arbitrage
   c. Issuer
   d. Initial margin

Chapter 16. Capital Structure Decisions: The Basics

6. The phrase _____ refers to the aspect of corporate strategy, corporate finance and management dealing with the buying, selling and combining of different companies that can aid, finance, or help a growing company in a given industry grow rapidly without having to create another business entity.

An acquisition, also known as a takeover, is the buying of one company (the 'target') by another. An acquisition may be friendly or hostile.

a. 529 plan
c. 7-Eleven
b. 4-4-5 Calendar
d. Mergers and acquisitions

7. The _____ is the rate that a company is expected to pay to finance its assets. WACC is the minimum return that a company must earn on existing asset base to satisfy its creditors, owners, and other providers of capital.

Companies raise money from a number of sources: common equity, preferred equity, straight debt, convertible debt, exchangeable debt, warrants, options, pension liabilities, executive stock options, governmental subsidies, and so on.

a. Weighted average cost of capital
c. Capital intensity
b. 4-4-5 Calendar
d. Cost of capital

8. In finance, _____ refers to the way a corporation finances its assets through some combination of equity, debt, or hybrid securities. A firm's _____ is then the composition or 'structure' of its liabilities. For example, a firm that sells $20 billion in equity and $80 billion in debt is said to be 20% equity-financed and 80% debt-financed.

a. Rights issue
c. Market for corporate control
b. Capital structure
d. Book building

9. An _____ is an economic concept that relates to the cost incurred by an entity (such as organizations) associated with problems such as divergent management-shareholder objectives and information asymmetry. The costs consist of two main sources:

1. The costs inherently associated with using an agent (e.g., the risk that agents will use organizational resource for their own benefit) and
2. The costs of techniques used to mitigate the problems associated with using an agent (e.g., the costs of producing financial statements or the use of stock options to align executive interests to shareholder interests.)

Though effects of _____ are present in any agency relationship, the term is most used in business contexts.

The information asymmetry that exists between shareholders and the Chief Executive Officer is generally considered to be a classic example of a principal-agent problem. The agent (the manager) is working on behalf of the principal (the shareholders), who does not observe the actions of the agent.

a. Agency cost
c. A Random Walk Down Wall Street
b. AAB
d. ABN Amro

Chapter 16. Capital Structure Decisions: The Basics 183

10. In business and accounting, _____s are everything of value that is owned by a person or company. The balance sheet of a firm records the monetary value of the _____s owned by the firm. The two major _____ classes are tangible _____s and intangible _____s.
   a. EBITDA
   b. Accounts payable
   c. Asset
   d. Income

11. In finance, _____ is the process of estimating the potential market value of a financial asset or liability. they can be done on assets (for example, investments in marketable securities such as stocks, options, business enterprises, or intangible assets such as patents and trademarks) or on liabilities (e.g., Bonds issued by a company.) _____s are required in many contexts including investment analysis, capital budgeting, merger and acquisition transactions, financial reporting, taxable events to determine the proper tax liability, and in litigation.
   a. Margin
   b. Procter ' Gamble
   c. Share
   d. Valuation

12. In economics and contract theory, _____ deals with the study of decisions in transactions where one party has more or better information than the other. This creates an imbalance of power in transactions which can sometimes cause the transactions to go awry. Examples of this problem are adverse selection and moral hazard.
   a. ABN Amro
   b. A Random Walk Down Wall Street
   c. AAB
   d. Information asymmetry

13. The term _____ has three unrelated technical definitions, and is also used in a variety of non-technical ways.

   - In financial economics, it refers to any asset used to make money, as opposed to assets used for personal enjoyment or consumption. This is an important distinction because two people can disagree sharply about the value of personal assets, one person might think a sports car is more valuable than a pickup truck, another person might have the opposite taste. But if an asset is held for the purpose of making money, taste has nothing to do with it, only differences of opinion about how much money the asset will produce. With the further assumption that people agree on the probability distribution of future cash flows, it is possible to have an objective _____ pricing model. Even without the assumption of agreement, it is possible to set rational limits on _____ value.
   - In governmental accounting, it is defined as any asset used in operations with an initial useful life extending beyond one reporting period. Generally, government managers have a 'stewardship' duty to maintain _____s under their control. See International Public Sector Accounting Standards for details.
   - In US tax accounting, it is defined as any property other than a list of exceptions. The main exceptions are anything held for sale, and any real estate or depreciable property used in business. Almost everything you own and use for personal purposes, pleasure or investment is a _____. If something is a _____ for tax purposes, gains or losses on sale or disposition are capital gains or capital losses. For individuals, however, capital losses on property held for personal use are generally not deductible. See the IRS publication Tax Facts about Capital Gains and Losses for details.

A well-known financial accounting textbook advises that the term be avoided except in tax accounting because it is used in so many different senses, not all of them well-defined. For example it is often used as a synonym for fixed assets or for investments in securities.

A common non-technical usage occurs when people ask that employees or the environment or something else be treated as a _____.

a. Settlement date
b. Solvency
c. Political risk
d. Capital Asset

14. In finance, the _____ is used to determine a theoretically appropriate required rate of return of an asset, if that asset is to be added to an already well-diversified portfolio, given that asset's non-diversifiable risk. The model takes into account the asset's sensitivity to non-diversifiable risk (also known as systemic risk or market risk), often represented by the quantity beta (β) in the financial industry, as well as the expected return of the market and the expected return of a theoretical risk-free asset.

The model was introduced by Jack Treynor (1961, 1962), William Sharpe (1964), John Lintner (1965a,b) and Jan Mossin (1966) independently, building on the earlier work of Harry Markowitz on diversification and modern portfolio theory.

a. Hull-White model
b. Capital Asset Pricing Model
c. Cox-Ingersoll-Ross model
d. Random walk hypothesis

15. _____ is normally any risk associated with any form of financing.

Depending on the nature of the investment, the type of 'investment' risk will vary. High risk investments have greater potential rewards, but you may lose your money instead by taking the risk for more money.

a. Financial risk
b. Revaluation
c. Stock market index option
d. Liquidating dividend

16. _____ is a legally declared inability or impairment of ability of an individual or organization to pay their creditors. Creditors may file a _____ petition against a debtor ('involuntary _____') in an effort to recoup a portion of what they are owed or initiate a restructuring. In the majority of cases, however, _____ is initiated by the debtor (a 'voluntary _____' that is filed by the bankrupt individual or organization.)

a. 529 plan
b. Debt settlement
c. Bankruptcy
d. 4-4-5 Calendar

17. _____ is the balance of the amounts of cash being received and paid by a business during a defined period of time, sometimes tied to a specific project. Measurement of _____ can be used

- to evaluate the state or performance of a business or project.
- to determine problems with liquidity. Being profitable does not necessarily mean being liquid. A company can fail because of a shortage of cash, even while profitable.
- to generate project rate of returns. The time of _____s into and out of projects are used as inputs to financial models such as internal rate of return, and net present value.
- to examine income or growth of a business when it is believed that accrual accounting concepts do not represent economic realities. Alternately, _____ can be used to 'validate' the net income generated by accrual accounting.

_____ as a generic term may be used differently depending on context, and certain _____ definitions may be adapted by analysts and users for their own uses. Common terms include operating _____ and free _____.

Chapter 16. Capital Structure Decisions: The Basics

_____s can be classified into:

1. Operational _____s: Cash received or expended as a result of the company's core business activities.
2. Investment _____s: Cash received or expended through capital expenditure, investments or acquisitions.
3. Financing _____s: Cash received or expended as a result of financial activities, such as interests and dividends.

All three together - the net _____ - are necessary to reconcile the beginning cash balance to the ending cash balance. Loan draw downs or equity injections, that is just shifting of capital but no expenditure as such, are not considered in the net _____.

a. Corporate finance
b. Cash flow
c. Shareholder value
d. Real option

18. In economics, business, and accounting, a _____ is the value of money that has been used up to produce something, and hence is not available for use anymore. In business, the _____ may be one of acquisition, in which case the amount of money expended to acquire it is counted as _____. In this case, money is the input that is gone in order to acquire the thing.

a. Marginal cost
b. Cost
c. Sliding scale fees
d. Fixed costs

19. _____ or financing is to provide capital (funds), which means money for a project, a person, a business or any other private or public institutions.

Those funds can be allocated for either short term or long term purposes. The health fund is a new way of _____ private healthcare centers.

a. Proxy fight
b. Product life cycle
c. Synthetic CDO
d. Funding

20. In corporate finance, _____ is a cash flow available for distribution among all the security holders of a company. They include equity holders, debt holders, preferred stock holders, convertible security holders, and so on.

Note that the first three lines above are calculated for you on the standard Statement of Cash Flows.

a. Safety stock
b. Funding
c. Free cash flow
d. Forfaiting

21. _____, is when a company issues common stock or shares to the public for the first time. They are often issued by smaller, younger companies seeking capital to expand, but can also be done by large privately-owned companies looking to become publicly traded.

In an _____ the issuer may obtain the assistance of an underwriting firm, which helps it determine what type of security to issue (common or preferred), best offering price and time to bring it to market.

a. Asian Financial Crisis
c. Insolvency
b. Interest
d. Initial public offering

22. An _____ is a lease whose term is short compared to the useful life of the asset or piece of equipment (an airliner, a ship etc.) being leased. An _____ is commonly used to acquire equipment on a relatively short-term basis.

a. ABN Amro
c. AAB
b. Operating lease
d. A Random Walk Down Wall Street

23. _____ is the area of law in which manufacturers, distributors, suppliers, retailers, and others who make products available to the public are held responsible for the injuries those products cause.

In the United States, the claims most commonly associated with _____ are negligence, strict liability, breach of warranty, and various consumer protection claims. The majority of _____ laws are determined at the state level and vary widely from state to state.

a. Foreclosure
c. Family and Medical Leave Act
b. Product liability
d. Business valuation

24. The institution most often referenced by the word '_____' is a public or publicly traded _____, the shares of which are traded on a public stock exchange (e.g., the New York Stock Exchange or Nasdaq in the United States) where shares of stock of _____s are bought and sold by and to the general public. Most of the largest businesses in the world are publicly traded _____s. However, the majority of _____s are said to be closely held, privately held or close _____s, meaning that no ready market exists for the trading of shares.

a. Corporation
c. Federal Home Loan Mortgage Corporation
b. Protect
d. Depository Trust Company

25. Leasing is a process by which a firm can obtain the use of a certain fixed assets for which it must pay a series of contractual, periodic, tax deductable payments. The lessee is the receiver of the services or the assets under the lease contract and the lessor is the owner of the assets. The relationship between the tenant and the landlord is called a _____, and can be for a fixed or an indefinite period of time (called the term of the lease.)

a. Tenancy
c. Real Estate Investment Trust
b. REIT
d. Real estate investing

26. In finance, _____ (or gearing) is borrowing money to supplement existing funds for investment in such a way that the potential positive or negative outcome is magnified and/or enhanced. It generally refers to using borrowed funds, or debt, so as to attempt to increase the returns to equity. Deleveraging is the action of reducing borrowings.

a. Financial endowment
c. Leverage
b. Pension fund
d. Limited partnership

27. In the most general sense, a _____ is anything that is a hindrance, or puts individuals at a disadvantage.

Chapter 16. Capital Structure Decisions: The Basics

Before we discuss the financial terms, we should note that a _____ can also have a much more important slang meaning.

This is best described in an example.

a. Covenant
b. Limited liability
c. McFadden Act
d. Liability

28. The _____ is a measure of how revenue growth translates into growth in operating income. It is a measure of leverage, and of how risky (volatile) a company's operating income is.

There are various measures of _____, which can be interpreted analogously to financial leverage.

a. Invested capital
b. Operating leverage
c. Average accounting return
d. Asset turnover

29. In economics and business, specifically cost accounting, the _____ is the point at which cost or expenses and revenue are equal: there is no net loss or gain, and one has 'broken even'. A profit or a loss has not been made, although opportunity costs have been paid, and capital has received the risk-adjusted, expected return.

For example, if the business sells less than 200 tables each month, it will make a loss, if it sells more, it will be a profit.

a. Market microstructure
b. Fixed asset turnover
c. Defined contribution plan
d. Break-even point

30. A standard, commercial _____ is a document issued mostly by a financial institution, used primarily in trade finance, which usually provides an irrevocable payment undertaking.

The _____ can also be the source of payment for a transaction, meaning that redeeming the _____ will pay an exporter. Letters of credit are used primarily in international trade transactions of significant value, for deals between a supplier in one country and a customer in another.

a. Bond indenture
b. Duty of loyalty
c. McFadden Act
d. Letter of credit

31. _____ measures the rate of return on the ownership interest (shareholders' equity) of the common stock owners. _____ is viewed as one of the most important financial ratios. It measures a firm's efficiency at generating profits from every dollar of shareholders' equity (also known as net assets or assets minus liabilities.)

a. Return of capital
b. Diluted Earnings Per Share
c. Return on sales
d. Return on equity

Chapter 16. Capital Structure Decisions: The Basics

32. _____ is the provision of resources (such as granting a loan) by one party to another party where that second party does not reimburse the first party immediately, thereby generating a debt, and instead arranges either to repay or return those resources (or material(s) of equal value) at a later date. The first party is called a creditor, also known as a lender, while the second party is called a debtor, also known as a borrower.

Movements of financial capital are normally dependent on either _____ or equity transfers.

a. Warrant
b. Clearing house
c. Comparable
d. Credit

33. A _____ is a profit that results from investments into a capital asset, such as stocks, bonds or real estate, which exceeds the purchase price. It is the difference between a higher selling price and a lower purchase price, resulting in a financial gain for the seller. Conversely, a capital loss arises if the proceeds from the sale of a capital asset are less than the purchase price.

a. Tax brackets
b. Capital gain
c. Payroll tax
d. Capital gains tax

34. In finance, a _____ is a debt security, in which the authorized issuer owes the holders a debt and, depending on the terms of the _____, is obliged to pay interest (the coupon) and/or to repay the principal at a later date, termed maturity.

Thus a _____ is a loan: the issuer is the borrower, the _____ holder is the lender, and the coupon is the interest. _____s provide the borrower with external funds to finance long-term investments, or, in the case of government _____s, to finance current expenditure.

a. Convertible bond
b. Bond
c. Puttable bond
d. Catastrophe bonds

35. _____ is the concept of adding accumulated interest back to the principal, so that interest is earned on interest from that moment on. The act of declaring interest to be principal is called compounding (i.e., interest is compounded.) A loan, for example, may have its interest compounded every month: in this case, a loan with $100 principal and 1% interest per month would have a balance of $101 at the end of the first month.

a. Penny stock
b. 4-4-5 Calendar
c. Compound interest
d. Risk management

36. A _____ is a financial contract whose value is derived from the value of something else (known as the underlying.) The underlying on which a _____ is based can be an asset, weather conditions bonds or other forms of credit.

a. 7-Eleven
b. 4-4-5 Calendar
c. 529 plan
d. Derivative

37. _____ occurs when an entity that has issued callable bonds calls those debt securities from the debt holders with the express purpose of reissuing new debt at a lower coupon rate. In essence, the issue of new, lower-interest debt allows the company to prematurely refund the older, higher-interest debt.

On the contrary, NonRefundable Bonds may be callable but they cannot be re-issued with a lower coupon rate.

Chapter 16. Capital Structure Decisions: The Basics

a. Systematic risk
b. No-arbitrage bounds
c. Refunding
d. Market neutral

38. _____ is the process of decreasing an amount over a period of time. The word comes from Middle English amortisen to kill, alienate in mortmain, from Anglo-French amorteser, alteration of amortir, from Vulgar Latin admortire to kill, from Latin ad- + mort-, mors death. Particular instances of the term include:

- _____ (business), the allocation of a lump sum amount to different time periods, particularly for loans and other forms of finance, including related interest or other finance charges.
  - _____ schedule, a table detailing each periodic payment on a loan (typically a mortgage), as generated by an _____ calculator.
  - Negative _____, an _____ schedule where the loan amount actually increases through not paying the full interest
- Amortized analysis, analyzing the execution cost of algorithms over a sequence of operations.
- _____ of capital expenditures of certain assets under accounting rules, particularly intangible assets, in a manner analogous to depreciation.
- _____ (tax law)

_____ is also used in the context of zoning regulations and describes the time in which a property owner has to relocate when the property's use constitutes a preexisting nonconforming use under zoning regulations.

- Depreciation

a. Intrinsic value
b. Option
c. Amortization
d. AT'T Inc.

39. _____ is a fee paid on borrowed assets. It is the price paid for the use of borrowed money , or, money earned by deposited funds . Assets that are sometimes lent with _____ include money, shares, consumer goods through hire purchase, major assets such as aircraft, and even entire factories in finance lease arrangements.

a. A Random Walk Down Wall Street
b. AAB
c. Interest
d. Insolvency

40. _____ is a life of security. It may also refer to the final payment date of a loan or other financial instrument, at which point all remaining interest and principal is due to be paid.

1, 3, 6 months _____ band can be calculated by using 30-day per month periods.

a. Replacement cost
b. False billing
c. Primary market
d. Maturity

41. A _____ is a fungible, negotiable instrument representing financial value. They are broadly categorized into debt securities (such as banknotes, bonds and debentures), and equity securities; e.g., common stocks. The company or other entity issuing the _____ is called the issuer.

a. Tracking stock
b. Book entry
c. Securities lending
d. Security

42. The U.S. _____ is an independent agency of the United States government which holds primary responsibility for enforcing the federal securities laws and regulating the securities industry, the nation's stock and options exchanges, and other electronic securities markets. The SEC was created by section 4 of the SEC of 1934 (now codified as 15 U.S.C. Â§ 78d and commonly referred to as the 1934 Act.)
a. 4-4-5 Calendar
b. 529 plan
c. Securities and Exchange Commission
d. 7-Eleven

43. A _____ is a situation that involves losing one quality or aspect of something in return for gaining another quality or aspect. It implies a decision to be made with full comprehension of both the upside and downside of a particular choice.

In economics the term is expressed as opportunity cost, referring the most preferred alternative given up.

a. Capital outflow
b. Total revenue
c. Break-even point
d. Trade-off

44. The _____ of Capital Structure refers to the idea that a company chooses how much debt finance and how much equity finance to use by balancing the costs and benefits. The classical version of the hypothesis goes back to Kraus and Litzenberger who considered a balance between the dead-weight costs of bankruptcy and the tax saving benefits of debt. Often agency costs are also included in the balance.
a. Financial distress
b. Rights issue
c. Trade-off theory
d. Firm commitment

45. In United States banking, _____ is a marketing term for certain services offered primarily to larger business customers. It may be used to describe all bank accounts (such as checking accounts) provided to businesses of a certain size, but it is more often used to describe specific services such as cash concentration, zero balance accounting, and automated clearing house facilities. Sometimes, private banking customers are given _____ services.
a. Global tactical asset allocation
b. Profitability index
c. Capitalization rate
d. Cash management

46. _____ is the set of processes, customs, policies, laws and institutions affecting the way a corporation is directed, administered or controlled. _____ also includes the relationships among the many stakeholders involved and the goals for which the corporation is governed. The principal stakeholders are the shareholders, management and the board of directors.
a. Foreign Corrupt Practices Act
b. Patent
c. Due diligence
d. Corporate governance

47. _____ is a term used in accounting, economics and finance to spread the cost of an asset over the span of several years.

In simple words we can say that _____ is the reduction in the value of an asset due to usage, passage of time, wear and tear, technological outdating or obsolescence, depletion or other such factors.

In accounting, _____ is a term used to describe any method of attributing the historical or purchase cost of an asset across its useful life, roughly corresponding to normal wear and tear.

a. Matching principle
c. Bottom line
b. Deferred financing costs
d. Depreciation

48. A _____ occurs when a financial sponsor acquires a controlling interest in a company's equity and where a significant percentage of the purchase price is financed through leverage (borrowing.) The assets of the acquired company are used as collateral for the borrowed capital, sometimes with assets of the acquiring company. The bonds or other paper issued for _____s are commonly considered not to be investment grade because of the significant risks involved.

a. Limited partnership
c. Leverage
b. Pension fund
d. Leveraged buyout

49. _____ is a term in Corporate Finance used to indicate a condition when promises to creditors of a company are broken or honored with difficulty. Sometimes _____ can lead to bankruptcy. _____ is usually associated with some costs to the company and these are known as Costs of _____.

a. Financial distress
c. Commercial paper
b. Capital structure
d. Cashflow matching

50. The _____ is an expected return that the provider of capital plans to earn on their investment.

Capital (money) used for funding a business should earn returns for the capital providers who risk their capital. For an investment to be worthwhile, the expected return on capital must be greater than the _____.

a. 4-4-5 Calendar
c. Cost of capital
b. Weighted average cost of capital
d. Capital intensity

51. _____ is part of the Federal income tax system of the United States. There is an _____ for those who owe personal income tax, and another for corporations owing corporate income tax. Only the _____ for those owing personal income tax is described here.

The _____ operates in effect as a parallel tax system, with its own definition of taxable income, exemptions, and tax rates. Taxpayers compute tax owed under the 'regular' and _____ systems and are liable for whichever is higher.

a. ABN Amro
c. AAB
b. Alternative minimum tax
d. A Random Walk Down Wall Street

52. A _____ is a payment made by a corporation to its shareholder members. When a corporation earns a profit or surplus, that money can be put to two uses: it can either be re-invested in the business (called retained earnings), or it can be paid to the shareholders as a _____. Many corporations retain a portion of their earnings and pay the remainder as a _____.

a. Dividend yield
c. Special dividend
b. Dividend puzzle
d. Dividend

Chapter 16. Capital Structure Decisions: The Basics

53. The _____ is one of several stock market indices, created by nineteenth-century Wall Street Journal editor and Dow Jones ' Company co-founder Charles Dow. Dow compiled the index to gauge the performance of the industrial sector of the American stock market. It is the second-oldest U.S. market index, after the Dow Jones Transportation Average, which Dow also created.
   a. 529 plan
   b. 7-Eleven
   c. 4-4-5 Calendar
   d. Dow Jones Industrial Average

54. A _____ is an international bond that is denominated in a currency not native to the country where it is issued. It can be categorised according to the currency in which it is issued. London is one of the centers of the _____ market, but _____s may be traded throughout the world - for example in Singapore or Tokyo.
   a. Education production function
   b. Economic entity
   c. Eurobond
   d. Interest rate option

55. In finance, a _____ (non-investment grade bond, speculative grade bond or junk bond) is a bond that is rated below investment grade at the time of purchase. These bonds have a higher risk of default or other adverse credit events, but typically pay higher yields than better quality bonds in order to make them attractive to investors.
   a. Private equity
   b. Volatility
   c. Sharpe ratio
   d. High yield bond

56. _____ are a class of computational algorithms that rely on repeated random sampling to compute their results. _____ are often used when simulating physical and mathematical systems. Because of their reliance on repeated computation and random or pseudo-random numbers, _____ are most suited to calculation by a computer.

_____ in finance are often used to calculate the value of companies, to evaluate investments in projects at corporate level or to evaluate financial derivatives. The method is intended for financial analysts who want to construct stochastic or probabilistic financial models as opposed to the traditional static and deterministic models.

   a. Sample size
   b. Correlation
   c. Semivariance
   d. Monte Carlo methods

57. A _____ is a private or public market for the trading of company stock and derivatives of company stock at an agreed price; these are securities listed on a stock exchange as well as those only traded privately.

The size of the world _____ is estimated at about $36.6 trillion US at the beginning of October 2008 . The world derivatives market has been estimated at about $480 trillion face or nominal value, 12 times the size of the entire world economy.

   a. Anton Gelonkin
   b. Stock market
   c. Adolph Coors
   d. Andrew Tobias

58. A _____ is the direction in which a financial market is moving. _____s can be classified as primary trends, secondary trends (short-term), and secular trends (long-term.) This principle incorporates the idea that market cycles occur with regularity and persistence.
   a. 4-4-5 Calendar
   b. 529 plan
   c. 7-Eleven
   d. Market trend

Chapter 16. Capital Structure Decisions: The Basics

59. In Modern Portfolio Theory, the _____ is the graphical representation of the Capital Asset Pricing Model. It displays the expected rate of return for an overall market as a function of systematic (non-diversifiable) risk (beta.)

The Y-Intercept (beta=0) of the _____ is equal to the risk-free interest rate.

  a. Divestment
  c. Rebalancing
  b. Security Market Line
  d. Certificate in Investment Performance Measurement

60. _____ is a financial measure used to determine the attractiveness of an investment. It is generally used as part of a capital budgeting process to rank various alternative choices. It is a modification of the Internal Rate of Return (IRR).

_____ ranks project efficiency consistently with the present worth ratio (variant of NPV/Discounted Negative Cash Flow), considered the gold standard in many finance textbooks.

MIRR is calculated as follows:

where n is the number of (equal) periods in which the cash flows occur.

  a. Binomial options pricing model
  c. Black-Scholes
  b. Current yield
  d. Modified Internal Rate of Return

61. _____ identifies the relationship of investment to payoff of a proposed project. The ratio is calculated as follows:

_____ is also known as Profit Investment Ratio, abbreviated to P.I. and Value Investment Ratio (V.I.R.). _____ is a good tool for ranking projects because it allows you to clearly identify the amount of value created per unit of investment, thus if you are capital constrained you wish to invest in those projects which create value most efficiently first.

  a. Total return
  c. Conditional prepayment rate
  b. Capitalization rate
  d. Profitability index

62. _____ is an estimate of the fair value of corporations and their stocks, by using fundamental economic criteria. This theoretical valuation has to be perfected with market criteria, as the final purpose is to determine potential market prices.

  a. Stock valuation
  c. Growth stocks
  b. 4-4-5 Calendar
  d. Security Analysis

63. _____ is the process of determining the fair price of a bond. As with any security or capital investment, the fair value of a bond is the present value of the stream of cash flows it is expected to generate. Hence, the price or value of a bond is determined by discounting the bond's expected cash flows to the present using the appropriate discount rate.
    a. Collateralized debt obligations
    b. Bond valuation
    c. Bond fund
    d. Catastrophe bonds

64. A _____ is the price of a single share of a no. of saleable stocks of the company. Once the stock is purchased, the owner becomes a shareholder of the company that issued the share.
    a. Whisper numbers
    b. Stock split
    c. Share price
    d. Trading curb

65. In some countries, including the United States and the United Kingdom, corporations can buy back their own stock in a share repurchase, also known as a _____ or share buyback. There has been a meteoric rise in the use of share repurchases in the U.S. in the past twenty years, from $5b in 1980 to $349b in 2005. A share repurchase distributes cash to existing shareholders in exchange for a fraction of the firm's outstanding equity.
    a. Trading curb
    b. Stock repurchase
    c. Common stock
    d. Stockholder

Chapter 17. Capital Structure Decisions: Extensions

1. In finance, _____ refers to the way a corporation finances its assets through some combination of equity, debt, or hybrid securities. A firm's _____ is then the composition or 'structure' of its liabilities. For example, a firm that sells $20 billion in equity and $80 billion in debt is said to be 20% equity-financed and 80% debt-financed.
   a. Market for corporate control
   b. Book building
   c. Rights issue
   d. Capital structure

2. _____ is part of the Federal income tax system of the United States. There is an _____ for those who owe personal income tax, and another for corporations owing corporate income tax. Only the _____ for those owing personal income tax is described here.

   The _____ operates in effect as a parallel tax system, with its own definition of taxable income, exemptions, and tax rates. Taxpayers compute tax owed under the 'regular' and _____ systems and are liable for whichever is higher.

   a. A Random Walk Down Wall Street
   b. ABN Amro
   c. AAB
   d. Alternative minimum tax

3. In economics and finance, _____ is the practice of taking advantage of a price differential between two or more markets: striking a combination of matching deals that capitalize upon the imbalance, the profit being the difference between the market prices. When used by academics, an _____ is a transaction that involves no negative cash flow at any probabilistic or temporal state and a positive cash flow in at least one state; in simple terms, a risk-free profit.
   a. Initial margin
   b. Efficient-market hypothesis
   c. Arbitrage
   d. Issuer

4. _____ is a term used in accounting, economics and finance to spread the cost of an asset over the span of several years.

   In simple words we can say that _____ is the reduction in the value of an asset due to usage, passage of time, wear and tear, technological outdating or obsolescence, depletion or other such factors.

   In accounting, _____ is a term used to describe any method of attributing the historical or purchase cost of an asset across its useful life, roughly corresponding to normal wear and tear.

   a. Matching principle
   b. Deferred financing costs
   c. Bottom line
   d. Depreciation

5. A _____ is a payment made by a corporation to its shareholder members. When a corporation earns a profit or surplus, that money can be put to two uses: it can either be re-invested in the business (called retained earnings), or it can be paid to the shareholders as a _____. Many corporations retain a portion of their earnings and pay the remainder as a _____.
   a. Special dividend
   b. Dividend yield
   c. Dividend puzzle
   d. Dividend

6. The phrase _____ refers to the aspect of corporate strategy, corporate finance and management dealing with the buying, selling and combining of different companies that can aid, finance, or help a growing company in a given industry grow rapidly without having to create another business entity.

Chapter 17. Capital Structure Decisions: Extensions

An acquisition, also known as a takeover, is the buying of one company (the 'target') by another. An acquisition may be friendly or hostile.

    a. 529 plan
    b. 7-Eleven
    c. Mergers and acquisitions
    d. 4-4-5 Calendar

7. _____ or financing is to provide capital (funds), which means money for a project, a person, a business or any other private or public institutions.

Those funds can be allocated for either short term or long term purposes. The health fund is a new way of _____ private healthcare centers.

    a. Proxy fight
    b. Product life cycle
    c. Synthetic CDO
    d. Funding

8. _____ is the set of processes, customs, policies, laws and institutions affecting the way a corporation is directed, administered or controlled. _____ also includes the relationships among the many stakeholders involved and the goals for which the corporation is governed. The principal stakeholders are the shareholders, management and the board of directors.

    a. Corporate governance
    b. Patent
    c. Due diligence
    d. Foreign Corrupt Practices Act

9. A _____ is a profit that results from investments into a capital asset, such as stocks, bonds or real estate, which exceeds the purchase price. It is the difference between a higher selling price and a lower purchase price, resulting in a financial gain for the seller. Conversely, a capital loss arises if the proceeds from the sale of a capital asset are less than the purchase price.

    a. Capital gains tax
    b. Tax brackets
    c. Payroll tax
    d. Capital gain

10. In finance, _____ is the process of estimating the potential market value of a financial asset or liability. they can be done on assets (for example, investments in marketable securities such as stocks, options, business enterprises, or intangible assets such as patents and trademarks) or on liabilities (e.g., Bonds issued by a company.) _____s are required in many contexts including investment analysis, capital budgeting, merger and acquisition transactions, financial reporting, taxable events to determine the proper tax liability, and in litigation.

    a. Procter ' Gamble
    b. Valuation
    c. Share
    d. Margin

11. In finance, _____ or 'shorting' is the practice of selling a financial instrument that the seller does not own at the time of the sale. _____ is done with intent of later purchasing the financial instrument at a lower price. Short-sellers attempt to profit from an expected decline in the price of a financial instrument.

    a. Short ratio
    b. 529 plan
    c. Short selling
    d. 4-4-5 Calendar

12. _____ refers to a tax levied by various jurisdictions on the profits made by companies or associations. It is a tax on the value of the corporation's profits.

The measure of taxable profits varies from country to country.

a. Corporate tax
b. First-mover advantage
c. Proxy fight
d. Trade finance

13. In finance, _____ (or gearing) is borrowing money to supplement existing funds for investment in such a way that the potential positive or negative outcome is magnified and/or enhanced. It generally refers to using borrowed funds, or debt, so as to attempt to increase the returns to equity. Deleveraging is the action of reducing borrowings.

a. Pension fund
b. Limited partnership
c. Financial endowment
d. Leverage

14. A _____ is the reduction in income taxes that results from taking an allowable deduction from taxable income. For example, because interest on debt is a tax-deductible expense, taking on debt creates a _____. Since a _____ is a way to save cash flows, it increases the value of the business, and it is an important aspect of business valuation.

a. Present value of benefits
b. Present value of costs
c. Refinancing risk
d. Tax shield

15. In economics, business, and accounting, a _____ is the value of money that has been used up to produce something, and hence is not available for use anymore. In business, the _____ may be one of acquisition, in which case the amount of money expended to acquire it is counted as _____. In this case, money is the input that is gone in order to acquire the thing.

a. Cost
b. Fixed costs
c. Marginal cost
d. Sliding scale fees

16. In finance, the _____ is the minimum rate of return a firm must offer shareholders to compensate for waiting for their returns, and for bearing some risk.

The _____ capital for a particular company is the rate of return on investment that is required by the company's ordinary shareholders. The return consists both of dividend and capital gains, e.g. increases in the share price.

a. Residual value
b. Cost of equity
c. Round-tripping
d. Net pay

17. _____ is a life of security. It may also refer to the final payment date of a loan or other financial instrument, at which point all remaining interest and principal is due to be paid.

1, 3, 6 months _____ band can be calculated by using 30-day per month periods.

a. Primary market
b. Replacement cost
c. False billing
d. Maturity

Chapter 17. Capital Structure Decisions: Extensions

18. An _____ is a contract written by a seller that conveys to the buyer the right -- but not the obligation -- to buy (in the case of a call _____) or to sell (in the case of a put _____) a particular asset, such as a piece of property such as, among others, a futures contract. In return for granting the _____, the seller collects a payment (the premium) from the buyer.

For example, buying a call _____ provides the right to buy a specified quantity of a security at a set strike price at some time on or before expiration, while buying a put _____ provides the right to sell.

　a. AT'T Mobility LLC　　　　　　　　　　　b. Option
　c. Annuity　　　　　　　　　　　　　　　　d. Amortization

19. _____ is typically a higher ranking stock than voting shares, and its terms are negotiated between the corporation and the investor.

_____ usually carry no voting rights, but may carry superior priority over common stock in the payment of dividends and upon liquidation. _____ may carry a dividend that is paid out prior to any dividends to common stock holders.

　a. Second lien loan　　　　　　　　　　　b. Follow-on offering
　c. Trade-off theory　　　　　　　　　　　d. Preferred stock

20. _____ occurs when an entity that has issued callable bonds calls those debt securities from the debt holders with the express purpose of reissuing new debt at a lower coupon rate. In essence, the issue of new, lower-interest debt allows the company to prematurely refund the older, higher-interest debt.

On the contrary, NonRefundable Bonds may be callable but they cannot be re-issued with a lower coupon rate.

　a. No-arbitrage bounds　　　　　　　　　b. Refunding
　c. Systematic risk　　　　　　　　　　　　d. Market neutral

21. _____ is an estimate of the fair value of corporations and their stocks, by using fundamental economic criteria. This theoretical valuation has to be perfected with market criteria, as the final purpose is to determine potential market prices.
　a. Security Analysis　　　　　　　　　　　b. Growth stocks
　c. 4-4-5 Calendar　　　　　　　　　　　　d. Stock valuation

22. In financial accounting, a _____ or statement of financial position is a summary of a person's or organization's balances. Assets, liabilities and ownership equity are listed as of a specific date, such as the end of its financial year. A _____ is often described as a snapshot of a company's financial condition.

　a. Statement of retained earnings　　　　b. Statement on Auditing Standards No. 70: Service Organizations
　c. Financial statements　　　　　　　　　d. Balance sheet

23. In finance, a _____ is a debt security, in which the authorized issuer owes the holders a debt and, depending on the terms of the _____, is obliged to pay interest (the coupon) and/or to repay the principal at a later date, termed maturity.

Chapter 17. Capital Structure Decisions: Extensions

Thus a _____ is a loan: the issuer is the borrower, the _____ holder is the lender, and the coupon is the interest. _____s provide the borrower with external funds to finance long-term investments, or, in the case of government _____s, to finance current expenditure.

a. Bond
b. Catastrophe bonds
c. Convertible bond
d. Puttable bond

24. _____ is the process of determining the fair price of a bond. As with any security or capital investment, the fair value of a bond is the present value of the stream of cash flows it is expected to generate. Hence, the price or value of a bond is determined by discounting the bond's expected cash flows to the present using the appropriate discount rate.

a. Catastrophe bonds
b. Collateralized debt obligations
c. Bond fund
d. Bond valuation

25. A _____ is a financial contract between two parties, the buyer and the seller of this type of option. Often it is simply labeled a 'call'. The buyer of the option has the right, but not the obligation to buy an agreed quantity of a particular commodity or financial instrument (the underlying instrument) from the seller of the option at a certain time (the expiration date) for a certain price (the strike price.)

a. Bull spread
b. Bear call spread
c. Bear spread
d. Call option

26. _____ is the planning process used to determine whether a firm's long term investments such as new machinery, replacement machinery, new plants, new products, and research development projects are worth pursuing. It is budget for major capital, or investment, expenditures.

Many formal methods are used in _____, including the techniques such as

- Net present value
- Profitability index
- Internal rate of return
- Modified Internal Rate of Return
- Equivalent annuity

These methods use the incremental cash flows from each potential investment, or project. Techniques based on accounting earnings and accounting rules are sometimes used - though economists consider this to be improper - such as the accounting rate of return, and 'return on investment.' Simplified and hybrid methods are used as well, such as payback period and discounted payback period.

a. Shareholder value
b. Preferred stock
c. Capital budgeting
d. Financial distress

27. _____ is that which is owed; usually referencing assets owed, but the term can cover other obligations. In the case of assets, _____ is a means of using future purchasing power in the present before a summation has been earned. Some companies and corporations use _____ as a part of their overall corporate finance strategy.

a. Partial Payment
b. Cross-collateralization
c. Credit cycle
d. Debt

28. In financial mathematics, _____ defines a relationship between the price of a call option and a put option--both with the identical strike price and expiry. To derive the _____ relationship, the assumption is that the options are not exercised before expiration day, which necessarily applies to European options. _____ can be derived in a manner that is largely model independent.
   a. Put-call parity
   b. Cox-Ingersoll-Ross model
   c. Rendleman-Bartter model
   d. Hull-White model

29. In business and finance, a _____ (also referred to as equity _____) of stock means a _____ of ownership in a corporation (company.) In the plural, stocks is often used as a synonym for _____s especially in the United States, but it is less commonly used that way outside of North America.

In the United Kingdom, South Africa, and Australia, stock can also refer to completely different financial instruments such as government bonds or, less commonly, to all kinds of marketable securities.

   a. Margin
   b. Bucket shop
   c. Share
   d. Procter ' Gamble

30. _____ is a legally declared inability or impairment of ability of an individual or organization to pay their creditors. Creditors may file a _____ petition against a debtor ('involuntary _____') in an effort to recoup a portion of what they are owed or initiate a restructuring. In the majority of cases, however, _____ is initiated by the debtor (a 'voluntary _____' that is filed by the bankrupt individual or organization.)
   a. 4-4-5 Calendar
   b. 529 plan
   c. Debt settlement
   d. Bankruptcy

31. In United States banking, _____ is a marketing term for certain services offered primarily to larger business customers. It may be used to describe all bank accounts (such as checking accounts) provided to businesses of a certain size, but it is more often used to describe specific services such as cash concentration, zero balance accounting, and automated clearing house facilities. Sometimes, private banking customers are given _____ services.
   a. Cash management
   b. Global tactical asset allocation
   c. Profitability index
   d. Capitalization rate

32. In retail sales, a _____ is a form of fraud in which the party putting forth the fraud lures in customers by advertising a product or service at an unprofitably low price, then reveals to potential customers that the advertised good is not available but that a substitute is. This term has lots of other meanings, even outside of the marketing sense.

The goal of the _____ is to convince some buyers to purchase the substitute good as a means of avoiding disappointment over not getting the bait, or as a way to recover sunk costs expended to try to obtain the bait.

   a. Price-to-book ratio
   b. Time value of money
   c. Bait and switch
   d. Zero-coupon bond

Chapter 17. Capital Structure Decisions: Extensions

33. In business and accounting, _____s are everything of value that is owned by a person or company. The balance sheet of a firm records the monetary value of the _____s owned by the firm. The two major _____ classes are tangible _____s and intangible _____s.
   a. Asset
   b. Income
   c. Accounts payable
   d. EBITDA

34. In finance, a _____ is a type of bond that can be converted into shares of stock in the issuing company, usually at some pre-announced ratio. It is a hybrid security with debt- and equity-like features. Although it typically has a low coupon rate, the holder is compensated with the ability to convert the bond to common stock, usually at a substantial discount to the stock's market value.
   a. Gilts
   b. Bond fund
   c. Convertible bond
   d. Corporate bond

35. A _____ is a fungible, negotiable instrument representing financial value. They are broadly categorized into debt securities (such as banknotes, bonds and debentures), and equity securities; e.g., common stocks. The company or other entity issuing the _____ is called the issuer.
   a. Security
   b. Book entry
   c. Securities lending
   d. Tracking stock

36. The coupon or _____ of a bond is the amount of interest paid per year expressed as a percentage of the face value of the bond.

For example if you hold $10,000 nominal of a bond described as a 4.5% loan stock, you will receive $450 in interest each year (probably in two installments of $225 each.)

Not all bonds have coupons.

   a. Puttable bond
   b. Zero-coupon bond
   c. Revenue bonds
   d. Coupon rate

37. A _____ is a situation that involves losing one quality or aspect of something in return for gaining another quality or aspect. It implies a decision to be made with full comprehension of both the upside and downside of a particular choice.

In economics the term is expressed as opportunity cost, referring the most preferred alternative given up.

   a. Break-even point
   b. Capital outflow
   c. Total revenue
   d. Trade-off

38. The _____ of Capital Structure refers to the idea that a company chooses how much debt finance and how much equity finance to use by balancing the costs and benefits. The classical version of the hypothesis goes back to Kraus and Litzenberger who considered a balance between the dead-weight costs of bankruptcy and the tax saving benefits of debt. Often agency costs are also included in the balance.
   a. Financial distress
   b. Firm commitment
   c. Rights issue
   d. Trade-off theory

39. In economics and contract theory, _____ deals with the study of decisions in transactions where one party has more or better information than the other. This creates an imbalance of power in transactions which can sometimes cause the transactions to go awry. Examples of this problem are adverse selection and moral hazard.
   a. A Random Walk Down Wall Street
   b. ABN Amro
   c. AAB
   d. Information asymmetry

Chapter 18. Distributions to Shareholders: Dividends and Repurchases

1. A _____ is a payment made by a corporation to its shareholder members. When a corporation earns a profit or surplus, that money can be put to two uses: it can either be re-invested in the business (called retained earnings), or it can be paid to the shareholders as a _____. Many corporations retain a portion of their earnings and pay the remainder as a _____.

   a. Dividend yield
   b. Special dividend
   c. Dividend puzzle
   d. Dividend

2. _____ is a business valuation method. _____ is the net present value of a project if financed solely by ownership equity plus the present value of all the benefits of financing. Usually, the main benefit is a tax shield resulted from tax deductibility of interest payments. Another one can be a subsidized borrowing.

   a. AAB
   b. ABN Amro
   c. Adjusted present value
   d. A Random Walk Down Wall Street

3. In economics and contract theory, _____ deals with the study of decisions in transactions where one party has more or better information than the other. This creates an imbalance of power in transactions which can sometimes cause the transactions to go awry. Examples of this problem are adverse selection and moral hazard.

   a. A Random Walk Down Wall Street
   b. Information asymmetry
   c. AAB
   d. ABN Amro

4. _____ is the fraction of net income a firm pays to its stockholders in dividends:

The part of the earnings not paid to investors is left for investment to provide for future earnings growth. Investors seeking high current income and limited capital growth prefer companies with high _____. However investors seeking capital growth may prefer lower payout ratio because capital gains are taxed at a lower rate.

   a. Dividend payout ratio
   b. Dividend puzzle
   c. Dividend imputation
   d. Dividend yield

5. _____ is the set of processes, customs, policies, laws and institutions affecting the way a corporation is directed, administered or controlled. _____ also includes the relationships among the many stakeholders involved and the goals for which the corporation is governed. The principal stakeholders are the shareholders, management and the board of directors.

   a. Due diligence
   b. Patent
   c. Foreign Corrupt Practices Act
   d. Corporate governance

6. _____ are the earnings returned on the initial investment amount.

In the US, the Financial Accounting Standards Board (FASB) requires companies' income statements to report _____ for each of the major categories of the income statement: continuing operations, discontinued operations, extraordinary items, and net income.

The _____ formula does not include preferred dividends for categories outside of continued operations and net income.

a. Inventory turnover
b. Average accounting return
c. Assets turnover
d. Earnings per share

7. _____ is typically a higher ranking stock than voting shares, and its terms are negotiated between the corporation and the investor.

_____ usually carry no voting rights, but may carry superior priority over common stock in the payment of dividends and upon liquidation. _____ may carry a dividend that is paid out prior to any dividends to common stock holders.

   a. Second lien loan   b. Preferred stock
   c. Follow-on offering   d. Trade-off theory

8. In economics and finance, _____ is the practice of taking advantage of a price differential between two or more markets: striking a combination of matching deals that capitalize upon the imbalance, the profit being the difference between the market prices. When used by academics, an _____ is a transaction that involves no negative cash flow at any probabilistic or temporal state and a positive cash flow in at least one state; in simple terms, a risk-free profit.

   a. Initial margin   b. Arbitrage
   c. Issuer   d. Efficient-market hypothesis

9. In finance, _____ refers to the way a corporation finances its assets through some combination of equity, debt, or hybrid securities. A firm's _____ is then the composition or 'structure' of its liabilities. For example, a firm that sells $20 billion in equity and $80 billion in debt is said to be 20% equity-financed and 80% debt-financed.

   a. Market for corporate control   b. Book building
   c. Rights issue   d. Capital structure

10. In finance, _____ are stocks that appreciate in value and yield a high return on equity (ROE.) Analysts compute ROE by taking the company's net income and dividing it by the company's equity. To be classified as a growth stock, analysts expect to see at least 15 percent return on equity.

   a. Stock valuation   b. Security Analysis
   c. 4-4-5 Calendar   d. Growth stocks

11. In business and finance, a _____ (also referred to as equity _____) of stock means a _____ of ownership in a corporation (company.) In the plural, stocks is often used as a synonym for _____s especially in the United States, but it is less commonly used that way outside of North America.

In the United Kingdom, South Africa, and Australia, stock can also refer to completely different financial instruments such as government bonds or, less commonly, to all kinds of marketable securities.

   a. Bucket shop   b. Share
   c. Procter ' Gamble   d. Margin

Chapter 18. Distributions to Shareholders: Dividends and Repurchases

12. In finance, _____ is the process of estimating the potential market value of a financial asset or liability. they can be done on assets (for example, investments in marketable securities such as stocks, options, business enterprises, or intangible assets such as patents and trademarks) or on liabilities (e.g., Bonds issued by a company.) _____s are required in many contexts including investment analysis, capital budgeting, merger and acquisition transactions, financial reporting, taxable events to determine the proper tax liability, and in litigation.
    a. Valuation
    b. Share
    c. Margin
    d. Procter ' Gamble

13. A _____ is a profit that results from investments into a capital asset, such as stocks, bonds or real estate, which exceeds the purchase price. It is the difference between a higher selling price and a lower purchase price, resulting in a financial gain for the seller. Conversely, a capital loss arises if the proceeds from the sale of a capital asset are less than the purchase price.
    a. Capital gains tax
    b. Payroll tax
    c. Capital gain
    d. Tax brackets

14. The _____ on a company stock is the company's annual dividend payments divided by its market cap, or the dividend per share divided by the price per share. It is often expressed as a percentage.

Dividend payments on preferred shares are stipulated by the prospectus.

    a. Special dividend
    b. Dividend yield
    c. Dividend imputation
    d. Dividend reinvestment plan

15. The _____ is one of several stock market indices, created by nineteenth-century Wall Street Journal editor and Dow Jones ' Company co-founder Charles Dow. Dow compiled the index to gauge the performance of the industrial sector of the American stock market. It is the second-oldest U.S. market index, after the Dow Jones Transportation Average, which Dow also created.
    a. 529 plan
    b. Dow Jones Industrial Average
    c. 7-Eleven
    d. 4-4-5 Calendar

16. The institution most often referenced by the word '_____' is a public or publicly traded _____, the shares of which are traded on a public stock exchange (e.g., the New York Stock Exchange or Nasdaq in the United States) where shares of stock of _____s are bought and sold by and to the general public. Most of the largest businesses in the world are publicly traded _____s. However, the majority of _____s are said to be closely held, privately held or close _____s, meaning that no ready market exists for the trading of shares.
    a. Corporation
    b. Protect
    c. Federal Home Loan Mortgage Corporation
    d. Depository Trust Company

17. _____ or financing is to provide capital (funds), which means money for a project, a person, a business or any other private or public institutions.

Those funds can be allocated for either short term or long term purposes. The health fund is a new way of _____ private healthcare centers.

a. Synthetic CDO
c. Funding

b. Product life cycle
d. Proxy fight

18. In finance, the term _____ describes the amount in cash that returns to the owners of a security. Normally it does not include the price variations, at the difference of the total return. _____ applies to various stated rates of return on stocks (common and preferred, and convertible), fixed income instruments (bonds, notes, bills, strips, zero coupon), and some other investment type insurance products (e.g. annuities.)

a. 4-4-5 Calendar
c. Yield to maturity

b. Macaulay duration
d. Yield

19. _____ represents the impact on the stock price that investors would cause in reaction to a change in policy of a company.

a. Trade date
c. Volatility clustering

b. Clientele effect
d. Bonus share

20. _____ is a life of security. It may also refer to the final payment date of a loan or other financial instrument, at which point all remaining interest and principal is due to be paid.

1, 3, 6 months _____ band can be calculated by using 30-day per month periods.

a. Replacement cost
c. False billing

b. Primary market
d. Maturity

21. _____ occurs when an entity that has issued callable bonds calls those debt securities from the debt holders with the express purpose of reissuing new debt at a lower coupon rate. In essence, the issue of new, lower-interest debt allows the company to prematurely refund the older, higher-interest debt.

On the contrary, NonRefundable Bonds may be callable but they cannot be re-issued with a lower coupon rate.

a. No-arbitrage bounds
c. Systematic risk

b. Refunding
d. Market neutral

22. In economics, business, and accounting, a _____ is the value of money that has been used up to produce something, and hence is not available for use anymore. In business, the _____ may be one of acquisition, in which case the amount of money expended to acquire it is counted as _____. In this case, money is the input that is gone in order to acquire the thing.

a. Fixed costs
c. Cost

b. Sliding scale fees
d. Marginal cost

23. _____ is that which is owed; usually referencing assets owed, but the term can cover other obligations. In the case of assets, _____ is a means of using future purchasing power in the present before a summation has been earned. Some companies and corporations use _____ as a part of their overall corporate finance strategy.

a. Cross-collateralization
c. Partial Payment

b. Debt
d. Credit cycle

Chapter 18. Distributions to Shareholders: Dividends and Repurchases 207

24. The key date to remember for dividend paying stocks is the _____. The _____ is different from the record date. The _____ is typically two trading days before the record date.

In order to receive the upcoming dividend payment payout, you must already own or you must purchase the stock prior to the _____. It is important to note that in most countries, when you buy or sell any stock, there is a three trading-day settlement period on your order.

- a. Insolvency
- b. Index number
- c. Asian Financial Crisis
- d. Ex-dividend date

25. _____ is a corporate finance term denoting a type of takeover bid. The _____ is a public, open offer or invitation (usually announced in a newspaper advertisement) by a prospective acquirer to all stockholders of a publicly traded corporation (the target corporation) to tender their stock for sale at a specified price during a specified time, subject to the tendering of a minimum and maximum number of shares. In a _____, the bidder contacts shareholders directly; the directors of the company may or may not have endorsed the _____ proposal.

- a. Follow-on offering
- b. Tender offer
- c. Cash is king
- d. Shareholder value

26. In some countries, including the United States and the United Kingdom, corporations can buy back their own stock in a share repurchase, also known as a _____ or share buyback. There has been a meteoric rise in the use of share repurchases in the U.S. in the past twenty years, from $5b in 1980 to $349b in 2005. A share repurchase distributes cash to existing shareholders in exchange for a fraction of the firm's outstanding equity.

- a. Common stock
- b. Stockholder
- c. Trading curb
- d. Stock repurchase

27. _____, is when a company issues common stock or shares to the public for the first time. They are often issued by smaller, younger companies seeking capital to expand, but can also be done by large privately-owned companies looking to become publicly traded.

In an _____ the issuer may obtain the assistance of an underwriting firm, which helps it determine what type of security to issue (common or preferred), best offering price and time to bring it to market.

- a. Asian Financial Crisis
- b. Interest
- c. Insolvency
- d. Initial public offering

28. In finance, a _____ is a debt security, in which the authorized issuer owes the holders a debt and, depending on the terms of the _____, is obliged to pay interest (the coupon) and/or to repay the principal at a later date, termed maturity.

Thus a _____ is a loan: the issuer is the borrower, the _____ holder is the lender, and the coupon is the interest. _____s provide the borrower with external funds to finance long-term investments, or, in the case of government _____s, to finance current expenditure.

- a. Convertible bond
- b. Catastrophe bonds
- c. Puttable bond
- d. Bond

Chapter 18. Distributions to Shareholders: Dividends and Repurchases

29. _____ (also trust indenture or deed of trust) is a legal document issued to lenders and describes key terms such as the interest rate, maturity date, convertibility, pledge, promises, representations, covenants, and other terms of the bond offering. When the Offering Memorandum is prepared in advance of marketing a Bond, the indenture will typically be summarised in the 'Description of Notes' section.
   a. McFadden Act
   b. Fair Labor Standards Act
   c. Court of Audit of Belgium
   d. Bond indenture

30. In United States banking, _____ is a marketing term for certain services offered primarily to larger business customers. It may be used to describe all bank accounts (such as checking accounts) provided to businesses of a certain size, but it is more often used to describe specific services such as cash concentration, zero balance accounting, and automated clearing house facilities. Sometimes, private banking customers are given _____ services.
   a. Cash management
   b. Profitability index
   c. Capitalization rate
   d. Global tactical asset allocation

31. The _____ is an expected return that the provider of capital plans to earn on their investment.

Capital (money) used for funding a business should earn returns for the capital providers who risk their capital. For an investment to be worthwhile, the expected return on capital must be greater than the _____.

   a. 4-4-5 Calendar
   b. Weighted average cost of capital
   c. Capital intensity
   d. Cost of capital

32. _____ is a payment of a dividend to stockholders that exceeds the company's retained earnings. Once retained earnings is depleted, capital accounts such as additional paid-in capital are decreased to make up for the remaining dividend to be paid to stockholders. When a _____ occurs, it is considered to be a return of investment instead of profits.
   a. Stock market index option
   b. Revolving credit
   c. Securities offering
   d. Liquidating dividend

33. In accounting, _____ refers to the portion of net income which is retained by the corporation rather than distributed to its owners as dividends. Similarly, if the corporation makes a loss, then that loss is retained and called variously retained losses, accumulated losses or accumulated deficit. _____ and losses are cumulative from year to year with losses offsetting earnings.
   a. Matching principle
   b. Historical cost
   c. Generally Accepted Accounting Principles
   d. Retained earnings

34. _____ is a legally declared inability or impairment of ability of an individual or organization to pay their creditors. Creditors may file a _____ petition against a debtor ('involuntary _____') in an effort to recoup a portion of what they are owed or initiate a restructuring. In the majority of cases, however, _____ is initiated by the debtor (a 'voluntary _____' that is filed by the bankrupt individual or organization.)
   a. 529 plan
   b. Debt settlement
   c. Bankruptcy
   d. 4-4-5 Calendar

35. In finance, the _____ is the minimum rate of return a firm must offer shareholders to compensate for waiting for their returns, and for bearing some risk.

Chapter 18. Distributions to Shareholders: Dividends and Repurchases

The _____ capital for a particular company is the rate of return on investment that is required by the company's ordinary shareholders. The return consists both of dividend and capital gains, e.g. increases in the share price.

   a. Residual value
   c. Net pay
   b. Round-tripping
   d. Cost of equity

36. The _____ is a capital budgeting metric used by firms to decide whether they should make investments. It is an indicator of the efficiency or quality of an investment, as opposed to net present value (NPV), which indicates value or magnitude.

The IRR is the annualized effective compounded return rate which can be earned on the invested capital, i.e., the yield on the investment.

   a. ABN Amro
   c. AAB
   b. A Random Walk Down Wall Street
   d. Internal rate of return

37. The phrase _____ refers to the aspect of corporate strategy, corporate finance and management dealing with the buying, selling and combining of different companies that can aid, finance, or help a growing company in a given industry grow rapidly without having to create another business entity.

An acquisition, also known as a takeover, is the buying of one company (the 'target') by another. An acquisition may be friendly or hostile.

   a. 7-Eleven
   c. 4-4-5 Calendar
   b. Mergers and acquisitions
   d. 529 plan

38. _____ or net present worth (NPW) is defined as the total present value (PV) of a time series of cash flows. It is a standard method for using the time value of money to appraise long-term projects. Used for capital budgeting, and widely throughout economics, it measures the excess or shortfall of cash flows, in present value terms, once financing charges are met.

   a. Tax shield
   c. Negative gearing
   b. Present value of costs
   d. Net present value

39. In corporate finance, _____ analysis applies put option and call option valuation techniques to capital budgeting decisions. A _____ itself, is the right--but not the obligation--to undertake some business decision; typically the option to make, or abandon, a capital investment. For example, the opportunity to invest in the expansion of a firm's factory, or alternatively to sell the factory, is a _____.

   a. Book building
   c. Real option
   b. Capital budgeting
   d. Cash flow

40. In financial accounting, a _____ or statement of financial position is a summary of a person's or organization's balances. Assets, liabilities and ownership equity are listed as of a specific date, such as the end of its financial year. A _____ is often described as a snapshot of a company's financial condition.

Chapter 18. Distributions to Shareholders: Dividends and Repurchases

a. Balance sheet

b. Statement on Auditing Standards No. 70: Service Organizations

c. Financial statements

d. Statement of retained earnings

41. An _____ is a contract written by a seller that conveys to the buyer the right -- but not the obligation -- to buy (in the case of a call _____) or to sell (in the case of a put _____) a particular asset, such as a piece of property such as, among others, a futures contract. In return for granting the _____, the seller collects a payment (the premium) from the buyer.

For example, buying a call _____ provides the right to buy a specified quantity of a security at a set strike price at some time on or before expiration, while buying a put _____ provides the right to sell.

a. Option

b. Amortization

c. AT'T Mobility LLC

d. Annuity

42. _____ is the value on a given date of a future payment or series of future payments, discounted to reflect the time value of money and other factors such as investment risk. _____ calculations are widely used in business and economics to provide a means to compare cash flows at different times on a meaningful 'like to like' basis.

The most commonly applied model of the time value of money is compound interest.

a. Present value

b. Present value of benefits

c. Negative gearing

d. Net present value

43. In economic models, the _____ time frame assumes no fixed factors of production. Firms can enter or leave the marketplace, and the cost (and availability) of land, labor, raw materials, and capital goods can be assumed to vary. In contrast, in the short-run time frame, certain factors are assumed to be fixed, because there is not sufficient time for them to change.

a. 529 plan

b. Long-run

c. 4-4-5 Calendar

d. Short-run

44. On a stock exchange, a _____ is the opposite of a stock split, i.e. a stock merge - a reduction in the number of shares and an accompanying increase in the share price. The ratio is also reversed: 1-for-2, 1-for-3 and so on.

There is a stigma attached to doing this so it is not initiated without very good reason.

a. Trade date

b. Conglomerate merger

c. Correlation trading

d. Reverse stock split

45. A _____ or stock divide increases or decreases the number of shares in a public company. The price is adjusted such that the before and after market capitalization of the company remains the same and dilution does not occur. Options and warrants are included.

a. Contract for difference

b. Stock split

c. Stop order

d. Stop price

46. _____ are those dividends paid out in form of additional stock shares of the issuing corporation or other corporation They are usually issued in proportion to shares owned (for example for every 100 shares of stock owned, 5% stock dividend will yield 5 extra shares). If this payment involves the issue of new shares, this is very similar to a stock split in that it increases the total number of shares while lowering the price of each share and does not change the market capitalization or the total value of the shares held
   a. Database auditing
   b. Time-based currency
   c. The Hong Kong Securities Institute
   d. Stock or scrip dividends

47. A _____ is an equity investment option offered directly from the underlying company. The investor does not receive quarterly dividends directly as cash; instead, the investor's dividends are directly reinvested in the underlying equity. It should be noted that the investor still must pay tax annually on his or her dividend income, whether it is received or reinvested.
   a. Dividend reinvestment plan
   b. Dividend decision
   c. Dividend puzzle
   d. Dividend payout ratio

Chapter 19. Initial Public Offerings, Investment Banking, and Financial Restructuring

1. _____, is when a company issues common stock or shares to the public for the first time. They are often issued by smaller, younger companies seeking capital to expand, but can also be done by large privately-owned companies looking to become publicly traded.

In an _____ the issuer may obtain the assistance of an underwriting firm, which helps it determine what type of security to issue (common or preferred), best offering price and time to bring it to market.

   a. Insolvency
   b. Asian Financial Crisis
   c. Interest
   d. Initial public offering

2. _____ is a term defined by various securities laws that delineates investors permitted to invest in certain types of higher risk investments, limited partnerships, hedge funds, and angel investor networks. The term generally includes wealthy individuals and organizations such as a corporation, endowment, or retirement plans.

In the United States, for an individual to be considered an _____, they must have a net worth of at least one million US dollars or have made at least $200,000 each year for the last two years ($300,000 with his or her spouse if married) and have the expectation to make the same amount this year.' This rule came into effect in 1933 by way of the Securities Act of 1933.

   a. Accredited investor
   b. Investing online
   c. Alternative investment
   d. Investment performance

3. _____ is the corporate management term for the act of reorganizing the legal, ownership, operational, or other structures of a company for the purpose of making it more profitable or better organized for its present needs. Alternate reasons for restructing include a change of ownership or ownership structure, demerger repositioning debt _____ and financial _____.

   a. Day trading
   b. Concentrated stock
   c. Cross-border leasing
   d. Restructuring

4. In the United States, a _____ is an offering of securities that are not registered with the Securities and Exchange Commission (SEC.) Such offerings exploit an exemption offered by the Securities Act of 1933 that comes with several restrictions, including a prohibition against general solicitation. This exemption allows companies to avoid quarterly reporting requirements and many of the legal liabilities associated with the Sarbanes-Oxley Act.
   a. Private placement
   b. 4-4-5 Calendar
   c. 7-Eleven
   d. 529 plan

5. A _____ is a fungible, negotiable instrument representing financial value. They are broadly categorized into debt securities (such as banknotes, bonds and debentures), and equity securities; e.g., common stocks. The company or other entity issuing the _____ is called the issuer.
   a. Securities lending
   b. Security
   c. Book entry
   d. Tracking stock

6. Congress enacted the _____, in the aftermath of the stock market crash of 1929 and during the ensuing Great Depression. It requires that any offer or sale of securities using the means and instrumentalities of interstate commerce be registered pursuant to the 1933 Act, unless an exemption from registration exists under the law.

Chapter 19. Initial Public Offerings, Investment Banking, and Financial Restructuring 213

a. Securities Act of 1933
b. 7-Eleven
c. 529 plan
d. 4-4-5 Calendar

7. _____ is a legally declared inability or impairment of ability of an individual or organization to pay their creditors. Creditors may file a _____ petition against a debtor ('involuntary _____') in an effort to recoup a portion of what they are owed or initiate a restructuring. In the majority of cases, however, _____ is initiated by the debtor (a 'voluntary _____' that is filed by the bankrupt individual or organization.)

a. Debt settlement
b. 529 plan
c. Bankruptcy
d. 4-4-5 Calendar

8. _____ is the set of processes, customs, policies, laws and institutions affecting the way a corporation is directed, administered or controlled. _____ also includes the relationships among the many stakeholders involved and the goals for which the corporation is governed. The principal stakeholders are the shareholders, management and the board of directors.

a. Patent
b. Foreign Corrupt Practices Act
c. Due diligence
d. Corporate governance

9. In finance, _____ is the process of estimating the potential market value of a financial asset or liability. they can be done on assets (for example, investments in marketable securities such as stocks, options, business enterprises, or intangible assets such as patents and trademarks) or on liabilities (e.g., Bonds issued by a company.) _____s are required in many contexts including investment analysis, capital budgeting, merger and acquisition transactions, financial reporting, taxable events to determine the proper tax liability, and in litigation.

a. Margin
b. Valuation
c. Share
d. Procter ' Gamble

10. _____ is a type of private equity capital typically provided to early-stage, high-potential, growth companies in the interest of generating a return through an eventual realization event such as an IPO or trade sale of the company. _____ investments are generally made as cash in exchange for shares in the invested company. It is typical for _____ investors to identify and back companies in high technology industries such as biotechnology and ICT.

a. Probability distribution
b. Venture capital
c. Treasury Inflation-Protected Securities
d. Tail risk

11. The _____ of 2002 (Pub.L. 107-204, 116 Stat. 745, enacted July 30, 2002), also known as the Public Company Accounting Reform and Investor Protection Act of 2002 and commonly called Sarbanes-Oxley, Sarbox or SOX, is a United States federal law enacted on July 30, 2002 in response to a number of major corporate and accounting scandals including those affecting Enron, Tyco International, Adelphia, Peregrine Systems and WorldCom.

a. Blue sky law
b. Duty of loyalty
c. Sarbanes-Oxley Act
d. Foreign Corrupt Practices Act

12. A _____ is a payment made by a corporation to its shareholder members. When a corporation earns a profit or surplus, that money can be put to two uses: it can either be re-invested in the business (called retained earnings), or it can be paid to the shareholders as a _____. Many corporations retain a portion of their earnings and pay the remainder as a _____.

a. Special dividend
b. Dividend puzzle
c. Dividend yield
d. Dividend

13. The _____ is the financial market where previously issued securities and financial instruments such as stock, bonds, options, and futures are bought and sold. The term '_____' is also used refer to the market for any used goods or assets, or an alternative use for an existing product or asset where the customer base is the second market

With primary issuances of securities or financial instruments, or the primary market, investors purchase these securities directly from issuers such as corporations issuing shares in an IPO or private placement, or directly from the federal government in the case of treasuries.

a. Delta neutral
b. Performance attribution
c. Financial market
d. Secondary market

14. The phrase _____ refers to the aspect of corporate strategy, corporate finance and management dealing with the buying, selling and combining of different companies that can aid, finance, or help a growing company in a given industry grow rapidly without having to create another business entity.

An acquisition, also known as a takeover, is the buying of one company (the 'target') by another. An acquisition may be friendly or hostile.

a. 4-4-5 Calendar
b. Mergers and acquisitions
c. 7-Eleven
d. 529 plan

15. The U.S. _____ is an independent agency of the United States government which holds primary responsibility for enforcing the federal securities laws and regulating the securities industry, the nation's stock and options exchanges, and other electronic securities markets. The SEC was created by section 4 of the SEC of 1934 (now codified as 15 U.S.C. Â§ 78d and commonly referred to as the 1934 Act.)

a. 4-4-5 Calendar
b. 7-Eleven
c. Securities and Exchange Commission
d. 529 plan

16. In the _____ contract the underwriter agrees to sell as many shares as possible at the agreed-upon price.

Under the all-or-none contract the underwriter agrees either to sell the entire offering or to cancel the deal.

Stand-by underwriting, also known as strict underwriting or old-fashioned underwriting is a form of stock insurance: the issuer contracts the underwriter for the latter to purchase the shares the issuer failed to sell under stockholders' subscription and applications.

a. Book building
b. Real option
c. Follow-on offering
d. Best efforts

17. Unemployment occurs when a person is available to work and currently seeking work, but the person is without work. The prevalence of unemployment is usually measured using the _____, which is defined as the percentage of those in the labor force who are unemployed. The _____ is also used in economic studies and economic indexes such as the United States' Conference Board's Index of Leading Indicators as a measure of the state of the macroeconomics.

a. A Random Walk Down Wall Street
b. ABN Amro
c. AAB
d. Unemployment rate

Chapter 19. Initial Public Offerings, Investment Banking, and Financial Restructuring 215

18. A _____ is a financial contract whose value is derived from the value of something else (known as the underlying.) The underlying on which a _____ is based can be an asset, weather conditions bonds or other forms of credit.

   a. 7-Eleven
   b. 529 plan
   c. 4-4-5 Calendar
   d. Derivative

19. _____ is an SEC filing used by public companies to register their securities with the U.S. Securities and Exchange Commission (SEC.) The S-1 contains the basic business and financial information on an issuer with respect to a specific securities offering. Investors may use the prospectus to consider the merits of an offering and make educated investment decisions.

   a. Form S-1
   b. 529 plan
   c. 7-Eleven
   d. 4-4-5 Calendar

20. The term _____, also known as a waiting period is a period extended from the time a company files a registration statement with the SEC until SEC staff declared the registration statement effective. During that period, the federal securities laws limited what information a company and related parties can release to the public.'

Under the rules of the Securities Act of 1933, as modified June 29, 2005, electronic communications, including electronic road shows and information located on or hyperlinked to an issuer's website are also governed. The rules changes of June 29, 2005 also included various changes which 'liberalize permitted offering activity and communications to allow more information' for certain qualifying organizations.

   a. Duty of loyalty
   b. Leasing
   c. Lien
   d. Quiet period

21. _____ occurs when an entity that has issued callable bonds calls those debt securities from the debt holders with the express purpose of reissuing new debt at a lower coupon rate. In essence, the issue of new, lower-interest debt allows the company to prematurely refund the older, higher-interest debt.

On the contrary, NonRefundable Bonds may be callable but they cannot be re-issued with a lower coupon rate.

   a. Systematic risk
   b. No-arbitrage bounds
   c. Refunding
   d. Market neutral

22. In finance, a _____ is a debt security, in which the authorized issuer owes the holders a debt and, depending on the terms of the _____, is obliged to pay interest (the coupon) and/or to repay the principal at a later date, termed maturity.

Thus a _____ is a loan: the issuer is the borrower, the _____ holder is the lender, and the coupon is the interest. _____s provide the borrower with external funds to finance long-term investments, or, in the case of government _____s, to finance current expenditure.

   a. Catastrophe bonds
   b. Convertible bond
   c. Puttable bond
   d. Bond

Chapter 19. Initial Public Offerings, Investment Banking, and Financial Restructuring

23. The free _____ of a public company is an estimate of the proportion of shares that are not held by large owners and that are not stock with sales restrictions (restricted stock that cannot be sold until they become unrestricted stock.)

The free _____ or a public _____ is usually defined as being all shares held by investors other than:

- shares held by owners owning more than 5% of all shares (those could be institutional investors, 'strategic shareholders,' founders, executives, and other insiders' holdings)
- restricted stocks (granted to executives that can be, but don't have to be, registered insiders)
- insider holdings (it is assumed that insiders hold stock for the very long term)

The free _____ is an important criterion in quoting a share on the stock market.

To _____ a company means to list its shares on a public stock exchange through an initial public offering (or 'flotation'.)

- Open market
- Outstanding shares
- Market capitalization
- Public _____ *loat*
- Reverse takeover

a. Golden parachute
c. Synthetic CDO
b. Trade finance
d. Float

24. The _____ is a stock exchange based in New York City, New York. It is the largest stock exchange in the world by dollar value of its listed companies securities. As of October 2008, the combined capitalization of all domestic _____ listed companies was $10.1 trillion.
   a. 4-4-5 Calendar
   b. 7-Eleven
   c. 529 plan
   d. New York Stock Exchange

25. A _____, securities exchange or (in Europe) bourse is a corporation or mutual organization which provides 'trading' facilities for stock brokers and traders, to trade stocks and other securities. _____s also provide facilities for the issue and redemption of securities as well as other financial instruments and capital events including the payment of income and dividends. The securities traded on a _____ include: shares issued by companies, unit trusts and other pooled investment products and bonds.
   a. Stock Exchange
   b. 4-4-5 Calendar
   c. 7-Eleven
   d. 529 plan

26. In United States banking, _____ is a marketing term for certain services offered primarily to larger business customers. It may be used to describe all bank accounts (such as checking accounts) provided to businesses of a certain size, but it is more often used to describe specific services such as cash concentration, zero balance accounting, and automated clearing house facilities. Sometimes, private banking customers are given _____ services.

Chapter 19. Initial Public Offerings, Investment Banking, and Financial Restructuring 217

a. Profitability index
c. Capitalization rate
b. Global tactical asset allocation
d. Cash management

27. In economics, business, and accounting, a _____ is the value of money that has been used up to produce something, and hence is not available for use anymore. In business, the _____ may be one of acquisition, in which case the amount of money expended to acquire it is counted as _____. In this case, money is the input that is gone in order to acquire the thing.
    a. Marginal cost
    c. Fixed costs
    b. Sliding scale fees
    d. Cost

28. The _____ is an electronic quotation system in the United States that displays real-time quotes, last-sale prices, and volume information for many over-the-counter (OTC) equity securities that are not listed on the NASDAQ stock exchange or a national securities exchange. Broker-dealers who subscribe to the system can use the _____ to look up prices or enter quotes for OTC securities.
    a. AT'T Inc.
    c. Insolvency
    b. Internal control
    d. OTC Bulletin Board

29. A _____ is a private or public market for the trading of company stock and derivatives of company stock at an agreed price; these are securities listed on a stock exchange as well as those only traded privately.

The size of the world _____ is estimated at about $36.6 trillion US at the beginning of October 2008 . The world derivatives market has been estimated at about $480 trillion face or nominal value, 12 times the size of the entire world economy.

    a. Anton Gelonkin
    c. Andrew Tobias
    b. Adolph Coors
    d. Stock market

30. _____ is the provision of resources (such as granting a loan) by one party to another party where that second party does not reimburse the first party immediately, thereby generating a debt, and instead arranges either to repay or return those resources (or material(s) of equal value) at a later date. The first party is called a creditor, also known as a lender, while the second party is called a debtor, also known as a borrower.

Movements of financial capital are normally dependent on either _____ or equity transfers.

    a. Clearing house
    c. Warrant
    b. Comparable
    d. Credit

31. The variation margin or _____ is not collateral, but a daily offsetting of profits and losses. Futures are marked-to-market every day, so the current price is compared to the previous day's price. The profit or loss on the day of a position is then paid to or debited from the holder by the futures exchange.
    a. Delivery month
    c. Total return swap
    b. Maintenance margin
    d. SPI 200 futures contract

218 *Chapter 19. Initial Public Offerings, Investment Banking, and Financial Restructuring*

32. In finance, a _____ is collateral that the holder of a position in securities, options, or futures contracts has to deposit to cover the credit risk of his counterparty (most often his broker.) This risk can arise if the holder has done any of the following:

- borrowed cash from the counterparty to buy securities or options,
- sold securities or options short, or
- entered into a futures contract.

The collateral can be in the form of cash or securities, and it is deposited in a _____ account. On U.S. futures exchanges, '_____' was formally called performance bond.

_____ buying is buying securities with cash borrowed from a broker, using other securities as collateral.

a. Margin
b. Credit
c. Share
d. Procter ' Gamble

33. The _____ is the amount required to be collateralized in order to open a position. Thereafter, the amount required to be kept in collateral until the position is closed is the maintenance requirement. The maintenance requirement is the minimum amount to be collateralized in order to keep an open position.

a. AAB
b. ABN Amro
c. A Random Walk Down Wall Street
d. Initial margin requirement

34. In the United States, the Financial Industry Regulatory Authority (FINRA) is a self-regulatory organization (SRO) under the Securities Exchange Act of 1934, successor to the _____, Inc.

FINRA is responsible for regulatory oversight of all securities firms that do business with the public; professional training, testing and licensing of registered persons; arbitration and mediation; market regulation by contract for The NASDAQ Stock Market, Inc., the American Stock Exchange LLC, and the International Securities Exchange, LLC; and industry utilities, such as Trade Reporting Facilities and other over-the-counter operations.

a. 7-Eleven
b. 4-4-5 Calendar
c. 529 plan
d. National Association of Securities Dealers

35. A _____ is a statement required of a United States firm when soliciting shareholder votes. The firm needs to file a _____ with the U.S. Securities and Exchange Commission. This statement is useful in assessing how management is paid and potential conflict-of-interest issues with auditors.

a. 529 plan
b. 4-4-5 Calendar
c. 7-Eleven
d. Proxy statement

36. A _____ is the price of a single share of a no. of saleable stocks of the company. Once the stock is purchased, the owner becomes a shareholder of the company that issued the share.

a. Trading curb
b. Stock split
c. Whisper numbers
d. Share price

37. The institution most often referenced by the word '_____' is a public or publicly traded _____, the shares of which are traded on a public stock exchange (e.g., the New York Stock Exchange or Nasdaq in the United States) where shares of stock of _____s are bought and sold by and to the general public. Most of the largest businesses in the world are publicly traded _____s. However, the majority of _____s are said to be closely held, privately held or close _____s, meaning that no ready market exists for the trading of shares.

- a. Protect
- b. Depository Trust Company
- c. Federal Home Loan Mortgage Corporation
- d. Corporation

38. In finance, the _____ is the minimum rate of return a firm must offer shareholders to compensate for waiting for their returns, and for bearing some risk.

The _____ capital for a particular company is the rate of return on investment that is required by the company's ordinary shareholders. The return consists both of dividend and capital gains, e.g. increases in the share price.

- a. Residual value
- b. Net pay
- c. Round-tripping
- d. Cost of equity

39. _____ is typically a higher ranking stock than voting shares, and its terms are negotiated between the corporation and the investor.

_____ usually carry no voting rights, but may carry superior priority over common stock in the payment of dividends and upon liquidation. _____ may carry a dividend that is paid out prior to any dividends to common stock holders.

- a. Second lien loan
- b. Trade-off theory
- c. Follow-on offering
- d. Preferred stock

40. In financial accounting, a _____ or statement of financial position is a summary of a person's or organization's balances. Assets, liabilities and ownership equity are listed as of a specific date, such as the end of its financial year. A _____ is often described as a snapshot of a company's financial condition.

- a. Statement of retained earnings
- b. Statement on Auditing Standards No. 70: Service Organizations
- c. Financial statements
- d. Balance sheet

41. In finance and economics, _____ or divestiture is the reduction of some kind of asset for either financial goals or ethical objectives. A _____ is the opposite of an investment.

Often the term is used as a means to grow financially in which a company sells off a business unit in order to focus their resources on a market it judges to be more profitable, or promising.

- a. Portfolio investment
- b. Certificate in Investment Performance Measurement
- c. Divestment
- d. Late trading

Chapter 19. Initial Public Offerings, Investment Banking, and Financial Restructuring

42. In business and finance, a _____ (also referred to as equity _____) of stock means a _____ of ownership in a corporation (company.) In the plural, stocks is often used as a synonym for _____s especially in the United States, but it is less commonly used that way outside of North America.

In the United Kingdom, South Africa, and Australia, stock can also refer to completely different financial instruments such as government bonds or, less commonly, to all kinds of marketable securities.

- a. Procter ' Gamble
- b. Margin
- c. Bucket shop
- d. Share

43. _____ is a structured finance process that involves pooling and repackaging of cash-flow-producing financial assets into securities, which are then sold to investors. The term '_____' is derived from the fact that the form of financial instruments used to obtain funds from the investors are securities. As a portfolio risk backed by amortizing cash flows - and unlike general corporate debt - the credit quality of securitized debt is non-stationary due to changes in volatility that are time- and structure-dependent.

- a. Securitization
- b. Reputational risk
- c. The Glass-Steagall Act of 1933
- d. Special journals

44. An _____ is a contract written by a seller that conveys to the buyer the right -- but not the obligation -- to buy (in the case of a call _____) or to sell (in the case of a put _____) a particular asset, such as a piece of property such as, among others, a futures contract. In return for granting the _____, the seller collects a payment (the premium) from the buyer.

For example, buying a call _____ provides the right to buy a specified quantity of a security at a set strike price at some time on or before expiration, while buying a put _____ provides the right to sell.

- a. AT'T Mobility LLC
- b. Annuity
- c. Amortization
- d. Option

45. A _____, also known by its legal title as an 'over-allotment option' (the only way it can be referred to in a prospectus), gives underwriters the right to sell additional shares in a registered securities offering if demand for the securities is in excess of the original amount offered. The _____ can vary in size up to 15% of the original number of shares offered.

The _____ option is popular because it is the only SEC-permitted means for an underwriter to stabilize the price of a new issue post-pricing.

- a. Business valuation standards
- b. Supply and demand
- c. Green Shoe
- d. Foreign Language and Area Studies

46. A _____ or secondary offering is an issuance of stock subsequent to the company's initial public offering. A _____ can be either of two types (or a mixture of both): dilutive and non-dilutive. A secondary offering is an offering of securities by a shareholder of the company (as opposed to the company itself, which is a primary offering).

- a. Second lien loan
- b. Follow-on offering
- c. Shareholder value
- d. Capital structure

Chapter 19. Initial Public Offerings, Investment Banking, and Financial Restructuring

47. A _____ or Capital increase is a new equity issue by a company after its IPO. It differs from a secondary equity offering, in which owners (not the company) sell their shares. In the latter case, the company gets no money and no ownership dilution happens, for the company does not issue new shares.
   - a. FATF Blacklist
   - b. Debt-for-equity swap
   - c. Sinking fund
   - d. Seasoned equity offering

48. _____ is an arrangement with the U.S. Securities and Exchange Commission that allows a single registration document to be filed that permits the issuance of multiple securities.

   _____ is a registration of a new issue which can be prepared up to two years in advance, so that the issue can be offered quickly as soon as funds are needed or market conditions are favorable.

   For example, current market conditions in the housing market are not favorable for a specific firm to issue a public offering.
   - a. Bought deal
   - b. Black Sea Trade and Development Bank
   - c. 4-4-5 Calendar
   - d. Shelf registration

49. A _____ occurs when a financial sponsor acquires a controlling interest in a company's equity and where a significant percentage of the purchase price is financed through leverage (borrowing.) The assets of the acquired company are used as collateral for the borrowed capital, sometimes with assets of the acquiring company. The bonds or other paper issued for _____s are commonly considered not to be investment grade because of the significant risks involved.
   - a. Leverage
   - b. Limited partnership
   - c. Pension fund
   - d. Leveraged buyout

50. In finance, _____ refers to the way a corporation finances its assets through some combination of equity, debt, or hybrid securities. A firm's _____ is then the composition or 'structure' of its liabilities. For example, a firm that sells $20 billion in equity and $80 billion in debt is said to be 20% equity-financed and 80% debt-financed.
   - a. Book building
   - b. Rights issue
   - c. Market for corporate control
   - d. Capital structure

51. _____ is a New York City-based private equity firm that sponsors and manages investment funds, focusing primarily on leveraged buyouts of mature businesses. Since inception, the firm has completed over $400 billion of private equity transactions and was one of the pioneers of the leveraged buyout industry.

   The firm was founded in 1976 by Jerome Kohlberg, Jr., and cousins Henry Kravis and George R. Roberts, all of whom had previously worked together at Bear Stearns where they completed some of the earliest leveraged buyout transactions.
   - a. Noise trader
   - b. Kohlberg Kravis Roberts ' Co
   - c. Coefficient of variation
   - d. Debtor-in-possession financing

52. _____ is that which is owed; usually referencing assets owed, but the term can cover other obligations. In the case of assets, _____ is a means of using future purchasing power in the present before a summation has been earned. Some companies and corporations use _____ as a part of their overall corporate finance strategy.

a. Partial Payment
b. Cross-collateralization
c. Debt
d. Credit cycle

53. _____ is a life of security. It may also refer to the final payment date of a loan or other financial instrument, at which point all remaining interest and principal is due to be paid.

1, 3, 6 months _____ band can be calculated by using 30-day per month periods.

a. Primary market
b. Replacement cost
c. False billing
d. Maturity

54. _____ or financing is to provide capital (funds), which means money for a project, a person, a business or any other private or public institutions.

Those funds can be allocated for either short term or long term purposes. The health fund is a new way of _____ private healthcare centers.

a. Synthetic CDO
b. Proxy fight
c. Funding
d. Product life cycle

55. _____ is a fee paid on borrowed assets. It is the price paid for the use of borrowed money, or, money earned by deposited funds. Assets that are sometimes lent with _____ include money, shares, consumer goods through hire purchase, major assets such as aircraft, and even entire factories in finance lease arrangements.

a. Interest
b. AAB
c. A Random Walk Down Wall Street
d. Insolvency

56. An _____ is the price a borrower pays for the use of money they do not own, and the return a lender receives for deferring the use of funds, by lending it to the borrower. _____ s are normally expressed as a percentage rate over the period of one year.

_____ s targets are also a vital tool of monetary policy and are used to control variables like investment, inflation, and unemployment.

a. AAB
b. Interest rate
c. ABN Amro
d. A Random Walk Down Wall Street

57. In economics and contract theory, _____ deals with the study of decisions in transactions where one party has more or better information than the other. This creates an imbalance of power in transactions which can sometimes cause the transactions to go awry. Examples of this problem are adverse selection and moral hazard.

a. A Random Walk Down Wall Street
b. AAB
c. ABN Amro
d. Information asymmetry

Chapter 19. Initial Public Offerings, Investment Banking, and Financial Restructuring

58. In lending agreements, _____ is a borrower's pledge of specific property to a lender, to secure repayment of a loan. The _____ serves as protection for a lender against a borrower's risk of default - that is, a borrower failing to pay the principal and interest under the terms of a loan obligation. If a borrower does default on a loan (due to insolvency or other event), that borrower forfeits (gives up) the property pledged as _____ ollateral - and the lender then becomes the owner of the _____.
   - a. Collateral
   - b. Refinancing risk
   - c. Future-oriented
   - d. Nominal value

59. _____ or net present worth (NPW) is defined as the total present value (PV) of a time series of cash flows. It is a standard method for using the time value of money to appraise long-term projects. Used for capital budgeting, and widely throughout economics, it measures the excess or shortfall of cash flows, in present value terms, once financing charges are met.
   - a. Present value of costs
   - b. Negative gearing
   - c. Tax shield
   - d. Net present value

60. _____ is the value on a given date of a future payment or series of future payments, discounted to reflect the time value of money and other factors such as investment risk. _____ calculations are widely used in business and economics to provide a means to compare cash flows at different times on a meaningful 'like to like' basis.

The most commonly applied model of the time value of money is compound interest.
   - a. Net present value
   - b. Present value of benefits
   - c. Negative gearing
   - d. Present value

61. _____ is the financing of long-term infrastructure and industrial projects based upon a complex financial structure where project debt and equity are used to finance the project, rather than the balance sheets of project sponsors. Usually, a _____ structure involves a number of equity investors, known as sponsors, as well as a syndicate of banks that provide loans to the operation. The loans are most commonly non-recourse loans, which are secured by the project assets and paid entirely from project cash flow, rather than from the general assets or creditworthiness of the project sponsors, a decision in part supported by financial modeling.
   - a. Project finance
   - b. Duration gap
   - c. FATF Blacklist
   - d. Standard of deferred payment

62. In business and accounting, _____s are everything of value that is owned by a person or company. The balance sheet of a firm records the monetary value of the _____s owned by the firm. The two major _____ classes are tangible _____s and intangible _____s.
   - a. Asset
   - b. EBITDA
   - c. Income
   - d. Accounts payable

63. An _____ is a security whose value and income payments are derived from and collateralized (or 'backed') by a specified pool of underlying assets. The pool of assets is typically a group of small and illiquid assets that are unable to be sold individually. Pooling the assets allows them to be sold to general investors, a process called securitization, and allows the risk of investing in the underlying assets to be diversified because each security will represent a fraction of the total value of the diverse pool of underlying assets.

Chapter 19. Initial Public Offerings, Investment Banking, and Financial Restructuring

a. ABN Amro
b. A Random Walk Down Wall Street
c. AAB
d. Asset-backed security

64. In the global money market, _____ is an unsecured promissory note with a fixed maturity of one to 270 days. _____ is a money-market security issued (sold) by large banks and corporations to get money to meet short term debt obligations (for example, payroll), and is only backed by an issuing bank or corporation's promise to pay the face amount on the maturity date specified on the note. Since it is not backed by collateral, only firms with excellent credit ratings from a recognized rating agency will be able to sell their _____ at a reasonable price.
a. Financial distress
b. Book building
c. Trade-off theory
d. Commercial paper

65. A _____ is an international bond that is denominated in a currency not native to the country where it is issued. It can be categorised according to the currency in which it is issued. London is one of the centers of the _____ market, but _____s may be traded throughout the world - for example in Singapore or Tokyo.
a. Eurobond
b. Education production function
c. Interest rate option
d. Economic entity

66. _____ are asset-backed securities of current and future revenues of the first 25 albums (287 songs) of David Bowie's collection recorded before 1990. Issued by David Bowie in 1997, they were bought for $55 million by the Prudential Insurance Company. The 287 included songs also acted as collateral to insure the bond.
a. Bowie Bonds
b. Corporate bond
c. Clean price
d. Revenue bonds

67. In finance, a _____ is a type of bond that can be converted into shares of stock in the issuing company, usually at some pre-announced ratio. It is a hybrid security with debt- and equity-like features. Although it typically has a low coupon rate, the holder is compensated with the ability to convert the bond to common stock, usually at a substantial discount to the stock's market value.
a. Bond fund
b. Gilts
c. Corporate bond
d. Convertible bond

68. A _____ is a bond issued by a corporation. The term is usually applied to longer-term debt instruments, generally with a maturity date falling at least a year after their issue date. (The term 'commercial paper' is sometimes used for instruments with a shorter maturity.)
a. Brady bonds
b. Serial bond
c. Corporate bond
d. Government bond

69. In finance, a _____ (non-investment grade bond, speculative grade bond or junk bond) is a bond that is rated below investment grade at the time of purchase. These bonds have a higher risk of default or other adverse credit events, but typically pay higher yields than better quality bonds in order to make them attractive to investors.
a. Private equity
b. Volatility
c. Sharpe ratio
d. High yield bond

70. _____ are a class of computational algorithms that rely on repeated random sampling to compute their results. _____ are often used when simulating physical and mathematical systems. Because of their reliance on repeated computation and random or pseudo-random numbers, _____ are most suited to calculation by a computer.

Chapter 19. Initial Public Offerings, Investment Banking, and Financial Restructuring 225

_____ in finance are often used to calculate the value of companies, to evaluate investments in projects at corporate level or to evaluate financial derivatives. The method is intended for financial analysts who want to construct stochastic or probabilistic financial models as opposed to the traditional static and deterministic models.

  a. Semivariance
  b. Monte Carlo methods
  c. Sample size
  d. Correlation

71. In the United States, a _____ is a bond issued by a city or other local government, or their agencies. Potential issuers of these bonds include cities, counties, redevelopment agencies, school districts, publicly owned airports and seaports, and any other governmental entity (or group of governments) below the state level. They may be general obligations of the issuer or secured by specified revenues.
  a. Puttable bond
  b. Premium bond
  c. Senior debt
  d. Municipal bond

72. A _____ is a generic term for any bond selling for more than 100% of par value, i.e., at a price greater than 100.00, which typically occurs for high coupon bonds in a falling interest rate climate.
  a. Municipal bond
  b. Revenue bonds
  c. Premium bond
  d. Nominal yield

73. _____ are government bonds issued by the United States Department of the Treasury through the Bureau of the Public Debt. They are the debt financing instruments of the U.S. Federal government, and they are often referred to simply as Treasuries or Treasurys. There are four types of marketable _____: Treasury bills, Treasury notes, Treasury bonds, and Treasury Inflation Protected Securities (TIPS.)
  a. Treasury Inflation Protected Securities
  b. 4-4-5 Calendar
  c. Treasury Inflation-Protected Securities
  d. Treasury securities

74. The _____ is a financial market where participants buy and sell debt securities, usually in the form of bonds. As of 2006, the size of the international _____ is an estimated $45 trillion, of which the size of the outstanding U.S. _____ debt was $25.2 trillion.

Nearly all of the $923 billion average daily trading volume in the U.S. _____ takes place between broker-dealers and large institutions in a decentralized, over-the-counter market.

  a. Bond market
  b. 4-4-5 Calendar
  c. Fixed income
  d. 529 plan

Chapter 20. Lease Financing

1. _____ is the removal or simplification of government rules and regulations that constrain the operation of market forces. _____ does not mean elimination of laws against fraud, but eliminating or reducing government control of how business is done, thereby moving toward a more free market.

The stated rationale for '_____' is often that fewer and simpler regulations will lead to a raised level of competitiveness, therefore higher productivity, more efficiency and lower prices overall.

   a. Deregulation
   b. Value added
   c. Demand shock
   d. Supply shock

2. _____ is a legally declared inability or impairment of ability of an individual or organization to pay their creditors. Creditors may file a _____ petition against a debtor ('involuntary _____') in an effort to recoup a portion of what they are owed or initiate a restructuring. In the majority of cases, however, _____ is initiated by the debtor (a 'voluntary _____' that is filed by the bankrupt individual or organization.)
   a. Bankruptcy
   b. 4-4-5 Calendar
   c. 529 plan
   d. Debt settlement

3. The institution most often referenced by the word '_____' is a public or publicly traded _____, the shares of which are traded on a public stock exchange (e.g., the New York Stock Exchange or Nasdaq in the United States) where shares of stock of _____s are bought and sold by and to the general public. Most of the largest businesses in the world are publicly traded _____s. However, the majority of _____s are said to be closely held, privately held or close _____s, meaning that no ready market exists for the trading of shares.
   a. Protect
   b. Depository Trust Company
   c. Federal Home Loan Mortgage Corporation
   d. Corporation

4. _____ or financing is to provide capital (funds), which means money for a project, a person, a business or any other private or public institutions.

Those funds can be allocated for either short term or long term purposes. The health fund is a new way of _____ private healthcare centers.

   a. Synthetic CDO
   b. Funding
   c. Product life cycle
   d. Proxy fight

5. _____ is a process by which a firm can obtain the use of a certain fixed assets for which it must pay a series of contractual, periodic, tax deductable payments. The lessee is the receiver of the services or the assets under the lease contract and the lessor is the owner of the assets. The relationship between the tenant and the landlord is called a tenancy, and can be for a fixed or an indefinite period of time (called the term of the lease).
   a. Royalties
   b. Leasing
   c. Quiet period
   d. Foreign Corrupt Practices Act

6. A finance lease or _____ is a type of lease. It is a commercial arrangement where:

- the lessee (customer or borrower) will select an asset (equipment, vehicle, software);
- the lessor (finance company) will purchase that asset;
- the lessee will have use of that asset during the lease;
- the lessee will pay a series of rentals or installments for the use of that asset;
- the lessor will recover a large part or all of the cost of the asset plus earn interest from the rentals paid by the lessee;
- the lessee has the option to acquire ownership of the asset (e.g. paying the last rental, or bargain option purchase price);

The finance company is the legal owner of the asset during duration of the lease.

However the lessee has control over the asset providing them the benefits and risks of (economic) ownership.

A finance lease differs from an operating lease in that:

- in a finance lease the lessee has use of the asset over most of its economic life and beyond (generally by making small 'peppercorn' payments at the end of the lease term.)

In an operating lease the lessee only uses the asset for some of the asset's life.

- in a finance lease the lessor will recover all or most of the cost of the equipment from the rentals paid by the lessee.

In an operating lease the lessor will have a substantial investment or residual value on completion of the lease.

- in a finance lease the lessee has the benefits and risks of economic ownership of the asset (e.g. risk of obsolescence, paying for maintenance, claiming capital allowances/depreciation.)

In an operating lease the lessor has the benefits and risks of owning the asset.

The U.S. Financial Accounting Standards Board and the International Accounting Standards Board announced in 2006 a joint project to comprehensively review lease accounting standards.

a. Cash concentration
c. Capitalization rate
b. Cash management
d. Capital lease

7. The _____ is a private, not-for-profit organization whose primary purpose is to develop generally accepted accounting principles (GAAP) within the United States in the public's interest. The Securities and Exchange Commission (SEC) designated the _____ as the organization responsible for setting accounting standards for public companies in the U.S. It was created in 1973, replacing the Accounting Principles Board and the Committee on Accounting Procedure of the American Institute of Certified Public Accountants. The _____'s mission is 'to establish and improve standards of financial accounting and reporting for the guidance and education of the public, including issuers, auditors, and users of financial information.'

Chapter 20. Lease Financing

The _____ is not a governmental body.

   a. Credit karma
   c. PlaNet Finance
   b. FASB
   d. MRU Holdings

8. Leasing is a process by which a firm can obtain the use of a certain fixed assets for which it must pay a series of contractual, periodic, tax deductable payments. The lessee is the receiver of the services or the assets under the lease contract and the lessor is the owner of the assets. The relationship between the tenant and the landlord is called a _____, and can be for a fixed or an indefinite period of time (called the term of the lease.)
   a. Real Estate Investment Trust
   c. Tenancy
   b. REIT
   d. Real estate investing

9. An _____ is a lease whose term is short compared to the useful life of the asset or piece of equipment (an airliner, a ship etc.) being leased. An _____ is commonly used to acquire equipment on a relatively short-term basis.
   a. A Random Walk Down Wall Street
   c. Operating lease
   b. AAB
   d. ABN Amro

10. _____ short for sale-and-_____ is a financial transaction, where one sells an asset and leases it back for a long-term: thus one continues to be able to use the asset, but no longer owns it.

This is generally done for fixed assets, notably real estate and planes, and the purposes are varied, but include financing, accounting, and tax reasons.

After purchasing an asset, the owner enters a long-term agreement by which the property is leased back to the seller, at an agreed-to rate.

   a. 7-Eleven
   c. 4-4-5 Calendar
   b. Leaseback,
   d. 529 plan

11. _____ LLP, based in Chicago, was once one of the 'Big Five' accounting firms among PricewaterhouseCoopers, Deloitte Touche Tohmatsu, Ernst ' Young and KPMG, providing auditing, tax, and consulting services to large corporations. In 2002, the firm voluntarily surrendered its licenses to practice as Certified Public Accountants in the United States after being found guilty of criminal charges relating to the firm's handling of the auditing of Enron, the energy corporation, resulting in the loss of 85,000 jobs. Although the verdict was subsequently overturned by the Supreme Court of the United States, it has not returned as a viable business.
   a. Institute of Financial Accountants
   c. Arthur Andersen
   b. Information Systems Audit and Control Association
   d. Accion USA

12. A _____ is a fungible, negotiable instrument representing financial value. They are broadly categorized into debt securities (such as banknotes, bonds and debentures), and equity securities; e.g., common stocks. The company or other entity issuing the _____ is called the issuer.
   a. Tracking stock
   c. Securities lending
   b. Book entry
   d. Security

Chapter 20. Lease Financing

13. The U.S. _____ is an independent agency of the United States government which holds primary responsibility for enforcing the federal securities laws and regulating the securities industry, the nation's stock and options exchanges, and other electronic securities markets. The SEC was created by section 4 of the SEC of 1934 (now codified as 15 U.S.C. Â§ 78d and commonly referred to as the 1934 Act.)

   a. 7-Eleven
   b. 529 plan
   c. 4-4-5 Calendar
   d. Securities and Exchange Commission

14. A _____ is a financing structure by which a company structures the ownership of an asset so that -

   - for financial accounting purposes (under pre-2003 U.S. financial accounting rules), the asset is owned by a special-purpose entity and leased to the operating company under an operating lease. The special-purpose entity (SPE) is usually owned by the lessee / operating company, and is given just enough independence so that it can be taken off the operating company's balance sheet. The asset is thus recorded as an asset on the balance sheet of the special purpose entity, not of the lessee / operating company. Thus, depreciation of the asset need not be charged against income of the operating company. Instead, the lease payments are recorded as an expense on the income statement.

   - for tax purposes, the asset is owned by the operating company (or the special-purpose entity is consolidated with the operating company, so that the two are treated as a single entity for tax accounting purposes.) Thus, the operating company can deduct depreciation of the asset for tax purposes, generally on an accelerated depreciation schedule.

   Effectively, the asset is owned indirectly by the lessee / operating company, and the company leases the asset to itself. The post-Enron rules of the Financial Accounting Standards Board, which require some measure of independence of a special purpose entity from the operating company, and genuine economic substance to the transaction in which the SPE is a party, made it difficult or impossible to structure a _____ SPE, so they have essentially passed out of existence.

   a. Demand deposit
   b. 529 plan
   c. 4-4-5 Calendar
   d. Synthetic lease

15. The _____ is the current method of accelerated asset depreciation required by the United States income tax code. Under _____, all assets are divided into classes which dictate the number of years over which an asset's cost will be recovered.

   Prior to the Accelerated Cost Recovery System (ACRS), most capital purchases were depreciated using a straight line technique, that allowed for the depreciation of the asset over its useful life.

   a. 4-4-5 Calendar
   b. 7-Eleven
   c. 529 plan
   d. Modified Accelerated Cost Recovery System

16. In economics, business, and accounting, a _____ is the value of money that has been used up to produce something, and hence is not available for use anymore. In business, the _____ may be one of acquisition, in which case the amount of money expended to acquire it is counted as _____. In this case, money is the input that is gone in order to acquire the thing.

a. Sliding scale fees
b. Fixed costs
c. Marginal cost
d. Cost

17. The role of the _____ is to issue accounting standards in the United Kingdom. It is recognised for that purpose under the Companies Act 1985. It took over the task of setting accounting standards from the Accounting Standards Committee (ASC) in 1990.
   a. ABN Amro
   b. AAB
   c. A Random Walk Down Wall Street
   d. Accounting Standards Board

18. In financial accounting, a _____ or statement of financial position is a summary of a person's or organization's balances. Assets, liabilities and ownership equity are listed as of a specific date, such as the end of its financial year. A _____ is often described as a snapshot of a company's financial condition.
   a. Statement of retained earnings
   b. Financial statements
   c. Statement on Auditing Standards No. 70: Service Organizations
   d. Balance sheet

19. _____ is the field of accountancy concerned with the preparation of financial statements for decision makers, such as stockholders, suppliers, banks, employees, government agencies, owners, and other stakeholders. The fundamental need for _____ is to reduce principal-agent problem by measuring and monitoring agents' performance and reporting the results to interested users.

   _____ is used to prepare accounting information for people outside the organization or not involved in the day to day running of the company.

   a. 4-4-5 Calendar
   b. 7-Eleven
   c. 529 plan
   d. Financial Accounting

20. The _____ is a private, not-for-profit organization whose primary purpose is to develop generally accepted accounting principles (GAAP) within the United States in the public's interest. The Securities and Exchange Commission (SEC) designated the _____ as the organization responsible for setting accounting standards for public companies in the U.S. It was created in 1973, replacing the Accounting Principles Board and the Committee on Accounting Procedure of the American Institute of Certified Public Accountants. The _____'s mission is 'to establish and improve standards of financial accounting and reporting for the guidance and education of the public, including issuers, auditors, and users of financial information.'

   The _____ is not a governmental body.

   a. World Congress of Accountants
   b. Federal Deposit Insurance Corporation
   c. KPMG
   d. Financial Accounting Standards Board

21. _____ are formal records of a business' financial activities.

Chapter 20. Lease Financing

_____ provide an overview of a business' financial condition in both short and long term. There are four basic _____:

1. **Balance sheet**: also referred to as statement of financial position or condition, reports on a company's assets, liabilities, and net equity as of a given point in time.
2. **Income statement**: also referred to as Profit and Loss statement (or a 'P'L'), reports on a company's income, expenses, and profits over a period of time.
3. **Statement of retained earnings**: explains the changes in a company's retained earnings over the reporting period.
4. **Statement of cash flows**: reports on a company's cash flow activities, particularly its operating, investing and financing activities.

a. Notes to the Financial Statements

b. Statement on Auditing Standards No. 70: Service Organizations

c. Statement of retained earnings

d. Financial statements

22. The _____ is a capital budgeting metric used by firms to decide whether they should make investments. It is an indicator of the efficiency or quality of an investment, as opposed to net present value (NPV), which indicates value or magnitude.

The IRR is the annualized effective compounded return rate which can be earned on the invested capital, i.e., the yield on the investment.

a. ABN Amro

b. Internal rate of return

c. AAB

d. A Random Walk Down Wall Street

23. _____ is one of the constituents of a leasing calculus or operation. It describes the future value of a good in terms of percentage of depreciation of its initial value.

Example: A car is sold at a list price of $20,000 today. After a usage of 36 months and 50,000 miles its value is contractually defined as 50% or $10,000. The credited amount, on which the interest is applied, thus is $20,000 present value minus $10,000 future value.

a. Days Sales Outstanding

b. Net pay

c. Residual value

d. Round-tripping

24. _____ is the balance of the amounts of cash being received and paid by a business during a defined period of time, sometimes tied to a specific project. Measurement of _____ can be used

- to evaluate the state or performance of a business or project.
- to determine problems with liquidity. Being profitable does not necessarily mean being liquid. A company can fail because of a shortage of cash, even while profitable.
- to generate project rate of returns. The time of _____s into and out of projects are used as inputs to financial models such as internal rate of return, and net present value.
- to examine income or growth of a business when it is believed that accrual accounting concepts do not represent economic realities. Alternately, _____ can be used to 'validate' the net income generated by accrual accounting.

_____ as a generic term may be used differently depending on context, and certain _____ definitions may be adapted by analysts and users for their own uses. Common terms include operating _____ and free _____.

_____s can be classified into:

1. Operational _____s: Cash received or expended as a result of the company's core business activities.
2. Investment _____s: Cash received or expended through capital expenditure, investments or acquisitions.
3. Financing _____s: Cash received or expended as a result of financial activities, such as interests and dividends.

All three together - the net _____ - are necessary to reconcile the beginning cash balance to the ending cash balance. Loan draw downs or equity injections, that is just shifting of capital but no expenditure as such, are not considered in the net _____.

a. Real option
b. Corporate finance
c. Cash flow
d. Shareholder value

25. _____ is that which is owed; usually referencing assets owed, but the term can cover other obligations. In the case of assets, _____ is a means of using future purchasing power in the present before a summation has been earned. Some companies and corporations use _____ as a part of their overall corporate finance strategy.
a. Partial Payment
b. Credit cycle
c. Cross-collateralization
d. Debt

26. _____, refers to consumption opportunity gained by an entity within a specified time frame, which is generally expressed in monetary terms. However, for households and individuals, '_____ is the sum of all the wages, salaries, profits, interests payments, rents and other forms of earnings received... in a given period of time.' For firms, _____ generally refers to net-profit: what remains of revenue after expenses have been subtracted.
a. Annual report
b. OIBDA
c. Accrual
d. Income

27. An _____ is a tax levied on the financial income of people, corporations, or other legal entities. Various _____ systems exist, with varying degrees of tax incidence. Income taxation can be progressive, proportional, or regressive.

Chapter 20. Lease Financing

a. A Random Walk Down Wall Street
b. ABN Amro
c. Income tax
d. AAB

28. In United States banking, _____ is a marketing term for certain services offered primarily to larger business customers. It may be used to describe all bank accounts (such as checking accounts) provided to businesses of a certain size, but it is more often used to describe specific services such as cash concentration, zero balance accounting, and automated clearing house facilities. Sometimes, private banking customers are given _____ services.

a. Profitability index
b. Cash management
c. Capitalization rate
d. Global tactical asset allocation

29. An _____ can be defined as a contract which provides an income stream in return for an initial payment.

An immediate _____ is an _____ for which the time between the contract date and the date of the first payment is not longer than the time interval between payments. A common use for an immediate _____ is to provide a pension to a retired person or persons.

a. Annuity
b. Intrinsic value
c. AT'T Inc.
d. Amortization

30. A standard, commercial _____ is a document issued mostly by a financial institution, used primarily in trade finance, which usually provides an irrevocable payment undertaking.

The _____ can also be the source of payment for a transaction, meaning that redeeming the _____ will pay an exporter. Letters of credit are used primarily in international trade transactions of significant value, for deals between a supplier in one country and a customer in another.

a. McFadden Act
b. Duty of loyalty
c. Bond indenture
d. Letter of credit

31. _____ is the provision of resources (such as granting a loan) by one party to another party where that second party does not reimburse the first party immediately, thereby generating a debt, and instead arranges either to repay or return those resources (or material(s) of equal value) at a later date. The first party is called a creditor, also known as a lender, while the second party is called a debtor, also known as a borrower.

Movements of financial capital are normally dependent on either _____ or equity transfers.

a. Credit
b. Clearing house
c. Comparable
d. Warrant

32. A _____ is a lease in which the lessor puts up some of the money required to purchase the asset and borrows the rest from a lender. The lender is given a senior secured interest on the asset and an assignment of the lease and lease payments. The lessee makes payments to the lessor, who makes payments to the lender.

a. Guaranteed consumer funding
b. Collection agency
c. Debt buyer
d. Leveraged lease

Chapter 20. Lease Financing

33. A '_____' is a 'Charge' that is paid to obtain the right to delay a payment. Essentially, the payer purchases the right to make a given payment in the future instead of in the Present. The '_____', or 'Charge' that must be paid to delay the payment, is simply the difference between what the payment amount would be if it were paid in the present and what the payment amount would be paid if it were paid in the future.
   a. Value at risk
   b. Risk aversion
   c. Discount
   d. Risk modeling

34. The _____ is an interest rate a central bank charges depository institutions that borrow reserves from it.

The term _____ has two meanings:

- the same as interest rate; the term 'discount' does not refer to the meaning of the word, but to the purpose of using the quantity, such as computations of present value, e.g. net present value / discounted cash flow

- the annual effective _____, which is the annual interest divided by the capital including that interest; this rate is lower than the interest rate; it corresponds to using the value after a year as the nominal value, and seeing the initial value as the nominal value minus a discount; it is used for Treasury Bills and similar financial instruments

The annual effective _____ is the annual interest divided by the capital including that interest, which is the interest rate divided by 100% plus the interest rate. It is the annual discount factor to be applied to the future cash flow, to find the discount, subtracted from a future value to find the value one year earlier.

For example, suppose there is a government bond that sells for $95 and pays $100 in a year's time.

   a. Stochastic volatility
   b. Fisher equation
   c. Black-Scholes
   d. Discount rate

35. _____ is subcontracting a process, such as product design or manufacturing, to a third-party company. The decision to outsource is often made in the interest of lowering cost or making better use of time and energy costs, redirecting or conserving energy directed at the competencies of a particular business, or to make more efficient use of land, labor, capital, (information) technology and resources. _____ became part of the business lexicon during the 1980s.
   a. Exchange Rate Mechanism
   b. OTC Bulletin Board
   c. AT'T Inc.
   d. Outsourcing

36. _____ is part of the Federal income tax system of the United States. There is an _____ for those who owe personal income tax, and another for corporations owing corporate income tax. Only the _____ for those owing personal income tax is described here.

The _____ operates in effect as a parallel tax system, with its own definition of taxable income, exemptions, and tax rates. Taxpayers compute tax owed under the 'regular' and _____ systems and are liable for whichever is higher.

a. AAB
b. Alternative minimum tax
c. A Random Walk Down Wall Street
d. ABN Amro

37. _____ is a structured finance process that involves pooling and repackaging of cash-flow-producing financial assets into securities, which are then sold to investors. The term '_____' is derived from the fact that the form of financial instruments used to obtain funds from the investors are securities. As a portfolio risk backed by amortizing cash flows - and unlike general corporate debt - the credit quality of securitized debt is non-stationary due to changes in volatility that are time- and structure-dependent.
   a. The Glass-Steagall Act of 1933
   b. Special journals
   c. Reputational risk
   d. Securitization

38. In structured finance, a _____ is one of a number of related securities offered as part of the same transaction. The word _____ is French for slice, section, series, or portion. In the financial sense of the word, each bond is a different slice of the deal's risk.
   a. 4-4-5 Calendar
   b. Yield curve spread
   c. Credit enhancement
   d. Tranche

39. The term _____ describes two different concepts:

   - The first is a recognition of partial payment already made towards taxes due.
   - The second is a state benefit paid to workers through the tax system, which has the effect of increasing (rather than reducing) net income.

Within the Australian, Canadian, United Kingdom, and United States tax systems, a _____ is a recognition of partial payment already made towards taxes due. A similar concept exists (fr:Avoir fiscal) in the French tax system. This situation arises, for example, when standard rate tax has been deducted at source , but the tax-payer is subject to further taxation at a higher rate. It also applies in dividend imputation systems.

   a. 7-Eleven
   b. 4-4-5 Calendar
   c. Tax credit
   d. 529 plan

40. In business and accounting, _____s are everything of value that is owned by a person or company. The balance sheet of a firm records the monetary value of the _____s owned by the firm. The two major _____ classes are tangible _____s and intangible _____s.
   a. Accounts payable
   b. Asset
   c. EBITDA
   d. Income

41. In finance, _____ is the process of estimating the potential market value of a financial asset or liability. they can be done on assets (for example, investments in marketable securities such as stocks, options, business enterprises, or intangible assets such as patents and trademarks) or on liabilities (e.g., Bonds issued by a company.) _____s are required in many contexts including investment analysis, capital budgeting, merger and acquisition transactions, financial reporting, taxable events to determine the proper tax liability, and in litigation.
   a. Share
   b. Valuation
   c. Margin
   d. Procter ' Gamble

42. In finance, the _____ is used to determine a theoretically appropriate required rate of return of an asset, if that asset is to be added to an already well-diversified portfolio, given that asset's non-diversifiable risk. The model takes into account the asset's sensitivity to non-diversifiable risk (also known as systemic risk or market risk), often represented by the quantity beta (β) in the financial industry, as well as the expected return of the market and the expected return of a theoretical risk-free asset.

The model was introduced by Jack Treynor (1961, 1962), William Sharpe (1964), John Lintner (1965a,b) and Jan Mossin (1966) independently, building on the earlier work of Harry Markowitz on diversification and modern portfolio theory.

   a. Random walk hypothesis
   c. Capital asset pricing model
   b. Cox-Ingersoll-Ross model
   d. Hull-White model

43. The term _____ has three unrelated technical definitions, and is also used in a variety of non-technical ways.

   - In financial economics, it refers to any asset used to make money, as opposed to assets used for personal enjoyment or consumption. This is an important distinction because two people can disagree sharply about the value of personal assets, one person might think a sports car is more valuable than a pickup truck, another person might have the opposite taste. But if an asset is held for the purpose of making money, taste has nothing to do with it, only differences of opinion about how much money the asset will produce. With the further assumption that people agree on the probability distribution of future cash flows, it is possible to have an objective _____ pricing model. Even without the assumption of agreement, it is possible to set rational limits on _____ value.
   - In governmental accounting, it is defined as any asset used in operations with an initial useful life extending beyond one reporting period. Generally, government managers have a 'stewardship' duty to maintain _____s under their control. See International Public Sector Accounting Standards for details.
   - In US tax accounting, it is defined as any property other than a list of exceptions. The main exceptions are anything held for sale, and any real estate or depreciable property used in business. Almost everything you own and use for personal purposes, pleasure or investment is a _____. If something is a _____ for tax purposes, gains or losses on sale or disposition are capital gains or capital losses. For individuals, however, capital losses on property held for personal use are generally not deductible. See the IRS publication Tax Facts about Capital Gains and Losses for details.

A well-known financial accounting textbook advises that the term be avoided except in tax accounting because it is used in so many different senses, not all of them well-defined. For example it is often used as a synonym for fixed assets or for investments in securities.

A common non-technical usage occurs when people ask that employees or the environment or something else be treated as a _____.

   a. Political risk
   c. Solvency
   b. Settlement date
   d. Capital Asset

Chapter 20. Lease Financing

44. _____ is the risk that the value of an investment will decrease due to moves in market factors. The five standard _____ factors are:

- Equity risk, the risk that stock prices will change.
- Interest rate risk, the risk that interest rates will change.
- Currency risk, the risk that foreign exchange rates will change.
- Commodity risk, the risk that commodity prices (e.g. grains, metals) will change.

As with other forms of risk, _____ may be measured in a number of ways. Traditionally, this is done using a Value at Risk methodology. Value at risk is well established as a risk management technique, but it contains a number of limiting assumptions that constrain its accuracy.

   a. Tracking error   b. Currency risk
   c. Market risk   d. Transaction risk

45. _____ is a type of risk faced by investors, corporations, and governments. It is a risk that can be understood and managed with proper aforethought and investment.

Broadly, _____ refers to the complications businesses and governments may face as a result of what are commonly referred to as political decisions--or 'any political change that alters the expected outcome and value of a given economic action by changing the probability of achieving business objectives.' .

   a. Single-index model   b. Capital asset
   c. Mid price   d. Political risk

46. _____ is the discipline of identifying, monitoring and limiting risks. In some cases the acceptable risk may be near zero. Risks can come from accidents, natural causes and disasters as well as deliberate attacks from an adversary.
   a. FIFO   b. Risk management
   c. Penny stock   d. 4-4-5 Calendar

47. _____ is a financial ratio that indicates the percentage of a company's assets are provided via debt. It is the ratio of total debt (the sum of current liabilities and long-term liabilities) and total assets (the sum of current assets, fixed assets, and other assets such as 'goodwill'.)

or alternatively:

For example, a company with $2 million in total assets and $500,000 in total liabilities would have a _____ of 25%

Like all financial ratios, a company's _____ should be compared with their industry average or other competing firms.

a. Cash management
c. Cash concentration
b. Capitalization rate
d. Debt ratio

Chapter 21. Hybrid Financing: Preferred Stock, Warrants, and Convertibles

1. In finance, a _____ is a type of bond that can be converted into shares of stock in the issuing company, usually at some pre-announced ratio. It is a hybrid security with debt- and equity-like features. Although it typically has a low coupon rate, the holder is compensated with the ability to convert the bond to common stock, usually at a substantial discount to the stock's market value.

   a. Convertible bond
   b. Gilts
   c. Corporate bond
   d. Bond fund

2. The _____, in terms of finance and investing, describes how the expected return of a stock or portfolio is correlated to the return of the financial market as a whole.

   An asset with a beta of 0 means that its price is not at all correlated with the market; that asset is independent. A positive beta means that the asset generally follows the market.

   a. Beta coefficient
   b. Current yield
   c. Perpetuity
   d. LIBOR market model

3. In finance, a _____ is a debt security, in which the authorized issuer owes the holders a debt and, depending on the terms of the _____, is obliged to pay interest (the coupon) and/or to repay the principal at a later date, termed maturity.

   Thus a _____ is a loan: the issuer is the borrower, the _____ holder is the lender, and the coupon is the interest. _____s provide the borrower with external funds to finance long-term investments, or, in the case of government _____s, to finance current expenditure.

   a. Bond
   b. Convertible bond
   c. Puttable bond
   d. Catastrophe bonds

4. A _____ is a fungible, negotiable instrument representing financial value. They are broadly categorized into debt securities (such as banknotes, bonds and debentures), and equity securities; e.g., common stocks. The company or other entity issuing the _____ is called the issuer.

   a. Book entry
   b. Tracking stock
   c. Security
   d. Securities lending

5. _____ is a legal term for a type of debt which is overdue after missing an expected payment. It is also used (in the form in _____) for payments that occur at the end of a period.

   _____ accrue from the date on the first missed payment was due.

   a. Interest
   b. A Random Walk Down Wall Street
   c. AAB
   d. Arrears

6. _____ is typically a higher ranking stock than voting shares, and its terms are negotiated between the corporation and the investor.

   _____ usually carry no voting rights, but may carry superior priority over common stock in the payment of dividends and upon liquidation. _____ may carry a dividend that is paid out prior to any dividends to common stock holders.

a. Preferred stock	b. Follow-on offering
c. Trade-off theory	d. Second lien loan

7. _____ is a multiple-winner voting system intended to promote proportional representation while also being simple to understand.

_____ is used frequently in corporate governance, where it is mandated by many U.S. states, and it was used to elect the Illinois House of Representatives from 1870 until its repeal in 1980. It was used in England in the late 19th century to elect school boards.

a. 529 plan	b. 4-4-5 Calendar
c. Cumulative voting	d. 7-Eleven

8. In business and finance, a _____ (also referred to as equity _____) of stock means a _____ of ownership in a corporation (company.) In the plural, stocks is often used as a synonym for _____s especially in the United States, but it is less commonly used that way outside of North America.

In the United Kingdom, South Africa, and Australia, stock can also refer to completely different financial instruments such as government bonds or, less commonly, to all kinds of marketable securities.

a. Procter ' Gamble	b. Margin
c. Bucket shop	d. Share

9. The coupon or _____ of a bond is the amount of interest paid per year expressed as a percentage of the face value of the bond.

For example if you hold $10,000 nominal of a bond described as a 4.5% loan stock, you will receive $450 in interest each year (probably in two installments of $225 each.)

Not all bonds have coupons.

a. Puttable bond	b. Revenue bonds
c. Zero-coupon bond	d. Coupon rate

10. A _____ is a payment made by a corporation to its shareholder members. When a corporation earns a profit or surplus, that money can be put to two uses: it can either be re-invested in the business (called retained earnings), or it can be paid to the shareholders as a _____. Many corporations retain a portion of their earnings and pay the remainder as a _____.

a. Dividend	b. Dividend puzzle
c. Dividend yield	d. Special dividend

11. A _____ is an entity formed between two or more parties to undertake economic activity together. The parties agree to create a new entity by both contributing equity, and they then share in the revenues, expenses, and control of the enterprise. The venture can be for one specific project only, or a continuing business relationship such as the Sony Ericsson _____.

Chapter 21. Hybrid Financing: Preferred Stock, Warrants, and Convertibles

    a. Pre-emption right
    c. Lien
    b. Fair Debt Collection Practices Act
    d. Joint venture

12. A _____ is the price of a single share of a no. of saleable stocks of the company. Once the stock is purchased, the owner becomes a shareholder of the company that issued the share.
    a. Trading curb
    c. Whisper numbers
    b. Stock split
    d. Share price

13. In finance, the term _____ describes the amount in cash that returns to the owners of a security. Normally it does not include the price variations, at the difference of the total return. _____ applies to various stated rates of return on stocks (common and preferred, and convertible), fixed income instruments (bonds, notes, bills, strips, zero coupon), and some other investment type insurance products (e.g. annuities.)
    a. Yield to maturity
    c. Yield
    b. 4-4-5 Calendar
    d. Macaulay duration

14. _____ is that which is owed; usually referencing assets owed, but the term can cover other obligations. In the case of assets, _____ is a means of using future purchasing power in the present before a summation has been earned. Some companies and corporations use _____ as a part of their overall corporate finance strategy.
    a. Cross-collateralization
    c. Credit cycle
    b. Debt
    d. Partial Payment

15. _____, refers to consumption opportunity gained by an entity within a specified time frame, which is generally expressed in monetary terms. However, for households and individuals, '_____ is the sum of all the wages, salaries, profits, interests payments, rents and other forms of earnings received... in a given period of time.' For firms, _____ generally refers to net-profit: what remains of revenue after expenses have been subtracted.
    a. Income
    c. Annual report
    b. Accrual
    d. OIBDA

16. _____ is a life of security. It may also refer to the final payment date of a loan or other financial instrument, at which point all remaining interest and principal is due to be paid.

1, 3, 6 months _____ band can be calculated by using 30-day per month periods.

    a. False billing
    c. Primary market
    b. Maturity
    d. Replacement cost

17. An _____ is a contract written by a seller that conveys to the buyer the right -- but not the obligation -- to buy (in the case of a call _____) or to sell (in the case of a put _____) a particular asset, such as a piece of property such as, among others, a futures contract. In return for granting the _____, the seller collects a payment (the premium) from the buyer.

For example, buying a call _____ provides the right to buy a specified quantity of a security at a set strike price at some time on or before expiration, while buying a put _____ provides the right to sell.

a. Amortization
b. Annuity
c. AT'T Mobility LLC
d. Option

18. In finance, the _____ is the global financial market for short-term borrowing and lending. It provides short-term liquidity funding for the global financial system. The _____ is where short-term obligations such as Treasury bills, commercial paper and bankers' acceptances are bought and sold.
    a. Cramdown
    b. Money market
    c. Consumer debt
    d. Debt-for-equity swap

19. _____ or net present worth (NPW) is defined as the total present value (PV) of a time series of cash flows. It is a standard method for using the time value of money to appraise long-term projects. Used for capital budgeting, and widely throughout economics, it measures the excess or shortfall of cash flows, in present value terms, once financing charges are met.
    a. Present value of costs
    b. Tax shield
    c. Net present value
    d. Negative gearing

20. In finance, a _____ is a security that entitles the holder to buy stock of the company that issued it at a specified price, which is usually higher than the stock price at time of issue.

    _____s are frequently attached to bonds or preferred stock as a sweetener, allowing the issuer to pay lower interest rates or dividends. They can be used to enhance the yield of the bond, and make them more attractive to potential buyers.

    a. Clearing
    b. Credit
    c. Clearing house
    d. Warrant

21. _____ is an economic concept with commonplace familiarity. It is the price that a good or service is offered at, or will fetch, in the marketplace. It is of interest mainly in the study of microeconomics.
    a. Market price
    b. Delta hedging
    c. Convertible arbitrage
    d. Central Securities Depository

22. _____ is the value on a given date of a future payment or series of future payments, discounted to reflect the time value of money and other factors such as investment risk. _____ calculations are widely used in business and economics to provide a means to compare cash flows at different times on a meaningful 'like to like' basis.

    The most commonly applied model of the time value of money is compound interest.

    a. Present value of benefits
    b. Negative gearing
    c. Present value
    d. Net present value

23. A _____ is a financial contract between two parties, the buyer and the seller of this type of option. Often it is simply labeled a 'call'. The buyer of the option has the right, but not the obligation to buy an agreed quantity of a particular commodity or financial instrument (the underlying instrument) from the seller of the option at a certain time (the expiration date) for a certain price (the strike price.)

Chapter 21. Hybrid Financing: Preferred Stock, Warrants, and Convertibles

   a. Bull spread
   c. Bear call spread
   b. Call option
   d. Bear spread

24. _____ or financing is to provide capital (funds), which means money for a project, a person, a business or any other private or public institutions.

Those funds can be allocated for either short term or long term purposes. The health fund is a new way of _____ private healthcare centers.

   a. Proxy fight
   c. Product life cycle
   b. Funding
   d. Synthetic CDO

25. The phrase _____ refers to the aspect of corporate strategy, corporate finance and management dealing with the buying, selling and combining of different companies that can aid, finance, or help a growing company in a given industry grow rapidly without having to create another business entity.

An acquisition, also known as a takeover, is the buying of one company (the 'target') by another. An acquisition may be friendly or hostile.

   a. 7-Eleven
   c. 4-4-5 Calendar
   b. 529 plan
   d. Mergers and acquisitions

26. In finance, _____ refers to the way a corporation finances its assets through some combination of equity, debt, or hybrid securities. A firm's _____ is then the composition or 'structure' of its liabilities. For example, a firm that sells $20 billion in equity and $80 billion in debt is said to be 20% equity-financed and 80% debt-financed.

   a. Book building
   c. Rights issue
   b. Market for corporate control
   d. Capital structure

27. In options, the _____ is a key variable in a derivatives contract between two parties. Where the contract requires delivery of the underlying instrument, the trade will be at the _____, regardless of the spot price (market price) of the underlying instrument at that time.

Definition - The fixed price at which the owner of an option can purchase, in the case of a call in the case of a put, the underlying security or commodity.

   a. Naked put
   c. Swaption
   b. Moneyness
   d. Strike price

28. _____ is an estimate of the fair value of corporations and their stocks, by using fundamental economic criteria. This theoretical valuation has to be perfected with market criteria, as the final purpose is to determine potential market prices.

   a. Growth stocks
   c. Security Analysis
   b. 4-4-5 Calendar
   d. Stock valuation

Chapter 21. Hybrid Financing: Preferred Stock, Warrants, and Convertibles

29. In economics and finance, _____ is the practice of taking advantage of a price differential between two or more markets: striking a combination of matching deals that capitalize upon the imbalance, the profit being the difference between the market prices. When used by academics, an _____ is a transaction that involves no negative cash flow at any probabilistic or temporal state and a positive cash flow in at least one state; in simple terms, a risk-free profit.
   a. Efficient-market hypothesis
   b. Issuer
   c. Initial margin
   d. Arbitrage

30. _____ is the process of determining the fair price of a bond. As with any security or capital investment, the fair value of a bond is the present value of the stream of cash flows it is expected to generate. Hence, the price or value of a bond is determined by discounting the bond's expected cash flows to the present using the appropriate discount rate.
   a. Catastrophe bonds
   b. Collateralized debt obligations
   c. Bond fund
   d. Bond valuation

31. In finance, _____ is the process of estimating the potential market value of a financial asset or liability. they can be done on assets (for example, investments in marketable securities such as stocks, options, business enterprises, or intangible assets such as patents and trademarks) or on liabilities (e.g., Bonds issued by a company.) _____s are required in many contexts including investment analysis, capital budgeting, merger and acquisition transactions, financial reporting, taxable events to determine the proper tax liability, and in litigation.
   a. Valuation
   b. Procter ' Gamble
   c. Margin
   d. Share

32. In economics, business, and accounting, a _____ is the value of money that has been used up to produce something, and hence is not available for use anymore. In business, the _____ may be one of acquisition, in which case the amount of money expended to acquire it is counted as _____. In this case, money is the input that is gone in order to acquire the thing.
   a. Marginal cost
   b. Fixed costs
   c. Sliding scale fees
   d. Cost

33. The _____ is a capital budgeting metric used by firms to decide whether they should make investments. It is an indicator of the efficiency or quality of an investment, as opposed to net present value (NPV), which indicates value or magnitude.

The IRR is the annualized effective compounded return rate which can be earned on the invested capital, i.e., the yield on the investment.

   a. AAB
   b. A Random Walk Down Wall Street
   c. ABN Amro
   d. Internal rate of return

Chapter 21. Hybrid Financing: Preferred Stock, Warrants, and Convertibles

34. An _____ is an economic concept that relates to the cost incurred by an entity (such as organizations) associated with problems such as divergent management-shareholder objectives and information asymmetry. The costs consist of two main sources:

   1. The costs inherently associated with using an agent (e.g., the risk that agents will use organizational resource for their own benefit) and
   2. The costs of techniques used to mitigate the problems associated with using an agent (e.g., the costs of producing financial statements or the use of stock options to align executive interests to shareholder interests.)

Though effects of _____ are present in any agency relationship, the term is most used in business contexts.

The information asymmetry that exists between shareholders and the Chief Executive Officer is generally considered to be a classic example of a principal-agent problem. The agent (the manager) is working on behalf of the principal (the shareholders), who does not observe the actions of the agent.

   a. A Random Walk Down Wall Street
   b. AAB
   c. ABN Amro
   d. Agency cost

35. In some countries, including the United States and the United Kingdom, corporations can buy back their own stock in a share repurchase, also known as a _____ or share buyback. There has been a meteoric rise in the use of share repurchases in the U.S. in the past twenty years, from $5b in 1980 to $349b in 2005. A share repurchase distributes cash to existing shareholders in exchange for a fraction of the firm's outstanding equity.

   a. Stock repurchase
   b. Trading curb
   c. Common stock
   d. Stockholder

36. In the _____ contract the underwriter agrees to sell as many shares as possible at the agreed-upon price.

Under the all-or-none contract the underwriter agrees either to sell the entire offering or to cancel the deal.

Stand-by underwriting, also known as strict underwriting or old-fashioned underwriting is a form of stock insurance: the issuer contracts the underwriter for the latter to purchase the shares the issuer failed to sell under stockholders' subscription and applications.

   a. Book building
   b. Real option
   c. Follow-on offering
   d. Best efforts

37. The _____ is a financial market where participants buy and sell debt securities, usually in the form of bonds. As of 2006, the size of the international _____ is an estimated $45 trillion, of which the size of the outstanding U.S. _____ debt was $25.2 trillion.

Nearly all of the $923 billion average daily trading volume in the U.S. _____ takes place between broker-dealers and large institutions in a decentralized, over-the-counter market.

   a. Bond market
   b. Fixed income
   c. 529 plan
   d. 4-4-5 Calendar

Chapter 21. Hybrid Financing: Preferred Stock, Warrants, and Convertibles

38. In retail sales, a _____ is a form of fraud in which the party putting forth the fraud lures in customers by advertising a product or service at an unprofitably low price, then reveals to potential customers that the advertised good is not available but that a substitute is. This term has lots of other meanings, even outside of the marketing sense.

The goal of the _____ is to convince some buyers to purchase the substitute good as a means of avoiding disappointment over not getting the bait, or as a way to recover sunk costs expended to try to obtain the bait.

   a. Time value of money
   b. Bait and switch
   c. Zero-coupon bond
   d. Price-to-book ratio

39. _____ is a legally declared inability or impairment of ability of an individual or organization to pay their creditors. Creditors may file a _____ petition against a debtor ('involuntary _____') in an effort to recoup a portion of what they are owed or initiate a restructuring. In the majority of cases, however, _____ is initiated by the debtor (a 'voluntary _____' that is filed by the bankrupt individual or organization.)

   a. 529 plan
   b. 4-4-5 Calendar
   c. Debt settlement
   d. Bankruptcy

40. The role of the _____ is to issue accounting standards in the United Kingdom. It is recognised for that purpose under the Companies Act 1985. It took over the task of setting accounting standards from the Accounting Standards Committee (ASC) in 1990.

   a. Accounting Standards Board
   b. ABN Amro
   c. A Random Walk Down Wall Street
   d. AAB

41. _____ is the field of accountancy concerned with the preparation of financial statements for decision makers, such as stockholders, suppliers, banks, employees, government agencies, owners, and other stakeholders. The fundamental need for _____ is to reduce principal-agent problem by measuring and monitoring agents' performance and reporting the results to interested users.

_____ is used to prepare accounting information for people outside the organization or not involved in the day to day running of the company.

   a. Financial Accounting
   b. 529 plan
   c. 4-4-5 Calendar
   d. 7-Eleven

42. The _____ is a private, not-for-profit organization whose primary purpose is to develop generally accepted accounting principles (GAAP) within the United States in the public's interest. The Securities and Exchange Commission (SEC) designated the _____ as the organization responsible for setting accounting standards for public companies in the U.S. It was created in 1973, replacing the Accounting Principles Board and the Committee on Accounting Procedure of the American Institute of Certified Public Accountants. The _____'s mission is 'to establish and improve standards of financial accounting and reporting for the guidance and education of the public, including issuers, auditors, and users of financial information.'

The _____ is not a governmental body.

a. World Congress of Accountants b. KPMG
c. Federal Deposit Insurance Corporation d. Financial Accounting Standards Board

Chapter 22. Working Capital Management

1. _____ is a financial metric which represents operating liquidity available to a business. Along with fixed assets such as plant and equipment, _____ is considered a part of operating capital. It is calculated as current assets minus current liabilities.
   a. Working capital
   b. Working capital management
   c. 529 plan
   d. 4-4-5 Calendar

2. In United States banking, _____ is a marketing term for certain services offered primarily to larger business customers. It may be used to describe all bank accounts (such as checking accounts) provided to businesses of a certain size, but it is more often used to describe specific services such as cash concentration, zero balance accounting, and automated clearing house facilities. Sometimes, private banking customers are given _____ services.
   a. Capitalization rate
   b. Profitability index
   c. Global tactical asset allocation
   d. Cash management

3. The _____ measures how long an investment with suppliers deprives a firm of cash -- it is (in the generic case of a retailer) the time between disbursement for inventory and collection on its sale. Thus, the _____ measures how risky it would be to increase this investment with suppliers in the course of expanding customer sales. However, shortening the _____ creates its own risks: while a firm could even achieve a negative _____ by collecting from customers before paying suppliers, a policy of strict collections and lax payments is not always sustainable.
   a. Return on sales
   b. Price/cash flow ratio
   c. Cash conversion cycle
   d. Return on capital employed

4. _____, in bookkeeping, refers to assets, liabilities, income, and expenses recorded on individual pages of the so called book of final entry or ledger. Changes in _____ value are made by chronologically posting debit (DR) and credit (CR) entries to its page. Examples of _____s are cash, _____s receivable, mortgages, loans, land and buildings, common stock, sales, services provided, wages, and payroll overhead.
   a. Account
   b. Alpha
   c. Accretion
   d. Option

5. _____ is one of a series of accounting transactions dealing with the billing of customers who owe money to a person, company or organization for goods and services that have been provided to the customer. In most business entities this is typically done by generating an invoice and mailing or electronically delivering it to the customer, who in turn must pay it within an established timeframe called credit or payment terms.

An example of a common payment term is Net 30, meaning payment is due in the amount of the invoice 30 days from the date of invoice.

   a. Accounting methods
   b. Income
   c. Impaired asset
   d. Accounts receivable

6. _____ is a business valuation method. _____ is the net present value of a project if financed solely by ownership equity plus the present value of all the benefits of financing. Usually, the main benefit is a tax shield resulted from tax deductibility of interest payments. Another one can be a subsidized borrowing.
   a. A Random Walk Down Wall Street
   b. Adjusted present value
   c. ABN Amro
   d. AAB

Chapter 22. Working Capital Management

7. _____ is a term used by inventory specialists to describe a level of extra stock that is maintained below the cycle stock to buffer against stockouts. _____ exists to counter uncertainties in supply and demand. _____ is defined as extra units of inventory carried as protection against possible stockouts .(shortfall in raw material or packaging.)
   a. Golden parachute   b. Counting house
   c. Funding   d. Safety stock

8. In business and finance, a _____ (also referred to as equity _____) of stock means a _____ of ownership in a corporation (company.) In the plural, stocks is often used as a synonym for _____s especially in the United States, but it is less commonly used that way outside of North America.

In the United Kingdom, South Africa, and Australia, stock can also refer to completely different financial instruments such as government bonds or, less commonly, to all kinds of marketable securities.

   a. Margin   b. Bucket shop
   c. Share   d. Procter ' Gamble

9. _____ is the planning process used to determine whether a firm's long term investments such as new machinery, replacement machinery, new plants, new products, and research development projects are worth pursuing. It is budget for major capital, or investment, expenditures.

Many formal methods are used in _____, including the techniques such as

- Net present value
- Profitability index
- Internal rate of return
- Modified Internal Rate of Return
- Equivalent annuity

These methods use the incremental cash flows from each potential investment, or project. Techniques based on accounting earnings and accounting rules are sometimes used - though economists consider this to be improper - such as the accounting rate of return, and 'return on investment.' Simplified and hybrid methods are used as well, such as payback period and discounted payback period.

   a. Capital budgeting   b. Shareholder value
   c. Financial distress   d. Preferred stock

10. Working capital requirements of a business should be monitored at all times to ensure that there are sufficient funds available to meet short-term expenses.

The _____ is basically a detailed plan that shows all expected sources and uses of cash

   a. Mitigating Control   b. Loans and interest, in Judaism
   c. Rate of return   d. Cash budget

Chapter 22. Working Capital Management

11. _____ or financing is to provide capital (funds), which means money for a project, a person, a business or any other private or public institutions.

Those funds can be allocated for either short term or long term purposes. The health fund is a new way of _____ private healthcare centers.

   a. Product life cycle   b. Synthetic CDO
   c. Proxy fight   d. Funding

12. _____ is used in finance as a measure of the returns that a company is realising from its capital employed. It is commonly used as a measure for comparing the performance between businesses and for assessing whether a business generates enough returns to pay for its cost of capital.

Net Profit / Capital Employed X 100

_____ compares earnings with capital invested in the company. It is similar to Return on Assets (ROA), but takes into account sources of financing.

   a. Sharpe ratio   b. Debt service coverage ratio
   c. Net assets   d. Return on capital employed

13. In economics and finance, _____ is the practice of taking advantage of a price differential between two or more markets: striking a combination of matching deals that capitalize upon the imbalance, the profit being the difference between the market prices. When used by academics, an _____ is a transaction that involves no negative cash flow at any probabilistic or temporal state and a positive cash flow in at least one state; in simple terms, a risk-free profit.

   a. Arbitrage   b. Initial margin
   c. Efficient-market hypothesis   d. Issuer

14. _____ has many definitions and is not easily analysed. In general, it represents the capital investment necessary for a business to function. Consequently, it is not a measure of assets, but of capital investment: stock or shares and long-term liabilities.

   a. Times interest earned   b. PEG ratio
   c. Capital employed   d. Return on assets

15. _____ is the balance of the amounts of cash being received and paid by a business during a defined period of time, sometimes tied to a specific project. Measurement of _____ can be used

- to evaluate the state or performance of a business or project.
- to determine problems with liquidity. Being profitable does not necessarily mean being liquid. A company can fail because of a shortage of cash, even while profitable.
- to generate project rate of returns. The time of _____s into and out of projects are used as inputs to financial models such as internal rate of return, and net present value.
- to examine income or growth of a business when it is believed that accrual accounting concepts do not represent economic realities. Alternately, _____ can be used to 'validate' the net income generated by accrual accounting.

Chapter 22. Working Capital Management 251

_____ as a generic term may be used differently depending on context, and certain _____ definitions may be adapted by analysts and users for their own uses. Common terms include operating _____ and free _____.

_____s can be classified into:

1. Operational _____s: Cash received or expended as a result of the company's core business activities.
2. Investment _____s: Cash received or expended through capital expenditure, investments or acquisitions.
3. Financing _____s: Cash received or expended as a result of financial activities, such as interests and dividends.

All three together - the net _____ - are necessary to reconcile the beginning cash balance to the ending cash balance. Loan draw downs or equity injections, that is just shifting of capital but no expenditure as such, are not considered in the net _____.

a. Corporate finance
c. Real option

b. Cash flow
d. Shareholder value

16. The free _____ of a public company is an estimate of the proportion of shares that are not held by large owners and that are not stock with sales restrictions (restricted stock that cannot be sold until they become unrestricted stock.)

The free _____ or a public _____ is usually defined as being all shares held by investors other than:

- shares held by owners owning more than 5% of all shares (those could be institutional investors, 'strategic shareholders,' founders, executives, and other insiders' holdings)
- restricted stocks (granted to executives that can be, but don't have to be, registered insiders)
- insider holdings (it is assumed that insiders hold stock for the very long term)

The free _____ is an important criterion in quoting a share on the stock market.

To _____ a company means to list its shares on a public stock exchange through an initial public offering (or 'flotation'.)

- Open market
- Outstanding shares
- Market capitalization
- Public _____ *loat*
- Reverse takeover

a. Float
c. Trade finance

b. Golden parachute
d. Synthetic CDO

Chapter 22. Working Capital Management

17. _____ occurs when an entity that has issued callable bonds calls those debt securities from the debt holders with the express purpose of reissuing new debt at a lower coupon rate. In essence, the issue of new, lower-interest debt allows the company to prematurely refund the older, higher-interest debt.

On the contrary, NonRefundable Bonds may be callable but they cannot be re-issued with a lower coupon rate.

a. No-arbitrage bounds
b. Market neutral
c. Refunding
d. Systematic risk

18. In financial accounting, the term _____ is most commonly used to describe any part of shareholders' equity, except for basic share capital. Sometimes, the term is used instead of the term provision; such a use, however, is inconsistent with the terminology suggested by International Accounting Standards Board. For more information about provisions, see provision (accounting.)

a. FIFO and LIFO accounting
b. Closing entries
c. Reserve
d. Treasury stock

19. The institution most often referenced by the word '_____' is a public or publicly traded _____, the shares of which are traded on a public stock exchange (e.g., the New York Stock Exchange or Nasdaq in the United States) where shares of stock of _____s are bought and sold by and to the general public. Most of the largest businesses in the world are publicly traded _____s. However, the majority of _____s are said to be closely held, privately held or close _____s, meaning that no ready market exists for the trading of shares.

a. Federal Home Loan Mortgage Corporation
b. Protect
c. Depository Trust Company
d. Corporation

20. An _____ can be defined as a contract which provides an income stream in return for an initial payment.

An immediate _____ is an _____ for which the time between the contract date and the date of the first payment is not longer than the time interval between payments. A common use for an immediate _____ is to provide a pension to a retired person or persons.

a. AT'T Inc.
b. Amortization
c. Intrinsic value
d. Annuity

21. _____ is a list for goods and materials held available in stock by a business. It is also used for a list of the contents of a household and for a list for testamentary purposes of the possessions of someone who has died. In accounting _____ is considered an asset.

a. AAB
b. Inventory
c. ABN Amro
d. A Random Walk Down Wall Street

22. _____ is the provision of resources (such as granting a loan) by one party to another party where that second party does not reimburse the first party immediately, thereby generating a debt, and instead arranges either to repay or return those resources (or material(s) of equal value) at a later date. The first party is called a creditor, also known as a lender, while the second party is called a debtor, also known as a borrower.

Movements of financial capital are normally dependent on either _____ or equity transfers.

a. Comparable
b. Clearing house
c. Warrant
d. Credit

23. A _____ is the system of organizations, people, technology, activities, information and resources involved in moving a product or service from supplier to customer. _____ activities transform natural resources, raw materials and components into a finished product that is delivered to the end customer. In sophisticated _____ systems, used products may re-enter the _____ at any point where residual value is recyclable.
   a. Supply chain
   b. 4-4-5 Calendar
   c. 7-Eleven
   d. 529 plan

24. In accountancy, _____ is a company's average collection period. A low number of days indicates that the company collects its outstanding receivables quickly. Typically, _____ is calculated monthly. The _____ figure is an index of the relationship between outstanding receivables and sales achieved over a given period. The _____ analysis provides general information about the number of days on average that customers take to pay invoices.
   a. Residual value
   b. Round-tripping
   c. Net pay
   d. Days sales outstanding

25. _____ is a file or account that contains money that a person or company owes to suppliers, but hasn't paid yet (a form of debt.) When you receive an invoice you add it to the file, and then you remove it when you pay. Thus, the A/P is a form of credit that suppliers offer to their purchasers by allowing them to pay for a product or service after it has already been received.
   a. Outstanding balance
   b. Accrual
   c. Earnings before interest, taxes, depreciation and amortization
   d. Accounts payable

26. Accrual, in accounting, describes the accounting method known as _____, whereby revenues and expenses are recognized when they are accrued, i.e. accumulated (earned or incurred), regardless when the actual cash is received or paid out.

E.g. a company delivers a product to a customer who will pay for it 30 days later in the next fiscal year starting a week after the delivery. The company recognizes the proceeds as a revenue in its current income statement still for the fiscal year of the delivery, even though it will get paid in cash during the following accounting period.

   a. Accrual basis
   b. A Random Walk Down Wall Street
   c. ABN Amro
   d. AAB

27. In economics, business, and accounting, a _____ is the value of money that has been used up to produce something, and hence is not available for use anymore. In business, the _____ may be one of acquisition, in which case the amount of money expended to acquire it is counted as _____. In this case, money is the input that is gone in order to acquire the thing.
   a. Cost
   b. Sliding scale fees
   c. Marginal cost
   d. Fixed costs

28. _____ is a type of trade policy that allows traders to act and transact without interference from government. Thus, the policy permits trading partners mutual gains from trade, with goods and services produced according to the theory of comparative advantage.

Chapter 22. Working Capital Management

Under a _____ policy, prices are a reflection of true supply and demand, and are the sole determinant of resource allocation.

a. Seasoned equity offering
c. Yield spread

b. Monte Carlo methods
d. Free trade

29. _____ is a life of security. It may also refer to the final payment date of a loan or other financial instrument, at which point all remaining interest and principal is due to be paid.

1, 3, 6 months _____ band can be calculated by using 30-day per month periods.

a. Primary market
c. Maturity

b. False billing
d. Replacement cost

30. In economics, the concept of the _____ refers to the decision-making time frame of a firm in which at least one factor of production is fixed. Costs which are fixed in the _____ have no impact on a firms decisions. For example a firm can raise output by increasing the amount of labour through overtime.

a. Long-run
c. Short-run

b. 529 plan
d. 4-4-5 Calendar

31. _____ exists when one firm provides goods or services to a customer with an agreement to bill them later, or receive a shipment or service from a supplier under an agreement to pay them later. It can be viewed as an essential element of capitalization in an operating business because it can reduce the required capital investment to operate the business if it is managed properly. _____ is the largest use of capital for a majority of business to business (B2B) sellers in the United States and is a critical source of capital for a majority of all businesses.

a. Trade credit
c. Going concern

b. 529 plan
d. 4-4-5 Calendar

32. _____ are securities that can be easily converted into cash. Such securities will generally have highly liquid markets allowing the security to be sold at a reasonable price very quickly. This is a usual feature in real estate.

a. Book entry
c. Tracking stock

b. Securities lending
d. Marketable

33. A _____ is a fungible, negotiable instrument representing financial value. They are broadly categorized into debt securities (such as banknotes, bonds and debentures), and equity securities; e.g., common stocks. The company or other entity issuing the _____ is called the issuer.

a. Securities lending
c. Security

b. Tracking stock
d. Book entry

34. A _____ is a situation that involves losing one quality or aspect of something in return for gaining another quality or aspect. It implies a decision to be made with full comprehension of both the upside and downside of a particular choice.

In economics the term is expressed as opportunity cost, referring the most preferred alternative given up.

Chapter 22. Working Capital Management

a. Break-even point
b. Capital outflow
c. Total revenue
d. Trade-off

35. The _____ of Capital Structure refers to the idea that a company chooses how much debt finance and how much equity finance to use by balancing the costs and benefits. The classical version of the hypothesis goes back to Kraus and Litzenberger who considered a balance between the dead-weight costs of bankruptcy and the tax saving benefits of debt. Often agency costs are also included in the balance.
   a. Trade-off theory
   b. Rights issue
   c. Firm commitment
   d. Financial distress

36. _____ is the process of decreasing an amount over a period of time. The word comes from Middle English amortisen to kill, alienate in mortmain, from Anglo-French amorteser, alteration of amortir, from Vulgar Latin admortire to kill, from Latin ad- + mort-, mors death. Particular instances of the term include:

   - _____ (business), the allocation of a lump sum amount to different time periods, particularly for loans and other forms of finance, including related interest or other finance charges.
     - _____ schedule, a table detailing each periodic payment on a loan (typically a mortgage), as generated by an _____ calculator.
     - Negative _____, an _____ schedule where the loan amount actually increases through not paying the full interest
   - Amortized analysis, analyzing the execution cost of algorithms over a sequence of operations.
   - _____ of capital expenditures of certain assets under accounting rules, particularly intangible assets, in a manner analogous to depreciation.
   - _____ (tax law)

_____ is also used in the context of zoning regulations and describes the time in which a property owner has to relocate when the property's use constitutes a preexisting nonconforming use under zoning regulations.

   - Depreciation

   a. Intrinsic value
   b. AT'T Inc.
   c. Amortization
   d. Option

37. The U.S. _____ is an independent agency of the United States government which holds primary responsibility for enforcing the federal securities laws and regulating the securities industry, the nation's stock and options exchanges, and other electronic securities markets. The SEC was created by section 4 of the SEC of 1934 (now codified as 15 U.S.C. Â§ 78d and commonly referred to as the 1934 Act.)
   a. 529 plan
   b. 4-4-5 Calendar
   c. 7-Eleven
   d. Securities and Exchange Commission

38. In finance, a _____ is a debt security, in which the authorized issuer owes the holders a debt and, depending on the terms of the _____, is obliged to pay interest (the coupon) and/or to repay the principal at a later date, termed maturity.

Thus a _____ is a loan: the issuer is the borrower, the _____ holder is the lender, and the coupon is the interest. _____s provide the borrower with external funds to finance long-term investments, or, in the case of government _____s, to finance current expenditure.

a. Bond
b. Puttable bond
c. Catastrophe bonds
d. Convertible bond

39. In financial accounting, _____s are precautions for which the amount or probability of occurrence are not known. Typical examples are _____s for warranty costs and _____ for taxes the term reserve is used instead of term _____; such a use, however, is inconsistent with the terminology suggested by International Accounting Standards Board.

a. Provision
b. Money measurement concept
c. Petty cash
d. Momentum Accounting and Triple-Entry Bookkeeping

40. A _____ is any credit facility extended to a business by a bank or financial institution. A _____ may take several forms such as cash credit, overdraft, demand loan, export packing credit, term loan, discounting or purchase of commercial bills etc. It is like an account that can readily be tapped into if the need arises or not touched at all and saved for emergencies.

a. Cash credit
b. Default Notice
c. Debt-snowball method
d. Line of credit

41. A _____, referred to as a note payable in accounting, is a contract where one party (the maker or issuer) makes an unconditional promise in writing to pay a sum of money to the other (the payee), either at a fixed or determinable future time or on demand of the payee, under specific terms. They differ from IOUs in that they contain a specific promise to pay, rather than simply acknowledging that a debt exists.

The terms of a note typically include the principal amount, the interest rate if any, and the maturity date.

a. Title loan
b. Credit repair software
c. Promissory note
d. Financial plan

42. _____ is a type of credit that does not have a fixed number of payments, in contrast to installment credit. Examples of _____s used by consumers include credit cards. Corporate _____ facilities are typically used to provide liquidity for a company's day-to-day operations.

a. Package loan
b. Reverse stock split
c. Revolving credit
d. Commercial finance

43. A _____ is a contractual provision in a loan agreement which provides that all loans must be repaid within a specified period, after which no further loans will be made available to the debtor for a specified 'cleanup' period.

It may also refer to revolving line of credit. Lender may require a cleanup period annually, like borrower may have to pay down the balance to zero for 30 days.

Chapter 22. Working Capital Management

a. Market neutral
c. Package loan
b. Holding period return
d. Cleanup clause

44. In the global money market, _____ is an unsecured promissory note with a fixed maturity of one to 270 days. _____ is a money-market security issued (sold) by large banks and corporations to get money to meet short term debt obligations (for example, payroll), and is only backed by an issuing bank or corporation's promise to pay the face amount on the maturity date specified on the note. Since it is not backed by collateral, only firms with excellent credit ratings from a recognized rating agency will be able to sell their _____ at a reasonable price.
   a. Book building
   c. Trade-off theory
   b. Commercial paper
   d. Financial distress

45. _____ is a fee paid on borrowed assets. It is the price paid for the use of borrowed money, or, money earned by deposited funds. Assets that are sometimes lent with _____ include money, shares, consumer goods through hire purchase, major assets such as aircraft, and even entire factories in finance lease arrangements.
   a. Insolvency
   c. Interest
   b. AAB
   d. A Random Walk Down Wall Street

46. An _____ is the price a borrower pays for the use of money they do not own, and the return a lender receives for deferring the use of funds, by lending it to the borrower. _____s are normally expressed as a percentage rate over the period of one year.

_____s targets are also a vital tool of monetary policy and are used to control variables like investment, inflation, and unemployment.

   a. AAB
   c. ABN Amro
   b. A Random Walk Down Wall Street
   d. Interest rate

47. In lending agreements, _____ is a borrower's pledge of specific property to a lender, to secure repayment of a loan. The _____ serves as protection for a lender against a borrower's risk of default - that is, a borrower failing to pay the principal and interest under the terms of a loan obligation. If a borrower does default on a loan (due to insolvency or other event), that borrower forfeits (gives up) the property pledged as _____ *ollateral* - and the lender then becomes the owner of the _____.
   a. Refinancing risk
   c. Collateral
   b. Future-oriented
   d. Nominal value

48. _____ is a legally declared inability or impairment of ability of an individual or organization to pay their creditors. Creditors may file a _____ petition against a debtor ('involuntary _____') in an effort to recoup a portion of what they are owed or initiate a restructuring. In the majority of cases, however, _____ is initiated by the debtor (a 'voluntary _____' that is filed by the bankrupt individual or organization.)
   a. Bankruptcy
   c. Debt settlement
   b. 4-4-5 Calendar
   d. 529 plan

49. In law, _____ refers to the process by which a company (or part of a company) is brought to an end, and the assets and property of the company redistributed. _____ can also be referred to as winding-up or dissolution, although dissolution technically refers to the last stage of _____. The process of _____ also arises when customs, an authority or agency in a country responsible for collecting and safeguarding customs duties, determines the final computation or ascertainment of the duties or drawback accruing on an entry.

    a. Debt settlement
    b. Liquidation
    c. 529 plan
    d. 4-4-5 Calendar

Chapter 23. Derivatives and Risk Management

1. The _____ is an American financial and commodity derivative exchange based in Chicago. The _____ was founded in 1898 as the Chicago Butter and Egg Board. Originally, the exchange was a non-profit organization.
   a. Financial Crimes Enforcement Network
   b. Public Company Accounting Oversight Board
   c. Chicago Mercantile Exchange
   d. Gamelan Council

2. _____ are financial instruments that can be used by organizations or individuals as part of a risk management strategy to reduce risk associated with adverse or unexpected weather conditions. The difference from other derivatives is that the underlying asset (rain/temperature/snow) has no direct value to price the weather derivative. Farmers can use _____ to hedge against poor harvests caused by drought or frost; theme parks may want to insure against rainy weekends during peak summer seasons; and gas and power companies may use heating degree days (HDD) or cooling degree days (CDD) contracts to smooth earnings.
   a. Volatility arbitrage
   b. Credit derivative
   c. Risk-neutral measure
   d. Weather derivatives

3. A _____ is a financial contract whose value is derived from the value of something else (known as the underlying.) The underlying on which a _____ is based can be an asset, weather conditions bonds or other forms of credit.
   a. 7-Eleven
   b. 4-4-5 Calendar
   c. 529 plan
   d. Derivative

4. In finance, a _____ is a standardized contract, to buy or sell a specified commodity of standardized quality at a certain date in the future, at a market determined price (the futures price.)

   The price is determined by the instantaneous equilibrium between the forces of supply and demand among competing buy and sell orders on the exchange at the time of the purchase or sale of the contract.

   In many cases, the items may be such non-traditional 'commodities' as foreign currencies, commercial or government paper [e.g., bonds], or 'baskets' of corporate equity ['stock indices'] or other financial instruments.

   a. Financial future
   b. Repurchase agreement
   c. Heston model
   d. Futures contract

5. The institution most often referenced by the word '_____' is a public or publicly traded _____, the shares of which are traded on a public stock exchange (e.g., the New York Stock Exchange or Nasdaq in the United States) where shares of stock of _____s are bought and sold by and to the general public. Most of the largest businesses in the world are publicly traded _____s. However, the majority of _____s are said to be closely held, privately held or close _____s, meaning that no ready market exists for the trading of shares.
   a. Corporation
   b. Protect
   c. Depository Trust Company
   d. Federal Home Loan Mortgage Corporation

6. _____ is the discipline of identifying, monitoring and limiting risks. In some cases the acceptable risk may be near zero. Risks can come from accidents, natural causes and disasters as well as deliberate attacks from an adversary.
   a. 4-4-5 Calendar
   b. FIFO
   c. Penny stock
   d. Risk management

7. A _____ is something for which there is demand, but which is supplied without qualitative differentiation across a market. It is a product that is the same no matter who produces it, such as petroleum, notebook paper, or milk. In other words, copper is copper.

Chapter 23. Derivatives and Risk Management

a. Commodity	b. 529 plan
c. 4-4-5 Calendar	d. 7-Eleven

8. _____ is the planning process used to determine whether a firm's long term investments such as new machinery, replacement machinery, new plants, new products, and research development projects are worth pursuing. It is budget for major capital, or investment, expenditures.

Many formal methods are used in _____, including the techniques such as

- Net present value
- Profitability index
- Internal rate of return
- Modified Internal Rate of Return
- Equivalent annuity

These methods use the incremental cash flows from each potential investment, or project. Techniques based on accounting earnings and accounting rules are sometimes used - though economists consider this to be improper - such as the accounting rate of return, and 'return on investment.' Simplified and hybrid methods are used as well, such as payback period and discounted payback period.

a. Shareholder value	b. Financial distress
c. Capital budgeting	d. Preferred stock

9. In economics, business, and accounting, a _____ is the value of money that has been used up to produce something, and hence is not available for use anymore. In business, the _____ may be one of acquisition, in which case the amount of money expended to acquire it is counted as _____. In this case, money is the input that is gone in order to acquire the thing.

a. Marginal cost	b. Fixed costs
c. Sliding scale fees	d. Cost

10. An _____ is a contract written by a seller that conveys to the buyer the right -- but not the obligation -- to buy (in the case of a call _____) or to sell (in the case of a put _____) a particular asset, such as a piece of property such as, among others, a futures contract. In return for granting the _____, the seller collects a payment (the premium) from the buyer.

For example, buying a call _____ provides the right to buy a specified quantity of a security at a set strike price at some time on or before expiration, while buying a put _____ provides the right to sell.

a. Amortization	b. AT'T Mobility LLC
c. Annuity	d. Option

Chapter 23. Derivatives and Risk Management

11. _____ (in a financial context) is the assumption of the risk of loss, in return for the uncertain possibility of a reward. Only if one may safely say that a particular position involves no risk may one say, strictly speaking, that such a position represents an 'investment.' Financial _____ involves the buying, holding, selling, and short-selling of stocks, bonds, commodities, currencies, collectibles, real estate, derivatives, or any valuable financial instrument to profit from fluctuations in its price as opposed to buying it for use or for income via methods such as dividends or interest. _____ represents one of four market roles in Western financial markets, distinct from hedging, long- or short-term investing, and arbitrage.
  a. Central Securities Depository
  b. Market anomaly
  c. Forward market
  d. Speculation

12. In finance, a _____ is a position established in one market in an attempt to offset exposure to the price risk of an equal but opposite obligation or position in another market -- usually, but not always, in the context of one's commercial activity. Hedging is a strategy designed to minimize exposure to such business risks as a sharp contraction in demand for one's inventory, while still allowing the business to profit from producing and maintaining that inventory. A typical hedger might be a farmer with 2000 acres of unharvested wheat in the ground, who would rather tend his crop without the distraction of uncertain prices.
  a. Hedge
  b. 7-Eleven
  c. 4-4-5 Calendar
  d. 529 plan

13. Procter is a surname, and may also refer to:

  - Bryan Waller Procter (pseud. Barry Cornwall), English poet
  - Goodwin Procter, American law firm
  - _____, consumer products multinational

  a. Valuation
  b. Clearing house
  c. Bucket shop
  d. Procter ' Gamble

14. A _____ is a stock market phenomenon occurring when investors sell what they perceive to be higher-risk investments and purchase safer investments, such as US Treasuries, gold or land. This is considered a sign of fear in the marketplace, as investors seek less risk in exchange for lower profits.
  a. Stock market index option
  b. Volatility clustering
  c. Flight-to-quality
  d. Specific risk

15. The _____ or cash market is a commodities or securities market in which goods are sold for cash and delivered immediately. Contracts bought and sold on these markets are immediately effective. _____s can operate wherever the infrastructure exists to conduct the transaction.
  a. Foreign exchange controls
  b. Currency swap
  c. Spot market
  d. Non-deliverable forward

Chapter 23. Derivatives and Risk Management

16. _____ LLP, based in Chicago, was once one of the 'Big Five' accounting firms among PricewaterhouseCoopers, Deloitte Touche Tohmatsu, Ernst ' Young and KPMG, providing auditing, tax, and consulting services to large corporations. In 2002, the firm voluntarily surrendered its licenses to practice as Certified Public Accountants in the United States after being found guilty of criminal charges relating to the firm's handling of the auditing of Enron, the energy corporation, resulting in the loss of 85,000 jobs. Although the verdict was subsequently overturned by the Supreme Court of the United States, it has not returned as a viable business.
   a. Information Systems Audit and Control Association
   b. Institute of Financial Accountants
   c. Accion USA
   d. Arthur Andersen

17. A standard, commercial _____ is a document issued mostly by a financial institution, used primarily in trade finance, which usually provides an irrevocable payment undertaking.

The _____ can also be the source of payment for a transaction, meaning that redeeming the _____ will pay an exporter. Letters of credit are used primarily in international trade transactions of significant value, for deals between a supplier in one country and a customer in another.

   a. Duty of loyalty
   b. Bond indenture
   c. McFadden Act
   d. Letter of credit

18. _____ is the provision of resources (such as granting a loan) by one party to another party where that second party does not reimburse the first party immediately, thereby generating a debt, and instead arranges either to repay or return those resources (or material(s) of equal value) at a later date. The first party is called a creditor, also known as a lender, while the second party is called a debtor, also known as a borrower.

Movements of financial capital are normally dependent on either _____ or equity transfers.

   a. Comparable
   b. Warrant
   c. Clearing house
   d. Credit

19. A _____ is an agreement between two parties to buy or sell an asset at a specified point of time in the future. The price of the underlying instrument, in whatever form, is paid before control of the instrument changes. This is one of the many forms of buy/sell orders where the time of trade is not the time where the securities themselves are exchanged.
   a. Derivatives markets
   b. Loan Credit Default Swap Index
   c. Constant maturity credit default swap
   d. Forward contract

20. A sole _____, or simply _____ is a type of business entity which legally has no separate existence from its owner. Hence, the limitations of liability enjoyed by a corporation and limited liability partnerships do not apply to sole proprietors. All debts of the business are debts of the owner.
   a. Just-in-time
   b. Free cash flow
   c. Proprietorship
   d. Product life cycle

21. A _____ is an exchange of promises between two or more parties to do an act which is enforceable in a court of law. It is where an unqualified offer meets a qualified acceptance and the parties reach Consensus ad Idem. The parties must have the necessary capacity to _____ and the _____ must not be either trifling, indeterminate, impossible or illegal.

a. 4-4-5 Calendar
c. 529 plan
b. 7-Eleven
d. Contract

22. _____ is the set of processes, customs, policies, laws and institutions affecting the way a corporation is directed, administered or controlled. _____ also includes the relationships among the many stakeholders involved and the goals for which the corporation is governed. The principal stakeholders are the shareholders, management and the board of directors.
   a. Patent
   b. Corporate governance
   c. Foreign Corrupt Practices Act
   d. Due diligence

23. In the original and simplified sense, _____ were things of value, of uniform quality, that were produced in large quantities by many different producers; the items from each different producer are considered equivalent. It is the contract and this underlying standard that define the commodity, not any quality inherent in the product.

_____ exchanges include:

- Chicago Board of Trade
- Kansas City Board of Trade
- Euronext.liffe
- Kuala Lumpur Futures Exchange
- Bhatinda Om ' Oil Exchange
- London Metal Exchange
- New York Mercantile Exchange
- Multi Commodity Exchange
- Dalian Commodity Exchange

Markets for trading _____ can be very efficient, particularly if the division into pools matches demand segments. These markets will quickly respond to changes in supply and demand to find an equilibrium price and quantity.

   a. 7-Eleven
   b. Commodities
   c. 4-4-5 Calendar
   d. 529 plan

24. _____ is a fee paid on borrowed assets. It is the price paid for the use of borrowed money, or, money earned by deposited funds. Assets that are sometimes lent with _____ include money, shares, consumer goods through hire purchase, major assets such as aircraft, and even entire factories in finance lease arrangements.
   a. A Random Walk Down Wall Street
   b. Interest
   c. AAB
   d. Insolvency

25. An _____ is the price a borrower pays for the use of money they do not own, and the return a lender receives for deferring the use of funds, by lending it to the borrower. _____s are normally expressed as a percentage rate over the period of one year.

_____s targets are also a vital tool of monetary policy and are used to control variables like investment, inflation, and unemployment.

a. A Random Walk Down Wall Street
b. ABN Amro
c. AAB
d. Interest rate

26. An _____ is a futures contract with an interest-bearing instrument as the underlying asset.

Examples include Treasury-bill futures, Treasury-bond futures and Eurodollar futures.

The global market for exchange-traded _____s is notionally valued by the Bank for International Settlements at $5,794,200 million in 2005.

a. Open interest
b. Interest rate future
c. Interest rate derivative
d. Equity swap

27. In finance, a _____ is a derivative in which two counterparties agree to exchange one stream of cash flows against another stream. These streams are called the legs of the _____.

The cash flows are calculated over a notional principal amount, which is usually not exchanged between counterparties.

a. Volatility arbitrage
b. Volatility swap
c. Local volatility
d. Swap

28. A _____ is a foreign exchange agreement between two parties to exchange principal and fixed rate interest payments on a loan in one currency for principal and fixed rate interest payments on an equal (regarding net present value) loan in another currency. They are motivated by comparative advantage.

a. Currency swap
b. Foreign exchange market
c. Currency pair
d. Forex swap

29. An _____ is a derivative in which one party exchanges a stream of interest payments for another party's stream of cash flows. _____s can be used by hedgers to manage their fixed or floating assets and liabilities. They can also be used by speculators to replicate unfunded bond exposures to profit from changes in interest rates.

a. Implied volatility
b. Interest rate swap
c. International Swaps and Derivatives Association
d. Equity swap

30. _____ or financing is to provide capital (funds), which means money for a project, a person, a business or any other private or public institutions.

Those funds can be allocated for either short term or long term purposes. The health fund is a new way of _____ private healthcare centers.

a. Product life cycle
b. Proxy fight
c. Synthetic CDO
d. Funding

Chapter 23. Derivatives and Risk Management

31. _____ is a structured finance process that involves pooling and repackaging of cash-flow-producing financial assets into securities, which are then sold to investors. The term '_____' is derived from the fact that the form of financial instruments used to obtain funds from the investors are securities. As a portfolio risk backed by amortizing cash flows - and unlike general corporate debt - the credit quality of securitized debt is non-stationary due to changes in volatility that are time- and structure-dependent.
   a. Securitization
   b. Special journals
   c. The Glass-Steagall Act of 1933
   d. Reputational risk

32. _____ are government bonds issued by the United States Department of the Treasury through the Bureau of the Public Debt. They are the debt financing instruments of the U.S. Federal government, and they are often referred to simply as Treasuries or Treasurys. There are four types of marketable _____: Treasury bills, Treasury notes, Treasury bonds, and Treasury Inflation Protected Securities (TIPS.)
   a. Treasury Inflation Protected Securities
   b. 4-4-5 Calendar
   c. Treasury Inflation-Protected Securities
   d. Treasury securities

33. A _____ is a bond bought at a price lower than its face value, with the face value repaid at the time of maturity. It does not make periodic interest payments, or so-called 'coupons,' hence the term zero-coupon bond. Investors earn return from the compounded interest all paid at maturity plus the difference between the discounted price of the bond and its par value.
   a. Municipal bond
   b. Zero coupon bond
   c. Callable bond
   d. Bowie bonds

34. In finance, a _____ is a debt security, in which the authorized issuer owes the holders a debt and, depending on the terms of the _____, is obliged to pay interest (the coupon) and/or to repay the principal at a later date, termed maturity.

Thus a _____ is a loan: the issuer is the borrower, the _____ holder is the lender, and the coupon is the interest. _____s provide the borrower with external funds to finance long-term investments, or, in the case of government _____s, to finance current expenditure.

   a. Puttable bond
   b. Convertible bond
   c. Bond
   d. Catastrophe bonds

35. A _____ is a financial debt vehicle that was first created in June 1983 by investment banks Salomon Brothers and First Boston for Freddie Mac. (The First Boston team was led by Dexter Senft.) Legally, a _____ is a special purpose entity that is wholly separate from the institution(s) that create it.
   a. Tranche
   b. Collateralized mortgage obligation
   c. 4-4-5 Calendar
   d. Yield curve spread

36. The coupon or _____ of a bond is the amount of interest paid per year expressed as a percentage of the face value of the bond.

For example if you hold $10,000 nominal of a bond described as a 4.5% loan stock, you will receive $450 in interest each year (probably in two installments of $225 each.)

Not all bonds have coupons.

a. Revenue bonds
b. Puttable bond
c. Coupon rate
d. Zero-coupon bond

37. An _____ is a type of bond or other type of debt instrument used in finance whose coupon rate has an inverse relationship to short-term interest rates (or its reference rate.) With an _____, as interest rates rise the coupon rate falls. The basic structure is the same as an ordinary floating rate note except for the direction in which the coupon rate is adjusted.
   a. A Random Walk Down Wall Street
   b. Inverse floater
   c. AAB
   d. ABN Amro

38. _____ is a term applied in many countries to a reference interest rate used by banks. The term originally indicated the rate of interest at which banks lent to favored customers, i.e., those with high credibility, though this is no longer always the case. Some variable interest rates may be expressed as a percentage above or below _____.
   a. Time deposit
   b. Reserve requirement
   c. Credit bureau
   d. Prime rate

39. A _____, referred to as a note payable in accounting, is a contract where one party (the maker or issuer) makes an unconditional promise in writing to pay a sum of money to the other (the payee), either at a fixed or determinable future time or on demand of the payee, under specific terms. They differ from IOUs in that they contain a specific promise to pay, rather than simply acknowledging that a debt exists.

The terms of a note typically include the principal amount, the interest rate if any, and the maturity date.

   a. Promissory note
   b. Financial plan
   c. Credit repair software
   d. Title loan

40. A _____ is a futures contract on a short term interest rate (STIR.) Contracts vary, but are often defined on an interest rate index such as 3-month sterling or US dollar LIBOR.

They are traded across a wide range of currencies, including the G12 country currencies and many others.

   a. Real estate derivatives
   b. Dual currency deposit
   c. Notional amount
   d. Financial future

41. _____ are bonds that have a variable coupon, equal to a money market reference rate, like LIBOR or federal funds rate, plus a spread. The spread is a rate that remains constant. Almost all _____ have quarterly coupons, i.e. they pay out interest every three months, though counter examples do exist.
   a. Floating rate notes
   b. CVECAs
   c. Loan participation
   d. Gordon growth model

42. In the most general sense, a _____ is anything that is a hindrance, or puts individuals at a disadvantage.

Before we discuss the financial terms, we should note that a _____ can also have a much more important slang meaning.

This is best described in an example.

Chapter 23. Derivatives and Risk Management

a. Covenant
c. McFadden Act
b. Limited liability
d. Liability

43. In finance, _____ trading is the trading of exchange listed securities in the over-the-counter (OTC) market. Bernard Madoff was engaged in _____ trading.
   a. 529 plan
   c. 7-Eleven
   b. Third market
   d. 4-4-5 Calendar

44. _____ is a term that refers both to:

- a formal discipline used to help appraise, or assess, the case for a project or proposal, which itself is a process known as project appraisal; and
- an informal approach to making decisions of any kind.

Under both definitions the process involves, whether explicitly or implicitly, weighing the total expected costs against the total expected benefits of one or more actions in order to choose the best or most profitable option.

A hallmark of _____ is that all benefits and all costs are expressed in money terms, and are adjusted for the time value of money, so that all flows of benefits and flows of project costs over time (which tend to occur at different points in time) are expressed on a common basis in terms of their present value.

   a. 529 plan
   c. 4-4-5 Calendar
   b. 7-Eleven
   d. Cost-benefit analysis

45. An _____ is a natural person, business, or corporation which provides goods or services to another entity under terms specified in a contract or within a verbal agreement. Unlike an employee, an _____ does not work regularly for an employer but works as and when required, during which time she or he may be subject to the Law of Agency. _____s are usually paid on a freelance basis.
   a. A Random Walk Down Wall Street
   c. ABN Amro
   b. AAB
   d. Independent contractor

46. A _____ is an entity formed between two or more parties to undertake economic activity together. The parties agree to create a new entity by both contributing equity, and they then share in the revenues, expenses, and control of the enterprise. The venture can be for one specific project only, or a continuing business relationship such as the Sony Ericsson _____.
   a. Joint venture
   c. Pre-emption right
   b. Lien
   d. Fair Debt Collection Practices Act

47. The phrase _____ refers to the aspect of corporate strategy, corporate finance and management dealing with the buying, selling and combining of different companies that can aid, finance, or help a growing company in a given industry grow rapidly without having to create another business entity.

An acquisition, also known as a takeover, is the buying of one company (the 'target') by another. An acquisition may be friendly or hostile.

a. 7-Eleven
b. 529 plan
c. 4-4-5 Calendar
d. Mergers and acquisitions

48. _____ is a type of risk faced by investors, corporations, and governments. It is a risk that can be understood and managed with proper aforethought and investment.

Broadly, _____ refers to the complications businesses and governments may face as a result of what are commonly referred to as political decisions--or 'any political change that alters the expected outcome and value of a given economic action by changing the probability of achieving business objectives.' .

a. Mid price
b. Capital asset
c. Single-index model
d. Political risk

49. _____ is the area of law in which manufacturers, distributors, suppliers, retailers, and others who make products available to the public are held responsible for the injuries those products cause.

In the United States, the claims most commonly associated with _____ are negligence, strict liability, breach of warranty, and various consumer protection claims. The majority of _____ laws are determined at the state level and vary widely from state to state.

a. Family and Medical Leave Act
b. Foreclosure
c. Business valuation
d. Product liability

50. _____ is used to assign the available resources in an economic way. It is part of resource management.

In strategic planning, a _____ decision is a plan for using available resources, for example human resources, especially in the near term, to achieve goals for the future.

a. Resource allocation
b. 7-Eleven
c. 529 plan
d. 4-4-5 Calendar

51. _____ is a legally declared inability or impairment of ability of an individual or organization to pay their creditors. Creditors may file a _____ petition against a debtor ('involuntary _____') in an effort to recoup a portion of what they are owed or initiate a restructuring. In the majority of cases, however, _____ is initiated by the debtor (a 'voluntary _____' that is filed by the bankrupt individual or organization.)

a. Debt settlement
b. Bankruptcy
c. 4-4-5 Calendar
d. 529 plan

52. _____ is a list for goods and materials held available in stock by a business. It is also used for a list of the contents of a household and for a list for testamentary purposes of the possessions of someone who has died. In accounting _____ is considered an asset.

a. ABN Amro
b. A Random Walk Down Wall Street
c. AAB
d. Inventory

53. The _____ is an equation that equals the cost of goods sold divided by the average inventory. Average inventory equals beginning inventory plus ending inventory divided by 2.

The formula for _____:

$$\text{Inventory Turnover} = \frac{\text{Cost of Goods Sold}}{\text{Average Inventory}}$$

The formula for average inventory:

$$\text{Average Inventory} = \frac{\text{Beginning inventory} + \text{Ending inventory}}{2}$$

A low turnover rate may point to overstocking, obsolescence, or deficiencies in the product line or marketing effort.

a. Information ratio
b. Earnings yield
c. Operating leverage
d. Inventory turnover

54. _____ is one of the Accounting Liquidity ratios, a financial ratio. This ratio measures the number of times, on average, the inventory is sold during the period. Its purpose is to measure the liquidity of the inventory.
a. ABN Amro
b. A Random Walk Down Wall Street
c. AAB
d. Inventory turnover ratio

55. In law, _____ refers to the process by which a company (or part of a company) is brought to an end, and the assets and property of the company redistributed. _____ can also be referred to as winding-up or dissolution, although dissolution technically refers to the last stage of _____. The process of _____ also arises when customs, an authority or agency in a country responsible for collecting and safeguarding customs duties, determines the final computation or ascertainment of the duties or drawback accruing on an entry.
a. Liquidation
b. 529 plan
c. Debt settlement
d. 4-4-5 Calendar

56. _____ is a political organization established in 2002 and dedicated to the protection of children from abuse, exploitation and neglect. It is a nonprofit, 501(c)(4) membership association with members in every U.S. state and 10 nations. _____ achieved great success in its first three years, winning legislative victories in eight state legislatures.
a. First Prudential Markets
b. The Depository Trust ' Clearing Corporation
c. Protect
d. Ford Foundation

57. A _____ s a time deposit, a financial product commonly offered to consumers by banks, thrift institutions, and credit unions.

They are similar to savings accounts in that they are insured and thus virtually risk-free; they are 'money in the bank'. They are different from savings accounts in that they have a specific, fixed term (often three months, six months, or one to five years), and, usually, a fixed interest rate.

a. Variable rate mortgage
b. Time deposit
c. Reserve requirement
d. Certificate of deposit

58. A _____ is an international bond that is denominated in a currency not native to the country where it is issued. It can be categorised according to the currency in which it is issued. London is one of the centers of the _____ market, but _____s may be traded throughout the world - for example in Singapore or Tokyo.
   a. Economic entity
   b. Eurobond
   c. Education production function
   d. Interest rate option

59. _____s are deposits denominated in United States dollars at banks outside the United States, and thus are not under the jurisdiction of the Federal Reserve. Consequently, such deposits are subject to much less regulation than similar deposits within the United States, allowing for higher margins. There is nothing 'European' about _____ deposits; a US dollar-denominated deposit in Tokyo or Caracas would likewise be deemed _____ deposits.
   a. ABN Amro
   b. A Random Walk Down Wall Street
   c. Eurodollar
   d. AAB

60. _____ are those dividends paid out in form of additional stock shares of the issuing corporation or other corporation They are usually issued in proportion to shares owned (for example for every 100 shares of stock owned, 5% stock dividend will yield 5 extra shares). If this payment involves the issue of new shares, this is very similar to a stock split in that it increases the total number of shares while lowering the price of each share and does not change the market capitalization or the total value of the shares held
   a. Time-based currency
   b. The Hong Kong Securities Institute
   c. Database auditing
   d. Stock or scrip dividends

61. A _____ is a payment made by a corporation to its shareholder members. When a corporation earns a profit or surplus, that money can be put to two uses: it can either be re-invested in the business (called retained earnings), or it can be paid to the shareholders as a _____. Many corporations retain a portion of their earnings and pay the remainder as a _____.
   a. Dividend
   b. Dividend yield
   c. Special dividend
   d. Dividend puzzle

62. The variation margin or _____ is not collateral, but a daily offsetting of profits and losses. Futures are marked-to-market every day, so the current price is compared to the previous day's price. The profit or loss on the day of a position is then paid to or debited from the holder by the futures exchange.
   a. SPI 200 futures contract
   b. Delivery month
   c. Maintenance margin
   d. Total return swap

63. In finance, a _____ is collateral that the holder of a position in securities, options, or futures contracts has to deposit to cover the credit risk of his counterparty (most often his broker.) This risk can arise if the holder has done any of the following:

   - borrowed cash from the counterparty to buy securities or options,
   - sold securities or options short, or
   - entered into a futures contract.

The collateral can be in the form of cash or securities, and it is deposited in a _____ account. On U.S. futures exchanges, '_____' was formally called performance bond.

_____ buying is buying securities with cash borrowed from a broker, using other securities as collateral.

a. Procter ' Gamble
b. Credit
c. Share
d. Margin

64. _____ are legal property rights over creations of the mind, both artistic and commercial, and the corresponding fields of law. Under _____ law, owners are granted certain exclusive rights to a variety of intangible assets, such as musical, literary, and artistic works; ideas, discoveries and inventions; and words, phrases, symbols, and designs. Common types of _____ include copyrights, trademarks, patents, industrial design rights and trade secrets.
   a. A Random Walk Down Wall Street
   b. ABN Amro
   c. AAB
   d. Intellectual property

65. A _____ is a fungible, negotiable instrument representing financial value. They are broadly categorized into debt securities (such as banknotes, bonds and debentures), and equity securities; e.g., common stocks. The company or other entity issuing the _____ is called the issuer.
   a. Securities lending
   b. Tracking stock
   c. Book entry
   d. Security

66. _____ provides protection against most risks to property, such as fire, theft and some weather damage. This includes specialized forms of insurance such as fire insurance, flood insurance, earthquake insurance, home insurance or boiler insurance. Property is insured in two main ways - open perils and named perils.
   a. 529 plan
   b. 4-4-5 Calendar
   c. Lenders Mortgage Insurance
   d. Property insurance

67. _____ is a process by which a firm can obtain the use of a certain fixed assets for which it must pay a series of contractual, periodic, tax deductable payments. The lessee is the receiver of the services or the assets under the lease contract and the lessor is the owner of the assets. The relationship between the tenant and the landlord is called a tenancy, and can be for a fixed or an indefinite period of time (called the term of the lease).
   a. Leasing
   b. Quiet period
   c. Royalties
   d. Foreign Corrupt Practices Act

Chapter 24. Bankruptcy, Reorganization, and Liquidation

1. _____ is a legally declared inability or impairment of ability of an individual or organization to pay their creditors. Creditors may file a _____ petition against a debtor ('involuntary _____') in an effort to recoup a portion of what they are owed or initiate a restructuring. In the majority of cases, however, _____ is initiated by the debtor (a 'voluntary _____' that is filed by the bankrupt individual or organization.)
   a. 529 plan
   b. Debt settlement
   c. Bankruptcy
   d. 4-4-5 Calendar

2. The institution most often referenced by the word '_____' is a public or publicly traded _____, the shares of which are traded on a public stock exchange (e.g., the New York Stock Exchange or Nasdaq in the United States) where shares of stock of _____s are bought and sold by and to the general public. Most of the largest businesses in the world are publicly traded _____s. However, the majority of _____s are said to be closely held, privately held or close _____s, meaning that no ready market exists for the trading of shares.
   a. Protect
   b. Federal Home Loan Mortgage Corporation
   c. Depository Trust Company
   d. Corporation

3. _____ is a term in Corporate Finance used to indicate a condition when promises to creditors of a company are broken or honored with difficulty. Sometimes _____ can lead to bankruptcy. _____ is usually associated with some costs to the company and these are known as Costs of _____.
   a. Financial distress
   b. Capital structure
   c. Cashflow matching
   d. Commercial paper

4. _____ means regulating, adapting or settling in a variety of contexts:

   In commercial law, _____ means the settlement of a loss incurred on insured goods. The calculation of the amounts of compensation to be paid by or to the several interests is a complicated matter. It involves much detail and arithmetic, and requires a full and accurate knowledge of the principles of the subject.

   a. Asset recovery
   b. Intelligent investor
   c. Equity method
   d. Adjustment

5. A _____ is an agreement among several creditors of a debtor, usually a business. Usually, the agreement involves paying a lessened amount over a period of time.
   a. Time-based currency
   b. Doctrine of the Proper Law
   c. Loans and interest, in Judaism
   d. Composiition of Creditors

6. A _____ is a party (e.g. person, organization, company, or government) that has a claim to the services of a second party. The first party, in general, has provided some property or service to the second party under the assumption (usually enforced by contract) that the second party will return an equivalent property or service. The second party is frequently called a debtor or borrower.
   a. False billing
   b. Redemption value
   c. NOPLAT
   d. Creditor

7. _____ is the corporate management term for the act of reorganizing the legal, ownership, operational, or other structures of a company for the purpose of making it more profitable or better organized for its present needs. Alternate reasons for restructing include a change of ownership or ownership structure, demerger repositioning debt _____ and financial _____.

a. Restructuring
b. Day trading
c. Cross-border leasing
d. Concentrated stock

8. In finance and economics, _____ or divestiture is the reduction of some kind of asset for either financial goals or ethical objectives. A _____ is the opposite of an investment.

Often the term is used as a means to grow financially in which a company sells off a business unit in order to focus their resources on a market it judges to be more profitable, or promising.

a. Divestment
b. Certificate in Investment Performance Measurement
c. Late trading
d. Portfolio investment

9. In law, _____ refers to the process by which a company (or part of a company) is brought to an end, and the assets and property of the company redistributed. _____ can also be referred to as winding-up or dissolution, although dissolution technically refers to the last stage of _____. The process of _____ also arises when customs, an authority or agency in a country responsible for collecting and safeguarding customs duties, determines the final computation or ascertainment of the duties or drawback accruing on an entry.

a. 4-4-5 Calendar
b. Liquidation
c. 529 plan
d. Debt settlement

10. A _____ is a fungible, negotiable instrument representing financial value. They are broadly categorized into debt securities (such as banknotes, bonds and debentures), and equity securities; e.g., common stocks. The company or other entity issuing the _____ is called the issuer.

a. Tracking stock
b. Book entry
c. Securities lending
d. Security

11. The U.S. _____ is an independent agency of the United States government which holds primary responsibility for enforcing the federal securities laws and regulating the securities industry, the nation's stock and options exchanges, and other electronic securities markets. The SEC was created by section 4 of the SEC of 1934 (now codified as 15 U.S.C. Â§ 78d and commonly referred to as the 1934 Act.)

a. 4-4-5 Calendar
b. 7-Eleven
c. 529 plan
d. Securities and Exchange Commission

12. _____ is the process of decreasing an amount over a period of time. The word comes from Middle English amortisen to kill, alienate in mortmain, from Anglo-French amorteser, alteration of amortir, from Vulgar Latin admortire to kill, from Latin ad- + mort-, mors death. Particular instances of the term include:

- _____ (business), the allocation of a lump sum amount to different time periods, particularly for loans and other forms of finance, including related interest or other finance charges.
    - _____ schedule, a table detailing each periodic payment on a loan (typically a mortgage), as generated by an _____ calculator.
    - Negative _____, an _____ schedule where the loan amount actually increases through not paying the full interest
- Amortized analysis, analyzing the execution cost of algorithms over a sequence of operations.
- _____ of capital expenditures of certain assets under accounting rules, particularly intangible assets, in a manner analogous to depreciation.
- _____ (tax law)

_____ is also used in the context of zoning regulations and describes the time in which a property owner has to relocate when the property's use constitutes a preexisting nonconforming use under zoning regulations.

- Depreciation

  a. Intrinsic value   b. Option
  c. AT'T Inc.   d. Amortization

13. The _____ is an economic situation which exists when goods are rival, but non-exclusive Since these resources are owned in common, individuals have no private incentive to preserve them, but rather will seek to exploit them before others can derive benefit. The classic example is of fish in the ocean.
  a. Package loan   b. Cash flow loan
  c. Fund Accounting   d. Common pool problem

14. _____ is the legal and professional proceeding in which a mortgagee usually a lender, obtains a court ordered termination of a mortgagor's equitable right of redemption. Usually a lender obtains a security interest from a borrower who mortgages or pledges an asset like a house to secure the loan. If the borrower defaults and the lender tries to repossess the property, courts of equity can grant the borrower the equitable right of redemption if the borrower repays the debt.
  a. Letter of credit   b. Foreclosure
  c. Federal Acquisition Regulations   d. Liability

15. In financial accounting, _____s are precautions for which the amount or probability of occurrence are not known. Typical examples are _____s for warranty costs and _____ for taxes the term reserve is used instead of term _____; such a use, however, is inconsistent with the terminology suggested by International Accounting Standards Board.
  a. Money measurement concept   b. Petty cash
  c. Momentum Accounting and Triple-Entry Bookkeeping   d. Provision

Chapter 24. Bankruptcy, Reorganization, and Liquidation

16. A _____ is a company that owns other companies' outstanding stock. It usually refers to a company which does not produce goods or services itself, rather its only purpose is owning shares of other companies. They allow the reduction of risk for the owners and can allow the ownership and control of a number of different companies.
    a. Privately held company
    b. MRU Holdings
    c. Federal National Mortgage Association
    d. Holding company

17. A _____ is the involuntary imposition by a court of a reorganization plan over the objection of some classes of creditors.

While typically used in a corporate context, the phrase has gained currency in a personal context the financial crisis of 2007-2009.

Under current United States law, bankruptcy courts are not allowed to perform a _____ on mortgages of bankruptcy filers' primary residences. The term has also gained currency to denote informally any transaction where existing investors (debt or equity) are forced by circumstance to accept an unappealing transaction, such as an expensive financing, a debt transaction that subordinates them, a dilutive equity raising, or an acquisition at an unappealingly low price.

   a. Security interest
   b. Dow Jones Indexes
   c. Netting
   d. Cramdown

18. _____ is that which is owed; usually referencing assets owed, but the term can cover other obligations. In the case of assets, _____ is a means of using future purchasing power in the present before a summation has been earned. Some companies and corporations use _____ as a part of their overall corporate finance strategy.
    a. Credit cycle
    b. Cross-collateralization
    c. Partial Payment
    d. Debt

19. _____ is a special form of financing provided for companies in financial distress or under Chapter 11 bankruptcy process. Usually, this security is more senior than debt, equity, and any other securities issued by a company. It gives a troubled company a new start, albeit under strict conditions.
    a. Free float
    b. Corporate tax
    c. Synthetic CDO
    d. Debtor-in-possession financing

20. In finance, a _____ is a type of bond that can be converted into shares of stock in the issuing company, usually at some pre-announced ratio. It is a hybrid security with debt- and equity-like features. Although it typically has a low coupon rate, the holder is compensated with the ability to convert the bond to common stock, usually at a substantial discount to the stock's market value.
    a. Gilts
    b. Corporate bond
    c. Bond fund
    d. Convertible bond

21. _____ or financing is to provide capital (funds), which means money for a project, a person, a business or any other private or public institutions.

Those funds can be allocated for either short term or long term purposes. The health fund is a new way of _____ private healthcare centers.

a. Product life cycle	b. Proxy fight
c. Funding	d. Synthetic CDO

22. In economics, business, and accounting, a _____ is the value of money that has been used up to produce something, and hence is not available for use anymore. In business, the _____ may be one of acquisition, in which case the amount of money expended to acquire it is counted as _____. In this case, money is the input that is gone in order to acquire the thing.

a. Fixed costs	b. Sliding scale fees
c. Marginal cost	d. Cost

23. _____ means the inability to pay one's debts as they fall due. Usually used in Business terms, _____ refers to the inability for a 'limited liability' company to pay off debts.

This is defined in two different ways:

Cash flow _____ -
    Unable to pay debts as they fall due.
Balance sheet _____ -
    Having negative net assets: liabilities exceed assets; or net liabilities.

a. A Random Walk Down Wall Street	b. AAB
c. Insolvency	d. Interest

24. An _____ is an economic concept that relates to the cost incurred by an entity (such as organizations) associated with problems such as divergent management-shareholder objectives and information asymmetry. The costs consist of two main sources:

1. The costs inherently associated with using an agent (e.g., the risk that agents will use organizational resource for their own benefit) and
2. The costs of techniques used to mitigate the problems associated with using an agent (e.g., the costs of producing financial statements or the use of stock options to align executive interests to shareholder interests.)

Though effects of _____ are present in any agency relationship, the term is most used in business contexts.

The information asymmetry that exists between shareholders and the Chief Executive Officer is generally considered to be a classic example of a principal-agent problem. The agent (the manager) is working on behalf of the principal (the shareholders), who does not observe the actions of the agent.

a. Agency cost	b. A Random Walk Down Wall Street
c. ABN Amro	d. AAB

25. The phrase _____ refers to the aspect of corporate strategy, corporate finance and management dealing with the buying, selling and combining of different companies that can aid, finance, or help a growing company in a given industry grow rapidly without having to create another business entity.

Chapter 24. Bankruptcy, Reorganization, and Liquidation

An acquisition, also known as a takeover, is the buying of one company (the 'target') by another. An acquisition may be friendly or hostile.

a. 7-Eleven
b. 4-4-5 Calendar
c. 529 plan
d. Mergers and acquisitions

26. In the _____ contract the underwriter agrees to sell as many shares as possible at the agreed-upon price.

Under the all-or-none contract the underwriter agrees either to sell the entire offering or to cancel the deal.

Stand-by underwriting, also known as strict underwriting or old-fashioned underwriting is a form of stock insurance: the issuer contracts the underwriter for the latter to purchase the shares the issuer failed to sell under stockholders' subscription and applications.

a. Follow-on offering
b. Best efforts
c. Book building
d. Real option

27. An _____ is a contract written by a seller that conveys to the buyer the right -- but not the obligation -- to buy (in the case of a call _____) or to sell (in the case of a put _____) a particular asset, such as a piece of property such as, among others, a futures contract. In return for granting the _____, the seller collects a payment (the premium) from the buyer.

For example, buying a call _____ provides the right to buy a specified quantity of a security at a set strike price at some time on or before expiration, while buying a put _____ provides the right to sell.

a. Annuity
b. Amortization
c. AT'T Mobility LLC
d. Option

28. The _____, was a law enacting several significant changes to the U.S. Bankruptcy Code. Referred to colloquially as the 'New Bankruptcy Law', the Act of Congress attempts to, among other things, make it more difficult for some consumers to file bankruptcy under Chapter 7; some of these consumers may instead utilize Chapter 13.

a. Foreclosure
b. Personal property
c. Covenant
d. Bankruptcy Abuse Prevention and Consumer Protection Act of 2005

29. In financial accounting, a _____ or statement of financial position is a summary of a person's or organization's balances. Assets, liabilities and ownership equity are listed as of a specific date, such as the end of its financial year. A _____ is often described as a snapshot of a company's financial condition.

a. Balance sheet
b. Statement of retained earnings
c. Financial statements
d. Statement on Auditing Standards No. 70: Service Organizations

30. _____ is the area of law in which manufacturers, distributors, suppliers, retailers, and others who make products available to the public are held responsible for the injuries those products cause.

In the United States, the claims most commonly associated with _____ are negligence, strict liability, breach of warranty, and various consumer protection claims. The majority of _____ laws are determined at the state level and vary widely from state to state.

    a. Business valuation
    c. Family and Medical Leave Act
    b. Product liability
    d. Foreclosure

31. In the most general sense, a _____ is anything that is a hindrance, or puts individuals at a disadvantage.

Before we discuss the financial terms, we should note that a _____ can also have a much more important slang meaning.

This is best described in an example.

    a. Covenant
    c. McFadden Act
    b. Liability
    d. Limited liability

32. _____ is the economic policy of restraining trade between nations, through methods such as tariffs on imported goods, restrictive quotas, and a variety of other restrictive government regulations designed to discourage imports, and prevent foreign take-over of local markets and companies. This policy is closely aligned with anti-globalization, and contrasts with free trade, where government barriers to trade are kept to a minimum. The term is mostly used in the context of economics, where _____ refers to policies or doctrines which 'protect' businesses and workers within a country by restricting or regulating trade between foreign nations.

    a. 7-Eleven
    c. 4-4-5 Calendar
    b. Protectionism
    d. 529 plan

33. _____ and the related Fisher's linear discriminant are methods used in statistics and machine learning to find the linear combination of features which best separate two or more classes of objects or events. The resulting combination may be used as a linear classifier, or, more commonly, for dimensionality reduction before later classification.

_____ is closely related to ANOVA (analysis of variance) and regression analysis, which also attempt to express one dependent variable as a linear combination of other features or measurements.

    a. 4-4-5 Calendar
    c. 7-Eleven
    b. 529 plan
    d. Linear discriminant analysis

Chapter 25. Mergers, LBOs, Divestitures, and Holding Companies

1. The phrase _____ refers to the aspect of corporate strategy, corporate finance and management dealing with the buying, selling and combining of different companies that can aid, finance, or help a growing company in a given industry grow rapidly without having to create another business entity.

   An acquisition, also known as a takeover, is the buying of one company (the 'target') by another. An acquisition may be friendly or hostile.

   a. Mergers and acquisitions
   b. 4-4-5 Calendar
   c. 7-Eleven
   d. 529 plan

2. In finance and economics, _____ or divestiture is the reduction of some kind of asset for either financial goals or ethical objectives. A _____ is the opposite of an investment.

   Often the term is used as a means to grow financially in which a company sells off a business unit in order to focus their resources on a market it judges to be more profitable, or promising.

   a. Certificate in Investment Performance Measurement
   b. Portfolio investment
   c. Late trading
   d. Divestment

3. A _____ is a company that owns other companies' outstanding stock. It usually refers to a company which does not produce goods or services itself, rather its only purpose is owning shares of other companies. They allow the reduction of risk for the owners and can allow the ownership and control of a number of different companies.

   a. Federal National Mortgage Association
   b. MRU Holdings
   c. Privately held company
   d. Holding company

4. _____, refers to consumption opportunity gained by an entity within a specified time frame, which is generally expressed in monetary terms. However, for households and individuals, '_____ is the sum of all the wages, salaries, profits, interests payments, rents and other forms of earnings received... in a given period of time.' For firms, _____ generally refers to net-profit: what remains of revenue after expenses have been subtracted.

   a. Annual report
   b. Accrual
   c. OIBDA
   d. Income

5. An _____ is a tax levied on the financial income of people, corporations, or other legal entities. Various _____ systems exist, with varying degrees of tax incidence. Income taxation can be progressive, proportional, or regressive.

   a. A Random Walk Down Wall Street
   b. ABN Amro
   c. AAB
   d. Income tax

6. A _____ occurs when a financial sponsor acquires a controlling interest in a company's equity and where a significant percentage of the purchase price is financed through leverage (borrowing.) The assets of the acquired company are used as collateral for the borrowed capital, sometimes with assets of the acquiring company. The bonds or other paper issued for _____s are commonly considered not to be investment grade because of the significant risks involved.

   a. Leverage
   b. Leveraged buyout
   c. Limited partnership
   d. Pension fund

7. A _____ is a fungible, negotiable instrument representing financial value. They are broadly categorized into debt securities (such as banknotes, bonds and debentures), and equity securities; e.g., common stocks. The company or other entity issuing the _____ is called the issuer.

a. Tracking stock
b. Securities lending
c. Book entry
d. Security

8. The U.S. _____ is an independent agency of the United States government which holds primary responsibility for enforcing the federal securities laws and regulating the securities industry, the nation's stock and options exchanges, and other electronic securities markets. The SEC was created by section 4 of the SEC of 1934 (now codified as 15 U.S.C. Â§ 78d and commonly referred to as the 1934 Act.)
a. Securities and Exchange Commission
b. 7-Eleven
c. 529 plan
d. 4-4-5 Calendar

9. _____ are securities that can be easily converted into cash. Such securities will generally have highly liquid markets allowing the security to be sold at a reasonable price very quickly. This is a usual feature in real estate .
a. Securities lending
b. Tracking stock
c. Book entry
d. Marketable

10. _____ is a business valuation method. _____ is the net present value of a project if financed solely by ownership equity plus the present value of all the benefits of financing. Usually, the main benefit is a tax shield resulted from tax deductibility of interest payments. Another one can be a subsidized borrowing.
a. A Random Walk Down Wall Street
b. AAB
c. ABN Amro
d. Adjusted present value

11. In business and accounting, _____s are everything of value that is owned by a person or company. The balance sheet of a firm records the monetary value of the _____s owned by the firm. The two major _____ classes are tangible _____s and intangible _____s.
a. EBITDA
b. Income
c. Accounts payable
d. Asset

12. _____ is a legally declared inability or impairment of ability of an individual or organization to pay their creditors. Creditors may file a _____ petition against a debtor ('involuntary _____') in an effort to recoup a portion of what they are owed or initiate a restructuring. In the majority of cases, however, _____ is initiated by the debtor (a 'voluntary _____' that is filed by the bankrupt individual or organization.)
a. 529 plan
b. Debt settlement
c. Bankruptcy
d. 4-4-5 Calendar

13. In United States banking, _____ is a marketing term for certain services offered primarily to larger business customers. It may be used to describe all bank accounts (such as checking accounts) provided to businesses of a certain size, but it is more often used to describe specific services such as cash concentration, zero balance accounting, and automated clearing house facilities. Sometimes, private banking customers are given _____ services.
a. Profitability index
b. Capitalization rate
c. Global tactical asset allocation
d. Cash management

14. _____ is the set of processes, customs, policies, laws and institutions affecting the way a corporation is directed, administered or controlled. _____ also includes the relationships among the many stakeholders involved and the goals for which the corporation is governed. The principal stakeholders are the shareholders, management and the board of directors.

Chapter 25. Mergers, LBOs, Divestitures, and Holding Companies

a. Corporate governance
b. Patent
c. Foreign Corrupt Practices Act
d. Due diligence

15. The institution most often referenced by the word '_____' is a public or publicly traded _____, the shares of which are traded on a public stock exchange (e.g., the New York Stock Exchange or Nasdaq in the United States) where shares of stock of _____s are bought and sold by and to the general public. Most of the largest businesses in the world are publicly traded _____s. However, the majority of _____s are said to be closely held, privately held or close _____s, meaning that no ready market exists for the trading of shares.

a. Corporation
b. Depository Trust Company
c. Federal Home Loan Mortgage Corporation
d. Protect

16. _____ in finance is a risk management technique, related to hedging, that mixes a wide variety of investments within a portfolio. Because the fluctuations of a single security have less impact on a diverse portfolio, _____ minimizes the risk from any one investment.

A simple example of _____ is the following: On a particular island the entire economy consists of two companies: one that sells umbrellas and another that sells sunscreen.

a. Diversification
b. 7-Eleven
c. 4-4-5 Calendar
d. 529 plan

17. In financial accounting, a _____ or statement of financial position is a summary of a person's or organization's balances. Assets, liabilities and ownership equity are listed as of a specific date, such as the end of its financial year. A _____ is often described as a snapshot of a company's financial condition.

a. Statement of retained earnings
b. Financial statements
c. Balance sheet
d. Statement on Auditing Standards No. 70: Service Organizations

18. _____ is a fee paid on borrowed assets. It is the price paid for the use of borrowed money , or, money earned by deposited funds . Assets that are sometimes lent with _____ include money, shares, consumer goods through hire purchase, major assets such as aircraft, and even entire factories in finance lease arrangements.

a. Interest
b. Insolvency
c. AAB
d. A Random Walk Down Wall Street

19. An _____ is the price a borrower pays for the use of money they do not own, and the return a lender receives for deferring the use of funds, by lending it to the borrower. _____s are normally expressed as a percentage rate over the period of one year.

_____s targets are also a vital tool of monetary policy and are used to control variables like investment, inflation, and unemployment.

a. A Random Walk Down Wall Street
b. AAB
c. ABN Amro
d. Interest rate

20. In economics, a _____ is the combination of two or more firms competing in the same market with the same good or service.

a. 4-4-5 Calendar
b. Fixed exchange rate system
c. Horizontal merger
d. Passive income

21. In finance, an _____ is the difference between the expected return of a security and the actual return. _____s are sometimes triggered by 'events.' Events can include mergers, dividend announcements, company earning announcements, interest rate increases, lawsuits, etc. all which can contribute to an _____.

a. A Random Walk Down Wall Street
b. Abnormal return
c. AAB
d. ABN Amro

22. _____ is that which is owed; usually referencing assets owed, but the term can cover other obligations. In the case of assets, _____ is a means of using future purchasing power in the present before a summation has been earned. Some companies and corporations use _____ as a part of their overall corporate finance strategy.

a. Partial Payment
b. Cross-collateralization
c. Credit cycle
d. Debt

23. _____ is a financial ratio that indicates the percentage of a company's assets are provided via debt. It is the ratio of total debt (the sum of current liabilities and long-term liabilities) and total assets (the sum of current assets, fixed assets, and other assets such as 'goodwill'.)

or alternatively:

For example, a company with $2 million in total assets and $500,000 in total liabilities would have a _____ of 25%

Like all financial ratios, a company's _____ should be compared with their industry average or other competing firms.

a. Cash concentration
b. Capitalization rate
c. Cash management
d. Debt ratio

24. In business, a _____ is the purchase of one company (the target) by another (the acquirer or bidder). In the UK the term refers to the acquisition of a public company whose shares are listed on a stock exchange, in contrast to the acquisition of a private company.

Before a bidder makes an offer for another company, it usually first informs that company's board of directors.

a. 529 plan
b. Takeover
c. Stock swap
d. 4-4-5 Calendar

Chapter 25. Mergers, LBOs, Divestitures, and Holding Companies

25. _____ is the largest provider of local, long distance telephone services in the United States, and also serves digital subscriber line Internet access. AT'T is the second largest provider of wireless service in the United States, with over 77 million wireless customers, and more than 150 million total customers.

   a. Intrinsic value
   b. Alpha
   c. Option
   d. AT'T Inc.

26. In finance, a _____ is a debt security, in which the authorized issuer owes the holders a debt and, depending on the terms of the _____, is obliged to pay interest (the coupon) and/or to repay the principal at a later date, termed maturity.

   Thus a _____ is a loan: the issuer is the borrower, the _____ holder is the lender, and the coupon is the interest. _____s provide the borrower with external funds to finance long-term investments, or, in the case of government _____s, to finance current expenditure.

   a. Puttable bond
   b. Convertible bond
   c. Catastrophe bonds
   d. Bond

27. _____ or financing is to provide capital (funds), which means money for a project, a person, a business or any other private or public institutions.

   Those funds can be allocated for either short term or long term purposes. The health fund is a new way of _____ private healthcare centers.

   a. Funding
   b. Product life cycle
   c. Proxy fight
   d. Synthetic CDO

28. A _____ is an event that may occur when a corporation's stockholders develop opposition to some aspect of the corporate governance, often focusing on directorial and management positions. Corporate activists may attempt to persuade shareholders to use their proxy votes (i.e. votes by one individual or institution as the authorized representative of another) to install new management for any of a variety of reasons.

   In a _____, incumbent directors and management have the odds stacked in their favor over those trying to force the corporate change.

   a. Procurement
   b. Proxy fight
   c. Trade finance
   d. Forfaiting

29. _____ is a corporate finance term denoting a type of takeover bid. The _____ is a public, open offer or invitation (usually announced in a newspaper advertisement) by a prospective acquirer to all stockholders of a publicly traded corporation (the target corporation) to tender their stock for sale at a specified price during a specified time, subject to the tendering of a minimum and maximum number of shares. In a _____, the bidder contacts shareholders directly; the directors of the company may or may not have endorsed the _____ proposal.

   a. Shareholder value
   b. Follow-on offering
   c. Cash is king
   d. Tender offer

Chapter 25. Mergers, LBOs, Divestitures, and Holding Companies

30. The _____ refers to amendments to the Securities Exchange Act of 1934 enacted in 1968 regarding tender offers. The legislation was proposed by Senator Harrison A. Williams of New Jersey.

The _____ requires that bidders must include all details of their tender offer in their filing to the SEC and the target company. Their file must include the terms, cash source, and their plans for the company after takeover. There are also time constraints that stipulate the minimum period of time the offer may be open and the number of days after the offering in which shareholders have the right to change their minds.

a. Prudent man rule
c. Rule 144A

b. Securities Investor Protection Corporation
d. Williams Act

31. In finance, the _____ approach describes a method of valuing a project, company, or asset using the concepts of the time value of money. All future cash flows are estimated and discounted to give their present values. The discount rate used is generally the appropriate cost of capital and may incorporate judgments of the uncertainty (riskiness) of the future cash flows.

a. Discounted cash flow
c. Net present value

b. Present value of benefits
d. Future-oriented

32. In corporate finance, _____ is a cash flow available for distribution among all the security holders of a company. They include equity holders, debt holders, preferred stock holders, convertible security holders, and so on.

Note that the first three lines above are calculated for you on the standard Statement of Cash Flows.

a. Funding
c. Safety stock

b. Forfaiting
d. Free cash flow

33. _____ is the balance of the amounts of cash being received and paid by a business during a defined period of time, sometimes tied to a specific project. Measurement of _____ can be used

- to evaluate the state or performance of a business or project.
- to determine problems with liquidity. Being profitable does not necessarily mean being liquid. A company can fail because of a shortage of cash, even while profitable.
- to generate project rate of returns. The time of _____s into and out of projects are used as inputs to financial models such as internal rate of return, and net present value.
- to examine income or growth of a business when it is believed that accrual accounting concepts do not represent economic realities. Alternately, _____ can be used to 'validate' the net income generated by accrual accounting.

_____ as a generic term may be used differently depending on context, and certain _____ definitions may be adapted by analysts and users for their own uses. Common terms include operating _____ and free _____.

_____s can be classified into:

1. Operational _____s: Cash received or expended as a result of the company's core business activities.
2. Investment _____s: Cash received or expended through capital expenditure, investments or acquisitions.
3. Financing _____s: Cash received or expended as a result of financial activities, such as interests and dividends.

All three together - the net _____ - are necessary to reconcile the beginning cash balance to the ending cash balance. Loan draw downs or equity injections, that is just shifting of capital but no expenditure as such, are not considered in the net _____.

a. Shareholder value
b. Corporate finance
c. Real option
d. Cash flow

34. In finance, _____ is the process of estimating the potential market value of a financial asset or liability. they can be done on assets (for example, investments in marketable securities such as stocks, options, business enterprises, or intangible assets such as patents and trademarks) or on liabilities (e.g., Bonds issued by a company.) _____s are required in many contexts including investment analysis, capital budgeting, merger and acquisition transactions, financial reporting, taxable events to determine the proper tax liability, and in litigation.
a. Margin
b. Valuation
c. Share
d. Procter ' Gamble

35. _____ is the value on a given date of a future payment or series of future payments, discounted to reflect the time value of money and other factors such as investment risk. _____ calculations are widely used in business and economics to provide a means to compare cash flows at different times on a meaningful 'like to like' basis.

The most commonly applied model of the time value of money is compound interest.

a. Present value of benefits
b. Net present value
c. Negative gearing
d. Present value

36. A _____ is the reduction in income taxes that results from taking an allowable deduction from taxable income. For example, because interest on debt is a tax-deductible expense, taking on debt creates a _____. Since a _____ is a way to save cash flows, it increases the value of the business, and it is an important aspect of business valuation.
a. Present value of costs
b. Refinancing risk
c. Present value of benefits
d. Tax shield

37. A _____ is a payment made by a corporation to its shareholder members. When a corporation earns a profit or surplus, that money can be put to two uses: it can either be re-invested in the business (called retained earnings), or it can be paid to the shareholders as a _____. Many corporations retain a portion of their earnings and pay the remainder as a _____.

a. Dividend yield
b. Special dividend
c. Dividend
d. Dividend puzzle

38. In the portfolio management field, Eugene Fama and Kenneth French developed the highly successful _____ to describe market behavior.

CAPM uses a single factor, beta, to compare the excess returns of a portfolio with the excess returns of the market as a whole. But it oversimplifies the complex market. Fama and French started with the observation that two classes of stocks have tended to do better than the market as a whole: small caps and (ii) stocks with a high book-to-market ratio (BM, customarily called value stocks, and different from growth stocks). They then added two factors to CAPM to reflect a portfolio's exposure to these two classes:

Here r is the portfolio's return rate, R_f is the risk-free return rate, and K_m is the return of the whole stock market. The 'three factor' $>\beta$ is analogous to the classical $>\beta$ but not equal to it, since there are now two additional factors to do some of the work. SMB stands for 'small minus big' and HML for 'high (book-to-price ratio) minus low'; they measure the historic excess returns of small caps over big caps and of value stocks over growth stocks.

   a. Guaranteed investment contracts   b. Reputational risk
   c. Fama-French three factor model   d. Mitigating Control

39. In finance, _____ refers to the way a corporation finances its assets through some combination of equity, debt, or hybrid securities. A firm's _____ is then the composition or 'structure' of its liabilities. For example, a firm that sells $20 billion in equity and $80 billion in debt is said to be 20% equity-financed and 80% debt-financed.
   a. Capital structure   b. Market for corporate control
   c. Book building   d. Rights issue

40. A _____ is the highest price that a buyer (i.e., bidder) is willing to pay for a good. It is usually referred to simply as the 'bid.'

In bid and ask, the _____ stands in contrast to the ask price or 'offer', and the difference between the two is called the bid/ask spread.

An unsolicited bid or offer is when a person or company receives a bid even though they are not looking to sell.

   a. Political risk   b. Mid price
   c. Bid price   d. Settlement date

41. The role of the _____ is to issue accounting standards in the United Kingdom. It is recognised for that purpose under the Companies Act 1985. It took over the task of setting accounting standards from the Accounting Standards Committee (ASC) in 1990.
   a. ABN Amro   b. A Random Walk Down Wall Street
   c. AAB   d. Accounting Standards Board

Chapter 25. Mergers, LBOs, Divestitures, and Holding Companies

42. The _____ is a private, not-for-profit organization whose primary purpose is to develop generally accepted accounting principles (GAAP) within the United States in the public's interest. The Securities and Exchange Commission (SEC) designated the _____ as the organization responsible for setting accounting standards for public companies in the U.S. It was created in 1973, replacing the Accounting Principles Board and the Committee on Accounting Procedure of the American Institute of Certified Public Accountants. The _____'s mission is 'to establish and improve standards of financial accounting and reporting for the guidance and education of the public, including issuers, auditors, and users of financial information.'

The _____ is not a governmental body.

   a. PlaNet Finance
   c. FASB
   b. MRU Holdings
   d. Credit karma

43. _____ is the field of accountancy concerned with the preparation of financial statements for decision makers, such as stockholders, suppliers, banks, employees, government agencies, owners, and other stakeholders. The fundamental need for _____ is to reduce principal-agent problem by measuring and monitoring agents' performance and reporting the results to interested users.

_____ is used to prepare accounting information for people outside the organization or not involved in the day to day running of the company.

   a. 4-4-5 Calendar
   c. 529 plan
   b. 7-Eleven
   d. Financial Accounting

44. The _____ is a private, not-for-profit organization whose primary purpose is to develop generally accepted accounting principles (GAAP) within the United States in the public's interest. The Securities and Exchange Commission (SEC) designated the _____ as the organization responsible for setting accounting standards for public companies in the U.S. It was created in 1973, replacing the Accounting Principles Board and the Committee on Accounting Procedure of the American Institute of Certified Public Accountants. The _____'s mission is 'to establish and improve standards of financial accounting and reporting for the guidance and education of the public, including issuers, auditors, and users of financial information.'

The _____ is not a governmental body.

   a. World Congress of Accountants
   c. Federal Deposit Insurance Corporation
   b. KPMG
   d. Financial Accounting Standards Board

45. _____ is an accounting term used to reflect the portion of the book value of a business entity not directly attributable to its assets and liabilities; it normally arises only in case of an acquisition. It reflects the ability of the entity to make a higher profit than would be derived from selling the tangible assets. _____ is also known as an intangible asset.
   a. Goodwill
   c. Consolidation
   b. Cost of goods sold
   d. Net profit

46. An _____ can be defined as a contract which provides an income stream in return for an initial payment.

An immediate _____ is an _____ for which the time between the contract date and the date of the first payment is not longer than the time interval between payments. A common use for an immediate _____ is to provide a pension to a retired person or persons.

a. Annuity
b. AT'T Inc.
c. Intrinsic value
d. Amortization

47. _____ are formal records of a business' financial activities.

_____ provide an overview of a business' financial condition in both short and long term. There are four basic _____:

1. **Balance sheet**: also referred to as statement of financial position or condition, reports on a company's assets, liabilities, and net equity as of a given point in time.
2. **Income statement**: also referred to as Profit and Loss statement (or a 'P'L'), reports on a company's income, expenses, and profits over a period of time.
3. **Statement of retained earnings**: explains the changes in a company's retained earnings over the reporting period.
4. **Statement of cash flows**: reports on a company's cash flow activities, particularly its operating, investing and financing activities.

a. Statement of retained earnings
b. Statement on Auditing Standards No. 70: Service Organizations
c. Notes to the Financial Statements
d. Financial statements

48. _____ is a term used to describe the value of an entity's assets less the value of its liabilities. The term is commonly used in relation to collective investment schemes. It may also be used as a synonym for the book value of a firm.

a. Financial intermediary
b. Retail broker
c. Net asset value
d. Passive management

49. An _____ is a financial statement for companies that indicates how Revenue is transformed into net income The purpose of the _____ is to show managers and investors whether the company made or lost money during the period being reported.

The important thing to remember about an _____ is that it represents a period of time.

a. A Random Walk Down Wall Street
b. AAB
c. ABN Amro
d. Income statement

50. _____ or amalgamation is the act of merging many things into one. In business, it often refers to the mergers or acquisitions of many smaller companies into much larger ones. The financial accounting term of _____ refers to the aggregated financial statements of a group company as consolidated account.

Chapter 25. Mergers, LBOs, Divestitures, and Holding Companies

a. Cost of goods sold
b. Retained earnings
c. Consolidation
d. Write-off

51. In finance, a _____ is a type of bond that can be converted into shares of stock in the issuing company, usually at some pre-announced ratio. It is a hybrid security with debt- and equity-like features. Although it typically has a low coupon rate, the holder is compensated with the ability to convert the bond to common stock, usually at a substantial discount to the stock's market value.
   a. Bond fund
   b. Gilts
   c. Corporate bond
   d. Convertible bond

52. A _____ is an agreement between a company and an employee (usually upper executive) specifying that the employee will receive certain significant benefits if employment is terminated. Sometimes, certain conditions, typically a change in company ownership, must be met, but often the cause of termination is unspecified. These benefits may include severance pay, cash bonuses, stock options, or other benefits.
   a. Debtor-in-possession financing
   b. Trade finance
   c. Market capitalization
   d. Golden parachute

53. _____ is typically a higher ranking stock than voting shares, and its terms are negotiated between the corporation and the investor.

   _____ usually carry no voting rights, but may carry superior priority over common stock in the payment of dividends and upon liquidation. _____ may carry a dividend that is paid out prior to any dividends to common stock holders.

   a. Trade-off theory
   b. Preferred stock
   c. Follow-on offering
   d. Second lien loan

54. A _____ is the price of a single share of a no. of saleable stocks of the company. Once the stock is purchased, the owner becomes a shareholder of the company that issued the share.
   a. Trading curb
   b. Stock split
   c. Whisper numbers
   d. Share price

55. _____ is an estimate of the fair value of corporations and their stocks, by using fundamental economic criteria. This theoretical valuation has to be perfected with market criteria, as the final purpose is to determine potential market prices.
   a. Security Analysis
   b. Stock valuation
   c. 4-4-5 Calendar
   d. Growth stocks

56. _____ measures the nominal future sum of money that a given sum of money is 'worth' at a specified time in the future assuming a certain interest rate rate of return; it is the present value multiplied by the accumulation function.

The value does not include corrections for inflation or other factors that affect the true value of money in the future. This is used in time value of money calculations.

a. Discounted cash flow
b. Future value
c. Present value of costs
d. Future-oriented

57. In finance, _____ are stocks that appreciate in value and yield a high return on equity (ROE.) Analysts compute ROE by taking the company's net income and dividing it by the company's equity. To be classified as a growth stock, analysts expect to see at least 15 percent return on equity.

a. Stock valuation
b. Security Analysis
c. Growth stocks
d. 4-4-5 Calendar

58. In business and finance, a _____ (also referred to as equity _____) of stock means a _____ of ownership in a corporation (company.) In the plural, stocks is often used as a synonym for _____s especially in the United States, but it is less commonly used that way outside of North America.

In the United Kingdom, South Africa, and Australia, stock can also refer to completely different financial instruments such as government bonds or, less commonly, to all kinds of marketable securities.

a. Procter ' Gamble
b. Bucket shop
c. Margin
d. Share

59. _____, also called fair price (in a commonplace conflation of the two distinct concepts), is a concept used in finance and economics, defined as a rational and unbiased estimate of the potential market price of a good, service, or asset, taking into account such objective factors as:

- acquisition/production/distribution costs, replacement costs, or costs of close substitutes
- actual utility at a given level of development of social productive capability
- supply vs. demand

and subjective factors such as

- risk characteristics
- cost of capital
- individually perceived utility

In accounting, _____ is used as an estimate of the market value of an asset (or liability) for which a market price cannot be determined (usually because there is no established market for the asset.) Under GAAP (FAS 157), _____ is the amount at which the asset could be bought or sold in a current transaction between willing parties, or transferred to an equivalent party, other than in a liquidation sale. This is used for assets whose carrying value is based on mark-to-market valuations; for assets carried at historical cost, the _____ of the asset is not used. One example of where _____ is an issue is a College kitchen with a cost of $2 million which was built 5 years ago.

a. 529 plan
b. 4-4-5 Calendar
c. 7-Eleven
d. Fair value

Chapter 25. Mergers, LBOs, Divestitures, and Holding Companies

60. In economics and finance, _____ is the practice of taking advantage of a price differential between two or more markets: striking a combination of matching deals that capitalize upon the imbalance, the profit being the difference between the market prices. When used by academics, an _____ is a transaction that involves no negative cash flow at any probabilistic or temporal state and a positive cash flow in at least one state; in simple terms, a risk-free profit.
   a. Initial margin
   b. Issuer
   c. Arbitrage
   d. Efficient-market hypothesis

61. An _____ is a statistical method to assess the impact of an event on the value of a firm. For example, the announcement of a merger between two firms can be analyzed to see whether investors believe the merger will create or destroy value. Event studies have been used in a large variety of studies, including [mergers and acquisitions], earnings announcements, debt or equity issues, corporate reorganisations, investment decisions and corporate social responsibility (MacKinlay 1997; McWilliams ' Siegel, 1997.)
   a. AAB
   b. A Random Walk Down Wall Street
   c. Event study
   d. ABN Amro

62. A _____ is an entity formed between two or more parties to undertake economic activity together. The parties agree to create a new entity by both contributing equity, and they then share in the revenues, expenses, and control of the enterprise. The venture can be for one specific project only, or a continuing business relationship such as the Sony Ericsson _____.
   a. Pre-emption right
   b. Joint venture
   c. Lien
   d. Fair Debt Collection Practices Act

63. _____ is a New York City-based private equity firm that sponsors and manages investment funds, focusing primarily on leveraged buyouts of mature businesses. Since inception, the firm has completed over $400 billion of private equity transactions and was one of the pioneers of the leveraged buyout industry.

The firm was founded in 1976 by Jerome Kohlberg, Jr., and cousins Henry Kravis and George R. Roberts, all of whom had previously worked together at Bear Stearns where they completed some of the earliest leveraged buyout transactions.

   a. Debtor-in-possession financing
   b. Coefficient of variation
   c. Noise trader
   d. Kohlberg Kravis Roberts ' Co

64. A _____ is a new organization or entity formed by a split from a larger one, such as a television series based on a pre-existing one, or a new company formed from a university research group or business incubator. In literature, especially in milieu-based popular fictional book series like mysteries, westerns, fantasy, or science fiction, the term sub-series is generally used instead of _____, but with essentially the same meaning.

_____s as a descriptive term can also include a dissenting faction of a membership organization, a sect of a cult, or a denomination of a church.

   a. 4-4-5 Calendar
   b. 529 plan
   c. Spin-off
   d. 7-Eleven

Chapter 25. Mergers, LBOs, Divestitures, and Holding Companies

65. A _____ is a financial contract whose value is derived from the value of something else (known as the underlying.) The underlying on which a _____ is based can be an asset, weather conditions bonds or other forms of credit.
    a. 4-4-5 Calendar
    b. 7-Eleven
    c. Derivative
    d. 529 plan

66. The term _____ has three unrelated technical definitions, and is also used in a variety of non-technical ways.

    - In financial economics, it refers to any asset used to make money, as opposed to assets used for personal enjoyment or consumption. This is an important distinction because two people can disagree sharply about the value of personal assets, one person might think a sports car is more valuable than a pickup truck, another person might have the opposite taste. But if an asset is held for the purpose of making money, taste has nothing to do with it, only differences of opinion about how much money the asset will produce. With the further assumption that people agree on the probability distribution of future cash flows, it is possible to have an objective _____ pricing model. Even without the assumption of agreement, it is possible to set rational limits on _____ value.
    - In governmental accounting, it is defined as any asset used in operations with an initial useful life extending beyond one reporting period. Generally, government managers have a 'stewardship' duty to maintain _____s under their control. See International Public Sector Accounting Standards for details.
    - In US tax accounting, it is defined as any property other than a list of exceptions. The main exceptions are anything held for sale, and any real estate or depreciable property used in business. Almost everything you own and use for personal purposes, pleasure or investment is a _____. If something is a _____ for tax purposes, gains or losses on sale or disposition are capital gains or capital losses. For individuals, however, capital losses on property held for personal use are generally not deductible. See the IRS publication Tax Facts about Capital Gains and Losses for details.

A well-known financial accounting textbook advises that the term be avoided except in tax accounting because it is used in so many different senses, not all of them well-defined. For example it is often used as a synonym for fixed assets or for investments in securities.

A common non-technical usage occurs when people ask that employees or the environment or something else be treated as a _____.

    a. Political risk
    b. Capital Asset
    c. Settlement date
    d. Solvency

67. In finance, the _____ is used to determine a theoretically appropriate required rate of return of an asset, if that asset is to be added to an already well-diversified portfolio, given that asset's non-diversifiable risk. The model takes into account the asset's sensitivity to non-diversifiable risk (also known as systemic risk or market risk), often represented by the quantity beta (β) in the financial industry, as well as the expected return of the market and the expected return of a theoretical risk-free asset.

The model was introduced by Jack Treynor (1961, 1962), William Sharpe (1964), John Lintner (1965a,b) and Jan Mossin (1966) independently, building on the earlier work of Harry Markowitz on diversification and modern portfolio theory.

a. Random walk hypothesis	b. Cox-Ingersoll-Ross model
c. Hull-White model	d. Capital Asset Pricing Model

68. A standard, commercial _____ is a document issued mostly by a financial institution, used primarily in trade finance, which usually provides an irrevocable payment undertaking.

The _____ can also be the source of payment for a transaction, meaning that redeeming the _____ will pay an exporter. Letters of credit are used primarily in international trade transactions of significant value, for deals between a supplier in one country and a customer in another.

a. Duty of loyalty	b. Letter of credit
c. Bond indenture	d. McFadden Act

69. _____ is the provision of resources (such as granting a loan) by one party to another party where that second party does not reimburse the first party immediately, thereby generating a debt, and instead arranges either to repay or return those resources (or material(s) of equal value) at a later date. The first party is called a creditor, also known as a lender, while the second party is called a debtor, also known as a borrower.

Movements of financial capital are normally dependent on either _____ or equity transfers.

a. Comparable	b. Clearing house
c. Warrant	d. Credit

70. _____ is a list for goods and materials held available in stock by a business. It is also used for a list of the contents of a household and for a list for testamentary purposes of the possessions of someone who has died. In accounting _____ is considered an asset.

a. AAB	b. ABN Amro
c. A Random Walk Down Wall Street	d. Inventory

71. The _____ is an equation that equals the cost of goods sold divided by the average inventory. Average inventory equals beginning inventory plus ending inventory divided by 2.

The formula for _____:

$$\text{Inventory Turnover} = \frac{\text{Cost of Goods Sold}}{\text{Average Inventory}}$$

The formula for average inventory:

$$\text{Average Inventory} = \frac{\text{Beginning inventory} + \text{Ending inventory}}{2}$$

A low turnover rate may point to overstocking, obsolescence, or deficiencies in the product line or marketing effort.

a. Inventory turnover
b. Information ratio
c. Earnings yield
d. Operating leverage

72. _____ is one of the Accounting Liquidity ratios, a financial ratio. This ratio measures the number of times, on average, the inventory is sold during the period. Its purpose is to measure the liquidity of the inventory.
a. A Random Walk Down Wall Street
b. AAB
c. ABN Amro
d. Inventory turnover ratio

Chapter 26. Multinational Financial Management 295

1. _____s are deposits denominated in United States dollars at banks outside the United States, and thus are not under the jurisdiction of the Federal Reserve. Consequently, such deposits are subject to much less regulation than similar deposits within the United States, allowing for higher margins. There is nothing 'European' about _____ deposits; a US dollar-denominated deposit in Tokyo or Caracas would likewise be deemed _____ deposits.
   a. ABN Amro
   b. A Random Walk Down Wall Street
   c. AAB
   d. Eurodollar

2. In finance, the _____ between two currencies specifies how much one currency is worth in terms of the other. For example an _____ of 102 Japanese yen to the United States dollar means that JPY 102 is worth the same as USD 1. The foreign exchange market is one of the largest markets in the world.
   a. ABN Amro
   b. AAB
   c. A Random Walk Down Wall Street
   d. Exchange rate

3. _____ is the planning process used to determine whether a firm's long term investments such as new machinery, replacement machinery, new plants, new products, and research development projects are worth pursuing. It is budget for major capital, or investment, expenditures.

Many formal methods are used in _____, including the techniques such as

- Net present value
- Profitability index
- Internal rate of return
- Modified Internal Rate of Return
- Equivalent annuity

These methods use the incremental cash flows from each potential investment, or project. Techniques based on accounting earnings and accounting rules are sometimes used - though economists consider this to be improper - such as the accounting rate of return, and 'return on investment.' Simplified and hybrid methods are used as well, such as payback period and discounted payback period.

   a. Shareholder value
   b. Preferred stock
   c. Financial distress
   d. Capital budgeting

4. The institution most often referenced by the word '_____' is a public or publicly traded _____, the shares of which are traded on a public stock exchange (e.g., the New York Stock Exchange or Nasdaq in the United States) where shares of stock of _____s are bought and sold by and to the general public. Most of the largest businesses in the world are publicly traded _____s. However, the majority of _____s are said to be closely held, privately held or close _____s, meaning that no ready market exists for the trading of shares.
   a. Federal Home Loan Mortgage Corporation
   b. Protect
   c. Depository Trust Company
   d. Corporation

5. _____ in finance is a risk management technique, related to hedging, that mixes a wide variety of investments within a portfolio. Because the fluctuations of a single security have less impact on a diverse portfolio, _____ minimizes the risk from any one investment.

A simple example of _____ is the following: On a particular island the entire economy consists of two companies: one that sells umbrellas and another that sells sunscreen.

a. 4-4-5 Calendar
b. 529 plan
c. 7-Eleven
d. Diversification

6. _____ is a type of risk faced by investors, corporations, and governments. It is a risk that can be understood and managed with proper aforethought and investment.

Broadly, _____ refers to the complications businesses and governments may face as a result of what are commonly referred to as political decisions--or 'any political change that alters the expected outcome and value of a given economic action by changing the probability of achieving business objectives.' .

a. Mid price
b. Capital asset
c. Political risk
d. Single-index model

7. A _____, securities exchange or (in Europe) bourse is a corporation or mutual organization which provides 'trading' facilities for stock brokers and traders, to trade stocks and other securities. _____s also provide facilities for the issue and redemption of securities as well as other financial instruments and capital events including the payment of income and dividends. The securities traded on a _____ include: shares issued by companies, unit trusts and other pooled investment products and bonds.

a. 529 plan
b. 7-Eleven
c. 4-4-5 Calendar
d. Stock Exchange

8. In finance, a _____ is a debt security, in which the authorized issuer owes the holders a debt and, depending on the terms of the _____, is obliged to pay interest (the coupon) and/or to repay the principal at a later date, termed maturity.

Thus a _____ is a loan: the issuer is the borrower, the _____ holder is the lender, and the coupon is the interest. _____s provide the borrower with external funds to finance long-term investments, or, in the case of government _____s, to finance current expenditure.

a. Catastrophe bonds
b. Puttable bond
c. Bond
d. Convertible bond

9. _____ is a fee paid on borrowed assets. It is the price paid for the use of borrowed money , or, money earned by deposited funds . Assets that are sometimes lent with _____ include money, shares, consumer goods through hire purchase, major assets such as aircraft, and even entire factories in finance lease arrangements.

a. Interest
b. Insolvency
c. AAB
d. A Random Walk Down Wall Street

10. An _____ is the price a borrower pays for the use of money they do not own, and the return a lender receives for deferring the use of funds, by lending it to the borrower. _____s are normally expressed as a percentage rate over the period of one year.

_____s targets are also a vital tool of monetary policy and are used to control variables like investment, inflation, and unemployment.

a. AAB
b. ABN Amro
c. A Random Walk Down Wall Street
d. Interest rate

11. _____ are a currency pair that does not include USD, such as GBP/JPY. Pairs that involve the EUR are called euro crosses, such as EUR/GBP. All other currency pairs (those that don't involve USD or EUR) are generally referred to as _____.

a. Cross rates
b. 529 plan
c. 4-4-5 Calendar
d. Foreign exchange risk

12. A _____ agreement is a contract between two or more parties where each party grants rights to their intellectual property to the other parties.

In patent law, a _____ agreement is an agreement according to which two or more parties grant a license to each other for the exploitation of the subject-matter claimed in one or more of the patents each owns. Very often, the patents that each party owns covers different essential aspects of a given commercial product.

a. Cross-licensing
b. 7-Eleven
c. 4-4-5 Calendar
d. 529 plan

13. _____ is a multiple-winner voting system intended to promote proportional representation while also being simple to understand.

_____ is used frequently in corporate governance, where it is mandated by many U.S. states, and it was used to elect the Illinois House of Representatives from 1870 until its repeal in 1980. It was used in England in the late 19th century to elect school boards.

a. 529 plan
b. 7-Eleven
c. 4-4-5 Calendar
d. Cumulative voting

14. _____ is a term used in accounting relating to the increase in value of an asset. In this sense it is the reverse of depreciation, which measures the fall in value of assets over their normal life-time.

_____ is a rise of a currency in a floating exchange rate.

a. A Random Walk Down Wall Street
b. Operating cash flow
c. Other Comprehensive Basis of Accounting
d. Appreciation

15. In economics and finance, _____ is the practice of taking advantage of a price differential between two or more markets: striking a combination of matching deals that capitalize upon the imbalance, the profit being the difference between the market prices. When used by academics, an _____ is a transaction that involves no negative cash flow at any probabilistic or temporal state and a positive cash flow in at least one state; in simple terms, a risk-free profit.

a. Initial margin
b. Issuer
c. Arbitrage
d. Efficient-market hypothesis

16. A _____ is a financial contract whose value is derived from the value of something else (known as the underlying.) The underlying on which a _____ is based can be an asset, weather conditions bonds or other forms of credit.
   a. 4-4-5 Calendar
   b. Derivative
   c. 529 plan
   d. 7-Eleven

17. A _____, sometimes called a pegged exchange rate, is a type of exchange rate regime wherein a currency's value is matched to the value of another single currency or to a basket of other currencies, or to another measure of value such as gold.

A _____ is usually used to stabilize the value of a currency, vis-a-vis the currency it is pegged to. This facilitates trade and investments between the two countries, and is especially useful for small economies where external trade forms a large part of their GDP.

   a. Market structure
   b. Fixed exchange rate
   c. Human capital
   d. Deflation

18. A _____ is a currency system in which governments try to keep the value of their currencies constant against one another.
   a. 4-4-5 Calendar
   b. Passive income
   c. Horizontal merger
   d. Fixed exchange rate system

19. _____ is exchange of capital, goods, and services across international borders or territories. In most countries, it represents a significant share of gross domestic product (GDP.) While _____ has been present throughout much of history, its economic, social, and political importance has been on the rise in recent centuries.
   a. United States Treasury security
   b. OTC Bulletin Board
   c. International trade
   d. Index number

20. _____ exists when one firm provides goods or services to a customer with an agreement to bill them later, or receive a shipment or service from a supplier under an agreement to pay them later. It can be viewed as an essential element of capitalization in an operating business because it can reduce the required capital investment to operate the business if it is managed properly. _____ is the largest use of capital for a majority of business to business (B2B) sellers in the United States and is a critical source of capital for a majority of all businesses.
   a. Trade credit
   b. Going concern
   c. 4-4-5 Calendar
   d. 529 plan

21. In economics, business, and accounting, a _____ is the value of money that has been used up to produce something, and hence is not available for use anymore. In business, the _____ may be one of acquisition, in which case the amount of money expended to acquire it is counted as _____. In this case, money is the input that is gone in order to acquire the thing.
   a. Marginal cost
   b. Fixed costs
   c. Sliding scale fees
   d. Cost

22. _____ is the provision of resources (such as granting a loan) by one party to another party where that second party does not reimburse the first party immediately, thereby generating a debt, and instead arranges either to repay or return those resources (or material(s) of equal value) at a later date. The first party is called a creditor, also known as a lender, while the second party is called a debtor, also known as a borrower.

Movements of financial capital are normally dependent on either _____ or equity transfers.

a. Clearing house
b. Comparable
c. Warrant
d. Credit

23. In economics, _____ is a rise in the general level of prices of goods and services in an economy over a period of time. The term '_____' once referred to increases in the money supply (monetary _____); however, economic debates about the relationship between money supply and price levels have led to its primary use today in describing price _____. _____ can also be described as a decline in the real value of money--a loss of purchasing power in the medium of exchange which is also the monetary unit of account.

a. A Random Walk Down Wall Street
b. ABN Amro
c. AAB
d. Inflation

24. A _____ secures the proper functioning of money by regulating economic agents, transaction types, and money supply.

They are traditionally formed by the policy decisions of individual governments and administrated as a domestic economic issue.

The current trend, however, is to use international trade and investment to alter the policy and legislation of individual governments.

a. Payback period
b. Pattern day trader
c. Bond credit rating
d. Monetary system

25. The _____ is the current method of accelerated asset depreciation required by the United States income tax code. Under _____, all assets are divided into classes which dictate the number of years over which an asset's cost will be recovered.

Prior to the Accelerated Cost Recovery System (ACRS), most capital purchases were depreciated using a straight line technique, that allowed for the depreciation of the asset over its useful life.

a. 7-Eleven
b. 4-4-5 Calendar
c. 529 plan
d. Modified Accelerated Cost Recovery System

26. In business and accounting, _____s are everything of value that is owned by a person or company. The balance sheet of a firm records the monetary value of the _____s owned by the firm. The two major _____ classes are tangible _____s and intangible _____s.

a. Income
b. EBITDA
c. Accounts payable
d. Asset

27. In finance, _____ is the process of estimating the potential market value of a financial asset or liability. they can be done on assets (for example, investments in marketable securities such as stocks, options, business enterprises, or intangible assets such as patents and trademarks) or on liabilities (e.g., Bonds issued by a company.) _____s are required in many contexts including investment analysis, capital budgeting, merger and acquisition transactions, financial reporting, taxable events to determine the proper tax liability, and in litigation.
   a. Share
   b. Procter ' Gamble
   c. Margin
   d. Valuation

28. The term _____ has three unrelated technical definitions, and is also used in a variety of non-technical ways.

   - In financial economics, it refers to any asset used to make money, as opposed to assets used for personal enjoyment or consumption. This is an important distinction because two people can disagree sharply about the value of personal assets, one person might think a sports car is more valuable than a pickup truck, another person might have the opposite taste. But if an asset is held for the purpose of making money, taste has nothing to do with it, only differences of opinion about how much money the asset will produce. With the further assumption that people agree on the probability distribution of future cash flows, it is possible to have an objective _____ pricing model. Even without the assumption of agreement, it is possible to set rational limits on _____ value.
   - In governmental accounting, it is defined as any asset used in operations with an initial useful life extending beyond one reporting period. Generally, government managers have a 'stewardship' duty to maintain _____s under their control. See International Public Sector Accounting Standards for details.
   - In US tax accounting, it is defined as any property other than a list of exceptions. The main exceptions are anything held for sale, and any real estate or depreciable property used in business. Almost everything you own and use for personal purposes, pleasure or investment is a _____. If something is a _____ for tax purposes, gains or losses on sale or disposition are capital gains or capital losses. For individuals, however, capital losses on property held for personal use are generally not deductible. See the IRS publication Tax Facts about Capital Gains and Losses for details.

A well-known financial accounting textbook advises that the term be avoided except in tax accounting because it is used in so many different senses, not all of them well-defined. For example it is often used as a synonym for fixed assets or for investments in securities.

A common non-technical usage occurs when people ask that employees or the environment or something else be treated as a _____.

   a. Political risk
   b. Capital Asset
   c. Solvency
   d. Settlement date

29. In finance, the _____ is used to determine a theoretically appropriate required rate of return of an asset, if that asset is to be added to an already well-diversified portfolio, given that asset's non-diversifiable risk. The model takes into account the asset's sensitivity to non-diversifiable risk (also known as systemic risk or market risk), often represented by the quantity beta (β) in the financial industry, as well as the expected return of the market and the expected return of a theoretical risk-free asset.

The model was introduced by Jack Treynor (1961, 1962), William Sharpe (1964), John Lintner (1965a,b) and Jan Mossin (1966) independently, building on the earlier work of Harry Markowitz on diversification and modern portfolio theory.

a. Random walk hypothesis
b. Cox-Ingersoll-Ross model
c. Capital Asset Pricing Model
d. Hull-White model

30. A _____ or a flexible exchange rate is a type of exchange rate regime wherein a currency's value is allowed to fluctuate according to the foreign exchange market. A currency that uses a _____ is known as a floating currency. The opposite of a _____ is a fixed exchange rate.

a. Floating exchange rate
b. Currency pair
c. Foreign exchange market
d. Spot market

31. _____ is the loss of value of a country's currency with respect to one or more foreign reference currencies, typically in a floating exchange rate system. It is most often used for the unofficial increase of the exchange rate due to market forces, though sometimes it appears interchangeably with devaluation. Its opposite is called appreciation.

a. 529 plan
b. Currency depreciation
c. 7-Eleven
d. 4-4-5 Calendar

32. _____ is a term used in accounting, economics and finance to spread the cost of an asset over the span of several years.

In simple words we can say that _____ is the reduction in the value of an asset due to usage, passage of time, wear and tear, technological outdating or obsolescence, depletion or other such factors.

In accounting, _____ is a term used to describe any method of attributing the historical or purchase cost of an asset across its useful life, roughly corresponding to normal wear and tear.

a. Depreciation
b. Deferred financing costs
c. Bottom line
d. Matching principle

33. _____ is a form of risk that arises from the change in price of one currency against another. Whenever investors or companies have assets or business operations across national borders, they face _____ if their positions are not hedged.

- Transaction risk is the risk that exchange rates will change unfavourably over time. It can be hedged against using forward currency contracts;
- Translation risk is an accounting risk, proportional to the amount of assets held in foreign currencies. Changes in the exchange rate over time will render a report inaccurate, and so assets are usually balanced by borrowings in that currency.

The exchange risk associated with a foreign denominated instrument is a key element in foreign investment. This risk flows from differential monetary policy and growth in real productivity, which results in differential inflation rates.

a. Currency risk
b. Market risk
c. Credit risk
d. Tracking error

34. In finance, a _____ is a type of bond that can be converted into shares of stock in the issuing company, usually at some pre-announced ratio. It is a hybrid security with debt- and equity-like features. Although it typically has a low coupon rate, the holder is compensated with the ability to convert the bond to common stock, usually at a substantial discount to the stock's market value.
   a. Corporate bond
   b. Gilts
   c. Bond fund
   d. Convertible bond

35. _____ is a reduction in the value of a currency with respect to other monetary units. In common modern usage, it specifically implies an official lowering of the value of a country's currency within a fixed exchange rate system, by which the monetary authority formally sets a new fixed rate with respect to a foreign reference currency. In contrast, (currency) depreciation is used for the unofficial decrease in the exchange rate in a floating exchange rate system.
   a. Petrodollar recycling
   b. Devaluation
   c. Currency board
   d. Reserve currency

36. _____ means a rise of a price of goods or products. This term is specially used as _____ of a currency, where it means a rise of currency to the relation with a foreign currency in a fixed exchange rate. In floating exchange rate correct term would be appreciation.
   a. Common pool problem
   b. Correlation trading
   c. Revaluation
   d. Holding period return

37. _____ is the balance of the amounts of cash being received and paid by a business during a defined period of time, sometimes tied to a specific project. Measurement of _____ can be used

   - to evaluate the state or performance of a business or project.
   - to determine problems with liquidity. Being profitable does not necessarily mean being liquid. A company can fail because of a shortage of cash, even while profitable.
   - to generate project rate of returns. The time of _____s into and out of projects are used as inputs to financial models such as internal rate of return, and net present value.
   - to examine income or growth of a business when it is believed that accrual accounting concepts do not represent economic realities. Alternately, _____ can be used to 'validate' the net income generated by accrual accounting.

_____ as a generic term may be used differently depending on context, and certain _____ definitions may be adapted by analysts and users for their own uses. Common terms include operating _____ and free _____.

_____s can be classified into:

1. Operational _____s: Cash received or expended as a result of the company's core business activities.
2. Investment _____s: Cash received or expended through capital expenditure, investments or acquisitions.
3. Financing _____s: Cash received or expended as a result of financial activities, such as interests and dividends.

All three together - the net _____ - are necessary to reconcile the beginning cash balance to the ending cash balance. Loan draw downs or equity injections, that is just shifting of capital but no expenditure as such, are not considered in the net _____.

Chapter 26. Multinational Financial Management

a. Corporate finance
c. Real option
b. Shareholder value
d. Cash flow

38. An _____ is a single market with a common currency. It is to be distinguished from a mere currency union, which does not involve a single market. This is the fifth stage of economic integration.

a. AAB
c. A Random Walk Down Wall Street
b. ABN Amro
d. Economic and Monetary Union

39. _____, refers to a globally traded currency that can serve as a reliable and stable store of value. Factors contributing to a currency's hard status can include political stability, low inflation, consistent monetary and fiscal policies, backing by reserves of precious metals, and long-term stable or upward-trending valuation against other currencies on a trade-weighted basis.

As of 2008, _____ could be argued to include the United States dollar, euro, Swiss franc, British pound sterling, Norwegian krone, Swedish krona, Canadian dollar, Japanese yen, and Australian dollar.

a. Devaluation
c. Petrodollar recycling
b. Reserve currency
d. Hard currency

40. _____ is a financial measure used to determine the attractiveness of an investment. It is generally used as part of a capital budgeting process to rank various alternative choices. It is a modification of the Internal Rate of Return (IRR).

_____ ranks project efficiency consistently with the present worth ratio (variant of NPV/Discounted Negative Cash Flow), considered the gold standard in many finance textbooks.

MIRR is calculated as follows:

width=747 border=0>

where n is the number of (equal) periods in which the cash flows occur.

a. Black-Scholes
c. Current yield
b. Binomial options pricing model
d. Modified internal rate of return

41. The _____ is a capital budgeting metric used by firms to decide whether they should make investments. It is an indicator of the efficiency or quality of an investment, as opposed to net present value (NPV), which indicates value or magnitude.

The IRR is the annualized effective compounded return rate which can be earned on the invested capital, i.e., the yield on the investment.

a. ABN Amro
b. A Random Walk Down Wall Street
c. Internal rate of return
d. AAB

42. In finance, _____, also known as return on investment is the ratio of money gained or lost on an investment relative to the amount of money invested. The amount of money gained or lost may be referred to as interest, profit/loss, gain/loss, or net income/loss. The money invested may be referred to as the asset, capital, principal, or the cost basis of the investment.
   a. Stock or scrip dividends
   b. Composiition of Creditors
   c. Doctrine of the Proper Law
   d. Rate of return

43. The _____ of a commodity, a security or a currency is the price that is quoted for immediate (spot) settlement (payment and delivery.) Spot settlement is normally one or two business days from trade date. This is in contrast with the forward price established in a forward contract or futures contract, where contract terms (price) are set now, but delivery and payment will occur at a future date.
   a. Spot rate
   b. Long position
   c. Limits to arbitrage
   d. Market anomaly

44.

In finance, the _____ can be the expected rate of return above the risk-free interest rate. When measuring risk, a common sense approach is to compare the risk-free return on T-bills and the very risky return on other investments. The difference between these two returns can be interpreted as a measure of the excess return on the average risky asset. This excess return is known as the _____.

   a. Risk aversion
   b. Risk premium
   c. Risk modeling
   d. Risk adjusted return on capital

45. A _____ is an international bond that is denominated in a currency not native to the country where it is issued. It can be categorised according to the currency in which it is issued. London is one of the centers of the _____ market, but _____s may be traded throughout the world - for example in Singapore or Tokyo.
   a. Interest rate option
   b. Education production function
   c. Eurobond
   d. Economic entity

46. _____ is an economic concept, expressed as a basic algebraic identity that relates interest rates and exchange rates. The identity is theoretical, and usually follows from assumptions imposed in economics models. There is evidence to support as well as to refute the concept.
   a. Interest rate parity
   b. AAB
   c. Unit price
   d. A Random Walk Down Wall Street

47. The _____ is an economic law stated as: 'In an efficient market all identical goods must have only one price.'

The intuition for this law is that all sellers will flock to the highest prevailing price, and all buyers to the lowest current market price. In an efficient market the convergence on one price is instant.

Commodities can be traded on financial markets, where there will be a single offer price, and bid price.

Chapter 26. Multinational Financial Management

a. Personal property
b. Liability
c. Letter of credit
d. Law of one price

48. _____ refers to a business or organization attempting to acquire goods or services to accomplish the goals of the enterprise. Though there are several organizations that attempt to set standards in the _____ process, processes can vary greatly between organizations. Typically the word '_____' is not used interchangeably with the word 'procurement', since procurement typically includes Expediting, Supplier Quality, and Traffic and Logistics (T'L) in addition to _____.

a. 4-4-5 Calendar
b. 529 plan
c. 7-Eleven
d. Purchasing

49. _____ is the value of goods/services compared to the amount paid with a currency. Currency can be either a commodity money, like gold or silver, or fiat currency like US dollars which are the world reserve currency. As Adam Smith noted, having money gives one the ability to 'command' others' labor, so _____ to some extent is power over other people, to the extent that they are willing to trade their labor or goods for money or currency.

a. 529 plan
b. 4-4-5 Calendar
c. 7-Eleven
d. Purchasing power

50. The _____ theory uses the long-term equilibrium exchange rate of two currencies to equalize their purchasing power. Developed by Gustav Cassel in 1920, it is based on the law of one price: the theory states that, in ideally efficient markets, identical goods should have only one price.

This purchasing power SEM rate equalizes the purchasing power of different currencies in their home countries for a given basket of goods.

a. Gross national product
b. TED spread
c. 4-4-5 Calendar
d. Purchasing power parity

51. _____ or financing is to provide capital (funds), which means money for a project, a person, a business or any other private or public institutions.

Those funds can be allocated for either short term or long term purposes. The health fund is a new way of _____ private healthcare centers.

a. Proxy fight
b. Product life cycle
c. Synthetic CDO
d. Funding

52. The _____ is the market for securities, where companies and governments can raise longterm funds. The _____ includes the stock market and the bond market. Financial regulators, such as the U.S. Securities and Exchange Commission, oversee the _____s in their designated countries to ensure that investors are protected against fraud.

a. Spot rate
b. Forward market
c. Delta neutral
d. Capital market

53. _____, in bookkeeping, refers to assets, liabilities, income, and expenses recorded on individual pages of the so called book of final entry or ledger. Changes in _____ value are made by chronologically posting debit (DR) and credit (CR) entries to its page. Examples of _____s are cash, _____s receivable, mortgages, loans, land and buildings, common stock, sales, services provided, wages, and payroll overhead.

a. Alpha
b. Accretion
c. Option
d. Account

54. A _____ is a futures contract on a short term interest rate (STIR.) Contracts vary, but are often defined on an interest rate index such as 3-month sterling or US dollar LIBOR.

They are traded across a wide range of currencies, including the G12 country currencies and many others.

a. Dual currency deposit
b. Real estate derivatives
c. Notional amount
d. Financial future

55. In finance, a _____ is a standardized contract, to buy or sell a specified commodity of standardized quality at a certain date in the future, at a market determined price (the futures price.)

The price is determined by the instantaneous equilibrium between the forces of supply and demand among competing buy and sell orders on the exchange at the time of the purchase or sale of the contract.

In many cases, the items may be such non-traditional 'commodities' as foreign currencies, commercial or government paper [e.g., bonds], or 'baskets' of corporate equity ['stock indices'] or other financial instruments.

a. Futures contract
b. Financial future
c. Heston model
d. Repurchase agreement

56. The _____ is a financial market where participants buy and sell debt securities, usually in the form of bonds. As of 2006, the size of the international _____ is an estimated $45 trillion, of which the size of the outstanding U.S. _____ debt was $25.2 trillion.

Nearly all of the $923 billion average daily trading volume in the U.S. _____ takes place between broker-dealers and large institutions in a decentralized, over-the-counter market.

a. Fixed income
b. 4-4-5 Calendar
c. 529 plan
d. Bond market

57. The _____ is one of several stock market indices, created by nineteenth-century Wall Street Journal editor and Dow Jones ' Company co-founder Charles Dow. Dow compiled the index to gauge the performance of the industrial sector of the American stock market. It is the second-oldest U.S. market index, after the Dow Jones Transportation Average, which Dow also created.

a. 529 plan
b. 4-4-5 Calendar
c. Dow Jones Industrial Average
d. 7-Eleven

58. A _____ is a private or public market for the trading of company stock and derivatives of company stock at an agreed price; these are securities listed on a stock exchange as well as those only traded privately.

The size of the world _____ is estimated at about $36.6 trillion US at the beginning of October 2008 . The world derivatives market has been estimated at about $480 trillion face or nominal value, 12 times the size of the entire world economy.

Chapter 26. Multinational Financial Management

a. Andrew Tobias
c. Anton Gelonkin

b. Adolph Coors
d. Stock market

59. A _____ is the direction in which a financial market is moving. _____s can be classified as primary trends, secondary trends (short-term), and secular trends (long-term.) This principle incorporates the idea that market cycles occur with regularity and persistence.

a. Market trend
c. 4-4-5 Calendar

b. 7-Eleven
d. 529 plan

60. An _____ represents the ownership in the shares of a foreign company trading on US financial markets. The stock of many non-US companies trades on US exchanges through the use of _____s. _____s enable US investors to buy shares in foreign companies without undertaking cross-border transactions.

a. AAB
c. ABN Amro

b. A Random Walk Down Wall Street
d. American Depository Receipt

61. The _____ is a stock exchange based in New York City, New York. It is the largest stock exchange in the world by dollar value of its listed companies securities. As of October 2008, the combined capitalization of all domestic _____ listed companies was $10.1 trillion.

a. 4-4-5 Calendar
c. 7-Eleven

b. New York Stock Exchange
d. 529 plan

62. The _____, in terms of finance and investing, describes how the expected return of a stock or portfolio is correlated to the return of the financial market as a whole.

An asset with a beta of 0 means that its price is not at all correlated with the market; that asset is independent. A positive beta means that the asset generally follows the market.

a. LIBOR market model
c. Current yield

b. Perpetuity
d. Beta coefficient

63. _____ is the risk that the value of an investment will decrease due to moves in market factors. The five standard _____ factors are:

- Equity risk, the risk that stock prices will change.
- Interest rate risk, the risk that interest rates will change.
- Currency risk, the risk that foreign exchange rates will change.
- Commodity risk, the risk that commodity prices (e.g. grains, metals) will change.

As with other forms of risk, _____ may be measured in a number of ways. Traditionally, this is done using a Value at Risk methodology. Value at risk is well established as a risk management technique, but it contains a number of limiting assumptions that constrain its accuracy.

a. Market risk
c. Transaction risk

b. Tracking error
d. Currency risk

64. _____ refers to confiscation of private property with the stated purpose of establishing social equality.

Unlike eminent domain, _____ takes place beyond the common law legal systems and refers to socially-motivated confiscations of any property rather than to taking away the real estate. Just compensation to owners is given.

_____ is one of the political risks involved with Foreign Direct Investment. It is characterized by confiscation of the foreign asset, and a pittance payment.

   a. AAB
   c. A Random Walk Down Wall Street
   b. ABN Amro
   d. Expropriation

65. When foreign currency is converted back to the currency of the home country it is referred to as _____. An example would be an American converting British Pounds back to U.S. Dollars.

_____ also refers to the payment of a dividend by a foreign corporation to a US corporation. This happens often where the foreign corporation is considered a 'controlled foreign corporation', which means that it more than 50% of the foreign corporation is owned by US shareholders.

   a. Repatriation
   c. Anton Gelonkin
   b. Adolph Coors
   d. Andrew Tobias

66. A _____ is a payment made by a corporation to its shareholder members. When a corporation earns a profit or surplus, that money can be put to two uses: it can either be re-invested in the business (called retained earnings), or it can be paid to the shareholders as a _____. Many corporations retain a portion of their earnings and pay the remainder as a _____.

   a. Dividend
   c. Dividend yield
   b. Special dividend
   d. Dividend puzzle

67. _____ is the difference between price and the costs of bringing to market whatever it is that is accounted as an enterprise (whether by harvest, extraction, manufacture, or purchase) in terms of the component costs of delivered goods and/or services and any operating or other expenses.

A key difficulty in measuring profit is in defining costs. Pure economic monetary profits can be zero or negative even in competitive equilibrium when accounted monetized costs exceed monetized price.

   a. Accounting profit
   c. Economic profit
   b. A Random Walk Down Wall Street
   d. AAB

68. _____ are a class of computational algorithms that rely on repeated random sampling to compute their results. _____ are often used when simulating physical and mathematical systems. Because of their reliance on repeated computation and random or pseudo-random numbers, _____ are most suited to calculation by a computer.

_____ in finance are often used to calculate the value of companies, to evaluate investments in projects at corporate level or to evaluate financial derivatives. The method is intended for financial analysts who want to construct stochastic or probabilistic financial models as opposed to the traditional static and deterministic models.

Chapter 26. Multinational Financial Management

a. Sample size
b. Correlation
c. Semivariance
d. Monte Carlo methods

69. _____ refers to the pricing of contributions (assets, tangible and intangible, services, and funds) transferred within an organization. For example, goods from the production division may be sold to the marketing division, or goods from a parent company may be sold to a foreign subsidiary. Since the prices are set within an organization (i.e. controlled), the typical market mechanisms that establish prices for such transactions between third parties may not apply.

a. Price discrimination
b. Transfer pricing
c. Price index
d. Discounts and allowances

70. The phrase _____ refers to the aspect of corporate strategy, corporate finance and management dealing with the buying, selling and combining of different companies that can aid, finance, or help a growing company in a given industry grow rapidly without having to create another business entity.

An acquisition, also known as a takeover, is the buying of one company (the 'target') by another. An acquisition may be friendly or hostile.

a. 4-4-5 Calendar
b. 529 plan
c. 7-Eleven
d. Mergers and acquisitions

71. _____ is the area of law in which manufacturers, distributors, suppliers, retailers, and others who make products available to the public are held responsible for the injuries those products cause.

In the United States, the claims most commonly associated with _____ are negligence, strict liability, breach of warranty, and various consumer protection claims. The majority of _____ laws are determined at the state level and vary widely from state to state.

a. Business valuation
b. Product liability
c. Family and Medical Leave Act
d. Foreclosure

72. In financial accounting, a _____ or statement of financial position is a summary of a person's or organization's balances. Assets, liabilities and ownership equity are listed as of a specific date, such as the end of its financial year. A _____ is often described as a snapshot of a company's financial condition.

a. Statement of retained earnings
b. Financial statements
c. Statement on Auditing Standards No. 70: Service Organizations
d. Balance sheet

73. In finance, _____ refers to the way a corporation finances its assets through some combination of equity, debt, or hybrid securities. A firm's _____ is then the composition or 'structure' of its liabilities. For example, a firm that sells $20 billion in equity and $80 billion in debt is said to be 20% equity-financed and 80% debt-financed.

a. Market for corporate control
b. Rights issue
c. Book building
d. Capital structure

74. In the most general sense, a _____ is anything that is a hindrance, or puts individuals at a disadvantage.

Before we discuss the financial terms, we should note that a _____ can also have a much more important slang meaning.

This is best described in an example.

a. Limited liability
b. McFadden Act
c. Covenant
d. Liability

75. In United States banking, _____ is a marketing term for certain services offered primarily to larger business customers. It may be used to describe all bank accounts (such as checking accounts) provided to businesses of a certain size, but it is more often used to describe specific services such as cash concentration, zero balance accounting, and automated clearing house facilities. Sometimes, private banking customers are given _____ services.

a. Global tactical asset allocation
b. Profitability index
c. Cash management
d. Capitalization rate

76. _____ is a financial metric which represents operating liquidity available to a business. Along with fixed assets such as plant and equipment, _____ is considered a part of operating capital. It is calculated as current assets minus current liabilities.

a. 4-4-5 Calendar
b. Working capital management
c. Working capital
d. 529 plan

77. Decisions relating to working capital and short term financing are referred to as _____. These involve managing the relationship between a firm's short-term assets and its short-term liabilities. The goal of _____ is to ensure that the firm is able to continue its operations and that it has sufficient cash flow to satisfy both maturing short-term debt and upcoming operational expenses.

a. 529 plan
b. Working capital management
c. Working capital
d. 4-4-5 Calendar

78. The _____ measures how long an investment with suppliers deprives a firm of cash -- it is (in the generic case of a retailer) the time between disbursement for inventory and collection on its sale. Thus, the _____ measures how risky it would be to increase this investment with suppliers in the course of expanding customer sales. However, shortening the _____ creates its own risks: while a firm could even achieve a negative _____ by collecting from customers before paying suppliers, a policy of strict collections and lax payments is not always sustainable.

a. Return on capital employed
b. Cash conversion cycle
c. Return on sales
d. Price/cash flow ratio

79. A standard, commercial _____ is a document issued mostly by a financial institution, used primarily in trade finance, which usually provides an irrevocable payment undertaking.

The _____ can also be the source of payment for a transaction, meaning that redeeming the _____ will pay an exporter. Letters of credit are used primarily in international trade transactions of significant value, for deals between a supplier in one country and a customer in another.

a. Duty of loyalty
b. Bond indenture
c. McFadden Act
d. Letter of credit

80. _____ is the discipline of identifying, monitoring and limiting risks. In some cases the acceptable risk may be near zero. Risks can come from accidents, natural causes and disasters as well as deliberate attacks from an adversary.
   a. Penny stock
   b. FIFO
   c. 4-4-5 Calendar
   d. Risk management

81. _____ is the set of processes, customs, policies, laws and institutions affecting the way a corporation is directed, administered or controlled. _____ also includes the relationships among the many stakeholders involved and the goals for which the corporation is governed. The principal stakeholders are the shareholders, management and the board of directors.
   a. Patent
   b. Corporate governance
   c. Due diligence
   d. Foreign Corrupt Practices Act

82. _____ is a list for goods and materials held available in stock by a business. It is also used for a list of the contents of a household and for a list for testamentary purposes of the possessions of someone who has died. In accounting _____ is considered an asset.
   a. ABN Amro
   b. Inventory
   c. AAB
   d. A Random Walk Down Wall Street

83. _____ is that which is owed; usually referencing assets owed, but the term can cover other obligations. In the case of assets, _____ is a means of using future purchasing power in the present before a summation has been earned. Some companies and corporations use _____ as a part of their overall corporate finance strategy.
   a. Debt
   b. Partial Payment
   c. Credit cycle
   d. Cross-collateralization

Chapter 1

1. d	2. d	3. d	4. d	5. d	6. d	7. b	8. d	9. d	10. d
11. a	12. c	13. c	14. b	15. d	16. c	17. d	18. a	19. d	20. a
21. d	22. d	23. d	24. b	25. d	26. d	27. d	28. d	29. b	30. d
31. d	32. b	33. b	34. b	35. d	36. d	37. d	38. d	39. c	40. a
41. c	42. d	43. d	44. b	45. d	46. b	47. b	48. c	49. a	50. d
51. d	52. a	53. d	54. a	55. d	56. d	57. a	58. b	59. b	60. c
61. b	62. b	63. a	64. d	65. d	66. b	67. b	68. a	69. d	70. b
71. d	72. d	73. d	74. b	75. d	76. a	77. d	78. d	79. d	80. c
81. d	82. b	83. d	84. d	85. a	86. a	87. c	88. c	89. a	90. d
91. d	92. a	93. d	94. d	95. d	96. d	97. c	98. c	99. b	100. d
101. d	102. b	103. d	104. a	105. d	106. d	107. d	108. b	109. a	

Chapter 2

1. d	2. b	3. c	4. b	5. c	6. d	7. b	8. b	9. d	10. b
11. d	12. a	13. b	14. d	15. a	16. b	17. b	18. d	19. c	20. b
21. d	22. d	23. d	24. b	25. d	26. c	27. a	28. a	29. c	30. c
31. d	32. b	33. a	34. b	35. c	36. d	37. d	38. a	39. d	40. d
41. b	42. c	43. d	44. a	45. b	46. c	47. a			

Chapter 3

1. d	2. d	3. d	4. d	5. d	6. d	7. c	8. a	9. d	10. d
11. d	12. a	13. a	14. d	15. d	16. b	17. a	18. d	19. d	20. d
21. d	22. c	23. d	24. d	25. c	26. c	27. d	28. b	29. a	30. c
31. b	32. d	33. d	34. d	35. d	36. a	37. d	38. c	39. d	40. d
41. b	42. b	43. d	44. a	45. b	46. d	47. c	48. b	49. d	50. c
51. b	52. b	53. d	54. d	55. b	56. b	57. b	58. c	59. d	60. b
61. a	62. b	63. c	64. a	65. d	66. d	67. c	68. d	69. d	70. c
71. d	72. d	73. a	74. c	75. d	76. b	77. d	78. c	79. b	80. a
81. b	82. d	83. d	84. d	85. d	86. b	87. d			

Chapter 4

1. d	2. d	3. c	4. c	5. c	6. d	7. a	8. b	9. d	10. b
11. d	12. d	13. a	14. c	15. d	16. a	17. d	18. d	19. a	20. d
21. d	22. d	23. d	24. b	25. b	26. d	27. d	28. b	29. d	30. c
31. d	32. d	33. d	34. d	35. c	36. d	37. a	38. c	39. a	40. a
41. a	42. d	43. d	44. a	45. d	46. d	47. d	48. a	49. d	50. b
51. b	52. a	53. b	54. d	55. d	56. d	57. c	58. d	59. d	60. c
61. b									

ANSWER KEY

Chapter 5
1. d   2. b   3. d   4. c   5. d   6. b   7. c   8. b   9. a   10. d
11. b   12. d   13. a   14. d   15. c   16. d   17. c   18. b   19. c   20. d
21. a   22. d   23. d   24. b   25. d   26. a   27. c   28. c   29. d   30. d
31. d   32. c   33. c   34. d   35. a   36. a   37. d   38. a   39. d   40. b
41. d   42. b   43. b   44. b   45. d   46. b   47. d   48. d   49. b   50. a
51. d   52. b   53. a   54. d   55. d   56. b   57. a   58. d   59. b   60. a
61. d   62. a   63. d   64. d   65. c   66. d   67. d   68. a   69. d   70. b
71. d   72. a   73. d   74. d   75. d   76. d   77. a   78. d   79. c   80. a
81. c   82. d   83. d   84. c   85. d

Chapter 6
1. d   2. c   3. d   4. d   5. c   6. d   7. d   8. a   9. d   10. d
11. a   12. d   13. a   14. b   15. d   16. c   17. b   18. a   19. b   20. d
21. d   22. d   23. d   24. d   25. b   26. c   27. d   28. a   29. d   30. b
31. b   32. d   33. a   34. a   35. d   36. b   37. d   38. a   39. d   40. a
41. b   42. b

Chapter 7
1. d   2. b   3. d   4. d   5. c   6. d   7. d   8. a   9. c   10. b
11. b   12. c   13. c   14. a   15. b   16. d   17. a   18. d   19. d   20. d
21. d   22. a   23. d   24. d   25. d   26. a   27. d   28. d   29. b   30. d

Chapter 8
1. d   2. a   3. d   4. d   5. d   6. d   7. d   8. d   9. d   10. b
11. d   12. a   13. a   14. d   15. d   16. d   17. d   18. d   19. a   20. d
21. d   22. d   23. d   24. a   25. c   26. d   27. c   28. d   29. d   30. a
31. b   32. b   33. a   34. d   35. a   36. a   37. d   38. a   39. b   40. d
41. d   42. a   43. d   44. d   45. b   46. b   47. c   48. d   49. b   50. d
51. d   52. c   53. d   54. a   55. d   56. d

Chapter 9
1. a   2. d   3. d   4. c   5. d   6. a   7. d   8. d   9. d   10. c
11. c   12. c   13. d   14. b   15. d   16. d   17. d   18. a   19. b   20. c
21. d   22. d   23. a   24. a   25. b   26. d   27. a   28. d   29. d   30. a
31. b   32. d   33. d   34. d   35. a   36. d   37. d   38. d   39. d   40. a
41. d

Chapter 10

1. a	2. d	3. d	4. d	5. a	6. d	7. d	8. a	9. d	10. a
11. d	12. d	13. a	14. c	15. d	16. c	17. a	18. b	19. d	20. c
21. d	22. c	23. a	24. b	25. d	26. d	27. d	28. d	29. d	30. d
31. d	32. b	33. d	34. d	35. d	36. d	37. b	38. d	39. a	40. d
41. b	42. d	43. d	44. d	45. c	46. d	47. d	48. d	49. b	50. d
51. a	52. d	53. b	54. b	55. c	56. d	57. d	58. b	59. a	60. d
61. c	62. b	63. d							

Chapter 11

1. d	2. b	3. d	4. b	5. a	6. b	7. a	8. a	9. d	10. d
11. a	12. c	13. d	14. d	15. b	16. b	17. a	18. d	19. b	20. d
21. d	22. a	23. a	24. a	25. c	26. a	27. b			

Chapter 12

1. b	2. d	3. d	4. b	5. b	6. d	7. d	8. c	9. c	10. d
11. d	12. b	13. d	14. b	15. d	16. a	17. b	18. b	19. b	20. b
21. d	22. a	23. c	24. d	25. d	26. b	27. d	28. c	29. d	30. c
31. d	32. c	33. d	34. d	35. d	36. d	37. d	38. d	39. d	40. d
41. b	42. b	43. b	44. a	45. d	46. a	47. c	48. b	49. a	50. b
51. c	52. b	53. c	54. a	55. d	56. d	57. b	58. a		

Chapter 13

1. d	2. b	3. d	4. d	5. d	6. d	7. c	8. d	9. a	10. c
11. b	12. d	13. d	14. c	15. a	16. a	17. c	18. d	19. a	20. b

Chapter 14

1. d	2. a	3. b	4. d	5. d	6. d	7. b	8. d	9. c	10. d
11. d	12. a	13. a	14. b	15. d	16. a	17. d	18. b	19. a	20. d
21. c	22. d	23. d	24. a	25. c	26. c	27. a	28. b	29. d	30. b
31. a	32. b	33. d	34. d	35. a	36. d	37. c	38. a	39. a	40. d
41. c	42. d	43. a	44. b	45. d	46. a	47. a	48. d	49. d	50. d
51. d									

Chapter 15

1. b	2. c	3. d	4. d	5. a	6. d	7. c	8. d	9. a	10. d
11. a	12. d	13. a	14. c	15. d	16. d	17. c	18. b	19. c	20. d
21. b	22. d	23. b	24. b	25. d	26. d	27. a	28. d	29. d	30. d
31. d	32. b	33. a	34. c	35. d	36. d	37. a	38. d	39. d	40. b
41. d	42. a	43. b	44. c	45. d	46. a				

ANSWER KEY

Chapter 16

1. d	2. b	3. d	4. c	5. b	6. d	7. a	8. b	9. a	10. c
11. d	12. d	13. d	14. b	15. a	16. c	17. b	18. b	19. d	20. c
21. d	22. b	23. b	24. a	25. a	26. c	27. d	28. b	29. d	30. d
31. d	32. d	33. b	34. b	35. c	36. d	37. c	38. c	39. c	40. d
41. d	42. c	43. d	44. c	45. d	46. d	47. d	48. d	49. a	50. c
51. b	52. d	53. d	54. c	55. d	56. d	57. b	58. d	59. b	60. d
61. d	62. a	63. b	64. c	65. b					

Chapter 17

1. d	2. d	3. c	4. d	5. d	6. c	7. d	8. a	9. d	10. b
11. c	12. a	13. d	14. d	15. a	16. b	17. d	18. b	19. d	20. b
21. d	22. d	23. a	24. d	25. d	26. c	27. d	28. a	29. c	30. d
31. a	32. c	33. a	34. c	35. a	36. d	37. d	38. d	39. d	

Chapter 18

1. d	2. c	3. b	4. a	5. d	6. d	7. b	8. b	9. d	10. d
11. b	12. a	13. c	14. b	15. b	16. a	17. c	18. d	19. b	20. d
21. b	22. c	23. b	24. d	25. b	26. d	27. d	28. d	29. d	30. a
31. d	32. d	33. d	34. c	35. d	36. d	37. b	38. d	39. c	40. a
41. a	42. a	43. b	44. d	45. b	46. d	47. a			

Chapter 19

1. d	2. a	3. d	4. a	5. b	6. a	7. c	8. d	9. b	10. b
11. c	12. d	13. d	14. b	15. c	16. d	17. d	18. d	19. a	20. d
21. c	22. d	23. d	24. d	25. a	26. d	27. d	28. d	29. d	30. d
31. b	32. a	33. d	34. d	35. d	36. d	37. d	38. d	39. d	40. d
41. c	42. d	43. a	44. d	45. c	46. b	47. d	48. d	49. d	50. d
51. b	52. c	53. d	54. c	55. a	56. b	57. d	58. a	59. d	60. d
61. a	62. a	63. d	64. d	65. a	66. a	67. d	68. c	69. d	70. b
71. d	72. c	73. d	74. a						

Chapter 20

1. a	2. a	3. d	4. b	5. b	6. d	7. b	8. c	9. c	10. b
11. c	12. d	13. d	14. d	15. d	16. d	17. d	18. d	19. d	20. d
21. d	22. b	23. c	24. c	25. d	26. d	27. c	28. b	29. a	30. d
31. a	32. d	33. c	34. d	35. d	36. b	37. d	38. d	39. c	40. b
41. b	42. c	43. d	44. c	45. d	46. b	47. d			

Chapter 21

1. a	2. a	3. a	4. c	5. d	6. a	7. c	8. d	9. d	10. a
11. d	12. d	13. c	14. b	15. a	16. b	17. d	18. b	19. c	20. d
21. a	22. c	23. b	24. b	25. d	26. d	27. d	28. d	29. d	30. d
31. a	32. d	33. d	34. d	35. a	36. d	37. a	38. b	39. d	40. a
41. a	42. d								

Chapter 22

1. a	2. d	3. c	4. a	5. d	6. b	7. d	8. c	9. a	10. d
11. d	12. d	13. a	14. c	15. b	16. a	17. c	18. c	19. d	20. d
21. b	22. d	23. a	24. d	25. d	26. a	27. a	28. d	29. c	30. c
31. a	32. d	33. c	34. d	35. a	36. c	37. d	38. a	39. a	40. d
41. c	42. c	43. d	44. b	45. c	46. d	47. c	48. a	49. b	

Chapter 23

1. c	2. d	3. d	4. d	5. a	6. d	7. a	8. c	9. d	10. d
11. d	12. a	13. d	14. c	15. c	16. d	17. d	18. d	19. d	20. c
21. d	22. b	23. b	24. b	25. d	26. b	27. d	28. a	29. b	30. d
31. a	32. d	33. b	34. c	35. b	36. c	37. b	38. d	39. a	40. d
41. a	42. d	43. b	44. d	45. d	46. a	47. d	48. d	49. d	50. a
51. b	52. d	53. d	54. d	55. a	56. c	57. d	58. b	59. c	60. d
61. a	62. c	63. d	64. d	65. d	66. d	67. a			

Chapter 24

1. c	2. d	3. a	4. d	5. d	6. d	7. a	8. a	9. b	10. d
11. d	12. d	13. d	14. b	15. d	16. d	17. d	18. d	19. d	20. d
21. c	22. d	23. c	24. a	25. d	26. b	27. d	28. d	29. a	30. b
31. b	32. b	33. d							

Chapter 25

1. a	2. d	3. d	4. d	5. d	6. b	7. d	8. a	9. d	10. d
11. d	12. c	13. d	14. a	15. a	16. a	17. c	18. a	19. d	20. c
21. b	22. d	23. d	24. b	25. d	26. d	27. a	28. b	29. d	30. d
31. a	32. d	33. d	34. b	35. d	36. d	37. c	38. c	39. a	40. c
41. d	42. c	43. d	44. d	45. a	46. a	47. d	48. c	49. d	50. c
51. d	52. d	53. b	54. d	55. b	56. b	57. c	58. d	59. d	60. c
61. c	62. b	63. d	64. c	65. c	66. b	67. d	68. b	69. d	70. d
71. a	72. d								

ANSWER KEY

Chapter 26

1. d	2. d	3. d	4. d	5. d	6. c	7. d	8. c	9. a	10. d
11. a	12. a	13. d	14. d	15. c	16. b	17. b	18. d	19. c	20. a
21. d	22. d	23. d	24. d	25. d	26. d	27. d	28. b	29. c	30. a
31. b	32. a	33. a	34. d	35. b	36. c	37. d	38. d	39. d	40. d
41. c	42. d	43. a	44. b	45. c	46. a	47. d	48. d	49. d	50. d
51. d	52. d	53. d	54. d	55. a	56. d	57. c	58. d	59. a	60. d
61. b	62. d	63. a	64. d	65. a	66. a	67. a	68. d	69. b	70. d
71. b	72. d	73. d	74. d	75. c	76. c	77. b	78. b	79. d	80. d
81. b	82. b	83. a